I0891542

ALGORITHM OF THE NIGHT

A. S. HAMRAH

"Unerring" (*Bookforum*), "hilarious" (Dana Spiotta), "our age's most irreplaceable critic" (Guernica), "a genius" (*Kenyon Review*), A. S. Hamrah returns with an extraordinary collection of his best film writing for *n+1*, the *Baffler*, the *New York Review of Books*, the Criterion Collection, and other publications. *Algorithm of the Night* assembles Hamrah's essays on films and filmmakers and his inimitable, aphoristic reviews—a body of work that, taken together, presents a powerful alternative to a culture mired in publicity and stale convention. A journey through the overlapping dystopias of the Trump years, the pandemic years, and the Trump years, *Algorithm of the Night* attends with remarkable style and precision to a film industry in self-imposed crisis, a chronicle of failures and occasional miracles from AI to *The Zone of Interest*. Against the tides of ignorance and solipsism, *Algorithm of the Night* is film criticism as literature and—perhaps—prophecy.

A. S. Hamrah is the author of *The Earth Dies Streaming: Film Writing, 2002–2018* (n+1 Books, 2018) and *Last Week in End Times Cinema* (Semiotext(e), 2025). He is the film critic for *n+1* and writes for a number of other publications, including *Harper's*, *Bookforum*, the *Nation*, the *New York Review of Books*, *Fast Company*, and the Criterion Collection. He has worked as a movie theater projectionist, a semiotic brand analyst in the television industry, a political pollster, a football cinematographer, and for the film director Raúl Ruiz. He produced the feature-length documentary *Bunker*, directed by Jenny Perlin, which was the opening night film at the Museum of Modern Art's Doc Fortnight in 2022. He lives in New York.

ALSO FROM n+1 BOOKS:

P.S. 1 Symposium: A Practical Avant-Garde

What We Should Have Known: Two Discussions

What Was the Hipster? A Sociological Investigation

The Trouble Is the Banks: Letters to Wall Street

No Regrets: Three Discussions

Buzz: A Play

Other Russias

Canon/Archive: Studies in Quantitative Formalism

The Earth Dies Streaming: Film Writing, 2002–2018

Missing Time: Essays

The Intellectual Situation: The Best of n+1's Second Decade

The Last Soviet Artist

ALGORITHM OF THE NIGHT

FILM WRITING, 2019–2025

A. S. HAMRAH

n+1 BOOKS

n+1 FOUNDATION NEW YORK

Published 2025 by n+1 Foundation

37 Greenpoint Avenue #316, Mailbox 18

Brooklyn, New York 11222

www.nplusonemag.com

ISBN 978-1-9538131-8-3

Printed by the Sheridan Press

Manufactured in the United States of America

Design by Rachel Ossip

First Printing

Algorithm of the Night *was published with support from the Ideas Workshop of the Open Society Foundations. The n+1 Foundation's programs are made possible in part by the New York State Council on the Arts with the support of the Office of the Governor and the New York State Legislature, as well as by public funds from the New York City Department of Cultural Affairs, in partnership with the City Council.*

For Kris Moran &
Ryan Webb

"Because in this sorry world, the night undoes the work of the day."

—*Diary of a Country Priest* (Robert Bresson, 1951)

CONTENTS

A TOTAL BREAKDOWN OF ALL THE EASTER EGGS

INTRODUCTION

IN DECEMBER 2019, THREE MONTHS BEFORE THE PANDEMIC, I WAS STANDING on a subway platform in Brooklyn when I recognized a prominent older film critic also waiting for the train. I had been reading his work for many years, so I decided I would introduce myself. It can be awkward or presumptuous to bother a stranger like that, but he didn't seem to mind. He was polite and engaging. It turned out that we lived in the same neighborhood, and later, after he'd read my book *The Earth Dies Streaming*, he emailed and we arranged to get coffee and breakfast.

We met in a tiny café with tables the size of half-dollars. We discussed filmmakers, film festivals, and other critics, and it was all very pleasant, though we were sitting at a table too small for two grown men to be eating at. As we left the café, we headed down the street in the same direction. "Scott, you've written a very good book," he said as we approached the intersection where we would part ways. "But writers could be film critics in this country from the 1940s to the 1980s. Not anymore. See ya!"

With that mic drop, he turned in the direction of the good part of the neighborhood where he lived. Awed by his restraint in not adding "don't quit your day job," I carried home the two books he'd given me, one he'd written and one he'd edited. Naturally, the period in which he said writers could be film critics in this country overlapped with his heyday. Still, I was somewhat dazed by the finality of his statement. Film criticism? Over. *O-v-u-r*, as it says at the end of the Jerry Lewis movie *Hardly Working*. A reason to continue? Not that he'd mentioned.

THIS ENCOUNTER WAS A FOREBODING way to end the year 2019, but at the time I had other things to think about. Soon after that breakfast, I was introducing Cocteau's *Orpheus* at the Quad in Manhattan and then, early in 2020, flying to Seattle to do the same for John Sayles's *Matewan* and to sign books at a bookstore. As far as I was concerned, film criticism was doing fine. On my flight back to New York, there was one person wearing a face mask on the plane, a man in his twenties. The mask was in a camouflage pattern. I thought to myself, "he's taking this coronavirus thing pretty seriously." I heard other people seated near me in the cabin wryly pointing him out to one another with a "get a load of this guy" attitude. A couple weeks later, movie theaters all over the country closed down. A lot of them remained shut until 2021, and many went out of business. Film criticism became something done at home, like baking bread.

These days when I think of 2019, what often comes to mind are Quentin Tarantino's remarks from the 2025 Sundance Film Festival, the second-to-last one that will happen in Utah, where Robert Redford, recently deceased, founded it. "What the fuck is a movie now?" Tarantino asked. "Something that plays in theaters for a token release . . . and by the second week you can watch it on television. I didn't get into all this for diminishing returns. . . . It was bad enough in 2019, and that was the last fucking year of movies." Tarantino, who had debuted *Reservoir Dogs* at Sundance thirty-three years earlier, ended his thoughts on this subject by claiming that theatrical releases of movies had become "a show pony exercise" designed to market films for the streamers.

As many literal-minded people pointed out, 2019 was not in fact the last year of movies. Many good films have been made since then.

Last year great films from all over the world were released in the US. A random list of disparate and original films seen on American screens in 2024 includes *La Chimera, About Dry Grasses, Christmas Eve in Miller's Point, The Settlers, A Different Man, Universal Language*, and, yes, *Megalopolis*. One of the best movies of the year summed it all up, not just in its title but in subject matter and style—in its whole approach to what a movie is and can be in the mid-2020s: Radu Jude's *Do Not Expect Too Much from the End of the World*. It's a film about a certain kind of filmmaking being done under certain conditions that seem, in their way, more perilous than the ones under which *Furiosa: A Mad Max Saga* was made.

I think 2019 will come to be seen in film history as a golden year and an inflection point, the same the way 1939 and its movies exist in the popular imagination as a series of classics constantly open to new investigation and debate—not just *The Wizard of Oz* and *Gone with the Wind* and *Mr. Smith Goes to Washington*, but also *The Rules of the Game* (of course), *Only Angels Have Wings, Ninotchka, Love Affair, Stagecoach* and *Young Mr. Lincoln*, and at least a couple dozen others. The 2019 version of these includes *Parasite, The Irishman, Uncut Gems*, Tarantino's *Once Upon a Time in Hollywood, The Souvenir, Ash Is Purest White, Portrait of a Lady on Fire*, and as in 1939, a number of other films whose reputations will grow and wane and grow again—*Peterloo, Atlantics, La Flor, Midsommar*. The films of 1939 arrived at a time of burgeoning right-wing authoritarianism around the world, and 2019 was similarly set on a precipice.

The difference between 2019 and now is that films from six years ago already seem the product of a different world. As it says onscreen in a film made at another turning point in film history, "That era has passed. Nothing that belongs to it exists anymore."

I have a strange relic from that vanished year that I've managed to hold onto. It's a *Cats* drink ticket. All the critics who attended the *Cats* press screening at the Landmark at 57 West in Manhattan on December 17, 2019 got one. Universal had little understanding of what they had done in adapting the Andrew Lloyd Webber musical to the screen. They didn't know that they had produced the worst film of the year, maybe the worst of the decade, maybe the worst ever. So little did they understand any of this that they were providing an open bar after the press screening. Each critic who received one of the golden-colored tickets was entitled to "One (1) Complimentary Wine, Beer or Specialty Cocktail COURTESY OF UNIVERSAL PICTURES." The idea, presumably, was that, having been delighted by *Cats*, the critics would gather at the bar to trade superlatives about Tom Hooper's direction and Idris Elba and Judi Dench's performances as singing felines, causing them to write sparkling encomia to the movie, which would then lead to big box office over Christmas.

I saw *Cats* with another film critic who was as appalled as I was when this bizarre, terrible movie ended. When we exited the theater and I suggested we go to the open bar, she wasn't having it. Nobody was. Not one critic stopped to use their drink ticket. It was as extraordinary as *Cats* itself, with its horrifying costumes and repellent cat-face makeup and its dancing cockroaches, with Taylor Swift and her CGI body and Jason Derulo as Rum Tum Tugger. Writers turning down free drinks. Another ominous sign for the new year.

The Landmark at 57 West, a huge, state-of-the-art eight-screen cineplex ridiculously located far from any subway stop, closed for good in the summer of 2020. *Cats* awaits rediscovery as a cult item, but in the meantime, more than any of the 2019 films that qualify as new classics, *Cats* looks like the kind of movie made for streaming services that tell us their movies have been watched by 300 million people and are number one on their weird charts, having broken every made-up record they can think of.

RECENTLY I WATCHED A CLIP ON YouTube of Woody Allen's appearance on Bill Maher's *Club Random* podcast. Allen was there to act as a second banana while Maher railed against cancel culture. Maher seemed agitated and vulgar compared to Allen, who came across as meek and old and like he would rather have been somewhere else, with someone who was not drinking from a large bottle of tequila.

Allen, director of one of the essential movie-theater films, *The Purple Rose of Cairo*, mentioned that he prefers to see movies in theaters, that that has always been his thing. That's what he makes films for, he said—to show them in theaters, to large groups of spectators all at once, not to isolated viewers at home. Maher reacted poorly to this. "You know this is a civilization gone with the wind?" the talk show host smirked, using the title of a 1939 movie to explain to a director who has been in the film industry for seven decades that he could get a lot more people to watch his movies if he made them for streaming television. Since Allen had already tried and failed to do that with an Amazon series starring Elaine May and Miley Cyrus, it probably would have been better not to bring that up.

As one of our more strident baby boomers, however, Maher could not help himself. He was compelled to voice an attitude that has contaminated his generation. A famously tech-loving cohort with money to burn, they have celebrated every new technology, right up to artificial intelligence, and presumably they will love the death robots because they, Immortan Joes all, will be in charge of them. As part of this new regime of anti-human technology, it has become imperative for them not only to believe that no one goes to the movies anymore, but also to mention this every time the subject of current movies comes up.

The continued existence of the cinema threatens their supremacy in the desiccated cultural life of our time. It has to be true for them in order for their resignation in the face of tech—and their total capitulation to it—not to become obvious as what it is: evidence of their own cultural stagnancy. Their self-perceived, long-term dominance in the cultural sphere won't allow for challenge. Saying at every opportunity that no one goes to the movies justifies their lack of interest in the possibility of new ones being good. *They* haven't heard of them. If good ones were being made, they'd somehow just know, without expending any effort.

This attitude plays into the hands of the right, whose obsession with being anti-Hollywood extends to a generalized hostility toward moviegoing. Whenever a celebrity says something the right doesn't like, a thousand social media posts appear announcing that "I haven't seen a movie in a theater in over eight years," or, more likely, ascribing a lack of interest to others: "This right here is why sooo many people checked out of watching anything Hollywood creates." Both of these are tweets I found in two seconds, the second from someone announcing his age and status (unless he's a bot): @silverfoxlife.

Or maybe this brand of generational solipsism is just a sign of age. Éric Rohmer, of all people, was not immune to it. In a documentary about him called *Moral Tales, Filmic Issues*, made in 2006, when he was 86 years old, Rohmer says the following to Barbet Schroeder, his interlocutor:

> I'll admit, some people might be outraged, but I don't go to the movies anymore. I can appreciate a film more, and judge it better, if I see it on video instead of in the movie theater. This is due to my age. I'm getting a bit claustrophobic and my eyesight is . . . I've lost the knack of choosing a seat at the right distance from the screen, because often I can't get to that seat and I can't sit just anywhere. That's why I prefer a film on video, despite what certain purists think.

The difference is that Rohmer, as one would expect, is wise enough not to make his preference into a universal fact. He "admits" he does it; he does not say it's better or that now nobody does it any other way.

Too often film critics get defensive about this screen agnosticism, responding to their implicatedness with non sequitur and cliché. Yes, cinephiles want to see everything all at once, for free if possible, and there are ways to do that from home or on the go. It's true that in most of the country there are fewer theaters showing fewer movies, and the local rep house is too often hosting a singalong screening of a musical. Martin Scorsese saw a lot of films for the first time on TV, and Truffaut wrote that if a film is good, its quality comes through even on a small black-and-white TV.

So what? We're always being told that for decades now most people's introduction to cinema has been via a TV screen or a computer screen. This is a truism. Repeating it gets us nowhere. And making a point of defending it is counterproductive to the future of cinema. Whenever David Lynch's cri de coeur against watching movies "on your fucking telephone" circulates online, it is met with hostility from certain people. As beloved as Lynch is, some of his viewers treat his assessment as an insult to their lifestyle choices. The implication of their overreactions is clear: a defense of laziness, convenience, and (cinephagic) gluttony—things they probably don't like in other people.

ON THE OTHER END OF THE SCALE, it is possible that the people who go to the movies less than anybody else, and who watch the fewest number of films, are members of the Hollywood film industry and the entertainment journalists who cover them. Binging once a year on for-your-consideration screeners of awards-nominated movies is also unhealthy. And since many of the people tasked with voting on awards don't actually watch all the movies under consideration, in 2025 the Academy of Motion Picture Arts and Sciences had to impose a rule requiring that voters in the industry watch all the Oscar-nominated films in their category to be eligible to vote on them. The rule doesn't insist they watch the whole movie, however, as that would be a crazy imposition on people already busy giving hearts to @emrata on social media while the film under consideration runs in the background.

In a recent interview with the *New York Times*, one of our most anti-cinema and TV-centric publications, Reese Witherspoon asserted that "usually people are seeing one movie a year in the theaters with their kids." When the *Times* reporter asked Witherspoon if there was a cognitive shift in attention spans being led by artificial intelligence, one that was causing decreased theater attendance in younger people, the actor-producer replied, "everybody knows it."

This is nonsense. First, the genres on which movie theaters reliably make money year after year are kids' movies, family movies, and animated movies. Box office stats bear that out. Second, if the reporter meant teens, what is unquestionably keeping most of them away is the rising price of theater admissions, coupled with a growing lack of employment opportunities for them to make money to spend at movie theaters. As for what "everybody knows" about artificial intelligence, that's another story. Yes, if AI takes over film production, audiences will stay away. That has nothing to do with attention spans and everything to do with the quality of the product that will emerge, something the studios are betting won't matter, or don't care about because their interest in theatrical exhibition has waned. Witherspoon adds that it is a waste of her time to try to get movies made that the studios won't greenlight. If even before the pandemic you were acting in and producing movies like *A Wrinkle in Time* and *Lucy in the Sky*, it makes sense why you might not bother.

The more these views are asserted, the more the box office has pushed back. It is to be remembered that Warner Bros. was so convinced that Ryan Coogler's *Sinners* wouldn't do well that they gave him a piece of the action (first-dollar gross and licensing rights). WBD then looked on bashfully as the Penske entertainment press (*Variety*, the *Hollywood Reporter*, Deadline, Gold Derby) recoiled in horror on WBD's behalf at *Sinners*' success and the money Coogler was making.

When *Revenge of the Sith* and *Jaws* were rereleased this year on their respective twentieth and fiftieth anniversaries, they cleaned up at the box office, despite being available streaming. But being number one at the movies is still not enough for Smilin' Ted Sarandos to press pause on his endless sales pitch for staying at home. Releasing movies in theaters, said the Netflix co-CEO as moviegoers lined up to see decades-old films, is "an outmoded idea for most people." One wonders who Sarandos means when he talks about *most people.* As early as 1954, the powerhouse screenwriter Ben Hecht was referring to Americans as "the TV watchers," yet this did not cause him to want to destroy theatrical exhibition. But he wasn't a co-CEO.

In the publicly traded world of Netflix and the breathless business reporting that follows it around, the growing success of arthouses and revival houses is an understandable inconvenience best ignored. Since news reports about the resurgence of these movie theaters cannot compete with stories about big tech and its oligarchs, and now their obsession with AI, it's also understandable why news of the continued existence of moviegoing has not permeated public consciousness. Widespread disbelief in the cinema is not amenable to hearing about it.

Yet over the past two years there have been many stories in the news about this very phenomenon. A headline in the *Telegraph* on November 24, 2023 read "Old Films, New Fans: Inside the Repertory Cinema Boom." From Screen Daily on February 20, 2024: "Why It's Boom Time for Theatrical Re-releases of Classic Films." NPR's Marketplace announced on June 27, 2024 that "Indie Theaters Are Using Repertory Films to Stay Afloat." The website Adolescent on December 31, 2024: "The Remarkable Movie Theater Boom of 2024." The *Christian Science Monitor*, two months later, on February 27, 2025: "'I Didn't Know I Needed It.' Why Neighborhoods Rally to Save Moviehouses." The Silver Spring, Maryland, news site Source of the Spring on March 6, 2025: "How AFI Silver and Maryland's Independent Theaters Are Thriving Amid Nationwide Closures." The *Orange County Register* the next month, on April 1, 2025: "Across the Region, Repertory Cinema Is Cool Once More." This all culminated in a piece on Sequoia Capital's controversial investment in MUBI (controversial because of Sequoia's ties to the Israeli military) in the *Financial Times* on May 31, 2025, in which the paper explained that Sequoia's investment was a response to the "rising global demand for arthouse cinema."

It is Hollywood that has ceded this ground. The studios don't make enough movies anymore. We have seen Christian movies, right-wing documentaries, and Bollywood movies take over screens in the big chains as the major studios decrease their output.

The big exhibitors have responded by booking movies from outside the pipeline of their traditional suppliers, but they are part of the problem too. In Kleber Mendonça Filho's 2023 documentary, *Pictures of Ghosts*, about his life as a moviegoer in his hometown, Recife, on Brazil's northeastern coast, Mendonça refers to movie theater marquees as "timepieces," because they so often show up in the backgrounds of photographs, which can be accurately dated by the release dates of the films playing at the theaters, their titles visible on the marquees. Marquees allow us to link pictures to certain dates, to periods in our own pasts and to history in general.

I drove by a fifteen-screen Cinemark multiplex in West Springfield, Massachusetts recently. This Cinemark had replaced the marquee with a huge billboard extolling the comfort of the seats in the theater. It made the building look like a chair factory. I guess this makes sense for places where the concession stand now sells two-person lap blankets, "the perfect costar for any movie." For the full airline experience, they could sell eye masks and ear plugs, too. Forget about the marquee. Why see the movie at all?

DURING THE PANDEMIC, when the studios were convinced moviegoing was a thing of the past and streaming had a headlock on the future, it became clear to them that the value of movie stars was linked to screen size—that stars were paid by the foot. So if a movie star appeared in a movie theater on a forty-foot screen, maybe they had to be paid $20 million. But what if their images could literally be cut down to size? On a two-foot screen at home, maybe they were only worth $2 million. And what about on a six-inch screen on a smartphone?

Scarlett Johansson had to sue Disney over a variation on this kind of thinking. When her 2021 superhero-starrer *Black Widow* was released simultaneously in theaters and on streaming because of the pandemic, she lost all the pay that, per her contract, was tied to box-office performance. She and Disney settled out of court, with the

Mouse allegedly compensating Johansson for her lost earnings. Now streamers like Apple have to once again pay stars like George Clooney and Brad Pitt in the low-to-mid eight figures for *Wolfs*, a movie that played in theaters for a week and then went to the studio's streaming channel, where it was watched by few and discussed by fewer, while the streamer touted it as the most popular movie it had ever made.

High salaries for actors contribute mightily to the studios' disappointment in the continuing success of a collective medium they would rather control at every stage in the process. Never in the history of cinema have producers had more power than they do now. Digital shooting and computer-generated images, coupled with AI, mean that every image falls out of the hands of directors and cinematographers and fully escapes the actors directed and photographed by them. If the studio owns the movie and there is no final cut in the director's contract, then there is no final cut, ever. Bob Iger, Disney's CEO, has mentioned that filmmakers in Hollywood must "embrace the change" represented by AI.

"While we are extremely proud of what's on screen," Iger said in 2023, "it's gotten to the point where it is enormously expensive." This from a company with almost $5 billion in net income in 2024, despite losing over $11 billion on streaming, against a profit of $5.5 billion in theatrical revenue. Streaming was profitable for Disney in 2024: they made $47 million—not billion—on it in the first half of the year. To put that in perspective, Iger's 2024 "total compensation" was $41 million, up about 30 percent from his 2023 package of $32 million.

With this kind of system in place, it is easy to see why studios are so eager to fully automate. While some actors, including Johansson, have come out against AI, others will be happy to lease or sign over their voices and faces for future animated product that can be used the way the late Peter Cushing is used in *Star Wars* product. James Earl Jones, the voice of Darth Vader, did exactly this before he died in 2024, ensuring that all future iterations of Vader will speak as the original. As I was writing this, an AI company announced that one of their creations, an AI-generated actress they call Tilly Norwood, had attracted the attention of talent agencies that were now trying to sign her, or it.

The new kind of fake actor will be a total reversal of the way movie stars have been seen throughout film history. In his 2023 biography of the Chinese American actor Anna May Wong (the only Hollywood movie star to ever make it onto US currency—her face appeared on an "American Women" series of quarters in 2022), Yunte Huang includes a trip Wong took to her father's hometown in China in 1936. People she met there were shocked to learn that she was a real person who actually existed. "They had seen me on screen, but they thought I was simply a picture invented by a machine," Wong wrote at the time. We should now prepare for the opposite of this kind of confusion. Some people will come to think that movie stars who don't exist are real.

This plan is pretty much in motion at Disney. Iger will continue to lay off staff while at the same time emphasizing what he calls "quality over quantity." Thus the upcoming releases from Disney are *Toy Story 5, Zootopia 2, Frozen III, Incredibles 3, The Mandalorian and Grogu, Avatar: Fire and Ash,* and *Tron: Ares,* all sequels based on previously existing intellectual property. It reminds me of a tweet from HBO Max (when it was still called that, before they renamed it MAX and then changed it back) about a forgotten movie they made in 2020 called *Superintelligence,* with Melissa McCarthy and disgraced talk-show host James Corden as the voice of evil: "An all-powerful AI decides humanity's fate—and it's hilarious."

Iger has explained that "politics is bad for business." "The bottom line," he says, "is that infusing messaging as a sort of number-one priority in our films and TV shows is not what we're up to." Their films and TV shows instead "need to be entertaining." According to a news report, one of Disney's problems is that "many audience members began to feel the company's content had grown overly existential and too concerned with social issues beyond the reach of children." Who were these *audience members*? I don't speak with many children, but I haven't heard any of them say they are leaving recent Disney and Pixar movies in a state of confusion and dread.

An unwillingness to come up with new material and an inability to sell it to audiences is a strange idea of what constitutes quality. It makes a virtue of playing it safe. It is a kind of filmmaking born of cowardice. Iger's version of "quality over quantity" is also appealing to those who approve corporate mergers in Washington. If Paramount Skydance can try to buy WBD, maybe Disney can absorb Universal. Then Sony and Lionsgate can merge, reducing Hollywood to three major studios making maybe forty-five movies a year. FCC Chairman Brendan Carr has written to Iger criticizing Disney for prioritizing their streaming service over the needs of local ABC-TV affiliates. Given their goals, which face government approval, it is amazing that after pulling Jimmy Kimmel and his late-night talk show off the air, they let him back on. But the only people Iger fears more than the Trump Administration are Hulu subscribers, who can cancel their streaming subscriptions. The trade-off is clear, however. The government wants to control TV news; owners of local affiliates want to consolidate; and the studios want to consolidate, too, just as Disney took over Hulu. This circle represents the death of knowledge and art in an age of extreme wealth inequality, a new paradigm that will generate garbage with as little human involvement as possible.

In Franz Kafka's story "In the Penal Colony," which is about an automated torture device, Kafka writes that "we used to have to adjust a few things by hand, but from now on the machine will work all by itself." I think this is exactly what people dread about AI and why they recoil from it, and also why large corporations are so excited about it. It is an aspect of the kind of fascism predicted by Kafka in the early 20th century. It removes the human element from the cinema just as the tech industry in general is removing showbiz from entertainment.

Here the news, entertainment, and the government all merge into a pool of toxic sludge. Because of AI, we could already picture a future in which another pandemic happens while we, as a species on lockdown, pass the hours in isolation viewing subpar art made by hallucination-prone nonentities. Today, videos of ICE raids scored to AI-generated nü-metal songs follow AI-generated jpegs of Donald Trump as Colonel Kilgore in *Apocalypse Now*, calling to mind "Ride of the Valkyries" from that film's score, solidifying the connection to the Wagner-loving Third Reich. We live under a mode of dehumanized production where the most human element is the images of dead Palestinians that show up in our feeds between the latest iterations of the official slop.

YOUNG CINEPHILES HAVE traveled a strange road in the 21st century, much to their credit. In general I think their trajectory went in this direction: a childhood of repeated exposure to animated family movies from Hollywood, occasionally enlivened by a Miyazaki, then onto violent, ugly horror films—the new ones also mostly made in Hollywood, the adolescent flipside of the kids' movies. And then, right after that: *Salò, or the 120 Days of Sodom*. With Letterboxd reviews.

I'm not especially interested in Letterboxd. I think it will eventually go the way of other social media into a *Salò*-esque enshittification, and I don't like watching celebrities being pestered to give up their favorite movies on camera, no matter how much they love John Cassavetes and Elaine May. At the same time, I think Letterboxd is preferable to the Roll Call of Shame that is Rotten Tomatoes. In the world of film criticism there is nothing sadder than seeing the phrase "Tomatometer-approved critic" in somebody's bio. I don't understand why critics seek approval from this content aggregator, owned by Comcast and WBD, which takes and republishes their work for free. (They approved me without my asking and I have occasionally sent in corrections to their evaluations of my work because once they claimed I thought *The Magnificent Ambersons* was "rotten." A scarring thing to see next to your name.)

The fact that Rotten Tomatoes has led to grade inflation in evaluating movies is well known. That alone demonstrates the herd mentality this kind of aggregation creates. I think Letterboxd is less susceptible to that, though on the other hand I have witnessed Letterboxd users announcing that they give every movie five stars because filmmakers try so hard. At least with Letterboxd we are not yet seeing actual news headlines like "*Guardians of the Galaxy Vol. 3* Rotten Tomatoes Score Revealed."

Most mainstream film criticism is of the average Rotten Tomatoes variety. Film critics prior to the 21st century existed to draw in readers and increase circulation. Their pieces often appeared in the final pages of magazines because many readers started from the back. This was one of the secrets of Pauline Kael's success and influence. Newspaper (and later TV) critics like Gene Siskel and Roger Ebert had a voice because they were compelling figures and struck readers as honest. Readers of hometown Chicago dailies often read them first when they picked up the paper.

Critics had personality, style, originality, wit, and deep knowledge borne of seeing many films, but for the most part publishers replaced them as they retired or died with people who could always be counted on to tell readers that *Good Time* was a bad movie and *Three Billboards Outside Ebbing, Missouri* or *1917* were good ones. I think of these critics as fake humanists, devoid of any of the values or pleasure I expect when I read film criticism.

The confluence of digital projection, streaming channels, AI, and the alleged death of criticism often makes it seem like we are dealing with the destruction of a worldview. I believe that this is indeed the goal of the corporations that control the studios and publishers. I don't think it means that people don't want to read criticism. What they don't want to read are writers who are afraid of their editors, who curry favor with Hollywood, and who want to be influencers. Critics like that don't consider one of the most important and necessary things about criticism today, that "struggle is always fighting the business world," as Noam Chomsky put it.

That should be foundational. The novelist Don DeLillo said the same thing in 2005, in an interview with a French horror-film magazine. Writers "must oppose systems. It's important to write against power, corporations, the state, and the whole system of consumption and of debilitating entertainments . . . I think writers, by nature, must oppose things, oppose whatever power tries to impose on us." It is significant that the author of *Libra* mentions "debilitating entertainments" (and only seventeen years before the Netflix version of *White Noise* came out). Studio product is too often wearying. There is a great sense of defeat that the new, would-be monoculture instills in all but the most here-for-it. We have to write against that. We can both "await the end of cinema with optimism" and understand film's value at the same time. There's a song by Momus called "What Will Death Be Like?" that is more about what death *won't* be like. "Death will be unlike the sea as it thunders on Liv Ullmann vanishing under the rollers," Momus sings. I know "the rollers" refers to the ocean waves in the movie *The Emigrants*, but when I hear it I always picture the rollers in a movie projector guiding the film between reels.

September 2025

WE CAN STILL THINK OUR OWN THOUGHTS

Crazy Rich Asians

If you go to a bachelorette party on an island and the other guests put a huge bloody fish head on your pillow, you are in a horror movie, not a rom-com. Maybe at this point in the history of capitalism there's not much difference. *Crazy Rich Asians* looks more like a glossy tourist magazine produced for an international economics summit than a movie.

While Henry Golding just misses the mark at being an actual Anglo-Asian Cary Grant (maybe next time), Constance Wu, playing an Asian American everywoman, comes off generic, a paper doll dressed first as a professor, then a Disney princess. Among the too numerous cast, Ronny Chieng and Victoria Loke stand out as a sarcastic, mean-spirited young husband and wife who despise each other, unlike the unmemorable Gemma Chan and Pierre Png, who play a more prominent, unfunny version of the same thing. I would gladly watch an entire movie about Chieng and Loke's shallow, disrespectful, well-dressed irritants wasting their fortune while struggling to maintain their status.

BlacKkKlansman

The film is framed by a satirical lecture featuring Alec Baldwin as a John Birch Society racist and documentary footage of the 2017 Unite the Right rally in Charlottesville, Virginia, in which Heather Heyer was killed by someone who could be this Baldwin character's grandson. What comes in between is an action-comedy that supposedly takes place in Colorado and mixes together, in standard Spike Lee style, police investigations, Black-history lessons, ruminations on genre cinema, and a dismantling of *The Birth of a Nation.*

Complaints that *BlacKkKlansman* valorizes cops are moot, since this film could not exist without them any more than a Sidney Lumet film like *Serpico* or *Prince of the City* could. Just like in those films, the cops here are a rogues' gallery of New York types, now transposed to Colorado. Their dialogue slips into a version of, "Eyyy, I'm John Turturro's brother, are we gonna get these Klan scumbags or what?" Adding to this Brooklyn feeling, a triumphant scene takes place in Sunny's waterfront bar in Red Hook. Lee establishes the scene with Sunny's red-and-green anchor-and-dolphin neon sign, showing us that this is just one of those nautical-themed saloons you find a county over from the Rocky Mountains.

Lee made the didactic *BlacKkKlansman* to move audiences, which he succeeds in doing despite the feeling that the film has been stitched together from everywhere. If the love scenes between John David Washington and Laura Harrier fall flat (unlike their period hairdos), it's because they are the bland good people in this movie, which foregrounds actors like Ashlie Atkinson, who plays the self-deluded, racist wife of a Klan goon like she's a transplant from the Bensonhurst of *The Honeymooners.* The film works well when Washington puts on his white voice to prank call Klansmen. He aspirates the word *white* with the precision Diane Keaton brought to the word *wheat* in *Love and Death,* without the crutch of being dubbed by a white comic as in *Sorry to Bother You.* His phone routines could have gone on longer, which would have added to the satiric intensity of the movie more than Alec Baldwin's slideshow meltdown.

Mission: Impossible – Fallout

Alec Baldwin is everywhere in 2018 as a bigheaded, squinty illustration of American authority's collapse. In the latest *Mission: Impossible* movie he returns as Tom Cruise's boss, the leader of a spy agency more rogue than the CIA. His confrontations with Angela Bassett, as the CIA's head, are tepid. They distract from Cruise's epic struggle to maintain his status as an action hero, a fight Cruise wins via grueling stunt work on the roofs of the world. Cruise is a live-action testament to his own ability to take punishment, a kind of human sacrifice. He is undiminished by both time and all the semi-comedy around him, which is the story of his career and his life.

Mission: Impossible – Fallout begins with a harrowing dream sequence, like *Vanilla Sky*. Called into question at his wedding as a failure who puts his loved ones in jeopardy, Cruise spends the rest of the film trying to make up for it by putting random people in danger, up to and including everyone in China, India, and Pakistan—a third of the world's population and a substantial market for films like this. Everyone who is not in Cruise's squad is formidable: Vanessa Kirby as a British arms dealer more threatening and coolly appealing than any woman in a recent Bond film; Sean Harris as a Steve Bannon-esque alleged mastermind strapped to a chair. Watching Cruise relentlessly pursue and destroy Henry Cavill's double-crossing CIA hunk, whose dialogue seems dubbed, was really satisfying. If anyone has earned the right to victory over a British superhero actor with a porn mustache who is twenty years his junior, it's the movie star who has managed to avoid the trite universes of DC and Marvel, even if it took being in that mummy film to do it.

The Equalizer 2

In the first *Equalizer*, Denzel Washington played an ex–intelligence agent working at a Home Depot in East Boston, Massachusetts. What made that movie work was how real Washington and director Antoine Fuqua made employment at Home Depot feel, as if someone involved had done time in the PVC pipe and lumber aisles. They had the layout down.

The new one starts with Washington disguised as an imam on a train in Turkey, with a big beard, a white skullcap, and black-frame eyeglasses, a look he pulls off better than anyone else in the past thousand years. While this is a change from working at Home Depot, *The Equalizer 2* is not quite a *Mission: Impossible* movie. Soon he is back in Boston, where he now works as a Lyft driver and still lives alone in a small apartment. During one of his shifts, he breaks into the hotel room of a drunken misogynist fare, a finance bro, to teach him and his buddies a lesson.

Between the train scene and the Lyft driving, *The Equalizer 2* begins with a lot of momentum. It dissipates as attention shifts to Washington's former spy colleagues. Confrontations with them in a suburban driveway and at a beach house in a deserted seaside town during a hurricane indicate movement away from the working class, toward the kind of real estate ex–intelligence agents are more likely to inhabit. Fuqua stages it all with a kind of Anthony Mann intensity and attention to space, but *The Equalizer 2* will probably end up being the only action movie to ever leave me wanting more scenes of the protagonist working for a rideshare app, or at least the only one since Jamie Foxx invented Uber in *Collateral*.

Leave No Trace

Will (Ben Foster), a veteran with PTSD, and his adolescent daughter, Tom (Thomasin McKenzie), live hardcore off the grid in a state forest in the Pacific Northwest. After yuppie hikers discover their lean-to and report them to the rangers, Will and Tom are relocated to a tree farm in an isolated community with a church and a school. There, Tom is exposed for the first time to people her own age. She makes contact with a dude who looks like a refugee from a Gus Van Sant film, or a guy from a grunge band like the Screaming Trees, a name that makes sense in this context. Tom wants to join 4-H with him so she can learn to take care of animals. Will, however, cannot abide the confinement of the small house he and his daughter have been assigned, nor can he tolerate the war-battle noise of the helicopters that haul away trees to be sold at Christmastime. "We can still think our own thoughts," he tells Tom when they move in, but the conformity of the simple life blots out thought for him, a man for whom peace of mind is impossible in human society.

Debra Granik's *Leave No Trace* is the director's belated return to feature filmmaking after *Winter's Bone* in 2010. Like *Captain Fantastic* from a couple of years ago, but with much more art, grace, and a sense of actual danger—perhaps because it is set among the homeless, perhaps because it was made by a woman—*Leave No Trace* restates the male Gen-X narrative of protecting children from the outside world and their eventual reintegration into it. For Foster's Will, there is no redemption, unlike Viggo Mortensen's character in *Captain Fantastic*. Will is a permanent exile who turns his back on the world, too damaged to change despite the chances offered him. Foster plays him somber and unlikable, in a performance of confusion and quiet self-righteousness that leads him to expose his daughter to frostbite, rides from truckers, and housebreaking. When Tom finally abandons him, he slinks back into the woods, a hermit turning his back on the film he's in. Granik pulls away to a God's-eye view of this figure as he disappears.

Gavagai

The enigmatic American filmmaker Rob Tregenza's last feature film before *Gavagai* came out twenty years ago. As in *Leave No Trace*, in *Gavagai* a man (Andreas Lust) goes into the woods alone. Unfriendly and embittered, he arrives in a remote Norwegian town and hires a driver (Mikkel Gaup) to take him farther north for reasons he doesn't explain. This is not a road film in which two men wax philosophical and overcome their differences on a journey through the European countryside, like in those *Trip* movies and TV shows with Steve Coogan and Rob Brydon, "from acclaimed director Michael Winterbottom." Tregenza shoots quiet people in long takes with complicated camera moves. The two men barely speak and never quite bond. Tregenza is not sketching the wistful unhappiness of the moneyed creative class so much as staring into the divide between souls.

The man's journey comes to an end short of his destination. In the rain on a cliff overlooking an expanse of forest, he rips up his late wife's translations of the Norwegian writer Tarjei Vesaas and flings them into the wind. His anger, destructive and futile, seems to compound his wife's death by destroying what's left of her work. *Gavagai* is a film about the impossibility of closure and the endlessness of grief. The title comes from the analytic philosopher W. V. Quine's *Word and Object*, in which Quine invents the word *gavagai* to use as an example of that-which-is-untranslatable. Tregenza and his co-scenarist Kirk Kjeldsen have translated, it seems, the poems of Vesaas into mood and atmosphere. The poems haunt *Gavagai* in this confrontation with the void. Sometimes they appear in the form of the man's wife, a ghost who shows up as an awkward memory-in-translation. In the end, the man and the film are both wise to abandon this image and return to life around a fire at dusk.

Let the Corpses Tan

This Belgian genre film, a delirious, unpleasant mash-up of a poliziottesco and a spaghetti western, shot in Corsica, is as violent as it is arty. A heist-gone-wrong set in and around a villa and a cave, it features a cast of treacherous, criminal zeroes, bohemians, and cops, and it doesn't let up on the violence or the artiness.

While adapting Jean-Patrick Manchette novels for the screen is as inevitable as it is desirable, this one seems to exist only as a music video for Ennio Morricone's score. As a music video, it's a shocker but too long. As a feature film, it's pointless and repetitive, especially the squeaking-leather-pants sound effect that recurs over and over again. Manchette's novels are latter-day séries noires, fast-paced, destructive critiques of capitalism from the era of urban terrorism in Europe. Few of their characters survive. In *Let the Corpses Tan* none do, and the grimness is not ironic or critical, just maggoty. The film does give off that "I'm on drugs" feel (specifically of bad speed), but it's so labor-intensive that, like many a trip, it should have ended sooner. Elina Löwensohn's presence as a witchy bisexual and often nude painter is almost as mysterious as Morricone's contract must have been. I hope Löwensohn made money, because busy-bee deconstructionists with many-itemed shot lists like codirectors Hélène Cattet and Bruno Forzani should pay their actors by the frame.

Mandy

The cinema is moving in all directions as endless new content crams itself into every available space. This is leading to new kinds of international cross-border weirdness, as films, more than ever, are shot wherever the money is. It's not just Belgians in Corsica imitating Italians, or Brooklyn playing Colorado, or North Carolina as California, or Toronto and Vancouver as anywhere else. Now, in *Mandy*, we get Belgium as both the Pacific Northwest and the bowels of hell, starring Nicolas Cage.

Emerging from the same cross-contaminated genre swamp as *Let the Corpses Tan*, *Mandy* achieves its goals with blunter and larger instruments, which is all the better, because where *Corpses* fails, *Mandy* succeeds. If *Corpses* was a music video, *Mandy* is a whole doom-metal opera in poisonous Technicolor, with an album cover depicting a landscape of magenta, indigo, and golden-yellow ruins. The film is like that Bell Witch album that only has one ninety-minute-long track.

It opens with King Crimson's "Starless" on the sound track, playing before a clip from a Ronald Reagan speech about "spiritual awakening." It's 1983 and Cage, a lumberjack, lives in the woods with his girlfriend (Andrea Riseborough), a weird-fiction fan who works in a tiny country grocery store and speaks like Patti Smith reading the poem at the beginning of "The Revenge of Vera Gemini"—a British person's version of unaffected Americanness. Riseborough's slight New Jersey inflection points to where *Mandy* lets in real life. One of the film's principle pleasures is that for all its splashy-morose color schemes and arty dissolves, its death cult maintains the feeling of unemployed oafs from Neptune, New Jersey, worshipping Satan in Ramapo Mountain State Forest.

The film is pure acid trip with a macaroni-and-cheese commercial thrown in. (TV commercials are the worst things to see on hallucinogenic drugs.) Cage howls in pain and screams in despair, breaking out in occasional intelligibility only to say things like, "Don't be negative." By the end, as a grimy, wounded Cage stands with a chain saw in front of a burning car and still hasn't avenged his girlfriend or saved anyone else from the drug-addicted demons/private-press recording artists, it becomes obvious what director Panos Cosmatos has delivered here: a parody of "the hero's journey" on par with Kanye West's use of that phrase in the Oval Office while describing Donald Trump to himself.

Burning

Panos Cosmatos knows a lot of things about making movies, including that you show the burning cars. And yet he's no Lee Chang-dong, who fails to fully reveal a burning Porsche that's an important plot point in his new film. Lee does show Donald Trump, however, on a TV in the protagonist's apartment, using the original Cheddar Goblin to add to the sense of unease in this unique serial-killer mystery. And unlike *Let the Corpses Tan*, *Burning* raises actual questions about money and its effects on people's lives.

Burning, like *Psycho* and *L'avventura*, starts off as a film about a woman, Hae-mi (Jeon Jong-seo), who appears to be its subject and star. While working her job hawking cell phone accessories in a miniskirt, she reconnects with Jong-su (Yoo Ah-in), a poverty-stricken aspiring writer she knew in high school. After they hook up, she leaves for a solo trip to Africa and returns with a new friend, Ben, played by the American actor Steven Yeun in a subtle, nuanced performance that shifts between friendly-classy and "I'm a secret arsonist." Ben is a young member of Gangnam's idle class, and neither Hae-mi nor Jong-su fit in there. After Hae-mi begins to date Ben, she disappears again. Jong-su quizzes Ben about her absence and slowly comes to realize something isn't quite right with this slick, fashionable dude who starts reading Faulkner because Jong-su mentioned him, one of the film's slyest condemnations of rich-person poaching.

Burning refuses to reveal what actually happened to Hae-mi, or what kind of person Ben really is, if he is any type at all, which leaves Jong-su in a terrifying moral limbo. All three of the film's main characters are dispensed with by Lee in this unsentimental movie that shows human connection as fragile and masked when the friends are unequal. Hae-mi, dismissed from the film the earliest and seemingly with ease, in a way gets off the easiest of these characters, because there's no way to know what happened to her. She's kooky and a searcher but also just an innocent victim. But of what? With the men it's all too clear.

Decline and recline

Cinephiles in New York have noted the difference between how 2018 began and how it is ending. In January it was possible to see a movie a day in almost any theater for $9.99 a month using MoviePass. It was possible to stream thousands of classic and foreign films at home through FilmStruck for about $8 a month. Now, out of the blue and with little explanation, but as the result of its monopolistic deal with AT&T, Time Warner has shut down FilmStruck. MoviePass still exists, but barely. For a while it managed to do something that seemed impossible: It changed theatrical exhibition for the better. Now it has (more predictably than the shuttering of FilmStruck, it must be said) become some new kind of con in which only the most mediocre and longest-running movies are available to see, and only three a month. Suddenly we are plunged into a world of $16 movies at theaters in a city with no video stores.

The cancellation of both services, at this point, seems like the end of the long tail. The blockbuster model has reasserted itself and as usual seeks to muscle everything else out of the way. At the height of corporate capitalism you pay full price for bad movies improperly projected in ugly theaters whose business is selling large sodas at a 1,000 percent markup. If you want to watch a movie at home, there's Netflix, now mostly a streaming television service, or Amazon. It's all an insult to cinephiles and to film history. Going mass means living in the moment and throwing away what came before. The moment is crap.

To rub it in, the large theatrical chains have implemented reserved seating policies, which, by slowing down ticket buying at the box office, herd filmgoers into making electronic purchases for which they have to pay an additional fee. Reserved seats are antithetical to moviegoing, which traditionally and democratically has been first come, first served. You could move to a different seat if a weirdo (or anybody) was sitting too close. This new nonegalitarian system is fancy and inappropriate. It takes too long and it huddles people together. Let's just go to the opera at this point, instead of seeing *The Girl in the Spider's Web* pinned in place next to someone texting "wyd?"

Meanwhile the ads shown before movies have gotten more aggressive about copping to how terrible and disgusting their products are. The one for Diet Coke with Netflix actress Gillian Jacobs is a masterpiece of the passive-aggressive come-on. "Look," Jacobs begins, like a pundit on a TV news show, "here's the thing about Diet Coke: life is short." As well as nasty and brutish. Next she implores people who want to live in yurts to "yurt it up" and "just do you." Yurt dwellers may not drink Diet Coke, but they still have rights. She concludes with a simple confession: "Diet Coke: because I can."

Has freedom of choice ever seemed less appealing? At least that particular ad wasn't made by a film student. The worst, most dystopian Coke ads shown in theaters—each one a little nightmare from a society that has gone full *Clockwork Orange*—are now also promos for higher education. They are contests that inculcate their lucky film-student winners into a world of meta-shilling, where the theatrical experience is reconfigured as an excuse to slurp Coke under dim lights. Doing that is so satisfying that the actors onscreen envy the soda guzzlers in their cushy seats with cup holders and reach out to grab their giant sodas.

This kind of audience flattery is a form of permission to use cell phones while the movie is on. If the actors are just dorks like you who need a Coke so bad, there isn't any need to pay attention to them. When I went to see *Crazy Rich Asians* my date and I sat next to three other couples in a row with eight seats. The young women in the other couples texted throughout the movie (which was sold as an important cultural event) while their boyfriends, careful not to mess up a date, sat passively and stared at the screen as if their girlfriends were watching the movie with them instead of paying attention to other people who weren't there.

I saw an Ingmar Bergman film at the Museum of Modern Art recently, where I was seated one row over from a family of four. The father texted throughout the first half hour of the movie, impervious to the nearby MoMA regulars hissing at him to stop. When they began turning around, jabbing their fingers in his face, and threatening to take his phone, he stood up, grabbed his children's hands, and marched out of the theater in a huff, his wife trailing behind. Somehow, he had been wronged. Similarly, at the New York Film Festival screening of *Burning*, a man seated a couple of rows ahead of me texted on and off for the first twenty minutes of the film until someone got an usher to shine a flashlight in his face and threaten to remove him. I understand why the texters went to see *Crazy Rich Asians*. I do not understand what they were doing at MoMA and the New York Film Festival.

It's true that excellent new theaters that show good movies have opened, and are opening, in New York City. They sell discount cards, and anyway, there are many different ways to see movies, some of them legal, without FilmStruck and MoviePass. But cash outlays for those discount cards are not small and the prices without them are steep. And when *Venom* came out last month to universal pans and no human being who liked it could be found anywhere, it still cleaned up at the box office. It's still playing. I looked just now and it has passed $200 million in ticket sales. It must be a great movie for texting.

Wobble Palace

A journey to the end of the night set in Los Angeles, like *Faces*, *Wobble Palace* is an anti-rom-com of debasement. Unlike *Faces* its characters are petulant, underemployed young whiners instead of confused, middle-class, middle-aged drunks. Times have changed in Los Angeles. No longer Cassavetes's city of nice houses with big dining rooms, *Wobble Palace* reveals LA living as downscale and codependent, even in open relationships. Scrolling text messages take up part of the frame sometimes and add to *Wobble Palace*'s mood of smarmy irritation. One gets used to them onscreen, where they are better than in the audience, but not to the artificial *click-click* sound of the keys. Put your shit on silent.

The Halloween night 2016 setting aids the film, as writer-director-star Eugene Kotlyarenko goes full Herzog's Nosferatu as his costume choice for the scenes before the final breakup. It's more flattering than the "fat Skrillex" look he is accused of sporting earlier. Costar and cowriter Dasha Nekrasova also gets to say things like "We're gonna have our first female president soon" in her distinctive world-weary drone of postironic predisappointment. Like Viva's bored drawl in the late 1960s Warhol films and in Varda's LA-set *Lions Love*, Nekrasova's voice is the voice of a generation—in tone at least. It is so distinctive I wish she would record the service interruption announcements on the subway so that the true sound of the stalled and waiting would come through the speakers.

Support the Girls

NO DRAMA is posted as rule No. 1 for the servers at the Hooters-esque restaurant in strip-mall Texas where *Support the Girls* takes place. Andrew Bujalski highlights his film's commitment to that as a concept, even as star Regina Hall, as the restaurant's manager, admits that banning drama is impossible with her half-dressed staff of twentysomething women. But when they get too provocative, she reminds them, "We are mainstream! We are mainstream!" Drama is mainstream, porn is not. Mumblecore isn't either, so Bujalski, who is now one of the best directors of actors in American filmmaking, has designed this unique, low-key film as a vehicle for Hall, the excellent actress from the *Think Like a Man* and *Scary Movie* movies who was overshadowed by the discovery of Tiffany Haddish in *Girls Trip*.

While the film descends into a bar-top riot and ends with women drinking and screaming in rage and frustration on a roof, it is men who are more likely to violate the "No Drama" rule. The restaurant owner (James Le Gros), for instance, subjects a captive Hall to his pointless fury as they speed in his truck, with boat attached, to pursue another driver who has annoyed him on the road. When Hall and her staff move over to a corporate chain restaurant called Man Cave, an HR manager, played with polished friendliness by Brooklyn Decker, reveals the true drama of our time. "We've built this super-well-thought-out culture of respect," she explains, "and we have a whole team of attorneys who are paid a crazy amount to make sure we lay that out clearly."

Like the manager she plays, Hall is a team player to the end. I'm not sure the ensemble cast doesn't overshadow her. Lea DeLaria as Bobo, a dyke regular at the bar, steals every scene she's in. Shayna McHayle, a.k.a. the Brooklyn rapper Junglepussy, draws attention away from everybody else with nothing more than baleful stares and a self-contained sick-of-it-all attitude. If someone put McHayle and Dasha Nekrasova in a movie, they would become a bored, indie Richard Pryor and Gene Wilder, at least for South by Southwest and Bushwick, if not the mainstream.

The Queen of Sheba Meets the Atom Man

Ron Rice's last film, unfinished at the time of his too-early death, is an essential document of bohemian New York City in 1963 as it was lived and thrashed in cheap apartments and on the streets. Taylor Mead, its star, the ultimate weird boho-hipster of the second half of the 20th century, finished a final cut of *The Queen of Sheba Meets the Atom Man* in 1981 after having screened other versions around the world for almost two decades. Mead's version has now been restored by Anthology Film Archives.

The film's black-and-white images demonstrate what the camp/avant-garde nexus meant in the Manhattan of Andy Warhol, Jill Johnston, and Frank O'Hara. The film was shot a year before Sontag's "Notes on Camp" was published, but Rice's movie is a living, breathing, leg-humping enactment more amusing, friendly, and connected to daily life than Jack Smith's *Flaming Creatures*. Smith, one of Sontag's inspirations, appears in the movie and almost takes over its second half from the coy, shier Mead and from Winifred Bryan, the implacable, overweight Black woman who is the Queen of Sheba to Mead's Atom Man. The film, having established the bizarre relationship between these two mismatched oddballs, can't stray too far from them no matter who piles on. *The Queen of Sheba Meets the Atom Man* should be projected twenty-four hours a day somewhere in Manhattan, so that before we're all pushed into the sea off Rockaway Beach people can be reminded of the strange form of life that once lived here.

The Jerry Lewis Gar-Ron movies

It turns out that self-conscious cinematic camp was not exactly invented by Jack Smith in New York. In an unimposing suburban home in Pacific Palisades, California, Jerry Lewis, unbeknownst to the avant-garde, had begun in 1951 to shoot black-and-white movie parodies and pre-Warholian color screen tests during his nights and weekends off from Paramount Pictures, where he and Dean Martin were employed as the nation's most popular comedy duo. Shown only once to friends at premiere parties at the same house where they were filmed, Lewis's Gar-Ron productions (named for his sons) remained unseen by anyone else until this past October, when the Lewis estate and the Library of Congress debuted them at the Museum of Modern Art. These films, which combine borscht belt humor and *Mad* magazine–style parody with vulgar put-downs and gay panic, reveal Lewis as a comic auteur and "total filmmaker" almost ten years before his official directorial debut, *The Bellboy*.

The Gar-Ron movies, like *The Queen of Sheba Meets the Atom Man*, also document their time and place, which in this case is the sunny Southern California of Hollywood movie stars partying at home. If you had been waiting to hear Dean Martin, Janet Leigh,

Tony Curtis, or Shelley Winters utter words like *orgasm, cock, shit,* and *vomit,* your wait was over if you made it to MoMA this past fall.

The series combined featurettes, shorts, and home movies from this period in which Jerry Lewis and America were both on the rise. Lewis's well-known neuroticism and aggressiveness are less hidden and more integrated in these productions than in the Freudian constructs Paramount put together for him and Dean, or in the later work for which he was solely responsible. In fact, these movies present a happy Jerry, not the lugubrious interviewee America got to know from his films in the 1960s, after he became an auteur and a philanthropist. One home movie, shot at a 1920s-themed jazz party in the Lewis rec room, is positively giddy, with Lewis and Patti, his wife, and Curtis and Leigh doing the Charleston in boaters, spats, and flapper outfits late into the night.

The films themselves present popular movies of the day in "Jewish" versions. *Sunset Boulevard* becomes *Fairfax Avenue,* the story of a handsome young delivery boy (Curtis) from a kosher deli forced to write a screenplay for a washed-up star of the silent screen (Leigh, caked in face powder). In *Come Back Little Shiksa,* Martin is a doctor "struggling to avoid sobriety." Each is like a Kuchar brothers film with big stars in it, too weird and offensive for TV sketch comedy, an emanation from a hip demimonde that only existed in Lewis's house when Curtis and Leigh dropped by. The Milton Berle screen test, which poses Uncle Miltie against a bright-red backdrop as it scrutinizes his face so Lewis can pepper him with rude, absurd questions offscreen, is more out-there than any Warhol screen test. I'd say it's one of the best films of the 1950s, and it clearly demonstrates Lewis's way with color and his ability to capture stylized discomfort onscreen.

Spatz in the face

In the MoMA lobby between Jerry Lewis screenings, a basketball-stomached older man wearing a large newsboy cap introduced himself to me as Spatz Donovan. He cornered me to tell me he used to be the film critic on Jackie Mason's radio show. Now he had a Broadway play and a reality TV series he was developing. "Hal Prince," said Spatz, "has my play on his desk, but he's booked up for the next three years." This play, a musical, takes place during the Woodstock rock music festival in 1969, but doesn't use any of the songs. It's all new, original music that Spatz has written. His TV show, *Celebrity Séance*, involves unsuspecting contestants speaking to famous dead people through the medium of Spatz's voice impressions, which he will provide offscreen.

At the very moment Spatz asked me, in the voice of Jerry Lewis, about getting some nookie, I got a text on my phone. A woman I know who works for Netflix was in town for the New York Film Festival. She was inviting me to meet her and two filmmakers for dinner at a fancy restaurant near Lincoln Center. While Spatz imitated Jerry Lewis and I looked at this text on my phone, a Brazilian artist named Romero Britto walked by dressed in a multicolored homemade suit and stopped to pose for photos fans of his wanted to take with him. The clowns had been sent in, and I was among them.

I couldn't go to dinner. There was another Jerry Lewis movie in half an hour that I planned to see, and besides I wasn't dressed for that kind of thing. If I had gone to meet my friend and two glamorous strangers, I would have become the Spatz of the dinner, explaining how I was a film critic.

That night, instead, I had committed myself to the bizarre and the asinine. Spatz exited onto 53rd Street, still doing his Jerry Lewis voice, and I went and sat down in the lobby to wait for the next show. A lady in a burgundy tracksuit sitting across from me pulled a container of macaroni salad out of a crinkly plastic shopping bag, pried off the clear plastic lid, and began eating it with a big metal soup spoon she had brought with her to the museum. At least I wasn't wearing a funny hat.

The Other Side of the Wind

A truer séance of dubbed voices, forgotten faces, and witchy art, Orson Welles's *The Other Side of the Wind* brings a lost work back to life. By the time of his death in 1985, Welles had been working on the film for fifteen years and hadn't finished it. Now it arrives complete, fully formed, a masterpiece and a shock to the system, courtesy of Netflix and all the money they have to burn. It is not a fragment like Welles's *It's All True* or *Don Quixote*. It is done. Never has a movie been as overwhelmed by the history of its production as this one, "this circus of scattered souls . . . a desperate venture shared by desperate men." That doesn't matter anymore. The desperate men and the scattered souls are now on the screen.

Near the beginning of the film, a busload of partygoers on the way to the desert house of the film director Jake Hannaford (John Huston) passes a drive-in theater where the huge marquee advertises two movies: I EAT YOUR SKINS and I DRINK YOUR BLOODS, fitting titles for this exposé of Hollywood vampirism. It's filmed alternately like *Zabriskie Point*, random Eurotrash, Kenneth Anger–ian avant-gardism, 1970s porn, Cassavetes, and cinema verité. Like *Faces* it is another SoCal journey to the end of the night; like the Jerry Lewis home movies, it inhabits a vulgar-sophisticated world of homosexual panic, here partially masked by lots of naked hippie hetero sex in a steam bath, in a moving car, and on a back lot in Hollywood, abandoned and in ruins.

In *The Other Side of the Wind*, Welles purposefully synthesized every film style that had come along since the late 1950s, in a bid for relevance the film mocks when Hannaford is accused of doing the same. Where Hannaford crashes and burns, Welles succeeds with brilliance, adding to the sense of tragedy surrounding the film. It should have come out in its time.

The film swings wildly between tones and tempos, black-and-white and ultravivid color. Michel Legrand's score and the other music in the film add to this. In the psychedelic film-within-a-film, Blue Cheer dominates the soundtrack like Can tried to at the beginning of *Inherent Vice*. In the party scenes, we hear the hip jazz pianist Jaki Byard, his music piped in as drunks spill booze on each other and sing "Glow Worm" in a haunting scene lit only by candles.

The film was cowritten by Welles's companion, Oja Kodar, who also costars. She is often nude and plays a mute Native American who is mocked as "Pocahontas" while an underage blonde girl (Cathy Lucas), a nonactor in an ARCHIE BUNKER FOR PRESIDENT T-shirt, is passed from Peter Bogdanovich, as a director in the flush of success, to Huston's Hannaford, a director who can't get his film made in the New Hollywood of the time. It's a sick, glorious movie that ends at another drive-in, a graveyard of the cinema with a train running past it, where Kodar, projected on the screen, stabs with scissors at these men's fantasies and dreams.

DOUBLE SQUIBS WITH HAMBURGER MEAT

THE WILD BUNCH

THE SHOOTING OF *THE WILD BUNCH* WAS NOT A PRETTY PICTURE. IF A FILM were made today the way Sam Peckinpah shot *The Wild Bunch* in Mexico in 1968, and if people found out, members of the cast and crew would be facing time in jail. The history of the film's production fascinates because it was all so wrong. What happened encompasses many vices and several crimes, including manslaughter and statutory rape. It is an often repellent tale, a stew of toxic masculinity feeding a movie designed to dismantle the very myths about heroic cowboys, gun violence, and la frontera that it succumbed to as a production.

W. K. Stratton, a Texas poet whose new book details the making of the film, begins by pointing out that while Peckinpah and company reveled in—or wallowed in—the violence of their fictional frontier village, American soldiers nine thousand miles away slaughtered hundreds of innocent Vietnamese "in what became known in the United States as the My Lai Massacre." What became known as *The Wild Bunch* inadvertently re-created on the screen scenes from the Vietnam War as they happened, and simultaneously reflected violence in the USA that included the assassinations of Martin Luther King Jr. and Robert Kennedy, both of whom were shot and killed while the film was in production in remote Parras de la Fuente, Coahuila.

The Wild Bunch starts with a mass shooting and ends with a mass shooting. The first, in the crowded square of a small town, gives the lie to the "good guy with a gun" idea of police protection. Caught in the crossfire between bank robbers on horseback and a railroad company militia, townspeople die in the street as bloody bullet holes explode on the actors playing them, who have been squibbed front and back, with hamburger meat added, "to give the illusion of tissue flying with the impact." Peckinpah devised his standards of gory realism as a Marine stationed in China after World War II, where he witnessed the bloody battles between the Maoists and the Kuomintang, as well as the subsequent atrocities committed by the winners. His experiences there determined his themes and his aesthetic. He first experienced the feeling of the slow-motion effects his films became known for while riding a train in China as Communists attacked, a scene he transposed to the US-Mexico border in *The Wild Bunch*.

The Wild Bunch's second massacre utilizes a Browning M1917, an early machine gun. Peckinpah illustrates, with plenty of fake blood, the all-too-real violence automatic weapons would bring to warfare and then to civilian populations, "when a lone killer with an assault rifle," as Stratton mentions, "could kill dozens of unsuspecting people in moments." At points in *The Wild Bunch*, this machine gun, a predictor of mechanized warfare beyond human control, fires randomly without a shooter into the mass of federal troops it is there to protect. A German adviser to the Mexican Army yells out to the soldiers who can't tame the gun that "it must be mounted on a tripod!" in order to kill with precision. His shouted instruction links this weapon to the six movie cameras cinematographer Lucien Ballard used to capture the inhuman mayhem of Peckinpah's finale.

While *The Wild Bunch* reflects the racist violence we witness daily on the border in the age of Trump, in the concurrent age of mass shootings the film also underscores the continuing psychosis of a militarized culture where gun violence is commonplace and expected. The film predicts the ongoing PTSD of American life, even though it is set in 1913 and specifically concerns itself with Mexico in the 1910s, "the years of sadness," as an elder Mexican villager in the film calls them. The Mexican Revolution, with its battles between the Federal Army of the Huertistas and Pancho Villa's rebels, lasted almost the entire decade. As Stratton describes it, the war was "the most horrifically violent conflict ever to occur in North America." By the time it ended, 10 percent of the Mexican population had perished in the fighting.

This conflict was watched over and prodded by US and German interests. Marauding bands of unemployed American cowboys rampaged on the border, competing with Texas lawmen in their brutality against the Mexican inhabitants of la frontera. In early October 1968, Mexico saw a return to such violence. Half a year after My Lai, in Mexico City's eerie Plaza de las Tres Culturas, soldiers gunned down hundreds of student protesters in another government-sanctioned mass killing, the Tlatelolco Massacre.

In the Minutemen song "The Punch Line," D. Boon sings about how "when they found the body of General George A. Custer. . . . He didn't die with any honor, any dignity, or any valor. . . . American general, patriot, and Indian-fighter. . . . He died with shit in his pants." That is exactly how Sam Peckinpah directed *The Wild Bunch*. Peckinpah was so afflicted with hemorrhoids that the film's first assistant director, in Stratton's words, "could smell Peckinpah before he saw him, the stench of Preparation H, shit, and blood assailing all noses in his vicinity." The director further demonstrated his unconcern with honor, dignity, and valor by habitually wearing white jeans on set.

"Still, he didn't allow [it] to slow him down," adds Stratton, whose portrait of the director does not shy away from showing Peckinpah as a blackout drunk, a bad loser with a violent temper, and a man who got into bar fights he knew he couldn't win, then depended on the street-fighting talents of stuntmen to extricate him before he got pulped.

Peckinpah's no-account character existed in contrast to his achievements as a director and to the loyalty he inspired in his casts and crew. Even so, another of *The Wild Bunch*'s ADs thrashed Peckinpah on set, and the actor L. Q. Jones, who appeared in many of Peckinpah's films and claimed he did not like to speak ill of the director, said he "wouldn't piss in Peckinpah's mouth if his brain was on fire." (Jones might not be the best witness. He was arrested in Mexico a dozen times for disorderly conduct while on location for *The Wild Bunch*.)

It was a stuntman who gave Peckinpah the idea for the film. Roy N. Sickner had portrayed the Marlboro Man in TV commercials and was known as a violent adherent of the "never hit the talent in the face" school of on-set behavior. He hooked up with Walon Green, a writer-producer on Jacques Cousteau and *National Geographic* documentaries for television who was acquainted with various semi-psycho Hollywood stuntmen, and had internalized their twisted code. One stuntman, a racist who had shot and killed a security guard during a robbery, was never turned in by his cohorts, even though they knew he was guilty. The sociopathic atmosphere of their milieu inspired the characters in *The Wild Bunch*.

The cast and crew were divided into three factions: stuntmen like Sickner, veterans of World War II (which included most of the American actors in the film), and Mexican movie directors cast in the roles of generals, majors, and peasant revolutionaries. The *directores* arrived on location armed, simply because they were never without their pistols, something Luis Buñuel, a Spaniard in Mexican exile who knew them, confirms in his autobiography, *My Last Sigh*.

Emilio "El Indio" Fernández, who plays the film's villain, General Mapache, had allegedly killed a man and was a veteran of the Mexican Revolution himself. Mexico's greatest director of the 1940s, he had modeled nude for the Oscar statuette after fleeing his home country for Hollywood in the 1920s. A man of many anecdotes, he was once asked by the pope to direct religious films for the Catholic Church in Mexico. "I still believe in Huitzilopochtli," he wrote the Holy Father, turning him down by referring to the Aztec god of war and human sacrifice. "Saints and miracles do not mean anything to me."

Since almost all the Americans involved in *The Wild Bunch* had seen action in the Second World War, the film can be read as a crypto-reenactment of the violence they witnessed and its subsequent trauma. William Holden, the film's star, was a particularly haunted vet. His younger brother had died in combat while Holden was on duty at a cushier post he had been assigned because of his star status. Holden, a suicidal alcoholic like Peckinpah, was a former gymnast who occasionally walked on his hands on hotel ledges while drunk. In 1966, driving his Ferrari a hundred miles an hour in Italy with two young women in the car, he rear-ended another driver and killed him. He was found guilty of manslaughter but let off by the Italian authorities with a suspended sentence. Outliers among the cast and crew were unsavory, too. Albert Dekker, the journeyman Hollywood actor and former California State assemblyman who played the corrupt railroad boss, showed up on location with a 13-year-old girl he claimed was his wife. When his role finished shooting, Dekker returned to Los Angeles, where days later he was found dead, hanging in his shower in Hollywood's most infamous and bizarre case of autoerotic asphyxiation.

For Peckinpah, the cinema was a ritual that excised violence from the human soul. The poet-translator Anne Carson has written that ancient Greek drama does the same thing, so it makes sense that the actor Robert Culp, who turned down the lead role in *The Wild Bunch*, awkwardly stated that Peckinpah "created a tragedy and put it up on the screen, which is perhaps as important in its way, in its very rude, empirical way, as any single work by Sophocles."

The special effects director thought *The Wild Bunch* so good that he considered it the culmination of his work in movies. After the bridge explosion scene was shot, he observed that he "just had the opportunity to hang a Rembrandt. It will probably never happen to me again." By the film's end, *The Wild Bunch* really does have the feel of the "Disasters of War" etchings by Goya to which Pauline Kael compared it. She went on to write that Peckinpah had poured "new wine into the bottle of the western" and then exploded the bottle.

As in *The Last Movie*, Dennis Hopper's meta-western that came out two years after *The Wild Bunch*, the making of the film itself was a debased ritual. Peckinpah, unaware he should be making excuses or apologizing for what went on during the production, explained his goals this way: "I deal in violence in terms of very sad poetry." He said he intended for that violence to purge the audience through "pity and fear." He thought *The Wild Bunch* would help get war and killing out of our collective system. By the end of his life in 1984 he'd reached a different conclusion: "I was wrong."

THE SHALLOW NOW

OSCAR MOVIES 2019

Vice

Dick Cheney is one of the most maleficent figures in American history. He is responsible for the deaths of hundreds of thousands of people in the war in Iraq, a war fought for spurious reasons that Cheney cooked up and supervised using the post–September 11 war on terror for cover. He condoned and promoted torture, commissioning bizarre legal justifications for it, and he ushered in the USA PATRIOT Act, which allows for the digital surveillance of everybody. Cheney's response to terror back then was hysterical, but not in the comedy sense.

Christian Bale and Sam Rockwell do excellent impressions of Cheney and George W. Bush in *Vice*. Bale has mastered Cheney's growly version of calm seriousness, Rockwell its whiny opposite. But a movie by Adam McKay, who made *The Big Short* and various beloved Will Ferrell comedies, should be better than an Oliver Stone biopic, and *Vice* is not. It should be a slam dunk, not a highlight reel. McKay has done the unthinkable: botched a takedown of Dick Cheney, a man who shot his friend in the face and then made him apologize.

In a postcredits sequence, McKay tells us what he really thinks, cutting to a focus group that shows Americans divided into stupid, angry camps. This follows a long, demonic speech from Cheney-Bale that blames Americans for wanting to be safe and protected after September 11. This audience-blaming precedes the audience-shaming in the focus group. Maybe this is a necessary form of Hollywood self-delusion. It's the way McKay avoids admitting that the nation that reelected Bush and Cheney also voted at the box office by making *Talladega Nights* and *The Other Guys* massive hits.

Green Book

Once the honchos at DreamWorks and Participant Media heard a screenplay existed that was *Driving Miss Daisy* in reverse, *Green Book* was a fait accompli. There is no way Hollywood could have resisted a true story about a white lout who gets a job as the chauffeur for an erudite Black man. That this is an old white person's idea of progressivism is the point, because *Green Book* is a film for old white people. The soundtrack is music from the 1950s and early 1960s, and the star is a turquoise Cadillac de Ville, a spotless machine that has never aged. It's a road trip movie, like 2017's *The Leisure Seeker*, with a certain amount of Alzheimer's built in. By the end it turns into a Hallmark Christmas movie with color-blind, non-homophobic hugs all around.

Mahershala Ali and Viggo Mortensen both really dig in as Don Shirley, the piano virtuoso on a tour of the South, and Frank "Tony Lip" Vallelonga, a Mob-adjacent bouncer in need of a job. As movie characters, they exist as vehicles for life lessons about discrimination, their shared ride a tour of the beautiful-ugly South of the past. The film provides a service in the same way *The Help* did: It makes a certain audience feel better about historical injustice while annoying pretty much everyone else. The fried chicken scene is a case in point. If Don had just said to Tony after being forced to try the chicken that it was only OK and really not his kind of thing, we all would have been better off as people.

Can You Ever Forgive Me?

Marielle Heller's film from Nicole Holofcener and Jeff Whitty's screenplay is an excellent evocation of the nonrich New York writer's life: low-key, desperate, and drained of what once might have been comedy. When Melissa McCarthy, as Lee Israel, the biographer and forger of letters from famous writers, steals a winter coat from a party in a huge Manhattan apartment by lying at the coat-check closet, we briefly glimpse the milieu of wealthy book agents and preening best-selling authors before Lee returns to the cold streets and to her cat-stink one-bedroom apartment. *Can You Ever Forgive Me?* is a movie for adults with a grown-up understanding of economic realities and the ways inner turmoil affects behavior.

Lee, who is an alcoholic, spends a lot of time in a gay bar in the West Village, where she and Jack Hock (Richard E. Grant) are reacquainted. The film takes place in the early 1990s. Years before, Jack and Lee had met at a different literary party, back when they were more carefree and maybe a little glamorous. Grant is as brazen a sophisticate as ever, even when playing someone down on his luck, an essentially sincere character who is not the smartest person in the movie for a change. Lee and Jack's wary alliance brings to mind a *Withnail and I* robbed of its last illusions.

Lee ultimately writes a book in which she confesses to her forgeries with a certain nonchalance, and the film exonerates her for participating in a crime based on other people's greed and desire. Yet *Can You Ever Forgive Me?* does not have what you would call a redemptive ending. After a final comfortless meeting, an infirm Jack, soon to be claimed by the AIDS epidemic, leaves Lee in the bar, where her new transgression is lying to her probation officer about going to AA. The evocation of a forgotten time and place—an early '90s New York without Sonic Youth or Jerry Seinfeld—lends Heller's film a nostalgic glow. The way Lee and Jack live feels close to home, but I can't quite tell if their unenviable circumstances are more or less dire for taking place in a New York before gentrification and the internet.

The Favourite

The elaborate chapter titles in *The Favourite* are a little hard to get used to, but not as hard as the extreme wide-angle lenses through which Yorgos Lanthimos shoots many of its scenes. Although the lenses no doubt have an analogue in 15th-century painting, their convex views give parts of the film a virtual-reality look, as if we have to feel around the heavy furniture onscreen. Similarly modern and as bro-ish as VR, a scene in which male aristocrats pelt a nude fellow toff with rotting oranges recalls paintball or *Jackass.* And Emma Stone gets pushed off a hillock by the fanciest bro in the film (Nicholas Hoult).

The film's anti-fairy-tale aspects and three female leads upstage the mise-en-scène and the men, however, as the mud-stained wretchedness of the poor country cousin (Stone) and the cruelty of a courtier management class represented by Rachel Weisz compete for the attention of the addled, grotesque monarch (Olivia Colman) they serve.

Colman's performance as Queen Anne is worthy of Charles Laughton in its lack of vanity and its ever building pathos. Anne keeps rabbits in her chambers (one for each dead child she gave birth to) and enjoys sex with both Stone and Weisz, until Weisz disappears to become a Lady Scarface bent on revenge. Stone, meanwhile, succeeds with the queen as Anne's dropsy worsens. Their final scene, with Stone permanently in the clutches of this needy royal, struck me as the ending to a Paul Thomas Anderson film more than a Lanthimos one. *The Favourite* is perverse and sadomasochistic, a gratifying evocation of doddering power and the jockeying that swarms it in decline.

The Ballad of Buster Scruggs

The film is a series of larks that look like they were expensive and grueling to make. Maybe that fits these gothic western tales about life and death in the Old West, where mankind's cruelty and nature's majesty compete for screen time. Eventually, the mordant screenwriting and acting take back seats to inventive shots of people getting arrows in the neck. Along those lines, the Coens, more softboiled than hardboiled, hang James Franco and let Zoe Kazan shoot herself in the forehead, but are too sentimental to kill off a cute dog or Tom Waits.

The section of *The Ballad of Buster Scruggs* titled "Meal Ticket" is the best in the film. The darkest, bleakest, and the most macabre, this vignette evokes the hellish carnival world of Tod Browning's *The Unknown* and *Freaks.* Liam Neeson plays a man who travels the West in a wagon exhibiting an actor without arms or legs, who is played by Harry Melling, the loathed cousin from the *Harry Potter* movies.

This torso with a head and a voice recites poems and patriotic speeches in front of grungy miners, trappers, and cowhands. As winter progresses with Neeson's westward trek, the crowds grow smaller. We can tell Neeson is beginning to question his role in show business when he comes across a chicken act that requires less maintenance than the helpless sideshow attraction he has to feed by hand, the way Dr. Caligari feeds Cesare. Neeson and Melling are pretty much the only characters in this cruel little burlesque; they don't speak to each other, and, as bodies onscreen, they are reduced by the Coens to a big lump in a fur coat and a rock in a bag, a unique diminution of humanity that rivals the stories of Ambrose Bierce.

Bohemian Rhapsody

> I'm just a poor boy, nobody loves me
> He's just a poor boy from a poor family
> Spare him his life from this monstrosity
> —Freddie Mercury

> I really want to work with you. I have a
> nice Ferrari.
> —Bryan Singer

If Beale Street Could Talk

Everyone is an expert on James Baldwin these days, so of course they had issues with Barry Jenkins's adaptation of Baldwin's 1974 novel, *If Beale Street Could Talk*. And there was undue pressure on Jenkins to repeat the near impossible feat of *Moonlight*, which combined the groundbreaking with the crowd-pleasing and produced a hit drama that also won awards. When so much love pours out from an audience to a movie, and the movie is successful, it becomes a revered object. It's hard to top reverence. Jenkins wrote his adaptation of *If Beale Street Could Talk* before the Baldwin revival took hold, and now he's being punished (or worse, ignored) because he didn't film it until after. That is a pitfall of working in an art form and an industry that used to be ahead of its time but now moves too slowly.

Jenkins and cinematographer James Laxton reinvented the way Florida and Georgia were filmed in *Moonlight*, and they do the same thing with Harlem in this movie. Immediately distinctive, their way of shooting actors in real places is without equal in current American feature films. Jenkins's work should be defining the mainstream—there is nothing more mainstream than winning the

Oscar for Best Picture—but since Jenkins makes movies about Black people, his work is not being received that way at all.

An illustration of Jenkins's style and approach is the scene in which Fonny (Stephan James) and a friend of his (Brian Tyree Henry), who just got out of prison, sit at a table in Fonny's basement apartment, which is also his art studio and workshop, drinking beers and talking (per the film's title, kind of). The scene, in Fonny's dark but light-pierced kitchen, foreshadows so much else that happens in the film. Its ominous tone is a misdirection leading the audience to believe something about Henry's character and motivations that is not true. Jenkins films this with circular camera movements that stop when Tish (KiKi Layne) arrives, defusing the intensity and the grief of Henry's subtle, underplayed speech.

Capernaum

Like *If Beale Street Could Talk*, *Capernaum* and *Shoplifters*, from Lebanon and Japan, are about families separated by injustice and prison. Debra Granik's *Leave No Trace* covered similar ground, and like Jenkins's film, it hasn't gotten enough attention. All four films exist outside the world of blockbusters, unlike *Roma*, which deals with a broken home, too, but from the perspective of a child of wealth who grows up to become a Hollywood movie director. *If Beale Street Could Talk* takes place in the past, like *Roma*, but despite the stylization of its vibrant yellow and blue, orange and brown 1970s color palette, its past seems more present than the black-and-white of *Roma*.

Nadine Labaki shot *Capernaum* in the slums of Beirut in the color palette of rubble. Her film refers to blockbusters—there is a character in it who calls himself Cockroach-Man (Joseph Jimbazian), a senior citizen who wears a baggy, modified Spider-Man costume and black-frame eyeglasses under his mask. He smokes on the bus he takes to his job luring customers into an amusement park. Among the other characters that the film's 12-year-old protagonist, Zain (Zain Al Rafeea), encounters, the seedy Cockroach-Man is relatively benign.

Those include Zain's family. His mother and father live in squalor with Zain and his siblings, an uncountable pack of toddlers. They sell his 13-year-old sister to Zain's employer, a corner-store owner, to pay a month's rent. A thick slab of neorealism that verges on melodrama and, at one point, seems about to break out in song like a Hindi musical, Labaki's film makes an implicitly pro-choice argument about family. After being arrested, Zain decides to sue his parents because he was born and because they won't stop having children.

The only smart or moral person in his family, Zain arrives at his decision after running away from home and falling in with a janitor at the amusement park, Rahil (Yordanos Shiferaw), an Ethiopian woman with a baby son and no immigration papers. When Rahil is arrested and disappears, Zain tries to take care of her baby before he's arrested himself. Labaki's ability with these nonprofessional actors, including the baby, is remarkable. Zain, a mini Alain Delon with a pushed-in Brando face, carries the film in a state of anger and frustration. Zain and his siblings sell some kind of juice they make in the street while inadvertently coughing into it. That gives Zain the training he needs to sell cheap drinks he makes with the opiate Tramadol to the many curbside idlers he encounters later in the film, including the ones who beat him up.

Shoplifters

If *Shoplifters* were an Ōshima or Imamura film from the 1960s, it would present its ad hoc family as a group of terrible scammers whose blatant activities expose a broken system of exploitation. In the 2010s, Hirokazu Kore-eda instead presents this same kind of family as a tight-knit group more loving than the real families in the film. They may be criminals hiding in plain sight in Tokyo, but since no one pays them any mind, their arrangement and their activities don't matter. They exist the way more and more people in the first world will probably learn to live in the coming decades—united and unnoticed.

A collection of strays posing as a nuclear family, the six main characters in *Shoplifters* live together in a small house with a matriarch figure (Kirin Kiki) who acts as a grandmother. They live off her pension and off the money she gets from her late husband's other family. The father figure, Osamu (Lily Franky), contributes through day labor on construction sites, by collecting workman's comp, and by shoplifting food and sporting goods, which he sells. The two youngest, Shota (Kairi Jyo, the film's equivalent of *Capernaum*'s Zain) and Yuri (Miyu Sasaki), are abandoned children learning to shoplift instead of going to school.

Osamu and Shota wear baggy track pants and walk in curious, shambling gaits to generic, quiet parks and fishing piers. Lily Franky's performance is a grab bag of little quirks and maladies. Kairi Jyo has an average-cute quality that would convince anyone he's a good kid. The film is the opposite of *Capernaum* because it is so low-key and everyone gets along so well. When the authorities bust up this family after a desperate act by Shota, jailing Nobuyo (Sakura Ando), Shota's mother figure and Osamu's significant other, the family becomes an exploited media sensation, reversing the use of media as savior in Labaki's film. By the end of *Shoplifters*, each character is alone in an individual cell, absorbed into the system. A sad little melting snowman is meant to encapsulate their solitary disappearances, a banal and sentimental image not up to the film's story and actors.

Roma

Seeing Alfonso Cuarón's *Roma* on a huge screen in 70mm and black-and-white was great, but since the film was shot in digital video in color, the whole thing kind of seemed like an art project. Roma is the name of the neighborhood in Mexico City where Cuarón grew up, and this autobiographical film takes place in 1970 and 1971. *Roma* is also the name of a semi-autobiographical Fellini film from 1972 that's in color—my favorite of his. Cuarón's *Roma* has a number of Felliniesque moments, but they're like the black-and-white Fellini movies of the 1950s and early 1960s, not his later color ones. This meta aspect of *Roma II* also confused me.

Characters in Cuarón's movie go to see other movies, ones playing in Mexico City at the time the film is set: *La grande vadrouille*, which I thought was a British *Carry On* comedy, and *Marooned*, a big Hollywood film about astronauts. Seeing *Marooned* led Cuarón to make *Gravity*. It made me wish Cuarón had watched better movies as a child. Maybe he has his main character, the housemaid Cleo (Yalitza Aparicio), go see *La grande vadrouille* because it's an army comedy and her date, Fermín (Jorge Antonio Guerrero), a threatening creep who abandons her, goes off to become a paramilitary.

Clearly I was concentrating on the wrong things, so I tried to snap out of it. I paid more attention to Cleo's life and Aparicio's stoic performance, how she has to clean the dog shit off the tile floors she mops in the family's carport, where they park their too-big car. The Felliniesque party section of the film, which starts with the taxidermied dog heads on the wall of a country house, reminded me of a Lucrecia Martel film, but a mild one, in which the bourgeoisie aren't so bad. That part of *Roma* takes place over Christmas; there's some kind of Krampus figure wandering through it all, scaring kids, and there's that party staple, a conga line. Cleo gets a cup of pulque broken on her at a nearby cantina, and then a fire breaks out in the woods, all quite beautifully. When the cup shatters it's startling, more of a wake-up than anything else in the film.

Much of *Roma*—its camera movements, long takes, black-and-white photography, its crowd scenes and protests—also reminded me of Mikhail Kalatozov's mind-blowing *I Am Cuba* from 1964, now playing in rerelease. *I Am Cuba* is an explicitly communist film, which *Roma* is not. The story in *Roma* was a lot like *The Royal Tenenbaums*, with a big house, multiple siblings, a terrible father, and an ethnic servant, a stock character from earlier Wes Anderson films people seem to have forgotten about. To *Roma*'s credit, Cleo is not a sidekick or played for laughs. She's in the foreground.

Her baby dies in the background, in a scene that disturbed me more for its virtuosity, which seemed out of touch with what was happening in it. I thought the same thing about the violent long-take battle scene in Cuarón's *Children of Men*. Only Cleo's rescue of the children in the waves really got to me. The film ends with *shantih shantih shantih* written on the screen, the final line from T. S. Eliot's *The Waste Land*, "the Peace which passeth understanding." Why end with that? The point in *Roma* was there was no "Death by Water," the opposite of the poem. In *Roma*, Cleo saved the children's lives, then had to go back to work and get them Twinkies. That is not past understanding.

Hale County This Morning, This Evening

A baby dies in RaMell Ross's documentary *Hale County This Morning, This Evening*, one of a set of infant twins we've briefly come to know. This happens offscreen, not in a show of bravura filmmaking, and yet Ross's nonwidescreen, not in 70mm, not in black-and-white documentary is, in every sense, a more brilliant piece of filmmaking than Cuarón's *Roma*. I have not seen a comparable documentary since *Iraq in Fragments* in 2006, by the long-lost James Longley.

Hale County, Alabama is an economically disadvantaged area where the principal employer is a factory catfish farm. Sixty percent of its residents are Black, and the county's median income is somewhere around $30,000. Ross doesn't go into statistics, however, instead presenting a luminous series of nonlinear, interlocking sections that place Hale County's younger Black residents in specific landscapes, different types of weather and times of day and night.

Without *shantih*-fying it, Ross introduces each section with a poetic phrase or question. Some of these relate directly to filmmaking: "How do we not frame someone?" Others are more obviously historical: "What happens when all the cotton is picked?"

How Ross films his subjects is maybe a little like Malick–Lubezki, but not in the derivative, self-conscious way of a movie like *At Eternity's Gate*. Ross has his own peculiar, attentive approach. He makes room for a lot of things: an eclipse, girls singing in silhouette under lamps at night, sweat dripping on the floor of a high school gym, *Star Wars* toys, blaring TVs and video games. The film's signature images are indelibly American: a town's empty Main Street awaiting a parade as we look into the distance at the point where the road disappears, then young men—not cowboys—riding horses through the town.

Cold War

The worst advice anyone ever got in a movie is in *Casablanca*. An underage, newly married Bulgarian girl (Joy Page) wants to leave Casablanca and go to America with her husband, but without having to sleep with the local corrupt cop (Claude Rains) to get them both visas. She asks café proprietor Humphrey Bogart what she should do. "You want my advice?" he says. "Go back to Bulgaria." *Cold War* is the story of that girl if she had gone back to Bulgaria.

Bulgaria here is Poland, and the girl is Zuzanna, also known as Zula (Joanna Kulig). The black-and-white in Paweł Pawlikowski's film is inkier than *Roma*'s, which brings out Kulig's silver-screen, movie-star qualities, which the film accentuates by introducing her in peasant clothes, like in a 1930s movie.

There have been a lot of films about singers this year. This one, a Red *Star Is Born*, counters them by rejecting notions of success from our side of the Iron Curtain. But life in Poland is not so great either. Zula is reduced to appearing in a black wig in a fake Mexican musical act after marrying a man she doesn't love and having his children. The beauty of the folk, classical, and jazz music Zula used to sing is corrupted by both party politics and commercialism.

Like Cuarón's film, Pawlikowski's is a biography of his parents. By the end things get lugubrious, as they often do in relationships at that point. Zuzanna and her long-suffering true love (Tomasz Kot) decide the whole thing wasn't worth it and end up facing suicide together. They forgot the rest of the advice Bogart gave Joy Page: "Everybody in Casablanca has problems. Yours may work out."

A Star Is Born

The new, Bradley Cooper–made version reconfigures *A Star Is Born* as a fairy tale of pop success in which dreams come true. Ally (Lady Gaga) checks off the items on a fantasy list by marrying an older rock star, performing in choreographed sold-out stadium shows, writing and recording songs that top the charts, winning a Grammy, and . . . going on *Saturday Night Live* with Alec Baldwin?

It was there that I realized this movie was not going to be the critical look at show business its ironic title used to imply (stars are made, not born). Instead, it is a film that from start to finish presents Gaga's Ally as perfection itself. Her only failing, before she meets Jack (Cooper), is thinking that she isn't pretty enough to make it big. For his part, Jack does his duty once he's fallen in love with her. Despite his alcoholism and pill popping, he writes her a song as his last will and testament that she turns into a megahit.

The humiliation of Jack's drunken appearance onstage as Ally collects her prize in the awards-show sequence does not allude to a world of showbiz manipulation and bitterness, but only to Jack's alcoholism. Being an illness, it's no one's fault. When Ally stands by her man despite the protests of her nonslimy realist of a British manager (Rafi Gavron), she achieves maturity, peace, and sainthood all at once—the things that success and money can't buy. This works because of Gaga, who is the history of American pop music personified in a well-adjusted, nondysfunctional form. She is Liza Minnelli, Barbra Streisand, Carole King, and Elton John all at once. Her brilliance conquers all.

But who is Cooper? The film is set in the present, and yet what fortysomething rock star, or outlaw-country star, exists today at the equivalent level of Jack's achievement and success? After three previous versions of *A Star Is Born*, this one is a hall of mirrors set at a flattering angle toward contemporary media, which is itself a circle of mirrors. Stating that this is "far from the shallow" does not make it true. *A Star Is Born* is a movie about what happens at an awards show, designed to collect awards at other awards shows.

The Wife

Glenn Close is an anti-Gaga in *The Wife*, a film that also prominently features an awards ceremony. Here it's the Nobel Prize honors in Sweden, to which Close travels with her novelist husband (Jonathan Pryce) so he can pick up the Nobel Prize in Literature for his life's work as a writer based on Philip Roth. Not merely a writer, the husband is also an annoyance who signs walnuts, which he gives to women he wants to sleep with. One of his books is called *The Walnut*.

If *A Star Is Born* is a youthful fantasy of success, *The Wife* is an aging fantasy of revenge. Close's character is the real talent in the family, a fact she has concealed since she was a student and he was her professor and she broke up his first marriage. She has hidden herself beneath his unearned glory ever since, because a sharp-tongued novelist (played by Elizabeth McGovern, who at first I thought was Paula Poundstone) told her at a faculty get-together in 1958 that people do not read books by women. Even though she's an English major, Close doesn't bring up Flannery O'Connor, Carson McCullers, or Mary McCarthy. The unspoken implication is that they were nobodies in 1958. Instead, she sets herself to the task of writing her husband's manuscripts for him.

Christian Slater, sly as ever, plays a biographer who has an inkling of the real story. He follows Pryce and Close to Sweden to needle them. Slater was the best thing in the movie. I wanted him to pick up one of Pryce's novels the way he picks up *Moby-Dick* in *Heathers*, underline the word *Eskimo*, then murder Pryce and make it look like a suicide. Then Close could have been vindicated by having to write and deliver Pryce's Nobel speech in his absence: "His body was in Stockholm, but his soul was in the Arctic Circle, freezing with the knowledge that fellow writers can be cruel."

At Eternity's Gate

Out of the eight Van Gogh movies I know of, I have now seen six, which is more than I needed. The most recent one before *At Eternity's Gate* was *Loving Vincent*, which came out in 2017 and animated Van Gogh's brushstrokes. The first, Alain Resnais's black-and-white documentary short, which merely showed the paintings, came out in 1948. It took eight years for the next to appear, Vincente Minnelli's *Lust for Life*, a big Hollywood biopic with Kirk Douglas as Van Gogh and Anthony Quinn as Paul Gauguin. In 1990 and 1991, three came out, including Maurice Pialat's, with Jacques Dutronc as Vincent, which is the best of them and covers the same period in Van Gogh's life as this new one by Julian Schnabel.

Like the auction prices of his paintings, Van Gogh biopics inflate over time. Now Schnabel has released the most prestigious one yet, a boutique production starring Willem Dafoe. THIS FILM IS DEDICATED TO AZZEDINE ALAÏA is the last thing seen onscreen in *At Eternity's Gate*, and why a film about a tortured artist who died penniless, insane, and alone would be dedicated to a world-famous designer who made dresses for Madonna, Rihanna, Lady Gaga, and Michelle Obama is not explained. Apparently Alaïa was the subject of some of Schnabel's own paintings. Schnabel should have ended with a shot of one of those, for the ultimate in hubris. Or maybe not. Schnabel's films are better than his paintings, yet the paintings are also the precondition that allows the films to exist.

As in *Lust for Life*, Van Gogh and Gauguin (Oscar Isaac) in *At Eternity's Gate* act like they're a comedy team. Van Gogh is ascetic, a visionary. Gauguin is worldly and robust. Both actors do an excellent, somewhat hammy job with what Schnabel has given them. They speak casually, in their own voices. "The impressionists? They're out of it!" "Wanna go to Martinique?" Dialogue is repeated over different scenes. Gauguin mentions "the painting surface" and "how the paint will sit on it" so much that I wanted Van Gogh to shut him up. *Sit on it yourself, Paul.*

The film's beauty, its feel for painting, its emotional intensity, Dafoe's soul-searching performance—none of these are new to the Van Gogh genre. But like Joan of Arc movies, new Van Gogh films must come out. That's because it becomes stranger, the farther we get from the lives of the postimpressionists, to see once again the crimped way people hated Van Gogh's paintings in their time. What's so odd about today is the way people love bad art with such boundless enthusiasm.

Never Look Away

This 188-minute movie is about the life of another painter, Gerhard Richter, in communist East Germany. But the main character in *Never Look Away* is not named Gerhard Richter, because Richter repudiated the film the same way the writer Christoph Hein repudiated *The Lives of Others*, Florian Henckel von Donnersmarck's earlier film, also set in Communist East Germany. Coincidentally, the new Nuri Bilge Ceylan film, *The Wild Pear Tree*, from Turkey, is also 188 minutes long. It's about a man who wants to be a writer, and I recommend it instead.

Henckel von Donnersmarck is the son of a count from what was once one of the wealthiest families in Germany. Now he lives in Los Angeles and is the Hollywood Teuton who followed *The Lives of Others* with *The Tourist*, starring Angelina Jolie and Johnny Depp, proving that failing up in Hollywood beats following up in Germany. Henckel von Donnersmarck went back to his homeland for this new movie, which prettifies Nazism and everything else in it, and has far less feel for art than *At Eternity's Gate*.

Its original title was *Werk ohne Autor* (*Work Without Author*). Changing the title to the authoritarian, entertainment-world command *Never Look Away* allows me to end with a song: *Look away, look away, look away, Deutschland!*

THE MOMA GRAMERCY

IT SEEMS LIKE THE MUSEUM OF MODERN ART IS ALWAYS UNDER CONSTRUCtion. In late 2002, not long after I'd moved to New York from Boston, MoMA was renovating, so they moved their film screenings from the movie theaters in the Museum to the Gramercy Theatre on East 23rd Street near Lexington Avenue. The Gramercy was "dark" at the time—a fully-equipped movie theater that wasn't showing movies. Few today remember this short but sweet period in New York City moviegoing history.

The Gramercy was an old theater that seated close to 700 people and had a balcony. The air conditioning was not up to cineplex standards. It had an odd lounge area, with the red sofas and upward-pointing wall lamps of the apartments in a David Lynch movie. During this period, all the cinephiles who had to switch to the Gramercy from the Museum, me included, had the same realization at the same time: this is way better than MoMA. This is where they should always show the films. My God, this is fun—we've been let out of school! This communal reaction said something about seeing films in a museum setting, no matter how well-designed the theater and how good the programming.

I had a full-time job in publishing then, but I used to ditch work sometimes to go see films at the Gramercy MoMA, even though my job was in Midtown right next to the actual Museum of Modern Art and the Gramercy was over thirty blocks away. I never would have considered leaving work early to go to MoMA on 53rd Street, but the MoMA Gramercy called to me. I distinctly remember slinking off one afternoon to see Agnès Varda's *Les Créatures*. And I had one of the great moviegoing experiences of my life there, seeing *We Can't Go Home Again* as part of a complete Nicholas Ray retrospective. It was a film I'd been waiting to see for years. It's an intense, emotionally volatile, experimental film Ray made in the 1970s with his film students after his Hollywood career had ended. Seeing it at the Gramercy was like being a part of the film in a way I don't think I would have felt at MoMA.

Before the renovation at the Museum was done, in the spring of 2004, MoMA stopped screening films at the Gramercy and never showed another movie there. Instead, they should have bought the theater. But maybe continuing to run it would have shown them up. A ratty old stand-alone theater with sluggish air conditioning and old sofas was in its way a better venue for seeing movies than what they had and what they built.

The MoMA Gramercy was one of the great missed opportunities in this city. If MoMA had continued to operate it, it would have done away with the awkward weirdness of the MoMA screenings, with their separate entrance and separate ticket-sales desk, with the indifferent-to-hostile security guards, and the random-seeming showtimes, half of which start after the museum is closed. The Gramercy is now a minor music venue still called the Gramercy Theatre. They ripped out the seats under the universal assumption that everyone prefers to stand for hours to see rock bands.

STAY NEAR THE TREE

TASTE OF CHERRY

CONSIDER THIS AN AFTERWORD TO *TASTE OF CHERRY* (1997), THE FEATURE that brought its director, Abbas Kiarostami, to full international prominence, after it became the first Iranian movie to win the Palme d'Or at the Cannes Film Festival (where it shared the prize with *The Eel,* by Shōhei Imamura). It is best to see *Taste of Cherry* without reading anything about it first. It should be seen cold—cold like the ground into which the film's protagonist, Mr. Badii (Homayoun Ershadi), seeks to consign himself.

Taste of Cherry uses the cinema to figure out if life is worth living, a hard question that seems superficial because so many films so easily reach the conclusion that it is. They show us a wedding, a happy family, a good job, a lottery winner. They indulge our desire to see things work out for the best. Kiarostami does none of that. *Taste of Cherry* excludes, cutting away plot and backstory, two things that can bog down a film. It goes in circles and meanders, the concision of its ninety-nine minutes becoming clear only in retrospect. It is meant to conceal, even to frustrate. Instead of tying the story up neatly, its ending does something else.

Kiarostami's unexpected death in a Paris hospital in the summer of 2016, at age 76, was a blow to cinephiles all over the world. It took a while for us to recover. A retrospective of his films traveled the United States in 2019, providing a much-needed summation of his career, which had started with 1970's *Bread and Alley,* the first of many films he made for Tehran's state-run Institute for the Intellectual Development of Children and Young Adults. Over the course of the decades that followed, he became the cinema's great poet of the ordinary and the everyday, of the unnoticed.

Kiarostami's films portray friendship and its difficulties, its fragility and uncertainty. Nowhere is that more striking than in *Homework* (1989), which begins as a documentary about schoolboys who haven't finished their homework, then proceeds through a series of interviews in which students face Kiarostami's camera alone to discuss their fraught relationships with their parents. Near the film's end, a boy named Majid becomes paralyzed in front of Kiarostami, unable to speak, distraught that he can't be interviewed accompanied by his friend Molai. Majid's anguish is wrenching and difficult to watch. Kiarostami records this child's breakdown, then the calming effect Molai has on him, in a way that suggests Majid's pain is a problem larger than just one boy's anxiety. The children in *Homework* are growing up neglected by their parents and teachers, who are quick to punish and unconcerned about nurturing them as fellow human beings.

By the '90s, Kiarostami had begun to complicate human relationships further, by folding and refolding them into issues of cinematic representation and narrative ambiguity. In *Close-up* (1990)—the true story of a man (Hossein Sabzian) who plays himself as the impostor he was—the yearning for human connection comes to the fore in new ways. In focusing on Sabzian, Kiarostami saw something that hadn't yet been identified in cinema: the exact point where, if for only a moment, the movies and real life dissolve into each other, before detaching again, as mirror images.

After Kiarostami's death, Mohsen Makhmalbaf—his fellow member of what is sometimes called the Iranian New Wave, who in *Close-up* plays himself, the filmmaker whom Sabzian was arrested for impersonating—summed up his colleague's life and career for the BBC: "He could show you how friendship could take you out of loneliness." The title of the 1987 film that begins the director's *Koker Trilogy* asks the main Kiarostamian question: *Where Is the Friend's House?* The following two films in the trilogy, *And Life Goes On* (1992) and *Through the Olive Trees* (1994), take place in the aftermath of the devastating 1990 Manjil–Rudbar earthquake. Those films put Kiarostami on the road to *Taste of Cherry,* in which he examines the precariousness of life without the backdrop of natural disaster. In *Taste of Cherry,* the calamity is private and subjective. We are never told what it is. Perhaps it is life itself.

MR. BADII KEEPS ASKING STRANGERS if they are his friends, or if he is their friend, because he wants to find someone who will aid him in his suicide, first by confirming that he has succeeded in killing himself, then by burying his body in the event that he has. Jonathan Rosenbaum, one of the great explicators of Kiarostami's work, notes how the director's films—often featuring nonprofessional actors, and fusing fiction and documentary—frequently depict the "strained interactions between big-city protagonists and the impoverished yet [to them] exotic villagers they're visiting," as is the case here. The cosmopolitan Mr. Badii drives around the outskirts of Tehran, soliciting assistance from a soldier, a seminary student, and a taxidermist, his extended interaction with each pushing the strained qualities Rosenbaum identifies into new areas of discomfort.

What Badii asks the men he meets to do is to permanently end a human connection, not create a new one. He wants them to help him commit an act that will lead to secrecy and guilt on their part, and one that is, furthermore, against Islamic law. In *Taste of Cherry,* each character becomes uneasy or threatening as Badii tries to cajole him with money, rather than with the kind of fleeting intimacy that comes from helping strangers.

In leaving out any reason for why Mr. Badii has reached this point—something that would usually be considered essential in a film about a suicidal man—Kiarostami subverts and undercuts his protagonist's talk of friendship. When Badii explains that he is "simply asking for a helping hand" while insisting that he can't say why because "it wouldn't help you to know," he is already severing himself from other people.

"You can't feel what I feel," the only explanation Badii is willing to offer, similarly challenges the movie itself. If no one can feel what others experience, then there is no point in watching. Badii's hesitations, the distress in his eyes, performed by Ershadi with restraint or reluctance, belie what he is saying, the same way certain actions and casual comments inadvertently reveal his will to live. He lets road workers help him get his Range Rover out of a rut on the side of a hill over which he could have plunged to his death. He refuses an offer of an omelet because "eggs are bad for me."

Seeing certain movies can wake you up to reality. The loose stories, contemplative style, and relative absence of plot in Kiarostami's films free us from feeling manipulated, even as we are patiently led to endings that are quite often emotionally shattering. This has the effect of bringing the viewer out into the world. And once we learn that it was often Kiarostami himself, sitting in the Range Rover, to whom the actors were responding during filming, that only adds to this feeling of being placed back in the world. At one point, Badii drives by some boys "playing car" in a rusted-out hulk in a junkyard—they are a reflection of Kiarostami and Ershadi making this film together.

WITH HIS PROMINENT NOSE, dimpled chin, stubble, and dark lips closed to match his stern, straight-ahead stare as he drives, Ershadi's right profile is the image that holds the film together. Kiarostami, in fact, had first spotted Ershadi, a Tehrani architect, driving one day. He stopped him and asked if he would appear in a film. Ershadi has since acted in other movies, but because he was new to the cinema in *Taste of Cherry,* his presence will always carry with it the permanent mystery of Badii's motivation. We never learn why Badii wants to die.

This allows the audience to project all sorts of things onto both the character and the actor who plays him.

The novelist Nicole Krauss recognized this. In her short story "Seeing Ershadi," which appeared in the *New Yorker* in 2018, Krauss's narrator sees *Taste of Cherry,* then later unexpectedly glimpses Ershadi in real life, in a Zen garden in Kyoto, the way the protagonist of Walker Percy's novel *The Moviegoer* suddenly sees William Holden on the street in New Orleans. "Everything we know about the depth contained within [Badii] we get from his face, which also tells us about the depth contained within the actor Homayoun Ershadi, about whose life we know even less," Krauss writes.

"The world seemed to bend toward Ershadi as if it needed him more than he needed it," she continues. "His face did something to me. Or, rather, the film, with its compassion and its utterly jarring ending, which I won't give away, did something to me." Later, the narrator does give away the ending, in relating that a friend, also a *Taste of Cherry* fan, had been flipping through TV channels one night when she came across Ershadi's face. She flipped by it, then went back, but somehow could not find the channel it was on again. Ershadi had disappeared.

One woman sees Ershadi in real life, the other as only a video image. These two encounters, sequential in Krauss's story, replicate the switch from the "real life" of Badii's quest to the video footage at the end of the film. Though their encounters with Ershadi are fleeting, the narrator and her friend reverse the intensity of his gaze. They project their feelings and ideas onto him, their fascination deepened, perhaps, by the fact that, in the film, Badii's own relations with women remain a mystery.

It is only about two-thirds of the way in, when the gruff museum taxidermist (Abdol Hossein Bagheri) asks Badii if he is willing to give up the taste of cherries, that we see women in this film, in long shot: a mother and daughter on a roof, taking laundry off a line. Shortly after this, outside the Darabad Museum of Natural History, a young woman hands Badii a camera and asks him to take a photo of her and her boyfriend. The boyfriend appears to be a man from the beginning of the film who threatened to punch Badii in the face when he offered him money, assuming Badii was propositioning him for sex.

IN HIS ONE-STAR PAN OF *Taste of Cherry* from 1998, when the film was released in the US, Roger Ebert accused Kiarostami of prurience for the movie's early sections, in which Badii's intentions are made purposefully unclear as he asks various men on the sidewalk for help from his car. Ebert calls the film "a lifeless drone," comparing it unfavorably to a 1992 Ulrike Ottinger movie: "I have abundant patience with long, slow films, if they engage me. I fondly recall *Taiga,* the eight-hour documentary about the yurt-dwelling nomads of Outer Mongolia." He concludes by declaring that *Taste of Cherry* is not worth seeing.

Ebert also describes the film's ending as "a tiresome distancing strategy to remind us we are seeing a movie." It is, in fact, quite the opposite. As Badii lies down in his grave, we see the full moon shrouded by black clouds—maybe the best image of the moon in cinema, and maybe the last thing Mr. Badii will ever see. After turning the camera back on Badii, as he gazes up at a gathering storm, Kiarostami fades in on video footage of soldiers marching up a hill in long shot. He then cuts to scenes of the crew at work on the film—including Ershadi, who smokes and offers Kiarostami a cigarette—soon accompanied by Louis Armstrong's 1928 recording of "St. James Infirmary," a song heard nowhere else in this film that is otherwise without a score or any nondiegetic music on the soundtrack. The graininess of this video footage transferred to film, the brightness of the sunny day, and the ease and friendliness of the film's cast and crew contrast sharply with Badii's dark night of the soul. This ending—so unexpected, because what film has ever ended like this?—seems at first like a mix-up.

There is no definitive explanation for this break in the narrative. It is several things at once: a scene of mournful tranquility, a contemplation of the happiness of being alive, relief from the film's tension, a rejection of sentimentality, a moment of rebirth, and an invitation to leave the theater. It also anticipates cinema's replacement with digital media, a form that will follow 35mm film after its "death." Above all, it is a memento mori that deepens the film's ambiguity, the final fate of Badii having been left unresolved. If, after this film's ninety-nine minutes, neither we nor Mr. Badii have come to know whether life is worth living, so be it.

The first two-thirds of *Taste of Cherry* are "a film found on a scrap heap," to borrow an intertitle from Jean-Luc Godard's *Weekend.* Badii drives through an arid, semi-industrial wasteland similar to the one in Barbara Loden's *Wanda.* He moves through the present in a pale car in a pale landscape, as Jack Nicholson does at the start of Michelangelo Antonioni's *The Passenger. Taste of Cherry* seems to have the same relationship to Iranian cinema as Roberto Rossellini's *Germany Year Zero* has to Italian neorealism: It's a work of despair and suicide, set amid the rubble. When Badii and an Afghan security guard at a cement factory discuss the location of Imam Ali's tomb, they point out that there are competing claims to where it really is. If Badii dies in the hole he has dug for himself, covered by the "twenty spadefuls of earth" he wants to pay someone to shovel over him, no one will know where he ended up either. More than once we see Badii's Range Rover disappear behind hills, leaving a landscape onscreen with no people in it.

Something about *Taste of Cherry* resists the melodrama or violence of the films mentioned above. The ending has a finality to it—"Tell your men to stay near the tree to rest. The shoot is over" are among the film's last words—but it is otherwise not an ending. It returns its protagonist to life outside the film. The story takes place on an unspecified holiday, maybe one of the martyrs' holidays that occur in Iran in the fall. Maybe *Taste of Cherry* was shot at different times of the year, but it seems to unfold in an autumn that occasionally turns to spring—the few trees and plants in the landscape appear to be both fading to brown and turning green. It's that promise of spring hidden in the movie that keeps everything alive.

WELCOME TO VIOLENCE

Ghostbox Cowboy

Immersed in our shared dollar-store world of travel-sized toiletries, useless trinkets, and selfie sticks, *Ghostbox Cowboy* investigates American and Chinese capitalism by presenting two sides of the same bad penny. "America is dead," explains a grifting American in China (Robert Longstreet) who is trying to make money from something called FreeDentures.com, which sells sets of Bluetooth-enabled false teeth online. His Chinese counterpart (Vincent Xie), a CEO and investor, longs to get out of Dongguan, a dismal factory town where he dines alone every night in the same restaurant. These two men conspire to stomp the dreams of Jimmy Van Horn (David Zellner), a Texan who has reinvented himself in China as the head of a start-up called Big Horn Global. Jimmy's big plans involve a small electronic device designed to communicate with the dead—a flimsy black box with a row of blinking colored lights on the front, priced to move.

Shot surreptitiously with DSLR cameras, documentarian John Maringouin's first narrative feature explores a corrupt investment economy in "sweaty betrayal season," the period in the Chinese summer when every deal goes wrong. An American expat fixer called the

Specialist, apparently playing himself, acts as guide to this hellish environment. He's a genius for business deals, he explains, though also suicidal.

Jimmy, the living embodiment of the phrase *all hat, no cattle,* depends on this twitching sharpie for guidance through the manufacturing warrens of Dongguan. His investors are the kinds of businessmen who have previously put money into products like "Bathtub Gargoyles," ugly statues that perch ominously on the corner of the tub, waiting to end up as landfill. As Jimmy pursues "influencers, agitators, violators, and jousters," every one of them fleeces him a little more. Penniless, he is reduced to playing a cowboy mascot on a Segway, prodded and berated by Chinese handlers who treat him like a circus animal and pay him in KFC coupons.

The film winds its way through Inner Mongolia to a city built to be the biggest in the world but inhabited by only twenty-five people. Maringouin, a self-consciously Herzogian director, has by that time turned Jimmy into a cartoon Kinski in a white *Fitzcarraldo* suit, a blond wig, and false teeth. A lost soul but eager to please, all he has left is a cyanide pill with an American flag printed on the capsule.

The Mule

Clint Eastwood is a Giacometti sculpture with a skull stuck on top. What skin he has left on his face is paper-thin, ready to be scraped and scratched. He looks dermabraded even before drug runners in *The Mule* push his face against a wall. Eastwood walks across motel parking lots in his latest movie with the careful certainty of a man who has always stayed on the hard line, a rule of life from a movie of his, *Blood Work,* he made seventeen years ago, when he already seemed old but was only 72. Since then he has become a wraith. In *The Mule* he drives back and forth along the border in a Ford truck from 1970. Later, dream-like, he finds himself driving a new black SUV, awakened like in a David Lynch film sitting in someone else's car.

Eastwood has not starred in any of the films he's directed since *Gran Torino* in 2008. *The Mule*, therefore, is something of a return to form after the strange, almost avant-garde films *Sully* and *The 15:17 to Paris*. *Gran Torino* and now *The Mule* allow Eastwood to resurrect himself as the aging embodiment of 20th-century America as it confronts crime in the non-Anglo world today—the Hmong community in Detroit in *Gran Torino*, a Mexican cartel in *The Mule*.

As a superannuated movie star, Eastwood's downscale portrayal of Walt Kowalski in *Gran Torino* had elements of distress and melancholy—his final suicidal act predicted various kinds of American deaths of despair even as Eastwood tried to show how his values of honor amid violence could be passed to a new generation that didn't look like him. *The Mule*, a variation on that, is equally a testament to Eastwood's life work and a revival of his persona in a new context.

Significantly, his daughter, Alison Eastwood, returns to a film by her father after an absence of over twenty years. Clint's character here, Earl Stone, is punished more for being a bad father and husband than he is for becoming a geriatric drug runner. The scenes of Earl using his newfound wealth to try to make things right with his family and friends are new in Eastwood's work, a late-stage apology.

Dianne Wiest's performance as Earl's ex-wife is repetitive and "acted," in the typical male-female dichotomy of Eastwood movies. It started with Jessica Walter's stalker hysteria in the first film he directed, 1971's *Play Misty for Me*, and continues through Meryl Streep's role in *The Bridges of Madison County* to Wiest in *The Mule*. Eastwood is terse and restrained, women are emotive and unhappy with him.

In Wiest's deathbed scenes with Eastwood, Earl confesses to the twin crimes of abandonment and drug running. Under the tender nagging of his former love, these scenes become the sappy exceptions in an otherwise dry, weird, and unsentimental film defined by road trips in which Earl prefers to be alone with his car radio, at least by day. It is significant that this film of reconciliation arrived on screens shortly before the death of Sondra Locke, Eastwood's romantic partner in the 1970s and '80s and the female lead in some of his best films.

After Eastwood ended their relationship, Locke sued him for palimony, then later for fraud. Eastwood's busy career and his lasting success, in this light, are the crimes for which he seeks to atone by making and appearing in *The Mule*. Like Earl, a florist before he turns to drug running, he just wanted to cultivate flowers (movies) in the sunshine. The film ends with Eastwood imprisoned, working in the penitentiary greenhouse, wearing a gardener's hat (not a cowboy hat), a frail old man but finally forgiven. The persistence of Eastwood as an icon in *The Mule* makes it easy to miss that as a director he was the one who forgave himself.

Welcome to Marwen

With its attention to long-legged, thin-waisted, big-busted living dolls, World War II, and male weakness, *Welcome to Marwen* should have been directed by the late Russ Meyer, not Robert Zemeckis. What holds the film back is that it does not go far enough in the direction of oomph, a hesitance Meyer would not have allowed. While the film's tragic story is fetishy and perverted, by trying to be tasteful or at least palatable it comes off a little self-deluded, and therefore wrong in a way Zemeckis could not have intended. Despite that, *Welcome to Marwen* retains a certain power, which comes from both the documentary on which it is based, and on Zemeckis's desire to make a career-enfolding late work so he could bare his soul. He puts it on display in thermoplastic polymers and CGI.

Playing with dolls and toys to make movies is how I've always suspected the Spielberg–Lucas–Zemeckis generation did it. They were always too chaste to do what normal kids would do with their dolls, which was to make Barbie and G.I. Joe fuck. Instead, they vocalized jet-fighter noises on the carpet and transmuted sex into crashes and explosions—the way of Hollywood since *Star Wars*. In retelling the story of Mark Hogancamp (Steve Carell), an artist with a brain injury whose photographs of miniatures in his backyard recreate the imaginary story of a Belgian village under Nazi attack, Zemeckis has found the perfect encapsulation of the Hollywood blockbuster process.

The miniature village is protected by Hogancamp's fighter-pilot alter ego and what must be described as a bevy of female soldiers whom Hogancamp has based on real women in his life. In his fiction they are cast as toy dolls in tight military garb, or in Frenchy striped tops, off-the-shoulder blouses and dirndls, and the stiletto heels Hogancamp sometimes likes to wear himself. In Zemeckis's movie, they are played by Leslie Mann, Janelle Monáe, Merritt Wever, Eiza González, Gwendoline Christie, and Leslie Zemeckis, the wife of the director cast as Hogancamp's favorite porn star, who is not exactly from his real life but appears in his favorite movie, *Wicked Hotel Encounters*. The magic of computer animation transforms these actresses into mannequins with Barbie physiques.

Hogancamp's photos are ready-made storyboards for Zemeckis's tribute to an alcoholic artist beaten senseless in a hate crime. *Welcome to Marwen* has much in common with *Back to the Future, Who Framed Roger Rabbit?, Forrest Gump, Flight,* and *Allied,* other Zemeckis movies that come in various shades of cartoonishness or seriousness or both. Hogancamp's memory is semi-shot. It relies on military history and fantasy to sublimate trauma. Zemeckis too seems to have a better memory for his own artistic creations than for anything else, and solves the film's (and Hogancamp's) problems by blasting Nazi action figures into the future, which is our present, and is where they reside today.

Aquaman

The way Robert Zemeckis threw his whole career into the stewpot for *Welcome to Marwen*, James Wan, the *Saw–Insidious–Conjuring* director, throws all of blockbuster cinema into a giant lobster pot for *Aquaman*. This comic-book movie ends with a message that purports to be pro-ecology and anti-pollution, but reads a little fascist: "The land and the sea are one!"

Aquaman (Jason Momoa), we learn, will now command a united ocean force, which is bigger than any individual ocean nation, just as the worldwide audience for movies like this is bigger and therefore better than the domestic audience. Aquaman becomes Jesus in a codpiece, with a trident instead of a cross. This ending calls to mind Fritz Lang's silent *Nibelungen*, supposedly Hitler's favorite movie, the same way *Star Wars* called to mind *The Triumph of the Will*. We've moved back in time, from 1935 to 1924, to a pre-fascist state. The film's interpolated credits scene sets up the next Aquaman movie, in which our half-American, half-Atlantean hero will be pitted against a Black villain (Yahya Abdul-Mateen II) and an Asian scientist (Randall Park).

The way superhero movies consistently threaten or depict CGI genocides has become predictable. Wan deflects from that by making this very long movie a gallery of set pieces that refer to previous blockbusters. Stormtroopers here are also Transformers. The undersea sets have a *Pirates of the Caribbean* look. Dinosaurs inhabit a lost world in the Antarctic. Black Manta, the Black villain, is Iron Man. The monsters are like the ones in *Alien*, *Arrival*, Spielberg's *War of the Worlds*, and a *Godzilla* remake. The heroine (Amber Heard) flies a semi-invisible plane like Wonder Woman used to. Since the film has a classic adventure quality more than a doom-and-gloom one, this fantasia where the world underwater is also outer space, Heaven, and Hell becomes more involving the more derivative it gets.

By the end it has the dream-like quality of the kind of silent-movie adventures that starred Douglas Fairbanks and were directed by Raoul Walsh or Allan Dwan, or an undersea Soviet fairy-tale film by Aleksandr Ptushko. Seahorse movements of the characters underwater, with their undulating hair and videogame bobbing, lull us into acceptance, as does Willem Dafoe, our guide here as Aquaman's mentor. Nicole Kidman, as Aquaman's mom, fights off bad guys in L.L. Bean outfits and Keds because she lives in Maine before getting divorced and moving to the Land of the Lost. Aquaman, unlike most superheroes, has a lot of nurturing support.

The film's simple-mindedness makes it work. When the characters end up in Sicily, a supertitle reads Sicily, Italy, so we know we are not in Sicily, Illinois. Momoa as Aquaman is more pro wrestler than actor, and Amber Heard is dressed and acts like a beauty queen. The movie is a New England *Black Panther*, as if the Nation of Hampton Beach finally got its own superhero, with a hot girlfriend who dyes her hair cosplay red.

The House That Jack Built

James Wan relies on the history of Saturday matinees, pumps it up, and resells it. On the other end of the spectrum, Lars von Trier wants to destroy the cinema entirely. His latest film is pedantic, stretched-out torture porn, with Matt Dillon as the serial killer in the title. *The House That Jack Built* is a PowerPoint presentation with gore between the slides, told in five "incidents," each of which, if this were Wan's *Saw* series, could have been its own separate franchise entry. The archival photos and explanations of things like Goethe's oak at Buchenwald, the Jericho sirens on Stuka dive bombers, Glenn Gould, and dessert wines would probably not make the cut in a franchise movie. All the material von Trier marshals to illustrate his lecture on how life is evil, human beings are stupid and soulless, and art is long would have to be relegated to the bonus features.

It's the first movie of von Trier's that's made him seem behind the times. His beef with modernity remains, but now he's repeating himself, using clips from his older films as if he's Godard, or maybe he's punishing Godard for not including von Trier footage in his own essay films. So we get to see *Aquaman* costar Willem Dafoe in an *Antichrist* clip. He also, through subtle-obvious references, tries to ruin Cassavetes, Wenders, Kiarostami, the done-to-death *Don't Look*

Back Bob Dylan clip with the signs, even Lucio Fulci. Fulci made a film called *Don't Torture a Duckling.* So von Trier does just that, just because an Italian genre director told him not to.

Amidst all the butchery and the arrangements of dead bodies into what Jack claims is architecture and art, the image of the duckling stands out. Whatever gimmick allowed von Trier to sever the duck's leg, the duckling is not a performer in the same way as Uma Thurman, Riley Keough, and the large number of other actors who signed up to play Jack's victims. Jack has contempt for them, calling them stupid and worse. He and the film are dedicated to showing how easily led people are, and how simple it is to convince cops that there's nothing to see at his crime scenes. Five minutes of bloodshed were cut from the film for theatrical release in the US, which may explain why the gore in *The House That Jack Built*, while disgusting, seems exactly as theoretical as von Trier's pontificating, much of which recalls the Übermensch dialogue in Hitchcock's *Rope*, a film from seventy years ago based on a crime that happened twenty-five years before it was made.

More than ever, all of this takes place in von Trier's mind, where windmill fantasies of American violence slowly turn, as they have throughout his career. As they rotate, he listens to David Bowie's *Young Americans* with his eyes closed, trying to figure out where songs from it go in his movies. Von Trier's America is supposedly near Mount St. Helens in Washington State. As filmed it's in Sweden, Denmark, and England, which I guess has something to do with his idea that in the rural US, peasant farmers clear fields with scythes like in 19th-century paintings. The whole movie is like that, a Thomas Bernhard novel about the Three Little Pigs, with Dillon in a Burt Reynolds mustache playing the Big Bad Wolf.

The film's wall-to-wall lecture plays over scenes in the form of a dialogue between Jack, American serial killer, and Virgil, the Roman poet, who is voiced by the great actor Bruno Ganz, who died shortly after the film came out in the US. Ganz played Hitler in *Downfall* (2004) and starred in Wim Wenders's *The American Friend* and

Wings of Desire. Von Trier must have chosen him for those reasons. Ganz was the embodiment of the post-1968 European art film. When he finally appears on screen in this film's last act to lead Jack into Hell, *The House That Jack Built* becomes a different film, one that is quite astonishing. It begins with filthy-sewer video footage, then crosses the River Styx in a Delacroix-inspired tableau vivant, before descending into crimson hues of hot lava. That is the thing with von Trier. Just when it seems like whatever he's trying to do has gone to hell, he will literally go there. If these scenes don't redeem the film's brutality, which von Trier must not care about anyway, they sure (as hell) make it entertaining, right up to Jack's drop into oblivion and the final cut to the blatant corny obviousness of the song over the end credits.

Vox Lux

The overly literary narration from Willem Dafoe that begins *Vox Lux*, along with its drab opening credits, which focus on an average street in a residential neighborhood in Staten Island, indicate that we are in the presence of art. Brady Corbet's second feature film proves that he has absorbed the nasty lessons he learned at the master's knee by playing one of the murderous preppy creeps in Michael Haneke's 2008 remake of his own *Funny Games*.

Vox Lux begins with a school shooting before its main character, Celeste (Raffey Cassidy, then Natalie Portman) becomes a jaded pop diva whose music video inspires a terrorist attack at a beach resort. By combining a Haneke film with *Katy Perry: Part of Me*, Corbet has invented a new genre of art film, one that fuses contemporary evil and violence to the backstage exposé and the concert film, then wraps it up in bad vibes. *Vox Lux* is too dark and stealthy to be pop art. It mingles with poptimism in an underhanded way. This mélange proves to be confounding, as the film, despite its many ideas, does not coalesce. It just ends with lots of concert footage.

This gradual inconclusive petering out is a strategy in itself. Its cold, tired repetitiveness, I guess, is the goal, although maybe it's meant to be redemptive or triumphant. Or maybe Corbet is rickrolling us.

Portman is up to the challenge of playing a hit singer with a choreographed stadium show and futuristic costumes. She and the rest of the British and Anglo-French cast (Cassidy, Jude Law, Stacy Martin) were sent by Corbet to the Arthur Fonzarelli School of Screen Acting so they could learn to talk like Andrew Dice Clay and Cyndi Lauper. *Vox Lux*, in fact, is *A Star Is Born* in negative, the first homegrown feel-bad art movie post-Gaga. Sia and Scott Walker did the music, another combination that demonstrates the film's objective of mixing austere European high art with *Glitter*. Portman again portrays a divine creature with many problems, blind in one eye, rolling her neck because of the bullet lodged there. Her presence and this film's unique jumble of elements will guarantee that *Vox Lux*'s stature grows when we remember this era of mass killing and audible pitch correction.

DUTCH ANGLES

MOVIE NIGHTS WITH THE REAGANS

"IF IT WAS A FRIDAY NIGHT, THE PRESIDENT'S HAIR WOULD LOOK MUCH softer and shinier than usual, because he had washed it that afternoon," Mark Weinberg remembers in *Movie Nights with the Reagans*, his 2018 memoir detailing the many evenings he spent at Camp David seeing films with President Ronald Reagan and his wife, Nancy. Throughout Reagan's two terms in the 1980s, Weinberg, then an assistant White House press officer, accompanied the Reagans on their weekend trips to Camp David, the compound located in the hills of Maryland that has been the official retreat of US presidents since 1942. Sitting in the dark with them for so many hours must have given him a good look at the back of Reagan's head.

They screened Hollywood movies at Camp David on each trip, usually new ones, everything from *Raiders of the Lost Ark* to *Oh, God! Book II*, after settling in with popcorn and glasses of water and removing a painting that hid the window of the Aspen Lodge's 35mm projection room. Weinberg was 23 when he began working in the White House. His youthful proximity to the power and glamour of our first real movie-star president colors his account with awe. To him, Reagan is inspiring and irreproachable, with an Honest Abe sense of fairness and decency.

Others who have written about Reagan's time in office are more likely to mention how the president would fall asleep during meetings with other heads of state. Those historians, however, did not bring Reagan "smooth-centered chocolates" when they watched movies together. Weinberg's loving account of the president is also a portrait of himself as an obsequious stooge, an earlier version of Gary Walsh, the assistant Tony Hale played on *Veep*. At another point in the book, Reagan over-apologizes to Weinberg for joking that something Weinberg said made him sound like a communist. Weinberg, touched by this, doesn't see it as the reaction of a man who had been a friendly witness before the House Un-American Activities Committee, one who secretly snitched to the FBI on fellow actors in Hollywood he considered communist sympathizers. The irony is lost because there is not a hint of anything less than total admiration in *Movie Nights with the Reagans*. To get permission to write it, Weinberg made a special pilgrimage to Bel Air, seeking approval from Nancy Reagan herself, weeks before she died.

MOVIE NIGHTS WITH THE REAGANS is hagiography, but it is also a personal document of Hollywood filmmaking in the 1980s from Ronald Reagan's point of view, recorded at his elbow. Weinberg makes sure to tell us that at Camp David, they "didn't screen movies based on their ideology." For the Reagans, he writes, movies were "an *escape* from politics" and a "diversion from the business of governing . . . a chance for the Reagans to relax and enjoy the art form." Ideology and politics, however, are notoriously hard to escape when enjoying art forms, which must be especially true if you're the living embodiment of national power. From the beginning of Weinberg's book, it's clear that however casual these screenings were, they were also a chance for the Reagans to hash out their thoughts on contemporary culture and politics, and then turn their movie-prompted insights into policies that would affect people's lives. There were ramifications for everyone if President Reagan happened to see, for instance, *Rocky IV* over the weekend. He saw that one in January 1986 and liked it because "it had a very happy ending. He beats the Russians." Hollywood and Reagan worked together to create the "dream life" that J. Hoberman (who quotes from Weinberg's memoir) identifies as replacing reality in his new book, *Make My Day: Movie Culture in the Age of Reagan*. For Hoberman, the dream life is the current in America's unconscious mind where ideology lives unseen, where it is shaped by movies.

The Reagans' reaction to *9 to 5*, the first movie Weinberg covers and one of the first the president screened in the Aspen Lodge, proves the point. A strongly feminist and prolabor workplace comedy released in 1980, the film costars Jane Fonda, a Hollywood prodigal daughter and demonized left-wing radical who appears more than once in Weinberg's book. That aside, according to Weinberg, it was the use of marijuana by the women in the film—while "sharing revenge fantasies against their boss"—that angered the Reagans. The scene would have been "truly funny," Reagan explained post-screening, "if the three gals had played getting drunk, but no, they had to get stoned on pot."

The Reagans seized on something harmless but illicit in *9 to 5* that allowed them to justify their disappointment with everything else in the film, and with what it reflected in modern life. The movie also reminded them of their opposition to the Equal Rights Amendment, but they glommed on to what Nancy later called "the notion of drug acceptability." The first lady alluded to *9 to 5* when she introduced her "Just Say No" antidrug campaign to the world, sarcastically describing a movie in which three women coworkers "get hilariously high on pot." Anti-ideology in action: When Reagan left office eight years later, drug offenses had doubled the US prison population. It was not office workers like the ones Jane Fonda, Dolly Parton, and Lily Tomlin played in *9 to 5* who made up that newly incarcerated population.

It is in the Reagan years that the right-wing impetus to identify pop-culture items as tacit instances of ideological support or opposition became entrenched in the Republican mindset. This process was aided in no small part by Hollywood, which began serving up productions geared to reflect the newly capitalistic, post-hippie values of boomers as they entered middle age. *Ghostbusters*, which the Reagans saw in July 1984, a month after it came out, shows how. Weinberg does "not recall the film making a major impression on the president," but he devotes an entire chapter to it anyway—here, Hoberman's dream life functions for Reagan's supporters while the president is sleeping.

The massive success of *Ghostbusters* "energized the 1984 campaign" for Reagan's reelection, according to Weinberg, with its catchy theme song and its branded logo, a proto-meme Americans saw everywhere that summer. Weinberg begins his chapter on the film by highlighting the "Fritzbusters," a troupe of College Republicans from Texas. They dressed up as *Ghostbusters* stars Bill Murray, Dan Aykroyd, and Harold Ramis and drove to college campuses in a tricked-out ambulance like the one in the movie, singing a satirical, pro-Reagan version of the theme song. According to the new lyrics, Reagan's opponent in the election, Democratic candidate Walter "Fritz" Mondale, represented "something strange in America."

When the Democrats tried to repurpose *Ghostbusters* to their own ends during their national convention, hawking "Reaganbuster" T-shirts using the *Ghostbusters* logo themselves, it was a typical lame gesture from the Democratic Party, offered too late in the game. Mondale was a ghost whose brand of liberal politics had already been busted. By 1984 the Democrats had lost the image war. They had ignored more than four years of genuine anti-Reagan youth rebellion, which had produced thousands of images like the cover of Jello Biafra's 1981 punk compilation, *Let Them Eat Jellybeans!*, trying instead to get in on the kind of mass-produced Hollywood action that always favors those in power.

Weinberg points out that *Ghostbusters* was named to a list of best conservative movies by *National Review* magazine in 2009 because "the bad guy" in it "is a regulation-happy buffoon from the EPA." Surely there is more to it than hating the Environmental

Protection Agency. *Ghostbusters* suggested to the Reagan youth who saw it that they could get away with a lot while their leader's eyes were closed. One of the main Fritzbusters was Jack Abramoff, then the National Committee chairman of the College Republicans. As a Fritzbuster, he wore "coveralls, black rubber gloves, and goggles." Less than a year into his tenure at Citizens for America, a pro-Contra group Abramoff joined after the election, he was fired for mishandling funds, the first in a long series of misdeeds. He went on to make millions as a shady lobbyist before eventually landing in federal prison. Locked up, he taught a screenwriting class for the other inmates, and ran, according to the *New York Times*, "a highly popular movie night."

Reagan's most well-known connection to 1980s movies is the Strategic Defense Initiative, accurately nicknamed the "Star Wars" defense system by Senator Teddy Kennedy. Reagan at first found the name annoying, but embraced it after he saw *Return of the Jedi*. He had started calling the Soviet Union the "evil empire" two months before the third *Star Wars* movie was released. After it came out, he realized he could say things like "the force is with us" when defending SDI to reporters. Weinberg compares Reagan to Luke Skywalker and speculates that the president saw his alcoholic father, Jack, in Darth Vader—an odd connection to make when discussing Reagan's so-called "Darth Vader" speech about the Soviet Union, which he called "the focus of evil in the modern world."

Fantasy was not Reagan's favorite genre, in any case: Its myths were too disconnected from the heroism of World War II. But he did host a screening of *E.T. the Extra-Terrestrial* at the White House in June 1982, a couple of weeks after the film came out. This was the infamous screening after which Reagan made a speech saying "everything on that screen is absolutely true," a bizarre moment even by the standards of a president who often confused real life with movies he acted in or had merely seen. Spielberg later claimed Reagan was so moved by the film that he "looked like a 10-year-old kid" while watching it. Both men wanted to transport the nation into a state of eternal childhood innocence.

Whatever emotions passed between Reagan and Spielberg that night, Reagan did say one thing to the director that made sense. He complained that the credits at the end of contemporary movies went on too long. "In my day, when I was an actor, our end credits were maybe fifteen seconds long," he explained. "Reduce your credits to fifteen seconds at the end," he suggested to Spielberg. If Reagan was right about anything, it was that. He may have declared ketchup a vegetable and claimed trees cause pollution, but his greatest achievement could have been making that a law. Now we're stuck with end credits that balloon like the federal deficit did while he was in charge.

A year into Reagan's second term, NBC-TV aired a tribute called *All-Star Party for "Dutch" Reagan*—"Dutch," Reagan's nickname as a toddler, had stuck into old age. Clad in tuxedos and gowns, the guests were a combo of classic Hollywood ham and 1980s cheese: James Stewart, Angie Dickinson, Sammy Davis Jr., Telly Savalas, Alex Trebek, John Ritter, and the stars of the TV show *Dynasty*. Frank Sinatra, "a favorite of Nancy's," hosted with Monty Hall, from the TV game show *Let's Make a Deal*. Charlton Heston delivered a grave and loony speech, telling the president, "You speak to mankind in our name." The show ended with Sinatra and Dean Martin, Democrats and Kennedy supporters in their Rat Pack days, duetting on a version of "Auld Lang Syne" directed at the president.

It was a send-off, three years early. When Reagan finally left the White House in 1989, he retired into Alzheimer's disease ("Should old acquaintance be forgot"). Weinberg worked for him in his Century City office, located in the building that had been christened "Nakatomi Plaza" for the Bruce Willis action movie *Die Hard* the year before. Asked to play the mayor of a western town in *Back to the Future Part III*, Reagan declined, missing a chance to bookend a series that had expressed good-natured incredulity at his presidency in its first entry, along with a chance to be in a movie with ZZ Top and Flea. Reagan and Nancy had seen *Back to the Future* at Camp

David. He liked it enough to quote it in a speech about the space program, which effectively ended with him after the *Challenger* exploded in 1986: "Where we're going, we don't need roads." This statement—drawn directly from the dream life—was the opposite of Barack Obama's "Somebody invested in roads and bridges." Obama's observation was boring, un-Hollywood, and uninspiring, but it had the virtue of being true.

GEORGE H. W. BUSH TRIED TO KEEP the movie glamour going after Reagan was gone. A month before taking office, while Reagan was still president, Bush hosted the premiere of the comedy *My Stepmother Is an Alien* in Washington, DC, hoping for some of that *E.T.* or *Ghostbusters* magic to rub off on him. It didn't, despite the photos of Poppy standing shoulder to shoulder with Kim Basinger and Dan Aykroyd in the cineplex lobby. The Bushes were wimpy, mean-spirited, and close-minded. They were *awkward*. Awkwardness was their defining feature, alongside greed. The gleam in their eye was for the wrong things, and they were not oblivious enough to project total sincerity at all times, or even very often. They just weren't movie people. They were oil people, baseball people, CIA people who knew the Hinckleys, the Texas family of John Hinckley Jr., who shot Reagan because *Taxi Driver* had driven him mad.

Strangely, Richard Nixon and Jimmy Carter were movie people. Mark Feeney's fascinating book *Nixon at the Movies* (2004) reveals that Nixon watched two or three movies a week while he was president. Nixon is known for finding inspiration in *Patton*, the George C. Scott military biopic, but Feeney makes the case that Nixon's relationship with Hollywood was more complicated than that. He loved movies and watched them seriously while at the same time hating and resenting the Hollywood of the late 1960s and early 1970s, which dismissed him as a corrupt warmonger and a square.

Carter saw more movies as president than anyone else who has held the office since the White House and Camp David installed projection rooms. In just his one four-year term, he saw over four hundred films, everything from *Buffalo Bill and the Indians* and *The Shining* to *The Marriage of Maria Braun* and *Annie Hall*, which he screened twice. Reagan may have had the Star Wars defense system, but Carter actually watched *Star Wars* at Camp David, in a secret meeting with Egyptian president Anwar Sadat.

Serious filmgoing in the White House ended after Reagan. When Obama told Katie Couric in a TV interview, "I'm a movie guy—I can rattle off a bunch of movies," he almost made Nixon seem hip. The first movie Obama made a point of seeing in office was *Avatar*, which he took his daughters to see at a mall. When he and Michelle gifted the British prime minister with a pile of classic American films on Region 1 DVDs that wouldn't play in England (Region 2), it was clear that this was no cinephile.

The first film the current occupant of the White House screened was *Finding Dory*, an animated movie evidently chosen for his son and his staffers' children to see. Trump, the only other president besides Reagan with a Screen Actors Guild pension, is more of a TV watcher, as we have learned: The current president's mass-entertainment apotheosis was small-screen all the way, playing a pumped-up version of himself on a boardroom set in a reality TV game show. Reality has merged with his game show as cable news covers his frolics and jests. But his taste in movies defines him nonetheless. His two favorites are said to be *Citizen Kane* and *Bloodsport*, a brutal 1988 martial arts movie starring Jean-Claude Van Damme, in which Van Damme has to fight blind. There it is, the Trump administration summed up in one weird double feature.

A Democratic member of the House, Representative Lee Hamilton from Indiana, once described Reagan as having made only one contribution in a meeting on nuclear missiles. The president interrupted the discussion to announce that he had seen *WarGames* the night before, then related how the teenage Matthew Broderick had mistakenly enabled a government supercomputer to launch nuclear weapons.

Thanks to *Movie Nights with the Reagans*, we now know what happened during that screening of *WarGames* at Camp David. Weinberg remembers one scene in particular. In the movie, a general at NORAD, standing under a portrait of Reagan, worries that a nuclear war has begun. He picks up the phone and yells, "Get me the president!" When that happened in the movie, everyone in the Aspen Lodge, including President Reagan, turned to look at the telephone on the table next to him, expecting it to ring.

DREAMS ARE LOST MEMORIES

The Dead Don't Die

Bill Murray, as the chief of police in a town beset by zombies, delivers a key line in *The Dead Don't Die*: "I was supposed to retire two years ago." Adam Driver, who plays his junior officer, asks him why he didn't, to which Murray, breaking the fourth wall, replies, "Are we improvising here?" They leave it at that. This scripted off-script moment and their deadpan delivery evade the question, which the characters, the actors playing them, and writer-director Jim Jarmusch never answer. *The Dead Don't Die* alludes to a gerontocracy that has refused to make way for the next generation, holding on to power even if it has to do it from beyond the grave. Tellingly, the first zombies reanimated are Iggy Pop and Sara Driver, playing 1970s rockers who crawl out of a graveyard and head for a vintage diner like the one in *American Graffiti*. Classic rock will never die, the 1950s will never end.

Murray and his subordinates dispatch members of the current generation swiftly and cruelly, without thinking much about it. They invade the motel room of three twentysomethings played, respectively, by a former TV tween turned pop idol, another former TV tween, and an influencer who makes money by wearing sunglasses on Instagram (Selena Gomez, Austin Butler, and Luka Sabbat). The cops find these tourists dead, attacked by the zombies. They chop off their heads preemptively, before they can turn.

The three dead tourists are a far cry from the Blank Generation hipster trio who ended up in a Florida motel in Jarmusch's *Stranger Than Paradise* thirty-five years ago, bohemians who came from nowhere and ended up nowhere. Back then, Jarmusch implies, such people could afford to be aimless wanderers, to kill time without getting assassinated themselves. Jarmusch does let some kids from juvie run off, but the movie's one real survivor is Tom Waits, the only hermit left alive, as unkillable as he was in *The Ballad of Buster Scruggs* last year.

The Dead Don't Die situates our unabated longing for the zombie apocalypse in the permanent October of rural areas where the Halloween store is open year-round. The exurban Jarmusch depicts both the sadness of half-empty towns upstate and the annoyance of having to live among neighbors like Steve Buscemi's farmer, a right-wing sourpuss in a modified MAGA cap. This is a film unhappy with humanity, right down to specific neighbors.

Mild and bleak, idyllic and enamored with hopelessness, the film is either Jarmusch's version of *The Trouble with Harry*, the autumnal Hitchcock film in which a dead body keeps reappearing, or one of those goofy William Castle horror comedies from the 1960s with Sid Caesar, in which bodies escape their coffins. In the end, it plays like a country version of Ivan Passer's bleak-funny 1974 movie *Law and Disorder*, which starred Carroll O'Connor and Ernest Borgnine as auxiliary policemen cruising the nighttime streets of the pre-Jarmusch Lower East Side. Back then, strung-out thieves and rapists outnumbered hipster artists in the city, the same way zombies outnumber the hipster cops in this movie. Jarmusch has moved upstate and found the same dead-eyed weirdos milling around.

From *Only Lovers Left Alive* to *The Dead Don't Die*, alive or dead has ceased to make much difference to Jarmusch. When the high-class vampire couple in the former murdered people so they could survive, they were different from these cops because they were aristocrats, not civil servants. What matters to Jarmusch is that there is a natural order in the universe. When Tilda Swinton removes herself from the scene to take her place among the aliens in this movie, that order is preserved, as it was when she was a vampire in *Only Lovers Left Alive.* For Jarmusch, these lumpen zombies lack panache, their brainlessness is not romantic, and they deserve what they get.

Us

Jordan Peele's follow-up to *Get Out* also mines country–city terror, though its point of view is Californian, not bohemian. Unlike Jarmusch, who would never do something so uncool, Peele channels the Steven Spielberg of the early 1980s, the Spielberg who hired director Tobe Hooper to make *Poltergeist* edgy, but then interfered to ensure it remained family friendly. In *Us*, Spielberg—as a concept, as a theme, and now as a memory—constrains Peele's vision the same way Spielberg constrained Hooper. *Poltergeist* is not *The Texas Chain Saw Massacre*, because whatever that movie was and however much money it made, *The Texas Chain Saw Massacre* was not commercial according to the aesthetic moralities of Hollywood.

Peele is haunted by his Reagan-era childhood and its pop-culture debris, which is understandable, but by compulsively inserting it into his movie Peele makes *Us* much less frightening than it could have been. Too much of the movie depends on what's on the T-shirts characters wear. Peele's wardrobe choices are supposed to ground the film in specific time periods but also have to perform the function of grounding it thematically. This is a recurrent tic of Hollywood filmmaking that is both distracting and flattering to an audience already primed to hunt for 1970s and '80s shout-outs in every Netflix show. In *Us*, it lessens the impact of the Hands Across America T-shirt at the film's climax. Peele presents a class-divided America using this ironic signifier, but it has the effect of implying that what will unite us as citizens is not class consciousness but liking this film, as one audience, because we get the references.

Lupita Nyong'o has no trouble being terrifying and disturbing as both the villain and the hero of *Us*. The scary, constricted voice she uses for her prison-jumpsuited doppelgänger was performance art, with Laurie Anderson vocals that seemed to come from an LP I couldn't quite remember. Tim Heidecker, as an evil version of the slightly more successful, back-slapping white neighbor, was more genuine in his dangerous frenzy and therefore more frightening. Heidecker comes across as an actual mirror version of himself, revealing in his violence a murderous id he's channeled from comedy.

Us exposes the shadow world of poverty and despair that undergirds the sunny lifestyle of people who are pretty sure, but not quite sure, that they've made it as middle-class Americans. It peaks during its home invasion scene, after way too much loving/winking establishment of regular family life, the kind of thing Hitchcock or a TV commercial would have done much quicker. Peele's slow buildup to the family's confrontation with the twisted, starved versions of themselves, who seek to eliminate them and take their place, brings something to the screen that Black audiences have been denied in Hollywood movies—a chance to see themselves in the Spielbergian glow of alleged American normalcy.

The nightmare image of the jumpsuit-clad doubles in the shadows of the driveway, a family car sticker come to life as menacing paper dolls holding their own scissors, is the highlight of *Us*. The home invasion is the film's best scene, but it doesn't last long enough after all the buildup. It could have been the whole movie from that point, and maybe would have been, in a cheaper film. Somehow the clash between the competing versions of this family ends up muddled in post–*Black Swan* ballet, the same way Luca Guadagnino's ponderous *Suspiria* remake did. Ballet, as a signifier of class privilege, lacks shock value in something as all-American as *Us*. Pretending that it's eerie and sinister is like hitting all the keys on the organ at once, *Phantom of the Opera* style; i.e., a cliché, not scary.

Captain Marvel

Captain Marvel takes place in 1995, the year of the Oklahoma City bombing and the O. J. Simpson trial, of "Gangsta's Paradise" and "Common People." That's why I went to see it. I wanted to find out how Marvel Studios handled the mid-'90s. It turns out they handled them like *Top Gun*, so more like the 1980s. The Blockbuster Video scene in the movie reminded me that people today think the former existence of Blockbuster Video is funny. I guess the existence of Netflix, the contemporary version of Blockbuster, is not funny because you don't have to go to a store.

It's hard to remember *Captain Marvel*, because it was boring. Brie Larson, who plays Captain Marvel and two other young women who are also Captain Marvel, gets to kick an old lady's ass on a bus. The old lady is a shape-shifting Skrull, however, so it's OK. Later, Larson becomes a god. Her apotheosis reminded me that before the film came out, Larson insisted that instead of the usual superhero-indoctrinated 40-year-old men attending her press junket, there should also be a young woman in a wheelchair in attendance.

I thought about this young woman as I watched the rest of *Captain Marvel*. I might resent Captain Marvel, it occurred to me, if I were in a wheelchair and Brie Larson had summoned me to watch her flying through the air and into outer space. In the movie, the Skrulls turn out to be the good aliens and the Kree, friendly at the beginning, are revealed as evil and destructive. The same thing could happen to an entertainment reporter who gets a special invitation from a movie star.

John Wick: Chapter 3 – Parabellum

There is an astonishing fight scene in *John Wick: Chapter 3* that takes place at night in a glass building with glass floors and walls. The inky set design in this scene, striking and ultra-contemporary, makes everything look like it's taking place under cracked iPhone screens. But the dynamic between Wick (Keanu Reeves) and the mewling sycophant he's fighting (Mark Dacascos) took a lot away from the action. There was no way this guy named Zero could get the upper hand for long. The choreography and the black-transparent look of that section of the film gave it a jolt and, for a while, a reason to exist. The rest lacked anything as involving, despite the aggressive, nonstop complication of every second of the film, including the title. There is also a ballet scene that is supposed to be moody and frightening and isn't.

Asia Kate Dillon, a nonbinary actor with a neatly shorn head, would have made a better foe for Wick, but Dillon is instead constricted to Helmut Newton–esque slinking and posing in tight black pencil skirts. Ian McShane's Winston, a traitorous hotelier, sleepwalks through his role like he's playing the Most Interesting Man in the World in the Dos Equis beer ads. As incessant gunfire in the lobby and corridors destroys his hotel, McShane responds with ever faker nonchalant bullshit acting, mirroring the overelaboration of everything else in the film. The John Wick franchise has an official weapons supplier, but the film's target audience isn't gun nuts. This is a movie for corporate travel agents upset that it costs so much to stay in hotels.

Domino

Brian De Palma, the director of the first *Mission: Impossible* movie with Tom Cruise in 1996, and therefore one of the architects of the genre, has, at this point, approximately zero chance of directing a $100 million action movie like *John Wick: Chapter 3* ever again. His reputation may have been enhanced by the 2015 documentary about him made by Noah Baumbach and Gwyneth Paltrow's brother, but his career got no bounce from it. The director of *Carrie, Dressed to Kill,* and *Scarface* depends these days on sketchy European producers, who have an unfortunate tendency to mirror the plots of his movies by betraying him. Thus *Domino*, his latest, arrives bitter and slapdash, more a plan for a movie buzzing or shimmering in De Palma's angry head.

Domino takes place in Copenhagen, where police detectives speak English and used to be in *Game of Thrones*. The director seems to have contempt for both his leads. Nikolaj Coster-Waldau, playing a not-bright cop who sets the plot in motion by forgetting his gun one morning, has a second-choice feel. Carice van Houten, who exists in *Domino* like she's waiting for each take to end so she can go outside and smoke, resembles Noomi Rapace in De Palma's earlier film *Passion*, but why? In the past, the resemblance would have been evidence of directorial obsession. Here, it's probably a coincidence.

Even in its partly realized form, *Domino*'s every frame is better than anything in *Game of Thrones*. In its less-than-ninety-minute running time, *Domino* links together CIA surveillance, terrorism, drone warfare, ISIS execution videos, and international film festivals. It all has a last-stand feel, in which De Palma excoriates today's regime of easy-to-make but disposable images, which people, now all spies, use to brutalize each other. Scene after scene features piles of red tomatoes, there for critics to throw at De Palma so they can be tabulated and scored by review aggregators.

Politics for De Palma is a bizarre excuse for exploitation. This is one of his films in which he spares no one. Everyone is a torturer and a victim at the same time in *Domino*—confused, compromised, in for punishment. With some irony, De Palma sets up a Libyan terrorist (Eriq Ebouaney) as the film's conscience. The CIA (in the person of the satanic-blasé Guy Pearce) forces him to work as a double agent, and the film's plot comes to depend on him. Yet by the end De Palma abandons this downhearted terrorist without any more hesitation than he gave a minor character whose face gets dunked in a fry cooker.

A final scene, which could be the last of De Palma's career, switches back and forth between a Spanish bullring and a hotel rooftop. The locations are linked by the threat of a mass killing and a camera drone, which De Palma uses to collapse the great distance between mass events and personal ones, a last gasp of mise-en-scène in the age of martyrdom videos on YouTube.

High Life

Robert Pattinson, the lone adult survivor on a spaceship destined for a black hole, jettisons the bodies of his dead fellow prisoner-astronauts, shoving them into body bags then dropping them one by one into the void. With his shaved and sculptural head, Pattinson would make a good match with *John Wick*'s Asia Kate Dillon, but in *High Life* he's saddled instead with Juliette Binoche's evil doctor-sorceress, a nefarious Beverly Crusher with a Renata Adler braid.

In this very dark (and orange) science-fiction movie, Claire Denis has provided her ship with a cell called the Box, a stainless-steel sex chamber that cleans itself like a car wash and comes equipped with a pneumatic dildo. *High Life*'s interest in bodily fluids is constant and intense. At one point, Binoche, an insomniac eugenicist, carries a handful of semen around the spaceship, while blood, shit, and breast milk smear its walls and floors. We meet the young co-ed crew in flashbacks. Criminals back on Earth, now institutionalized in the name of science, they are abusive and sexually violent—ugly-minded people who lash out at each other because they're trapped.

Denis pushes bodies to their limit while sending humanity to the margins of the universe in this frustration endurance test posing as space exploration. Technology exists in the film only as a way to experiment on helpless people. The opposite of *Interstellar*, *High Life* presents sci-fi without hope, its ship a borstal. In the crew scenes, *High Life* becomes an Alan Clarke movie in outer space. It's a companion piece to another arty genre film Denis made, 2001's blood-smeared *Trouble Every Day*. Hard to take, unclear in its intentions, it nonetheless delivers hard truths in a new way.

High Life's ending lacks the awesome evolutionary psychedelics of *2001: A Space Odyssey,* opting instead for a hookup with an earlier, abandoned spaceship inhabited only by sick dogs who survive in artificial green light. Denis contrasts it with the yellow nimbus surrounding the black hole. The end credits remind us, more than once, that the Icelandic artist Olafur Eliasson somehow owns this yellow light, along with his redesign for the supermarket vegetable sprayer misting plants in the ship's garden.

Non-Fiction

Juliette Binoche also costars in *Non-Fiction.* The new Olivier Assayas movie about the Parisian publishing world has things in common with *Things to Come,* the 2016 film by Mia Hansen-Løve, Assayas's ex-wife, which starred Isabelle Huppert as a Parisian philosophy professor and author. The difference is that *Things to Come* was a clear-eyed case study in middle age and *Non-Fiction* is an immature French farce.

Binoche plays a TV actress named Selena to whom another character mentions Juliette Binoche, a bit of self-referentiality drawn from the "he looks like that fellow in the movies, you know, Ralph Bellamy" gag in *His Girl Friday. The Dead Don't Die* does this kind of thing, too, only more so, with the actors breaking character to switch into script discussions. Maybe Jarmusch and Assayas's generation of arthouse directors feels trapped by storytelling and wants to leave it behind. The Lettrist ending of Assayas's *Irma Vep* pointed in that direction; in the years since, Assayas has become a more conventional filmmaker.

Here, he mistakes *His Girl Friday* for a zany romp instead of understanding that it's a cynical, fast-talking adventure-romance, like all Hawks's movies, as well as a comedy about the warlike nature of mass communication. The world of big-city newspaper reporters in the US in the late 1930s must have struck him as akin to the publishing world in contemporary Paris, where the big issues are not capital punishment and government corruption, like in *His Girl Friday*, but whether ebooks are the future. That adds up to French people saying the word *Kindle* a lot. This is a variation on the hand-wringing over the future of the cinema in *Irma Vep*—one thing Assayas keeps telling us is that it's a changing world out there, with all this technology. Vincent Macaigne is better and funnier than all that as an autobiographical novelist kind of inspired by Philip Roth in the same way this film is inspired by screwball comedies.

In the end, whatever happens to book publishing doesn't matter as long as these French people can sleep with each other's spouses and have young mistresses and go to their summer houses. In *His Girl Friday*, when Cary Grant promises to remarry Rosalind Russell then cons her into going away with him to cover a breaking story instead, it was important to the film that they weren't married anymore. Grant was exploiting Russell and stringing her along to get what he wanted for his newspaper. In *Non-Fiction*, nobody can get back together again because they never leave each other in the first place.

The Souvenir

Joanna Hogg's roman à clef of a movie covers her years in film school in early 1980s London, when she was figuring out how she wanted to make movies and living on and off with an upper-class junkie boyfriend employed by the Foreign Office. Julie (Honor Swinton Byrne), naive, from a good home, doesn't at first understand that the semi-comatose but well-dressed and handsomely flawed Anthony (Tom Burke) is a user. Her slow realization that something is wrong, and her polite, matter-of-fact introduction to Anthony's addiction, which they don't discuss, are the stuff of a horror movie.

Hogg downplays the lurid aspects of their love affair, replacing them with the familiarity of everyday life as their relationship unfolds. Strange, awkward scenes begin to pile up. Anthony brings Julie lingerie from Paris, asks her to put it on, tells her, "You're a dark horse, Julie." Then she sees the tracks on his arm, not knowing what they are. Their meals at Harrods have a sleepy, well-mannered mood that becomes nerve-racking and narcotic as Anthony runs out of money and begins to steal and sell Julie's possessions. Burke plays Anthony as Peter Lorre in an Evelyn Waugh novel. He's creepy but since he's unaware of it, Julie doesn't see it either. We never see him away from Julie, so his scoring and shooting up are not part of the film, nor his last hours.

The blown-out white light from the windows in their apartment and the pillow shots Hogg uses between scenes, accompanied by snippets of songs from the period by Robert Wyatt, Joe Jackson, and the Pretenders, shield the film from becoming too novelistic—it reminded me of a Margaret Drabble novel crossed with Ozu. *The Souvenir* is a beautifully realized, painful movie that only hits the viewer in the hours and days after seeing it. Tilda Swinton, in gray hair, plays her own daughter's mother, communing human-to-human for a change, instead of with the astral beings her muse or casting directors usually put her in touch with.

Her Smell

I never thought I'd see Elisabeth Moss singing "Another Girl, Another Planet" as Courtney Love in *The Kat Bjelland Story.* In Alex Ross Perry's *Her Smell,* set in the 1990s post-grunge Amerindie rock scene, Moss plays Becky Something, an alcoholic, drug-addicted guitarist and singer in a band with drummer Ali (Gayle Rankin) and bass player Marielle Hell (Agyness Deyn). Becky is a mess. A thrower of dressing-room tantrums, by the time she is finally able to make it onstage, she insults the audience and can only plow through a song or two before tottering into the drums and collapsing. Between gigs, she annoys everyone by hauling around her shaman, an irritant named Ya-Ema (Eka Darville). In the studio she fumbles between ill-prepared nothingness and rage.

Perry and Moss follow Becky's descent into addict hell and eventual recovery with true commitment to Cassavetes-style self-destruction and enlightenment. The difference is that John Cassavetes did not make period pieces. The 1990s evoked in *Her Smell* are as cleaned-up as Becky isn't. A new all-girl band comes to supplant Something She, Becky's weirdly named combo, and Perry presents them as more post-tween Green Day than post-Hole Veruca Salt. They're nice, studious, and millennial, like they got extra credit in a college course on riot grrrl for being in this movie. This removes the film by one step from the rawness of Becky's damaged life, turning *Her Smell* into an acting exercise with '90s touches.

The film's five-act structure brings Becky up-to-date at a reunion show, where she almost pulls her disappearing act sober. That could have been more interesting than all the coven-based female empowerment on display in the scenes where other women musicians sit cross-legged on the floor, light candles, and praise her. Those scenes came off as both pandering to a contemporary audience and a rejection of the generation Becky represents. I guess that's realistic. By act four she had already moved upstate to strum her guitar alone in a big house and ruminate on her misdeeds, a trajectory artists from her era know well. Becky wins her battle with herself, but when it was over I felt bruised and tired, as if she'd been pummeling me, too. Like Roberto Durán fighting Sugar Ray Leonard, she had me holding up my hands and muttering, "No Moss." Then the credits rolled and snapped me out of it with their fake album covers from the '90s.

The Hustle

The Hustle is very low stakes and I only saw it because I was stuck in a mall in New Jersey for two hours and it was the next thing playing.

The point of this remake of a remake is that the genders have been switched. Anne Hathaway and Rebel Wilson now play roles played by men in the other two versions. Yet by the end, it is a man who fools these two women con artists, blackmailing them into being his employees. Not the ending I was expecting from a film that begins by asserting that all men are suckers.

Alex Sharp plays this unconvincing man-boy grifter as a bland nothing whose initial guise is colorless and empty—a nice-guy tech billionaire shy around women. Hathaway has to pretend, by turns, that she is a member of the British leisure class and a German psychoanalyst femme fatale. She excels in the latter put-on, opening a new path for herself she will probably never explore again. Wilson, meanwhile, must pretend she is blind, an acting stunt which I guess is only not offensive because blind people won't see it. At one point Hathaway demonstrates to Wilson how to produce tears on cue, giving the lie to her award-winning crying jag in *Les Misérables*. It's a secret of her craft she reveals too cheap.

Long Day's Journey into Night

With his second feature, following his excellent debut, 2015's *Kaili Blues*, Bi Gan has done something radical. An incursion into form, *Long Day's Journey into Night* reveals the trick of 3D. Instead of a continuous, pseudo-immersive experience that starts at the beginning, here 3D infiltrates more than halfway through the film's nearly two-and-a-half-hour running time. When it finally enters, Bi reemphasizes its alleged immersiveness, 3D's main selling point, by having this last, hour-long section comprise one continuous take, a single shot that floats from a gondola lift through a nighttime market and elsewhere through the end of the film. Before this shot begins, the viewer must figure out when it's time to put on the clunky 3D glasses, a point in the film Bi signals by having his protagonist, Luo Hongwu (Huang Jue), sit down in a movie theater.

Bi has established himself as a significant artist with just two films partially by being a synthesist of all previous auteur cinema. *Long Day's Journey into Night* combines many strains, from the poetic realism of *Le jour se lève* to *Hiroshima mon amour* and *In the Mood for Love*, from Warhol (a character eats an entire apple in one shot) to Tarkovsky (a glass shakes itself off a table). It all seems put together in a calm, hypnotic state, using the gliding camera of Theo Angelopoulos to move through the torture and violence of Johnnie To and Tarantino gangster movies via the observational modernism of Apichatpong Weerasethakul.

That all of this becomes present in the viewer's mind without taking away from what's original about his film is a testament to Bi's skill. He's an artist who learned online, like some poker champions, watching films at home, and it's significant that he comes from provincial China, not the NYU Tisch School of the Arts. We inhabit the romance and fatalism of *Long Day's Journey into Night* as in a dream—someone says in the film that "dreams are lost memories." Bi's camera follows Luo as he searches his hometown for his lost love (the enchanting Tang Wei from *Lust, Caution*) and his best friend from twenty years ago, Wildcat, probably murdered.

I happened to see *Long Day's Journey into Night* at the Metrograph at a morning show at which I was the only person present. During the 3D sequence, a woman came into the theater and sat down right next to me, which I thought was odd. I turned to her, wearing the 3D glasses over my regular glasses, wondering what was going on. She looked at me, and in an Australian accent she asked, "Is this the *appatmint*?" I had no idea what she was saying. I was fully inhabiting the film and her entrance seemed like part of it.

She repeated the same question—*Is this the appatmint?*—and this time I understood. She wanted to know if this was *The Apartment*. Billy Wilder's movie of that name was showing at Metrograph in the other theater.

"No," I told her, "this is a new Chinese movie in 3D." She looked at me wearing the 3D glasses, then at the screen, and instead of leaving she watched the movie for a while. Something about what was going on froze her in place in front of images that were out of focus for her because she didn't have 3D glasses on. Suddenly she got up and walked out. Maybe I should have followed her out and gone to see *The Apartment*, starting my own journey into night, but by then Bi Gan had me pinned in place, stuck in the flow with his moving camera.

Ash Is Purest White

Jia Zhangke's latest film also focuses on events in the early 2000s, but since Jia has come to his mastery the hard way, his view of the interrupted relationship between a gangster (Liao Fan) and his moll (Zhao Tao) expands not just in filmic memory, but out into the real world of contemporary Chinese history. His vistas are bigger, plainer, and harder on the people who inhabit them. If this is a genre story in some ways, just as *Long Day's Journey into Night* is, it's a more tragic one, with bitter, unromantic repercussions. There is fatalism and then there is stoicism.

Here, it is a woman's longing, not a man's, that propels the film. Zhao is one of the greatest actresses in cinema, and her journey in *Ash Is Purest White* is hardboiled and subtly melodramatic. She begins as the realist daughter of an outmoded communist ideologue, then transforms herself into a cool money-making criminal in the provincial jianghu underworld. She takes the fall on a gun charge for her lover and ends up a jailbird. To get back to him after prison, she passes through the Three Gorges area of the Yangtze River on a ship where her identity and money are stolen. The new Chinese capitalism erases her past, rendering her sacrifice meaningless.

Zhao's Qiao is absorbed into a vast audience singing along with pop performers onstage, a wider angle on the individual karaoke in Bi Gan's film. Jia's tour of his country displays a 21st-century China that is dirty and mean, punishing its characters for coming into adulthood in a petty, greedy time. There is no progress in their lives, only aging. Qiao ends up where she started, doubly abandoned in her old hometown, serving the old gangsters who never made it out. For Bi Gan, only love can break your heart. In *Ash Is Purest White*, there are many more things that can break your spirit.

Diamantino

This soccer-refugee satire from Portugal by Gabriel Abrantes and Daniel Schmidt is cute as hell and as fluffy and pink as the enormous Pekingese puppies Diamantino Matamouros (Carloto Cotta) pictures in his head when he's on the field about to score a goal. Unfortunately, it's also about as savage as those puppies.

Diamantino is a modern Candide, a pampered star athlete without a thought in his head. He adopts a refugee as his son after a sudden burst of compassion, then allows himself to be experimented on by scientists who are after his perfect superman genes. Diamantino is too clueless to realize his refugee son is actually a queer girl (Cleo Tavares) scamming him, and that his doctors are slowly turning him into a woman, a side effect of their gene-mapping drugs. On top of all this he is duped into running for office by a fascist, anti-immigrant political party.

The plot sounds like next-generation Almodóvar or latter-day John Waters, but because *Diamantino* is so gentle and nice in its intersectionality, it ends up somewhat hapless, with a downbeat, wistful ending. Surely big pharma, right-wing manipulation, and the endless greed of the already wealthy deserve something a little harsher than this ninety-seven-minute underwear ad, an example of present-day camp too sane and well-behaved to have much bite.

Jobe'z World

Shot by Sean Price Williams, the dexterous cinematographer who also filmed *Her Smell*, Michael M. Bilandic's *Jobe'z World*, which is set, I think, in the present, is way more forthright and weird than Alex Ross Perry's film. The kind of micro-budget New York indie that exists to get gloriously terrible, out-of-it reviews in the *Hollywood Reporter* and *Variety*, *Jobe'z World* is pretty glorious and out-of-it itself.

The film follows Jason Grisell as Jobe, an idiotic former semi-pro inline skater ("There's some vids floating around of me on the internet") turned drug delivery man. He makes his rounds through an absurd demimonde where he encounters an actor, a doomsday prepper, a brain-damaged stand-up comic, a barefoot bum, and his mother, who is a fan of Bono's music in *Spider-Man: Turn Off the Dark*, and whom he tells he wants to get a face tattoo.

Jobe has an annoying voice and looks like he's aging in front of the camera. When his employer (Lindsay Burdge) sends him out on a special delivery, the customer turns out to be his favorite actor, Royce David Leslie (Theodore Bouloukos), a highfalutin sci-fi stalwart in films with names like *The Skull Machine*. The two discuss the big questions and Jobe shows him a comic book he's made. After Jobe leaves, Leslie begins livestreaming his drug experience, frothing at the mouth and becoming incoherent. Bilandic multiplies Leslie's head across the screen in a trip scene set against a backdrop of the cosmos. His death throes resemble the welcome-to-the-movies snipe they project before the feature at the Cobble Hill Cinema.

The cast in *Jobe'z World* is excellent and will do anything, no matter how stupid. Stephen Payne, as the armed and bunkered-down prepper, gets some big threatening closeups from Bilandic and Williams. They hold on him as he regales Jobe with his theories on movies and points the business end of a rocket launcher at the camera. All the characters in the film have made bad lighting choices for the interiors they inhabit, and the nighttime exteriors are similarly cheap green and purple displays. The stand-up comic (Owen Kline, the younger brother from *The Squid and the Whale*) is barely coherent and wears a large button that reads LICENSE TO BULLSHIT. This feature film is a concise and action-packed sixty-seven minutes long, and I could have easily watched another half hour of it. Or definitely another ten minutes.

The Proposal

"Does the angle between two walls have a happy ending?" asked J. G. Ballard. Jill Magid's epic troll of a documentary on the Mexican architect Luis Barragán suggests that it does not. Magid, who features herself in her film as prominently as Barragán (he died in 1988), visits the architect's house in Mexico, where she stays on a one-person residency to make Barragán-centric art of some kind using his personal archives. In this section of *The Proposal,* we see shots of Barragán's monumental, colorful, slab-like work, which photographs beautifully and is a pleasure to look at.

Magid then reveals that Barragán's estate and the rights to depicting his work are owned by an Italian woman, Federica Zanco. Zanco is an art historian married to the Swiss billionaire whose family owns Vitra, a design firm that manufactures high-end modernist furniture, runs a museum, and has headquarters that feature buildings by famous architects including Frank Gehry and Zaha Hadid. Zanco owns the Barragán estate because her husband, Rolf, bought it for her as a $2.5 million engagement present in 1995. Federica and Rolf have subsequently trademarked Barragán's name. They don't allow researchers to see his professional archives, nor do they allow any of his work to be displayed in other museums, including ones in Mexico. Photographers who take pictures of the architect's buildings are supposed to pay them, as are publishers who reproduce the photos. This villainous European couple has got the Barragán intellectual property rights in copyright lockdown.

Understandably, Barragán's family finds these horrible capitalists obnoxious and creepy, so they allow Magid to dig up the urn containing the architect's ashes and turn a portion of them into a diamond. Magid sets this new diamond in an engagement ring she offers to Zanco in exchange for freeing the Barragán rights. Zanco will finally get an engagement ring if she accepts Magid's macabre offer.

Magid films her meeting with Zanco from across the street using a long lens, like a police surveillance video. Zanco is barely glimpsed, inaccessible to the public, protected by her wealth. This could be the subject for a Hitchcock or a De Palma movie, and Magid comports herself with a certain allure and mystery even though she is open and cheerful. Her necrophilia is loving and all-American. She contrasts it with the secrecy of these austere Swiss oddballs and their exploitative scheme. Much of the film is epistolary because it takes Magid forever to get Zanco to meet her. In Magid's letters she compares herself and Zanco to Barragán's lovers, while Zanco responds with an excessive, perfect cordiality that seems both ultra-cultured and psycho. Somehow the precepts of the art world allow Magid to execute this giant prank flawlessly, hiring workers to dig up the cemetery and paying scientists to make the diamond in a commercial lab, all just to freak out one avaricious Italian woman who lives in the splendor of a great artist's work, poring over his records and objects in secret.

EVERY MOMENT BETWEEN HUMAN BEINGS

THE CONVERSATION

FRANCIS FORD COPPOLA HAS BEEN ON A TEAR RECENTLY, SHORING UP HIS reputation as a principal architect of New Hollywood by rereleasing, last August, his serpentine, grandiose Vietnam War epic *Apocalypse Now* (1979) in a third "final cut" and restoring *The Cotton Club* (1984) to its original length. *The Cotton Club Encore*, which premiered in October, revealed a new film, one much better than the studio-cut version that bombed on release, with subplots featuring its Black cast and musical numbers led by Gregory Hines allowed to play at length. Then last fall, fresh from those successes, the 80-year-old director, à la Scorsese, went on record to describe today's blockbuster superhero movies as "despicable," "not cinema," and "the same movie over and over."

Perhaps energized by his defiance, Coppola has now turned his attention to *The Conversation*, which debuted in 1974, won the top prize at Cannes, and was nominated for a Best Picture Oscar, losing to *The Godfather Part II*, which he also directed. *The Conversation* didn't need restoring, just new 35mm prints. It's the most uncompromising movie of Coppola's career, a summation and proof of New Hollywood aesthetics before *Jaws* washed them out in the tide. Filmed and edited in San Francisco under the aegis of Coppola's American Zoetrope film studio, *The Conversation* made no accommodations to the box office. As surveillance expert Harry (Gene Hackman) asks his assistant, Stan (John Cazale), early in the film, "Are you here to be entertained?"

Hackman's nuanced, self-effacing performance as a soul-sick, uneasy man burrows into crevices and bores through brutalist architecture. In the lobby of an Embarcadero building where his client, a CEO played by Robert Duvall, has his offices, a receptionist instructs Harry to make himself comfortable. The heavy, blocky concrete of the interior was designed to deny comfort to anyone, not least someone who exists at Harry's level of dread.

His discomfort is a twin aspect of his lack of identity. Finding a surprise birthday gift in his apartment, Harry calls his landlord to tell him he doesn't want him to have an extra key. "I would be perfectly happy to have all my personal things burn up in a fire," he explains, "because I don't have anything personal." Hackman wanders through *The Conversation* in a semi-transparent raincoat, head down, on an uncertain mission, but his signature posture in the film is folded and cramped under a sink next to a toilet in a hotel room, drilling holes in the wall to hear into the room next door.

Coppola's starting point in this ultimate existential thriller was to remove a layer. He changed the focus from the people who would be the leads in a routine crime film: the adulterous couple under surveillance, here played by Cindy Williams (later of the sitcom *Laverne & Shirley*) and Frederic Forrest (who would star in Coppola's *One from the Heart* in 1982). As he told fellow New Hollywood director Brian De Palma in an interview a month after *The Conversation* premiered, Coppola wanted "to do a film about eavesdropping and privacy" but make it about a professional listener, not the people he surveils and records. All Harry wants is "a nice, fat recording," but every encounter threatens him, just as every space he enters is a challenge or a dare.

The film begins with the couple as they weave in and out of a crowd in the city's Union Square, where a jazz band plays "I Found a New Baby," a drummer beats bongos, a mime accosts them, and a homeless man sleeps on a bench. Harry and his hired team of free-lance spies, ex-cops, and weird dudes (one of them is Michael Higgins, the bank robber from Barbara Loden's *Wanda*) observe the pair through long lenses and from a van with tinted windows, recording the couple's conversation from several vantage points. Their seemingly banal exchange will, in due time, reveal itself as foreboding. Harry listens to it again and again, a process that recalls the way the photograph in Antonioni's *Blowup* (1966), an obvious inspiration here, becomes more ominous but less understandable the more closely it is examined.

To Harry's chagrin, Stan leers at two young women outside the van who use the vehicle's windows to fix their lipstick, unable to see the men inches from their faces. Coppola cuts between the hidden and the seen throughout the film, putting Hackman behind and in front of translucent screens and sheer curtains as he goes about his business. He prefers to be unseen when not at work, too, spying on his soon-to-be-ex girlfriend (Teri Garr, who would costar with Forrest in *One from the Heart*). She's seen him watching her from her staircase "for a whole hour." Too paranoid to reveal his phone number, Harry conducts business from a payphone on the street, trying to ignore people waiting for their turn who tap on the glass: Harry is a cinematic embodiment of Camus's absurd man, enclosed in a phone booth and gesticulating and moving his mouth, unheard by the queue outside.

At a wiretapper's convention, Harry meets his main rival in the biz, Bernie Moran, an aggressive, short, heavyset loudmouth played by Allen Garfield, who, as he always does, brings menace and vigor to his role as a pest. Things begin to unravel for Harry as he tries to evade his peers and placate them at the same time. When he confronts Duvall's corporate henchman, a handsome, quiet thug played by a young Harrison Ford, their mutual coiled passivity comes to a blank standstill.

The Conversation is also Walter Murch's sound design manifesto. Murch emphasizes repeated tape loops of the same exchange multiple times, in this film in which no one else is ever quite able to have an actual conversation. He combines this loop with musique-concrète blipping and manipulated electronic dialogue, crowd noise, and competing music. His sound design counterpoints David Shire's moody, Satie-like piano score and the live jazz records Harry listens to and plays along with on his tenor sax, another form of one-way communication. By the time Harry ends up in the hotel room's bathroom, every kind of sound that water can make in an enclosed space has been explored and catalogued, from troubling dribble to whoosh and flush.

The film itself appears and disappears in this water, like a code in invisible ink. All movies disappear after you've seen them, until you see them again, yet somehow *The Conversation* remains at once hauntingly indelible and just beyond consciousness, coming and going like sounds from the street at night. And more than overt political-conspiracy thrillers from the same time period, such as *Three Days of the Condor* and *The Parallax View*, which depend on star performances from Robert Redford and Warren Beatty, standard leading men, *The Conversation* survives as the coldest, most alienated Hollywood film from the post-1960s era of suspicion and anxiety, a time in American life when we first realized that ordinary discourse had to be decoded, that the unseen forces controlling our lives were sinister, and knowledge was fragmentary.

"There is no moment between human beings that I cannot record," Moran brags to Harry. As in today's world of data collection and machine learning, there are also none he can understand. Harry can try to figure it all out, but he can't stop anything from happening. When the tape decks are turned and the mic is pointed at him, his interior deconstruction begins, isolating him even more.

ALL WE GOT IN COMMON

MATEWAN

MATEWAN OPENS IN THE PITCH-BLACK DARKNESS OF A WEST VIRGINIA coal mine. A miner lights the carbide lamp on his helmet. The small open flame he wears provides the only flicker of light in this cramped space next to a coal seam. A couple of minutes later, the miner yells out, "Shootin' coal! Shootin' coal!" and soon enough, an explosion goes off.

With this version of "Action!" that we see and hear onscreen, John Sayles brings his 1987 movie out of the darkness and starts it with a bang, as if he has simultaneously rolled camera on the scene he is filming and flipped the switch on the projector showing it. Right away, he gives the film over to one of its workers, a gesture from a writer-director more interested in the drama of history than in movie stars. We realize only later that this man is Sephus Purcell (Ken Jenkins), unofficial leader of the native-born Matewan miners.

In Sayles's book *Thinking in Pictures: The Making of the Movie "Matewan,"* which was released concurrently with the film and is perhaps the best (or only?) how-to memoir by a director about a single one of his works, he mentions that the miners' carbide headlamps, though difficult to photograph, were important to the film; they had often provided the only light in the actual West Virginia mines where he and his cinematographer, Haskell Wexler, were shooting—just "a few foot-candles' worth of illumination." That was all the light the miners had during the long hours of grueling labor in the tight, low spaces of the coal seams. Wexler created a palette for the film that emphasizes diffused blacks, browns, and gray-blues. He and Sayles eliminated primary colors to better convey the feeling of lives "spent crawling in coal" in work clothes that had been through "a thousand washings in harsh lye soap," as Sayles writes.

The Battle of Matewan, also known as the Matewan Massacre, took place in 1920, in "Bloody" Mingo County, West Virginia, home of the Hatfield family, who had feuded with the McCoys in the previous century. Sid Hatfield was the chief of police in Matewan at the time of the massacre, the rare lawman who refused to be bought off by the coal companies. He sided with the miners, many of whom had recently joined the United Mine Workers of America (UMWA), against the "gun thugs" of the Baldwin-Felts Detective Agency, brought in by the Stone Mountain Coal Company to break the union by threatening or murdering its members and harassing their families, as well as to ensure at gunpoint that scab labor brought in from out-of-state Black and Italian communities would work longer hours for less money than the striking miners.

By 1987, Sayles had made four films, one of which, *The Brother from Another Planet* (1984), had been started, finished, and released during the lengthy process of trying to produce *Matewan.* Used to working on low-budget, independent films, Sayles and producer Maggie Renzi eventually raised nearly $4 million to make *Matewan.* They filmed in Thurmond, West Virginia, over a seven-week period in autumn 1986. Sayles's early movies look prescient two decades into the 21st century. *Return of the Secaucus 7* (1980), a comedy-drama, deals with baby boomer friends who remain true to their youthful ideals but must face the failure of their generation to change the world. *Lianna* (1983) is an explicitly feminist film, a drama in which a woman who has married her college professor leaves him for another woman, also a professor. The socioeconomic gap between these lovers ultimately separates them, as it does Rosanna Arquette's college girl and her working-class boyfriend (Vincent Spano) in *Baby It's You,* also released in 1983.

Almost unique among movies from the first half of the '80s, *The Brother from Another Planet* deals with immigration, racism, and slavery. In it, we experience Reagan-era social reality through the eyes of the mute main character (Joe Morton), who appears to be an ordinary Black man but is really an alien from outer space. His pursuit by "men in black" (played by David Strathairn and the director himself) is a reminder that Sayles's working-class dramas influenced Hollywood and were repurposed in unexpected ways. *Secaucus 7,* with its ensemble cast gathered for a weekend, bears a resemblance to *The Big Chill,* made four years later, just as *Brother* now can't help but remind viewers of the *Men in Black* franchise that began in 1997.

Sayles's earlier films had had some success, but when he, Renzi, and coproducer Peggy Rajski began work on *Matewan,* the feature-film landscape did not favor what the director calls in his book a "semi-epic period piece" in which "the story was political, the hero a socialist, the ending not upbeat, and there was no room . . . for a rock soundtrack." The distributor Cinecom kicked in a big percentage of the budget to get the film made, and ultimately it was *Matewan* that established Sayles as a writer-director of leftist Americana and working-class crime drama (though one who has also made the occasional foray abroad, setting films in Ireland, Mexico, and the Philippines).

Sayles followed *Matewan* with *Eight Men Out* (1988), a baseball drama starring John Cusack, about the 1919 Black Sox scandal and the unfair labor practices in the major leagues at the end of the deadball era. Since then, Sayles, nearly always with Renzi producing (she has done so on fourteen of his eighteen total features), has made a dozen more movies, each one furthering their commitment to political filmmaking in narrative features. His career is unique in American cinema. No other writer-director who began making his own films post–*Star Wars* has managed to achieve as much while staying as true to his ideals.

Sheriff Hatfield—whom Strathairn, in his third Sayles film, plays with an inscrutable agenda—is not the hero of *Matewan.* It has two: Chris Cooper's Joe Kenehan, an outside agitator and pacifist sent in by the UMWA, and Will Oldham's teenage preacher-miner, Danny. They are the film's twin conscience and heart. Danny narrates the film as an old man, a survivor of the massacre. J. K. "Kent" Lilly, a Mercer County, West Virginia, native, provides Danny's present-day voice in the real accent of the mines and hollers. This triple focus in *Matewan,* in which Danny looks back at his younger self while that self watches Joe organize the miners and oppose the company, allows Sayles to build a kind of quiet, unshowy heroism into the film's structure. *Matewan* is the story of Danny's radicalization as it emerges not just from the violence around him but also from his first exposure to ideas from outside his small community.

Cooper was making his film debut at age 35 and has the thin face of a silent-movie star here; it is clear why he has become a Sayles regular. He plays Joe, a former Wobbly and an ex-con, with quiet dignity and friendly stoicism. Oldham, 16 at the time and a native of nearby Louisville, Kentucky, had appeared in one other movie but had not yet recorded any of the music he would become known for. His surprising authenticity in *Matewan* is feral but thoughtful, grounded in the Bible stories his character knows so well. Danny must come to the decision to reject the "hardshell" antiunion, antisocialist dogma of the preacher he has grown up admiring (played by Sayles, looking like a twisted Gregory Peck, as a mean-spirited shouter) so that he can reconcile the principles of the union with his Christian beliefs. We can see in Oldham's eyes the change taking place in his character when the beefy, red-faced Hickey (Kevin Tighe), the main Baldwin-Felts thug, insults him at the dinner table in the boardinghouse run by his mother, Elma (Mary McDonnell), a young widow. Hickey calls Danny dumb and describes Matewan as a "shithole," then pulls a gun on him because he won't pass the peas.

When the boy goes to live in the camp with Joe and the striking miners, he realizes he "ain't never seen everybody all together like this" before, and his conversion is complete.

Sayles deliberately rejects the kinds of hillbilly portrayals of Appalachians commonly found in American movies, from *Sergeant York* (1941) to *Deliverance* (1972). Each character in *Matewan* gets a moment to show his or her reasons, including Bridey Mae (Nancy Mette). Hickey calls her "that tramp who meets the passenger train," and C. E. Lively (Bob Gunton) coerces her into lying about Kenehan in order to discredit him. Sayles, however, has already allowed her to tell her own story, near the beginning of the film. Elma, for her part, sees that Kenehan is not telling the truth about himself at first but seals their friendship with a bloody handshake, a portent of the film's ending and the first in a series of sage, silent decisions she will make about people.

Joe, Danny, Bridey Mae, and Elma are Sayles inventions, but James Earl Jones's Few Clothes and Gunton's Lively, like Strathairn's Sid Hatfield, are not. Few Clothes fought in the Spanish-American War beside Teddy Roosevelt's Rough Riders. As a spokesman for the Black miners, he agrees to join the union, which leads to his being enlisted to commit murder. That's because among the union men there is a traitor and spy working for the coal company. The real-life Lively, posing as a fired miner, owned a restaurant in Matewan where the union men held meetings. The film's plot turns on Gunton's portrayal of this snake in the grass, who smears Kenehan and does not shy away from torture and cold-blooded killing. Lively died in West Virginia in 1962 at age 75. He exited this world unpunished and presumably untroubled, unlike villains in movies.

Matewan brings to life an important moment of solidarity in labor history. The Appalachian miners learn to get along with the Black and Italian men and their families who have been relocated to Mingo County by the coal companies, all to the tune of the Italian labor anthem "Avanti popolo." Music provides a link among these groups, with Sayles showing how bluegrass, the blues, and bel canto can blend. He and composer Mason Daring give Hazel Dickens, who also appears in the movie as a townswoman, songs to sing in the haunting and expressive high lonesome of the hills, a cappella on the soundtrack and onscreen during *Matewan*'s inevitable funeral scene.

The miners' union was broken by 1921, after President Warren G. Harding put the entire state of West Virginia under martial law and sent the army to the coalfields to defend the companies against their employees. By then, hundreds of miners had been killed, thousands arrested and jailed. It was not until 1935, under Franklin Roosevelt's New Deal, that union organizing was legally protected in the United States. *Matewan* came out on August 28, 1987, at the high-water mark of Ronald Reagan's America, six years after Reagan fired more than eleven thousand air traffic controllers for not ending a strike, and on a weekend between the premieres of *Dirty Dancing* and *Fatal Attraction.* Most of the thousands of coal jobs that would disappear over the course of Reagan's two terms were already gone. That year in American movies was defined somewhere between *Moonstruck* and *Lethal Weapon,* with a swampy hint of *Predator* mixed in. Nostalgia was sweet, as in *Dirty Dancing,* or hyperstylized and big-budgeted, as in Brian De Palma's *The Untouchables.* There was just as much a need then for *Matewan*—a film that presents real conflicts in American history, without a happy ending—as there is today.

When Sayles shot the movie in Thurmond (after deciding that the actual town of Matewan had become too modern), the population was "around sixty or seventy people," as he writes. In 1920, the population had been 285. Today, just five people live there. Similarly, in 1920 there were 850 people in Matewan itself; now there are fewer than 450, although the town still has the vibrancy to establish and maintain, along with UMWA Local 1440, the West Virginia Mine Wars Museum, dedicated to preserving the history that was once buried. Even with such exceptions, towns like these are among the so-called sacrifice zones in the US, places where heavy industry has permanently ruined the environment, lowered life expectancy, increased poverty and drug abuse, and led to depopulation. When strip mining and mountaintop removal replaced digging and blasting as the primary way coal is extracted from rock, coal companies eliminated jobs. The UMWA, strong through the early '60s, has seen a steady decline from its height of about half a million members.

In their 2012 book *Days of Destruction, Days of Revolt,* journalist Chris Hedges and artist Joe Sacco investigate the current situation in the coal-mining counties of Appalachia, focusing in particular on Welch, West Virginia, which is where Baldwin-Felts operatives assassinated Sid Hatfield in August 1921. There were a hundred thousand people living in McDowell County, of which Welch is the seat, in the middle of the 20th century. Now there are fewer than twenty thousand. In the counties they visited, Hedges and Sacco found towns covered in coal dust, unbreathable air, and contaminated water. Mountaintop removal has eliminated plant and animal life in parts of West Virginia, erasing eons of geological and natural history that will never return, even if beautiful woodlands and teeming wildlife remain in other abandoned hills and hollers in the state. But the coal companies, as the authors note, have erased labor history, too, by carting away the very soil on which union men clashed with capitalist thugs, and won.

Matewan, as Sayles writes, has the structure of a western. It's not that different in its way from *High Noon* or *The Wild Bunch* or any other movie where gunmen threaten a town. But, Sayles is careful to point out, "the purpose of the story is not nostalgia." Two moments in particular encapsulate what that purpose is, illustrating the film's continued relevance. "There ain't but two sides to this world: them that work and them that don't," Joe explains, in a scene in Lively's restaurant in which he has to prove himself to the miners. Instead of urging them to violence, he insists on solidarity across racial and ethnic lines. Later, when the striking miners are building their camp, Danny, in Lilly's voice-over, recalls how Joe explained to them, "All we got in common is our misery, and the least we can do is share it."

From Harding to Reagan and now to Donald Trump, the leaders of this country have lied to coal miners, used them up, riddled their landscape with bullets, and flooded it with slurry and ash. At one of his non-election-year rallies, in West Virginia in 2018, Trump told coal miners he was putting them back to work. "Great people," he called them. "Brave people. I don't know how the hell you do that, I'll tell ya. You guys have a lot of courage. But we love clean, beautiful West Virginia coal." He told them that wind energy, pipelines, and solar panels are fragile and hard to fix, and concluded by asking and answering his own question. "You know what you can't hurt? Coal," he said in front of a sign that read "Trump Digs Coal."

Pun aside, Trump does not actually dig any coal—he is one of them that don't work. He loves coal miners for the same reason the bosses at the Stone Mountain Coal Company did in 1920: for their capacity to be hurt, again and again. The opportunity to inflict unlimited pain and damage on workers and on the land, it goes without saying, requires the absence of unions. *Matewan* is one of the few movies produced in the US to make the need for them its subject. The gun-toting, non-miner hillbillies who stealthily materialize out of the woods in the film know that the coal companies stole their land. We, however, have to be shown. For the past four decades, a new John Sayles film has emerged every two years or so to show us the lives and struggles official histories and other movies ignore. From New Jersey and West Virginia to Florida and Texas, Sayles has made films all over the country. Every place in America has a Matewan.

MONEY IS AN IRON

OSCAR MOVIES 2020

The Two Popes

Hollywood Anglophilia reached new heights in 2019 and *The Two Popes* is Exhibit A: two old British men in dresses speaking in foreign accents pretending they're popes. Because of this movie, Adam Sandler and Eddie Murphy didn't get Oscar nominations for *Uncut Gems* and *Dolemite Is My Name*. That's strange, because Sandler and Murphy are comedians who started out on *Saturday Night Live*, and *The Two Popes* would have worked better as a sketch on *Monty Python's Flying Circus*.

So instead of Terry Jones in a frock, Anthony Hopkins plays Benedict XVI, the ex-Nazi pope, as if he's the doddering ghost of Rutger Hauer. Jonathan Pryce, a veteran of four Terry Gilliam films, plays Pope Francis as a warm, life-loving nebbish who seems Jewish in his self-doubt. Even so, the pair's dynamic lacks spark. Suitably for a Netflix film, they resolve their differences by watching TV together on the couch at home before nodding off to sleep. By the final scene, these two elderly priests dance the tango, exchanging a whisper *Viaggio in Italia*-style, like Bill Murray and Scarlett Johansson at the end of *Lost in Translation*, bringing the weird, conservative pedophile wing of the Catholic Church together with the less weird wing that flirted with liberation theology when it was younger.

Jojo Rabbit

In *The Two Popes* we are supposed to find it significant that Benedict doesn't know the music of the Beatles. In *Jojo Rabbit* we get to hear the Beatles sing "I Want to Hold Your Hand" in German as Taika Waititi compares the Third Reich to Beatlemania in an opening montage featuring scenes from *Triumph of the Will.* This unasked-for pop-culture critique sets up a silly movie about friendship and acceptance—all those Nazis needed was love. Either that, or Waititi couldn't secure the rights to "Get Back."

Waititi plays Hitler in *Jojo Rabbit,* with blue eyes like Robert De Niro's in *The Irishman.* Hitler, acted by Waititi below Fred Armisen-level, is here a wacky sitcom neighbor more than he is deranged or even odd. It's just that he's touchy about Jews. At one point Waititi-Hitler blurts out "correctamundo!" to Jojo (Roman Griffin Davis), the Hitler youth who fantasizes the Fuhrer is his best friend. Hitler saying "correctamundo" is only not arbitrary here because it's a word from a sitcom.

"Let everything happen to you" is the film's final message, a line from Rilke, who even if he hadn't died in 1926 probably could not have imagined a movie that is the equivalent of hugging a teddy bear with Hitler's face on it. While Jerry Lewis killed Hitler in *Which Way to the Front?* and had the audacity to imagine children led to the gas chamber in his unreleased movie *The Day the Clown Cried,* Waititi's Hitler is an imaginary friend, not a deadly fantasy projection come to life. "Let everything happen to you" seems like the exact wrong advice when dealing with the Nazis. Compare this to last year's *Hidden Life* by Terrence Malick, a serious film told from the exact opposite point of view as *Jojo Rabbit,* to find an ending more in line with reality.

Jojo Rabbit combines Quentin Tarantino and Wes Anderson in the worst, cop-out ways. While an obscure song by Love called "Everybody's Gotta Live" plays over a tricky parallel-tracking dolly shot that could come from an Anderson film, we are supposed to think of Anne Frank's plight. When Jojo's mother (Scarlett Johansson), the one humanizing force in his life and a member of the Resistance, is hanged in public by the Nazis, Waititi mars her tragedy by focusing too long on the spectator pumps on her feet dangling in the air, an image that is supposed to be disturbing and heartbreaking, not clever and artistic. Tarantino, like Lewis, killed Hitler in *Inglourious Basterds,* and I prefer the purposefully stupid "Anybody order fried sauerkraut? Burn, you Nazi bastards!" of *The 14 Fists of McCluskey* in *Once Upon a Time in Hollywood* to this mélange of other people's styles that is cutesy, fake-subtle, emotionally manipulative, and soft on fascism.

1917

In Sir Sam Mendes's *1917,* form and content meet in perfect harmony: the pointlessness of the film exactly mirrors the pointlessness of World War I.

Mendes has shot the entire film to look as though it were made in one continuous take, like *Russian Ark* was, but he has done it with computers, stitching everything together into a continuous flow of bombings, crashes, chases, carnage, fires, and death. As experiments go, it is, in addition to being pointless, also exactly as noble as the war was. Here, history is a video game in which a soldier (George MacKay) goes from level to level trying to deliver a message to Benedict Cumberbatch, playing Colonel Mustard in his prime.

I'm fairly certain that the film is pro-Brexit, but exactly how I don't know, and after *Dunkirk* I don't care. At this current level of Hollywood production, expressionistic British militarism is all the same to me and it's worn me out, which is perhaps its intention. I do know that *1917* buries the achievement of *Russian Ark* the same way calling a movie *1917* tends to obscure other things that happened that year. I guess part of the pointlessness is that a lot of things happened in 1917, and here is one of them. The war was going on in the trenches. Why it was happening we understand less from *1917* than we understand why the buffalo stampeded in *The Revenant.*

Joker

A month before *Joker* came out, there was a mass shooting in Midland-Odessa, Texas. A man fired from his job drove through those cities shooting at pedestrians from his car and then from a US Post Office van he hijacked. He killed seven people and wounded twenty-two others. The shooter lived alone in a metal, dirt-floor shack without electricity or plumbing, his only companion a dog. Police chased him in the postal van to the Cinergy Entertainment Permian Basin cineplex, "the largest community entertainment center in Texas," where they shot and killed him in front of theaters showing already-forgotten movies including *Don't Let Go, Bennett's War, The Peanut Butter Falcon, Overcomer, Angel Has Fallen, Ready or Not, Good Boys, 47 Meters Down: Uncaged, The Angry Birds Movie 2,* and *Dora and the Lost City of Gold.*

On the TV news show *CBS This Morning,* their "Lead National Correspondent" David Begnaud, wearing a dark burgundy button-down shirt the color of blood, showed up at the cineplex and said to the camera, "We are at the movie theater here in Odessa. We're here because this is where the rampage ended. But what police don't know, and what they may *never* know, is was the gunman coming *here* to continue his rampage?"

Joker was released in this atmosphere, in this kind of world, where after a deadly tragedy a man like Begnaud, who should know better, goes on national TV and says idiotic things at a crime scene because that's his job. So *Joker* seemed to a lot of film critics, who should also know better, like it was part of the problem. *Joker* is about a lonely man (Joaquin Phoenix) with a terrible life and mental health issues who loses his job and then kills people. In his case, he also goes on TV and kills a talk show host (Robert De Niro). As a Batman spin-off, it was thought that *Joker* could lead to a real-life mass murder like the one in Aurora, Colorado, where in 2012 a deranged, orange-haired lunatic shot and killed twelve people and wounded fifty-eight others during a screening of *The Dark Knight Rises*. Some critics said *Joker* should be banned to prevent that from happening again, or at least shunned, and *Entertainment Weekly*, which comes out monthly, was so appalled by it that they took a bold stand by refusing to give it a letter grade at the end of their review.

I dismissed these reactions, but when I went to see *Joker*, there was a man at the same show as me who had two large emotional support dogs with him. This man wore sunglasses throughout the entire screening, along with a tool belt that had a dozen items dangling from it, including a flashlight and bunches of Ziploc baggies, presumably for dog shit. At several points in the film he got up and walked the aisles of the theater, jangling and grunting, while the dogs, back in their seats, whined in his absence. This man's presence had a real "Emergo" effect, like the skeleton that flew over the audience's heads in the original *House on Haunted Hill*. His presence was unsettling and his random strolls added to the menace of what was on the screen. I wondered whether he was armed, so I moved to a seat closer to an exit door at the front of the theater, where I had a better chance of escaping if he opened fire.

When *Joker* was over, several members of the audience confronted the employees of the Cobble Hill Cinema to ask about this man's behavior, which they explained was somewhat threatening. A young man holding a lobby broom had to answer to them. "By law, we have to let in people with emotional support animals," he explained, "and wearing sunglasses is a personal preference, which we are not allowed to bring up to customers." Anyway, *Joker* is a one-man show featuring an undirected actor and cinematography that uses the *Piss Christ* filter on every shot so that everything looks yellow and corroded. Its fictional 1981 New York City is haphazard but not all that different from the more real 2012 New York of *Uncut Gems*, if New York had a clown district as well as a diamond district. The riot scenes near the end of *Joker* reflect something true in society, and they brought the film out of its shell. If you see *Joker*, it would be best to see it in a theater with a potential psychopath for that added thrill of maybe not surviving it. Seeing it at home will be a waste of time unless you live with someone who might kill you while it's on.

Judy

Like Joaquin Phoenix as the Joker, Renée Zellweger plays Judy Garland as an emaciated exemplary sufferer. With tiny-twitchy head movements, pursed lips, little laughs and quips, and squinting, she portrays Garland in the last year of her life as doomed and drunk, a reluctant trouper not ready to go on and unwilling to accept that there is any good reason to go on except money. And unlike Phoenix, Zellweger has to sing and sound like Garland in *Judy*, and her fake bad dancing is better than his. Instead of being an antihero to the alienated, she has to clearly mark the line between theater kids and show people, a line that the survivors of *High School Musical*, *Glee*, *Pitch Perfect*, and various TV talent shows would be wise to note.

Wearing a black mink over summer outfits inappropriate to the end of the year in London, Zellweger's Judy cycles through a variety of punk looks depending on what time of day it is in the movie. She's Stiv Bators before her shows, wasted and smeared, Sid Vicious after them, momentarily triumphant with spiky hair, and Holly Vincent when she wakes up in the morning, still alive. Zellweger finds the tragedy of Garland's life in odd moments—staring at a pretty slice of cake she is afraid to eat, turning the plate around.

Judy takes place in London in 1968 in winter. After films with Michelle Williams as Marilyn Monroe in England (*My Week with*

Marilyn, 2011) and Annette Bening as Gloria Grahame in England (*Film Stars Don't Die in Liverpool*, 2017), the "Hollywood actress in decline in Great Britain" genre officially exists. Seeing the most glamorous American women of their time shivering palely in the cold under gray skies next to stagnant little pools in damp parks is how England gets its revenge on Malibu. We learn that British fans will love these women no matter what, even after they've been rejected by the industry, by various husbands, and by a fickle public who has moved on to Audrey Hepburn. If we find out that Barbara Payton spent the winter in Folkestone in 1960, Jennifer Lawrence will have a comeback film.

Bombshell

With its trio of competing blondes at different stages in their careers, and a large group of character actors playing other clownish Fox News personalities, *Bombshell* could have been a sharp combination of Fassbinder and Christopher Guest. Instead, director Jay Roach, of the Austin Powers movies (and *Trumbo*), stages it as a set of intergenerational realizations that lead to individual empowerment. If Roach had really wanted to empower this film's audience, he and screenwriter Charles Randolph would have bluntly stated the salaries news anchors like Megyn Kelly (Charlize Theron) and Gretchen Carlson (Nicole Kidman) were paid to lie to their aging right-wing audience for so many years, and how their lying was further incentivized and rewarded with bonuses. After that had been established, the film could have had a meta ending like *Little Women* or *A Beautiful Day in the Neighborhood*, except in this case, in one last twist, we would also learn how much money Theron and Kidman made pretending to be the deluded sellouts they were playing underneath the prosthetics.

Alas, as a Hollywood movie about TV news, *Bombshell* is not *Tout va bien*. Roach has no insight into Roger Ailes as an auteur, except to have Ailes shouting the dumbest thing certain film directors also yell to excuse their worst impulses: "It's a visual medium!" Played by John Lithgow in a fat suit as a hunchbacked ogre with a cane, Ailes in *Bombshell* could have been a medieval grotesque or a repellent double-crosser like Charles Laughton in *The Big Clock*. By the end of the film, however, we are expected to pity this fat, limping predator. Rupert Murdoch, who discards Ailes to save his TV network, is played in turn by Malcolm McDowell, a man twelve years younger than Murdoch and a hundred years better-looking, proving a woman should have directed *Bombshell*. On the less debonair end of the spectrum, Richard Kind plays Rudy Giuliani in *Bombshell*, and that is a whole movie I'd like to see, but only if it's directed by the Safdie Brothers.

Harriet

Kasi Lemmons's *Harriet*, a biopic of the Black freedom fighter and Civil War commander who escaped slavery on her own and then risked her life to free dozens of others, has a perfunctory quality that renders Tubman's story a little dull. The most brutal scene in the film is one of Black-on-Black violence, in which a slave catcher (Omar Dorsey) beats to death a freedwoman played by Janelle Monáe. Cynthia Erivo, an award-winning English theater actress, plays Harriet, and Joe Alwyn, also English, plays her former owner. This acting arrangement implies, unfortunately, that the sick, exploitative history of the American South is classy drama for English people to play, but when it comes to Americans like Dorsey and Monáe, it's something more basic.

In the contemporary, Ohio-to-Louisiana-set crime drama *Queen & Slim* that also came out last year, two British actors (Daniel Kaluuya and Jodie Turner-Smith) played the African American leads, and these top-of-the-bill casting choices have become another area in which Black professionals in the United States are ignored, even when African American directors tell stories about their own history or the difficulty of Black lives today. There were no Americans who could have played even one of these three leading roles in *Harriet* or *Queen & Slim*? I know Samuel L. Jackson discussed this a couple of years ago, and took heat for it, but I think his criticism was valid. He pointed out that there is universal experience across the Black diaspora, but that not all experience is universal. Some of it is local.

Given the severe economic disadvantages American actors face competing with British (and Canadian and Australian) actors, disadvantages that are growing with the wealth gap, this seems especially unfair when it comes to stories about historical and contemporary injustice faced by African Americans. As the Oscars nominations prove, there are fewer roles deemed award-worthy for Black actors, so this Anglophilic system is more unfair to them than it is to white actors. I'm not suggesting American filmmakers should never employ Brits, but I do mean they should think through the implications of doing so in a more serious way than just choosing who's best by the industry standards which have been imposed on them. Without access to inexpensive education and health care from early in their lives, American actors are taking a beating because our country isn't civilized compared to the rest of the Anglophone world.

Harriet's good intentions, the careful way it exposes how families were separated under slavery, and its acknowledgment of the mystical aspects of Tubman's mission—all that was lost to me as I watched the last scene between Harriet and her former owner. The film just becomes *Masterpiece Theatre*, historical drama based on something classic. It is important to tell Harriet Tubman's story, especially now, when former film producer Steve Mnuchin has so blithely decided Tubman doesn't deserve her promised spot on the twenty-dollar bill, where she was supposed to replace a slave-owning president. Importing an actor to portray her, no matter how talented Erivo is, strikes the wrong note, so to speak.

I blame the casting of Vivien Leigh in *Gone with the Wind* for this. That's where this started, in a racist Hollywood epic. As moviegoers we should ask ourselves why it is that British people seem more natural to American audiences when they play Southerners, whether the characters are Black or white. Why are we more comfortable with that? This aristocratic mode is preserving something ugly, through the medium of highly trained British acting, instead of interrogating our shared history so we can write it and put it on screen in new ways for the future. Maybe it's time for a new approach, instead of treating the Antebellum South like it was invented at the Globe Theatre. We should be responsible for our own history, but we are outsourcing it and fancying it up.

Little Women

Little Women takes place during the same period in American history as *Harriet*, and Greta Gerwig's adaptation of the beloved classic features a bunch of Irish, British, and Australian actors as the title characters—Saoirse Ronan is Jo, Emma Watson is Meg, Florence Pugh is Amy, and Eliza Scanlen is poor, doomed Beth, who dies, as she always does. Laura Dern, a pure product of Southern California, beams over them as put-upon Marmee, their weirdly nicknamed mother. Was her name pronounced "Mahmee" when *Little Women* was written in Concord, Massachusetts, in 1868? I think it must have been, because if there's one thing young people from New England who move to New York to become writers like Jo does should know, it's that the hardest *r*'s are the ones we leave behind.

Gerwig's *Little Women* is an adaptation for a new century. She has reimagined the narrative, cutting it into large chunks and reordering them so Alcott's story is told out of sequence. This was a gamble with a book that is familiar to readers all over the world, and it works. The film is something of a masterpiece, with long, loping scenes shot on location in Massachusetts. Even Paris is in Ipswich here. Each scene is so lovingly crafted and sincere, and everyone in this film seems so committed to getting it right. It's the ultimate in professional cinema, a standard that other directors should look to. Gerwig has outdone contemporary Hollywood (and *Masterpiece Theatre*) in every respect. Each actor in *Little Women* shines, with Pugh and Timothée Chalamet (as Laurie) standing out, even as they revolve around Jo and then slide out of her orbit. Pugh was especially effective sitting next to Meryl Streep, who plays the girls' rich aunt in purple makeup.

Marriage Story

Seeing *Marriage Story* on the Upper West Side, its natural habitat even though the main characters live in Brooklyn, was so perfect that by the time the movie was over I felt kind of giddy. On the way out I thought to myself, "Now here is a serious film about important things, with real acting in it. So grueling, and yet ultimately so at peace with the reality of relationships."

Unfortunately for me, seeing it at the newly reopened Paris Theater was also like going to the Trader Vic's in the Plaza Hotel across the street afterward and having four mai tais to celebrate, if the Trader Vic's was still there and hadn't been closed by Donald Trump when he bought the Plaza because he thought it was tacky. The next morning I had a post-*Marriage Story* hangover and I hated myself for liking it. I swore I'd never go see another movie about some bougie fools and their inconsequential divorce and their real love, which is Stephen Sondheim.

Adam Driver plays a working-class dude from Indiana who is such a genius director of downtown avant-garde theater that he has won a MacArthur. We see part of one of his plays with Scarlett Johansson in it, his wife and star. The play seems to be a cross between Anne Carson and the Wooster Group that looks like it's from the early 2000s, the same way this couple's Los Angeles divorce lawyers, Laura Dern and Ray Liotta, seem to be from the Coen Brothers' *Intolerable Cruelty*. I was curious how many working-class guys from Indiana get Genius grants so I looked up the previous recipients for avant-garde theater direction. The closest I found was a Manhattan native whose father was on the Council of Foreign Relations and who has two advanced degrees from Yale.

Johansson, for her part, has to dress like one of the Beatles on the cover of *Sgt. Pepper's Lonely Hearts Club Band* and tie her ex-husband's shoe, the same way she has to wear a Tyrolean hat and tie her son's shoe in *Jojo Rabbit*. Earlier in the film, she dressed like *Let's Dance*-era David Bowie. I'm not sure what this impetus to further costume the Black Widow is, but I read that the next film Noah Baumbach is writing, with Greta Gerwig, is based on Barbie, the doll. Will Barbie extract herself from her box the way Johansson escapes her marriage and finds herself a nice place in LA and wins an Emmy to put in it? As for the emotional horror of some of the breakup scenes in *Marriage Story*, this is also a film in which Driver has to cut his arm with a box cutter to prove the film isn't bloodless.

A Beautiful Day in the Neighborhood

Marielle Heller's new film, like her previous one, *Can You Ever Forgive Me?*, is set in New York in the 1990s and is also about an angry writer struggling to get by. Lloyd (Matthew Rhys) has so much integrity his editor at *Esquire* (Christine Lahti) is mad at him, so she sends him on an assignment they both think is beneath him: interviewing Fred Rogers (Tom Hanks), the host of the PBS children's show, *Mister Rogers' Neighborhood*. Heller's film explicitly asks the question, "Why do we write for magazines for a living?" and answers it by stating that we do it because "we get to change a broken world with our words." It's a nice sentiment from a very strange film, aimed at Gen X writers from bad homes who are trying not to let life make them bitter, and probably failing.

The film's strangeness makes this convincing, and it's what saves it from gooeyness. One of the most unexpected and evocative scenes in any film last year is in *A Beautiful Day in the Neighborhood.* It's the scene with Lloyd and Fred eating lunch together in a Chinese restaurant in Pittsburgh, where Fred demands a moment of silence that spreads across the dining room and out into the world. Things like that are delicate and hard to make work, as are two other important elements in this film. One is the mix of models from Rogers's TV set with real life. The other is Tom Hanks. I am starting to really enjoy late-period Hanks, and this film states right up front that it is Hanks's sometimes otherworldly weirdness that saves him as actor, and then goes on to imply it can save all of us. Hanks-as-Rogers can talk to his puppets like they are real people, sing his simple songs about liking you, and ask grownups disarming questions: "When did you become angry? Did something happen?"

All this comes in a broken world where publishing is so decrepit and people are so damaged by their smartphones that Heller felt she had to include an old industrial film about how magazines are made. Chris Cooper is in this movie as Lloyd's drunk father, who sings "Something Stupid" at a wedding and starts a fight. Cooper was in *Little Women* as the kindly, rich neighbor, Mr. Laurence, and part of the reason I liked this film better than that one is because Cooper gets to do more here, and also because Jody Lee Lipes's hard-edge cinematography impressed me more than the cinematography in *Little Women*, which edged right up to the line of the too-fancy and peered over.

Ford v Ferrari

So many of these films are about fatherlessness. Either fathers are absent from them, or, if they are present, are terrible, active forces that ruin lives. *Ford v Ferrari* is different in that it shows the way a father can be lost to a dangerous profession—a slow but sudden process in a job that's all about speed. This Spielbergizes the film by concentrating too much attention on Ken Miles's (Christian Bale's) son, Peter (Noah Jupe), and reducing his sexy wife, Mollie (Caitríona Balfe), to motherhood when all we want is cars, machinery, more speed. In *Red Line 7000* (1965), Howard Hawks customized his characters to be without those kinds of bonds. Mangold, whose way with actors is so sure, seeks to reinstall cinematic values into mainstream factory production. He has ended up making an auto racing film far more clean-cut than Hawks's.

As with magazines in the Mister Rogers movie, so with cars in *Ford v Ferrari*. Objects from another era now becoming passé, their value must be restated for the new audiences of a digital world. Mangold's film is about how "the machine becomes weightless" and "everything fades" at 7000 RPMs, the point at which the machinery is working at top capacity. This metaphor for the cinema, about "a body moving through space and time" requires explanation because digital technology erases all that—weightlessness and other forms of non-being are built in.

So *Ford v Ferrari*, set around the same time as *Once Upon a Time in Hollywood*, coincidentally features some of the same things as Tarantino's film—a fight with canned food, a hero who lives in a trailer, lots of aimless driving, competition from an Italian industry that is doing it better than the inventors of the form. The central relationship here, between two men as in certain Hawks films, is the same as in Tarantino's movie. Matt Damon's Carroll Shelby employs and relies on Bale's Ken Miles to do dangerous work he can't do himself.

Since Mangold lives on the humane side of the Hawksian Fallacy, *Ford v Ferrari* doesn't go as far as *Once Upon a Time in Hollywood*, where Tarantino pushes Hawks's cold, brutal side into new areas, exposing acting as a non-dangerous profession, a series of poses against the inner turmoil of obsolescence. *Ford v Ferrari*'s meta-cinematic qualities remain buried, the men are not Hollywood bozos, and the whole enterprise can be enjoyed on a basic level, even, or perhaps especially, the part where Tracy Letts's blustery Henry Ford II explains that James Bond is a degenerate.

Once Upon a Time in Hollywood

Ford v Ferrari sticks to the facts: Ken Miles died in a car crash. *Once Upon a Time in Hollywood*, a shaggy dog story wrapped in a fairy tale, saves people who were killed and kills people who are still alive. One person it does not kill is Cliff Booth (Brad Pitt), stuntman for cowboy actor Rick Dalton (Leonardo DiCaprio). Instead, Booth is wheeled out to an ambulance, into another life, one where he no longer works for Dalton. As at the end of Hawks's *Red River*, we do not want to see either of the film's main characters die, anymore than we want to see Sharon Tate and her friends killed by the Manson Family.

Dalton is given his moment of heroism in the film when he torches one of the Mansons (Mikey Madison) with a flamethrower he conveniently has in his poolside cabana, implicitly comparing the Mansons to the Nazis it was used against in one of Dalton's films. Tarantino respects the Chekhovian rule that if you show a flamethrower earlier in the movie, you have to use it later. This weapon had appeared as a prop in a film within the film, where it was established as real—as real as anything else here. Similarly, when Dalton imagines himself into *The Great Escape*, replacing Steve McQueen, we see this onscreen. Tarantino digitally grafts DiCaprio into a role Dalton never played. We then cut to Margot Robbie as Sharon Tate in a movie theater seeing the real Tate onscreen in *The Wrecking Crew*. Dalton/DiCaprio ends up in a film he wasn't in, but Tate/Robbie does not appear in place of the real Tate in a film Tate was really in.

The way the film positions the Manson Family as real and threatening, more real than Hollywood, is turned around by the end. The face of evil is crushed by a dog food can. Tarantino changes the Mansons from encrustations of Hollywood who inhabit abandoned sets into cartoon characters, like people in a Frank Tashlin movie. This shock ending offended older critics, who revealed themselves as wed to the precious 1960s narratives they think they own. But as we already learned, in a movie, you can kill Hitler. We know it's harder in real life. We know what happened to Sharon Tate.

The real enemy of such critics is not Tarantino but the passage of time, just as the future, in the form of the 8-year-old actor Trudi Fraser (Julia Butters), at first seems like a tiny nemesis for Dalton, who will render him one more humiliation. Studious, serious, worshipping Disney, young Trudi represents the future of the movies and of American culture. She helps Dalton get himself together after an eight-whiskey-sour night, and if he throws her to the floor with a little too much force in their scene together, so what? She's wearing pads, of course, and taking falls is part of acting. If the Trudi Frasers of the world will someday replace the Rick Daltons, for now at least they know they're both in the same game.

Richard Jewell

A film about an officious, unlikable oaf (Paul Walter Hauser) who is accused of being the perpetrator of a deadly bombing is not the stuff of Hollywood success any more than the story-actor combo in Clint Eastwood's *The 15:17 to Paris* was in 2018. Eastwood, of late, has become interested in real-life disaster and terrorism. *Richard Jewell* combines his 2016 film *Sully*, which was about the 2009 US Airways landing on the Hudson River and forefronted Tom Hanks in a courtroom drama with minute repetitiveness, with *The 15:17 to Paris*, in which the young men who stopped a terrorist on a train in France played themselves. Hauser combines the quiet-awkward star-power performance of Hanks with the unquiet awkward naturalism of having real people act in a Hollywood movie. Hauser does not look like a lead actor, he closely resembles the real Jewell, and he gives an unsettling performance that exists in an obscure area where busy-bodying and stolidity meet the worship of law and order.

"A little power can turn a person into a monster," Jewell's lawyer (Sam Rockwell) tells him early in the film. This is Eastwood's theme. He drives it home by having Jon Hamm and Olivia Wilde represent law enforcement and the news media. These good-looking, TV-ish actors play an FBI agent and a newspaper reporter soullessly, as boring hacks unconcerned with truth and justice because they are preoccupied with success and fame, and always think they're right. In a time when, because of Trump, we are all supposed to have a newfound love for our protectors in the intelligence agencies and the media, Eastwood has decided to show them in the most perfunctory way possible, as handsome zeroes.

While Hamm and Wilde meet in bars and carry on a boring affair during which they barely look at each other, Jewell's mother (Kathy Bates) sits at home trying to watch movies like *Sands of Iwo Jima* while she worries about her son going to prison the way everybody worried every second that Sully might be found guilty of being a hero. The whole film has an uncomfortable, tense feeling which Eastwood establishes in the masterful Centennial Park bombing scenes and carries throughout. Set in 1996, filled with brand name products, tense with worry but stuck at home, *Richard Jewell* is an accurate portrait of the USA. Eastwood insists it hasn't changed much in twenty-three years.

The Irishman

By getting the streaming service Netflix to produce and release into movie theaters a hugely expensive, three-and-a-half-hour-long movie, Martin Scorsese proved something about the cinema today and how moviegoing is different than watching TV. *The Irishman*, which onscreen is called *I Heard You Paint Houses*, which is a better title, is a story of friendship and the false sense of duty that can come from it as it deteriorates over fifty years. I saw *The Irishman* in a huge theater on a giant screen, and I did not want to get up, didn't want it to end, and could have watched another hour of it if there was one. It seems like most everybody who watched it at home complained it was too long, redundant, and looked funny. It did not seem like entertainment to them. That was the message they sent out into the world and it reached me loud and clear.

What does that mean? Do I have a false sense of duty to the cinema? Or have people who watch movies at home, even great ones, been trained by their quality-TV habit to want things to be bingeable in forty-five-minute chunks, easy to ignore, and better to listen to than to watch? Most people seemed to have viewed *The Irishman* over the Christmas holiday. Could it be that their bad mood about it has something to do with frustration with their own families, and with the sense of entrapment that comes with being home for Christmas? That's where I think the real false duty is. The cinema may be an escape, but the living room couch in your parents' house definitely is not one.

A web of entrapment and manipulation surrounds the character played by Robert De Niro in *The Irishman*. A truck driver and union man who learned to kill in World War II, his Frank Sheeran explodes myths about the Greatest Generation, revealing the brutality that shaped them and made them into conformists. For men who came back and worked in the insurance industry, maybe that worked out. Working for the mobster Russell Bufalino (Joe Pesci) and the union organizer Jimmy Hoffa (Al Pacino), however, was not good for Frank's character or his soul. Bufalino and Hoffa supersede Frank's own family and expect loyalty without question. They represent a post-war employment economy that continues as the two styles of work—insurance companies and the mob—have merged into the same kind of corporate extortion racket.

While the florid Hoffa is the lesser of the two evils in Frank's life, his ideals make him less convincing than the corrupt and ruthless Bufalino, who wields a quiet mastery over others. The exception is Frank's daughter (Lucy Gallina, then Anna Paquin) who is repelled by Russell and fond of Jimmy. The awards banquet scene in this film, with Paquin and Pacino dancing while Pesci plots his demise with a reluctant De Niro, more than justifies the film's running time, just as certain scenes justify the enormous running times of films like *The Leopard*, and that scene probably also has a basis in all the awards shows Scorsese has had to attend over the years.

Pain and Glory

Pedro Almodóvar's elegy to memory and loss in the life of a film director is the exact opposite of *The Irishman* or *Uncut Gems*. This is the story of a man who wants to stay at home, see nobody, and do nothing. He doesn't even want to go to awards shows. His pain is completely internalized, as we learn in a beautifully colorful animated sequence that combines PowerPoint art and medical graphics. Salvador (Antonio Banderas), a respected film director, has learned that Pascal was right when he said that all of humanity's problems stem from our inability to sit quietly in a room alone. That's also a description of dying, as Salvador has slowly learned while reaching the point where he can't do anything to get better. Then film programmers reunite him with Alberto (Asier Etxeandia), the junkie actor he blames for fucking up one of his films.

The two of them have been asked to introduce a restored version of one of Salvador's early movies, *Sabor*, from the 1980s. (Almodóvar has become a master at looking back at the '80s.) Alberto, the actor, asks to read a memoir Salvador has been working on, which describes Salvador's life at that time. After reading it, Alberto decides he should turn it into a stage monologue. Its performance, not credited to Salvador, will reunite him with his lost love (Leonardo Sbaraglia) from the time of *Sabor*.

Almodóvar's ability to be both ultra-contemporary in his settings and ultra-modern in describing the past are unique in the cinema. Much of the film concerns Salvador's childhood when, as it happens, he lived in cave with his mother (Penelope Cruz), and a hunky local handyman (César Vicente) painted his portrait. Almodóvar is perhaps the only director in the world who can make cave-dwelling feel like living in an art gallery, and definitely the only one who could convince us that Penelope Cruz is Antonio Banderas's mother. As a film about filmmaking, *Pain and Glory* pivots on the mechanics of how screenwriting becomes cinema. Its meta-cinematic ending rivals *Little Women*'s but refuses to try to impress anyone watching it, a perfect encapsulation of Salvador's character as he comes back to life.

Knives Out

This whodunit is light entertainment at its finest, a surprising movie with an enjoyable sense of complication and a dream cast. It showed up like it came out of nowhere even though it was made by Rian Johnson, who directed *Star Wars: The Last Jedi*.

As in *Parasite*, three generations end up in the same mansion, here a towering Victorian pile somewhere in Massachusetts. The patriarch (Christopher Plummer) of a wealthy family, a successful and prolific mystery writer who refuses to franchise his work to movies or TV, dies under mysterious circumstances. Naturally, each member of his family becomes a suspect. His refusal to option his work is an amusing plot point from the best director of a *Star Wars* movie. Among his family, I thought Toni Collette was the most excellent as a purveyor of Goop-ish lifestyle products in from Los Angeles, but Don Johnson, Jamie Lee Curtis, and Michael Shannon all really rose to the challenge of the genre.

Each of them was appropriately bold and squirmy while questioned by Daniel Craig, playing an incongruous Southern detective with the unlikely name Benoit Blanc. We are told he is from a long line of master police detectives down South. Maybe Blanc's father was Sheriff J. W. Pepper from *Live and Let Die* and he met James Bond when Bond was Roger Moore and not Daniel Craig. Who associates police detectives from Mississippi with getting to the truth? Blanc, however, proves to be a friend of the working class when he helps the family's Latina housekeeper (Ana de Armas) negotiate the schemes of the duplicitous family she works for, and Craig, in his absurd Southern accent, gets to ask the strangest question in movies this year, about the patriarch's alt-right grandson (Jaeden Martell): "What were the overheard words of the Nazi child masturbatin' in the bathroom?"

Parasite

No detective comes to anyone's rescue in Bong Joon ho's *Parasite*, and the ghost-man hidden in the basement (Park Myung-hoon) is not set free like the Anne Frank surrogate in the attic in *Jojo Rabbit*. He's just replaced with another invisible man, the father of a poor family who is also the star of this film (Song Kang-ho). The Kim family, who live in a tiny basement apartment and have to suffer the humiliation of having drunks on the street piss in it through their half-window, all understand that "money is an iron" that smooths things out for the lives of the rich. So when they see the opportunity to move one at a time into the mansion of a wealthy family by getting jobs there, they take it. They revel in the successful scheme they put over on these distracted, self-involved rich people, until the family's condescension causes Mr. Kim to lash out at a party for the Parks' son (Jung Hyeon-jun). The birthday party is a real eye-opener, the best scene about killing the rich that the cinema has produced in a long, long time.

Between *Parasite* and *The Irishman*, I've got to stop looking at Twitter. I saw a very intelligent person I know very cynically tweeting that *Parasite*'s success came down to canny decisions on the part of its American distributor, and then announcing that the film wasn't sufficiently socialist. This has got to be the least predictable effect of social networking: someone in the United States upset because a successful Korean genre film doesn't address the concerns of the DSA in the exact right way.

At the same time that was happening, other critics were picking through Hong Sangsoo's fifteen or so films trying to determine which one was the best so they could put it on their Top Ten Films of the Decade lists. None of that has anything to do with film criticism as far as I'm concerned, and denying that Bong's work was leading to this galvanizing movie which has really shocked people into further questioning the wealth gap and understanding the precariousness of the urban underclass in an era of climate change was reactionary in some kind of new pop culture way.

It is not just those things that make *Parasite* an excellent movie, and there is plenty of room in the cinema for both Bong Joon ho and Hong Sangsoo. It may be that the few people who grumbled about *Parasite* are just allergic to peaches, but I think what they're really allergic to is class-based criticism in works of popular entertainment, especially when they are fueled by violence, comedy, clever screenwriting, and sharp acting. If popular movies become too leftist and continue to improve, they are going to be really annoyed.

THREAD COUNT

PAUL THOMAS ANDERSON

IN JUDD APATOW'S MOVIE *THIS IS 40*, FROM 2012, A MARRIED COUPLE played by Leslie Mann and Paul Rudd take a weekend trip to a hotel, where they get in bed and discuss their relationship. Rudd tells Mann that sometimes he feels like she wants to kill him. She admits that's true, so he asks her how she'd do it. "I'd poison your cupcakes," she answers, explaining that she would put in just enough toxin to slowly debilitate him. "I would enjoy our last few months together," she tells her husband, "because you'd be so weak and sweet, and I would take care of you, but while killing you."

Fans of recent American cinema will recognize this as the plot of Paul Thomas Anderson's *Phantom Thread*, which came out exactly five years after *This Is 40*, but with poison mushrooms instead of poisoned cupcakes. Judd Apatow, a more explicitly comic Hollywood contemporary of Anderson's, had already imagined the slow poisoning of an annoying husband by a loving wife. Apatow cast his own spouse as the wife, and made the incident into a short conversation, not a whole movie. Anderson, for his part, did not cast his own actor wife, Maya Rudolph, in the role in *Phantom Thread*. Instead, he found the Luxembourger Vicky Krieps to sauté poison mushrooms and feed them to Daniel Day-Lewis, so she could sicken him, then nurture him back to health.

Adam Nayman does not mention *This Is 40* in *Paul Thomas Anderson: Masterworks,* his large, colorful monograph on the director of *Boogie Nights* and *There Will Be Blood.* He does bring up the music video for the 1992 R.E.M. song "Everybody Hurts," pointing out the striking resemblance the six-minute clip has to Anderson's three-hour epic of LA life, *Magnolia,* from 1999. In both, "sad-eyed" citizens are "lost in private reveries" in separate stories, ready to break into lip-synching before a strange phenomenon unites them. Nayman might have added that both share references to books of the Bible—Psalms in "Everybody Hurts," Exodus in *Magnolia,* which signaled the film's rain of frogs.

No matter. Anderson's movies are always greater than the sum of their parts, as Nayman demonstrates by including a sidebar in each chapter on an unexpected but related older film—*The Manchurian Candidate* for *The Master, Shoot the Piano Player* for *Punch-Drunk Love.* Anderson says that the idea for *Phantom Thread* came to him while he was sick in bed and thinking Rudolph wanted him to stay there longer than he needed to, so she could take care of him while he watched *Rebecca, Beauty and the Beast,* and *The Story of Adele H.* It's a certain kind of filmmaker's dream, to be tended to maternally, unable to do anything besides absorb cinema classics, the whole time pretending he should really be somewhere else, working.

Anderson might have added *The Story of a Cheat* to his list of bedridden movies. Sacha Guitry's film is about a boy who ends up the only survivor of his family after all his relatives die from eating poison mushrooms while he is being punished in his room without dinner. Like the boy in Guitry's film, Anderson comes from a huge family. One of nine children, he was born in Los Angeles in 1970 to Ernie and Edwina Anderson. Ernie was a popular TV horror-movie host in Cleveland who moved his family to the San Fernando Valley when he got a job working for the ABC television network. His son's production company is named Ghoulardi, for Ernie's old TV character. Anderson began making films as a child when his father gave him a video camera. He went to NYU for a little while, but quit (wisely, as time has proved) to return to LA and get to work.

The films he has made since reflect his upbringing. In them, father figures and their male protégés negotiate rivalries, often with the lonely younger man looking for a love like the older one has, while both are surrounded by a gaggle of cultish oddballs who can turn threatening, violent, or just freaky. *Phantom Thread*, Anderson's most recent film, breaks this cycle by eliminating the father and finally wrapping the protagonist in the arms of true love, a woman who can be muse, lover, and twisted nurse mommy all in one.

THE STRUCTURE OF NAYMAN'S BOOK presents the Anderson oeuvre as a history lesson overlaying a bildungsroman. So instead of writing about each of Anderson's eight films in the order they were made, starting with 1997's *Hard Eight*, he writes about them in the order they take place, with the notable exception of *Phantom Thread*, which is set in the 1950s and which Nayman covers last.

The book, therefore, starts with 2007's *There Will Be Blood*, Anderson's fifth film, which begins its story in 1898. This schema works because, before that film, it still wasn't entirely clear what kind of filmmaker Anderson was. *There Will Be Blood*'s title announced its seriousness after the five-year gap between it and Anderson's arty, kooky Adam Sandler rom-com, *Punch-Drunk Love*, a surprising, concentrated film that curbed *Magnolia*'s sprawl.

There Will Be Blood, with Daniel Day-Lewis in the lead role as an oil prospector in old California, was a self-conscious and successful attempt to make the Great American Movie, a violent, masculine exposé of the capitalist psyche, in every way the opposite of romantic comedy. The frightening combination of Day-Lewis as an American, the vast landscapes he exploits, and the often bizarre dialogue he barks—"I drink your milkshake!" "You're a bastard from a basket!"—established Anderson's intensity beyond the obvious proficiency of his porn-industry fresco *Boogie Nights* (1997), and prepared him for *The Master* (2012) and *Inherent Vice* (2014), arguably his best films to date, one a cryptic riff on the early days of Scientology, the other an enigmatic Pynchon adaptation.

In *Magnolia,* Anderson had predicted a Jordan Peterson–style men's-rights guru, but one with the screen magnetism of Tom Cruise. As Frank T. J. Mackey, the author of a book called *Seduce and Destroy,* Cruise exhorted his followers to understand that "Men are *shit.* Because we do bad things, don't we? We do horrible, heinous, *heinous,* terrible things." This exorcism-celebration of male outrage seeps into all the lead performances in Anderson's films, in which violence and love fight for dominance.

In *Punch-Drunk Love,* Adam Sandler and Emily Watson's pillow talk expresses the depth of their mutual attraction with as much force of harm as possible. After Sandler tells Watson that the way he feels for her is like squeezing a puppy to death, he adds that he's so in love with her that he wants to smash her with a sledgehammer. Watson, in turn, replies that she wants to chew his face and remove his eyeballs with an ice cream scoop and eat them.

Anderson, it seems, based *Punch-Drunk Love* in part on a trip he took to Hawaii with the musician Fiona Apple, his then-girlfriend, a pop star whose intensity matched his own. Apple, in a recent interview, mentions that after Anderson, nominated for *Boogie Nights,* lost the 1998 Best Original Screenplay Oscar to Matt Damon and Ben Affleck, who won for *Good Will Hunting,* he threw a chair across the room, a signal, she realized, that he probably wasn't the one she should spend her life with.

An act of ill-temper, to be sure, but who wouldn't be tempted to hurl a chair at the wall after losing to those two? The difference between them is not an award, but that Affleck and Damon have not gone on to greater screenwriting glory, and Anderson has. And unlike them, he has never had to make a franchise film, or anything that reeks of mere entertainment, or any kind of compromise at all.

Anderson is, as Nayman points out, a one-film filmmaker, who gets an idea and follows it through from research to screenplay, and from casting to shooting and premiere, before he starts another.

Alone among Hollywood filmmakers, he has apparently never been tempted to do anything else. He has found a way to make films the way they are supposed to be made. Whether you view him as privileged and spoiled or talented and committed, Anderson seems well-adjusted and content, surrounded by his own large family, unswayed by the meretriciousness of the entertainment world (with the possible exception of Haim). The poison that is Hollywood nurtures more than sickens him.

It's interesting to note that Burt Reynolds and Mark Wahlberg both disavowed *Boogie Nights* years after it came out, saying they wished they had not been in it. Since it's the film that rescued them at crucial points in their careers, that really says something about Hollywood. After all, these are actors who also starred in *Cannonball Run II* and *Transformers: The Last Knight,* films they didn't renounce. If there is something essentially non-Hollywood about Anderson, he has learned to tamp it down. He's no longer the interviewee who once wished testicular cancer on fellow director David Fincher.

In interviews these days, Anderson presents a sunny disposition in which all is well in the cinema and in the world as long as he has a new movie out. As far as Hollywood goes, he is practically Goethe at this point, yet still squarely San Fernando Valley. Among current filmmakers he is the only one who has combined the looseness of Robert Altman and the control of Stanley Kubrick and lived to tell his tales, without giving in to despair like Lars von Trier or somebody. As we learn in Nayman's book, no matter what Paul Thomas Anderson puts his characters through, for some people there are still happy endings.

THE WORK OF FATE

INTRODUCTION TO *ORPHEUS*

ORPHEUS, JEAN COCTEAU'S 1950 FILM, "AN IMMORTAL THRILLER" AS IT was described in the movie's advertising when it was released, is a film about death and artistic creation, perhaps the best film ever made on those twin subjects. So I'd like to dedicate today's screening to two great artists of the cinema who died this week.

The first is Peter Wollen, who died yesterday. He was a British film critic, film theorist, screenwriter, and director who worked with Laura Mulvey, Tilda Swinton, and Michelangelo Antonioni. He cowrote Antonioni's 1975 film, *The Passenger*, which starred Jack Nicholson.

Wollen's book *Signs and Meaning in the Cinema* was one of the first books in English to discover and explain how semiotics, the study of how signs create meaning in culture, could be applied to film theory and film criticism. It is a groundbreaking book that had an enormous influence on the work of many writers and on my thinking as I was learning about film.

Orpheus is a film that deals in the interpretation of signs and meaning. It is one of the few films that deals with that in a direct and palpable way. Others from the same period as *Orpheus* are detective films and film noirs. This decoding is not just subtext nor is it merely somehow inscribed in the film for us to discover using our critical faculties. It is the film's subject matter. That's why *Orpheus* was also called, when it came out, "a detective story from the beyond."

The poet Orpheus, played by Jean Marais, one of Cocteau's lovers, here in a contemporary-to-1950 setting, becomes obsessed with transcribing the random words and numbers he hears on his car radio. He doesn't know it at first, but these are emanations from beyond reality. In other words, they are poetry. Similarly, Peter Wollen understood the cinema as a language that had to be decoded and reconstructed. It had to be made to make sense in a new way for new audiences, for a new generation, as Cocteau has done with this myth, the Greek myth of Orpheus and Eurydice. Soon after *Orpheus* came out, the great French writer and theorist Roland Barthes described and collected his work as *Mythologies*, because his series of essays took apart contemporary reality to expose the ideologies that control our lives and that we are often not consciously aware of. Wollen followed Barthes in applying this to the cinema, creating a circle with Cocteau, in this case, tonight, at least.

The other person I'd like to dedicate tonight's screening to is Anna Karina, who died last Saturday. Karina will be forever known as the woman who made the early films of Jean-Luc Godard what they are: pinnacles of cinema. As long as people watch movies, the collaboration of Anna Karina and Godard will stand as an example of everything the cinema can be, of all its possibilities. Like Cocteau and Barthes and Wollen, Godard deconstructed the movies, shaping them into new forms. Anna Karina was the first post-movie actress, the first one whose appearance in the films she was in was also self-consciously a comment on filming and cinema itself, as the well-known scene in Godard's *Vivre sa Vie*, from 1962—in which she watches the silent film *The Passion of Joan of Arc*—attests most starkly and most obviously.

According to Richard Roud, Godard cited no other filmmaker in his written film criticism as much as he cited Jean Cocteau. Cocteau's influence is clear and apparent in more than one Godard film, but it is especially pronounced in *Alphaville*, with Anna Karina, from

1965, a black-and-white science-fiction film shot in contemporary Paris, in which Cocteau's voyage into the land of the dead returns to the world of detectives and film noir. It could be said that *Alphaville* is more advanced than *Orpheus*. A computer, for instance, replaces the radio of Cocteau's film. But *Alphaville* is also somehow behind *Orpheus*, too. Godard's love of genre films and American cinema necessitated a return to the earlier forms Cocteau had done away with, because Cocteau was already his own form.

Jill Mulleady's show at the Swiss Institute is indebted to Cocteau in subtle ways, with its large painting of a male figure strapped down in Cocteau-esque landscape with ruins in the background, like the ruins you will see in *Orpheus*. Mulleady's use of an ATM in an otherwise empty bank vault can be seen as referring to Cocteau's zone of the dead, and her large wood-block prints of a rat looming over a cityscape recall Cocteau's debt to German expressionist cinema, one of his only influences still traceable in *Orpheus*.

Orpheus, like the German films of the silent era, relies on what in Hollywood are called practical effects for all its special effects. Unlike today's digital cinema, the cinema of Jean Cocteau is a low-tech art form that proves how everything imagined can be done in front of the camera, without computer-generated imagery. All cinematic problems have a solution in reality and in imagination. Everything can be created in front of the camera. This is Lesson Number One in filmmaking, too often forgotten.

For Cocteau, such solutions are death-defying, like poetry is. The simple act of recording them on film does that. It saves those solutions for posterity and for other artists and viewers. Sometimes their flatness, which Cocteau learned as a painter, illustrator, and scenic designer, occupations at one time he had been more known for than writing and directing films, calls attention to itself in the space of his film frames, such as the wide-open eyes painted on the closed eyelids of the actors you will see in *Orpheus*. These effects, again, go beyond animation, they obviate animation. They are achieved on set with the simplest of means. Without trying to, because they didn't exist yet, they show how high-tech digital effects are redundant.

There is much talk of death in *Orpheus*. Cocteau famously said that the cinema is the only art form that records death at work. In every shot a director and cinematographer make of an actor, that actor has aged, no matter how short the duration of the shot, or where it is placed in a film. A shot may appear in a film outside the chronology in which it was made, but it still records moments of aging, "death at work," even when a shot made later is placed next to a shot made earlier.

A new *Up* film came out recently, *63 Up*, one of a series of British documentaries that follow a group of ordinary people by catching *up* with them every seven years to see what time has done to them, how their lives have progressed, or not, to see how they have aged as they approach their inevitable ends. I confess that these celebrated documentaries bore me to death. They are an example of Cocteau's axiom made banal. I would rather watch *Orpheus*. The *Up* films make death *into* work, instead of showing it *at* work, almost invisibly.

Most of the people in *Orpheus* are now dead. Except for Juliette Gréco, the great chanteuse of 1950s bohemian Paris, here seen as Eurydice's somewhat threatening feminist best friend, who like María Casares's "Death of Orpheus" character also usually dresses all in black. She is now 92 years old.

Fate has spared her and allowed her to live to a very old age. Cocteau said something about that, and about the possibilities inherent in cinema. "Realism in unreality is a constant pitfall," he said. "People always tell me that this is possible, that that is impossible. But do we understand anything about the workings of fate?"

Orpheus is a film of mirrors and windows. For Cocteau the answer to the question of whether the cinema is a window through which we observe others or a mirror in which we observe ourselves is that it is both and neither. It is more than a combination of both. It is a portal, and so in *Orpheus* mirrors show us ourselves and then take us elsewhere. One of the radio transmissions in the film is cut off because there is dialogue over it. It says, in full, "Mirrors would do well to reflect a little more before sending us back images of ourselves." That is because, as one character says in *Orpheus*, "if you look in the mirror every day, you will see death working away like bees in a glass hive." The cinema, like certain illicit drugs, in certain rare cases, allows us to see that, to understand that, to feel it and observe it by turns intensely and dispassionately.

Everything in *Orpheus* is true like that and everything in it is about today. The film remains contemporary. The first line we hear in the film is narration in Cocteau's own voice: "The story of Orpheus is well-known," he says. It's so well-known, in fact, that I don't want to spoil it by saying anything more about it. Thank you for coming tonight to see it.

THE OTHER GUY BEING SOCIALISM

IN A MISGUIDED ATTEMPT TO BE COMPREHENSIVE, I BOUGHT A ROKU BOX and subscribed to Netflix so I could stream movies. There were too many films I should see coming out that way, I was thinking. Even though most of them have theatrical runs in New York City, I couldn't picture myself going to a movie theater to watch *Horse Girl* or *The Last Thing He Wanted*. Films like that were not *The Irishman* or even *Marriage Story*. They were the new fodder for the virtual content mound, even if they promised to be a little better than franchise films, which people have begun to describe simply as "IP," for intellectual property, a term that implies the *Maze Runner* movies are something more elevated than other kinds of assets. Like some people, it's not enough for them just to be worth money.

So if Dee Rees was going to adapt a Joan Didion novel, or if the Duplass Brothers were going to produce original screenplays written by actors, or if Barack and Michelle Obama were starting a documentary film company, I figured I should be able to see what they came up with without having to go to a movie theater each time and expose myself to coronavirus. What I've learned so far is that it's very hit or miss, I don't like staying home, and Netflix is quite interested in delving into my tastes and preferences. They send a lot of emails. They keep in touch. And they've found some things out.

If there's one thing Netflix knows about me, it's that I'm Black. Which I'm not, but that doesn't matter to the algorithm. The first two movies I watched when I got Netflix happened to be the Rudy Ray Moore biopic, *Dolemite Is My Name*, with Eddie Murphy, and *Atlantics*, the debut feature by Mati Diop, from Senegal. *Dolemite Is My Name* was highly entertaining; Murphy was excellent. *Atlantics*, a supernatural art film about women's lives under capitalism, set in motion when the men of Dakar disappear at sea, was one of the best films of last year. I should have seen it in a movie theater.

One of these films was written and directed by white guys in Hollywood. I think it's Alexander and Karaszewski's best screenplay, on their favorite subject: to be alive is to make a movie, let nothing stop you. *Dolemite* was in English, *Atlantics* mostly in Wolof. The fact that I watched both, however, meant only one thing to Netflix. Their recommendation engine clunked into motion, and the first movie they suggested I see was *How High 2*, a sequel to the stoner classic that starred Method Man and Redman, now with Lil Yachty and somebody else in their parts.

When I rated both *Dolemite* and *Atlantics* with a thumbs up, more recs from Netflix poured in. The streaming giant wanted me to see a new movie called *Miss Virginia*, with Uzo Aduba, and *Braxton Family Values*, the reality TV show, along with *Who Killed Malcolm X?*, a Netflix docuseries, and *Booty Call*, the 1997 comedy with Jamie Foxx. Those last two were presented in tandem, a double feature Netflix must have suggested knowing I would never think of it myself. Now Netflix wants me to see Tyler Perry's latest, *A Fall from Grace*, and *Queen Sono*, a South African crime series.

I can't believe how wrong they've got me. They think I want to watch TV shows. The most disturbing thing about Netflix is how all content is the same to them, one thing replaces another, and they don't want you to stop watching to read the credits. You see movies but you watch TV, and Netflix doesn't admit there's a difference. They just want to know what you like, which to them is who you are. One thing they didn't recommend was their new movie *The Last*

Thing He Wanted, even though it was directed by a Black woman. Maybe they thought I didn't want to watch it because it stars Anne Hathaway and Ben Affleck. I saw it anyway. But they were right, I shouldn't have. I'm learning that the last thing I wanted was Netflix.

The Last Thing He Wanted

Based on a Joan Didion novel set in the 1980s about a newspaper reporter (Anne Hathaway) at the *Washington Post* who becomes a gunrunner in Central America and then a problem for the CIA, Dee Rees's adaptation fails in scene after scene, flunking the basics of screenwriting and directing again and again. It's impossible to tell that *The Last Thing He Wanted* was made by the same director as *Mudbound*, except for their shared lugubriousness. When the producers (Netflix) demanded the name of the newspaper be switched to the *Atlantic Post*, Rees should have pulled the plug on the whole thing.

Instead the film drowns on its own. Hathaway reads the Didion narration like it's full of words and ideas she's never heard yet knows are important and literary. She uses smoky-voiced gravitas, aiming in the vague direction of William S. Burroughs reading his monologue about Thanksgiving in America. Meanwhile, Ben Affleck is becoming late-period Dana Andrews. He looks and acts pickled and bored playing a CIA agent named Treat, Hathaway's love interest. He lumbers through his part in a stupor, like it's a chore, looking sadly at his Rolex, knowing it's five o'clock somewhere. Details add up to nothing. A dog runs over a landmine and explodes—*woof! poof!* Hathaway has a CGI mastectomy scar. Affleck, explaining realpolitik to gritty news photographer Rosie Perez, nods knowingly about "the other guy." "The other guy being socialism," he says to make sure she understands, bolstering and predicting, in the most plodding way, how socialism always gets screwed in the Americas.

Horse Girl

Everything produced by the Duplass Brothers is hollow and superficial and cutesy. Their examinations of the bourgeoisie lack depth and flatter their audience by showing mild, recognizable foibles among bland people who can't change. Since it's not their characters' fault that they are the way they are, it isn't Mark and Jay Duplass's fault either. It's just how it is. People are imperfect and do dumb shit without thinking; they don't mean it. So when the subject of mental illness comes up, the Duplasses are really in their element. We can't blame people who are mentally ill for what they do, and we can't change them. But we can watch.

Horse Girl, which was cowritten by its star, Alison Brie, and directed by her cowriter, Jeff Baena, almost avoids the Duplassian shruggie. It swerves by taking us on an inner journey that successfully does what drug-trip movies want to do, which is make us feel like we are losing our minds along with the protagonist. The very end of *Horse Girl* is a cop-out, a metaphorical suicide done West Coast Kooky, but before that, Brie, in this acting showcase, pulls us into the frustrating loop of her character's derangement. An air of ordinary tragedy hangs over the life of the craft store worker she plays. Her family history includes mental illness and suicide; her best friend has brain damage due to a horseback riding accident she may have been part of; her prettier, conventional-shallow roommate (Debby Ryan) pities her and tries to help her but can't.

Sarah (Brie) is obsessed with a TV show called *Purgatory* that she binge watches. She compares people in her real life to characters on this cheesy series that is supposed to be like a supernatural show on a broadcast TV network. Her dedication to it is one of the early signs that Sarah is not all there, but it is also meta-commentary on Netflix itself. This viewpoint marks *Horse Girl* as a holdover from indiedom coming to grips with an insane new era, just as the presence of Molly Shannon as Sarah's coworker does, since Shannon, one of our great cracked actors, could have had Brie's part twenty years ago. When one of the other patients in a psychiatric hospital wears a Sub Pop T-shirt in Sarah's recurring dream of alien abduction and examination, we know that we, too, have been transported to a place where we, like Sarah, are culled for data then deposited back on the couch, in a recurring loop that precludes change or advancement.

American Factory

The workers at the Fuyao auto glass factory in Dayton, Ohio, may still only make $14 an hour, but they voted against joining a union, and elections have consequences. Things work out differently in America for different people. After the economy collapsed in 2008, for instance, President Obama did nothing for workers and homeowners, bailing out the banks and Wall Street instead. Now, post-presidency, he and Michelle have signed a multimillion-dollar deal with Netflix to produce content, which they can feel good about because the first documentary they released, *American Factory,* studies the plight of the workers Obama didn't help. And it won an Oscar for its filmmakers, Julia Reichert and Steve Bognar, the crowning glory of their long career in filmmaking that stretches back to movies about feminism, socialism, and labor unrest in the 1970s and 1980s.

We learn in *American Factory* that it all comes down to hard work. The factory workers in Dayton, out of jobs for over two years, are happy to take a 50 percent pay cut when a Chinese company reopens a GM factory in their town. Once employed again, they can't keep up with Chinese notions of efficiency because in China there are lax safety regulations, few limits to overtime, and workers only get "one or two" days off a month. One of their Chinese managers in Dayton buys a box of Twinkies every week and keeps it at work so he can eat just one for lunch every day and nothing else, because he doesn't want to waste money he could send back to his family in China. That's weird, we are supposed to think, but also: if only Americans could have that kind of discipline.

Fuyao sends a group of American workers to Fuqing in Fujian Province so they can observe the Chinese at work in their home country, but apparently nobody tells them that Chinese workers wear uniforms, so they shouldn't wear a *Jaws* T-shirt to meetings, and that Chinese safety vests are smaller, so they should bring their own. These workers are set up to fail but have to perform in a workers' variety show in China, dancing to "Y.M.C.A." then watching as the Chinese workers numbly sing in praise of Fuyao while nailing every dance move. Back home in Dayton, the microwave in the break room doesn't work.

This might sound comic, like Jacques Tati's mailman in *Jour de Fête* trying to learn American efficiency and speed from newsreels about the United States Postal Service. It's not. It's sad, bleak, and humiliating. We meet Chairman Cao, the CEO of Fuyao, who longs for the impoverishment of his youth, mentioning how the industrialized China he has helped bring into being has eliminated the "croaking frogs and chirping bugs" of his childhood. Even so, Cao hires American consultants from "the union avoidance consulting industry" to come lecture workers in his American plant, intimidating them into voting against their interests.

Here, the film's 180 really kicks in. We are supposed to feel pity for Cao, a man who is getting millions in tax subsidies from the state of Ohio. Then *American Factory* wrenches us again, like in *Modern Times*, with a supertitle at the end that informs us that by 2030, 375 million people around the world will have lost their jobs to automation, unions or not. Why this ideological muddle? Because this is cinema verité in the service of power, not people, made to win awards. A success story in the film, about an unemployed forklift operator named Jill who has to live in her sister's basement until she gets a job at Fuyao and moves into a tiny apartment by herself, turns sour when she's fired for bringing up safety violations. As for the Chinese workers in Dayton, they only look happy when their new American friends are teaching them to shoot pistols and shotguns in their backyards, where they can pose for photos holding firearms and wearing cool suits.

Greed

Steve Coogan plays Sir Richard McCreadie, a fictional British fast-fashion magnate, in Michael Winterbottom's new satire, which probably should have been called *Greedie* instead of *Greed* because that's the billionaire's nickname, it's funnier, and it avoids annoying Erich von Stroheim fans. As in most all Winterbottom films, *Greed* is a grab bag of flashy mockumentary techniques, predictable needle drops, and obvious references, its half-baked feeling the only thing keeping it afloat. As a comedy of economics and a burlesque of the super-wealthy, its didactic over-explanations of concepts in high finance are understandable and clear, which makes it more enjoyable than *The Big Short*, if somehow less pressing.

McCreadie, turning sixty, decides to throw himself an elaborate *Gladiator*-themed party on a Greek island he shares uncomfortably with Syrian refugees. All the important people in his life are asked to attend, *Rules of the Game*-style, as well as some celebrities, including the ever more fatuous and useless Stephen Fry, playing himself, and the dreadful, ubiquitous Alexa Chung, who Skypes in a perfunctory greeting. The constant references to *Gladiator* are wearisome, proving once again how British people love to genuflect before Ridley Scott, but they do pay off when McCreadie faces a circus lion whose dinner has been sprinkled with cocaine. Unlike in *Call of the Wild* and *Dolittle*, here an elaborate CGI lion is a violent joke and a digital deus ex machina, not the star lie in a kiddie movie.

Weaving themselves in and out of the plot, and on and off McCreadie's yacht, Isla Fisher and Shirley Henderson are underutilized considering their potential as the mogul's ex-wife and mother. Henderson's damaged malice and covetous spite make every scene she's in better, but Fisher has to carry too much of the plot, explaining tax havens and business liquidation while trying to moon over her ex unnoticed. The film's revenge plot, about a young Sri Lankan employee of McCreadie's (Dinita Gohil) whose mother died working in a sweatshop, is a necessary component that Winterbottom defangs by making everyone involved nice because he also thinks the film is like *A Midsummer Night's Dream*, which it's not. As a grace note, the film dashes our hopes for the future by reminding us that the children of the rich are no better than their parents, even if they seem like they might be. Statistics then enumerate how many people in the world are employed in sweatshops, how little they earn each day, how much money the men who own H&M and Zara have, and how little they pay in taxes.

Les Misérables

Lions have heraldic meaning as national symbols in Britain and France, so it's significant that a lion also moves through this French film about impoverished youth defying the cops who harass and abuse them daily. Ladj Ly's *Les Misérables* tells its story from the exact opposite end of the wealth gap as Winterbottom's *Greed*. Here, Muslims live in poverty in a banlieue that happens to be the same one in which Victor Hugo set part of his great novel. Today's African and Arab inhabitants know the title refers to them, too. Ly, the son of Malian immigrants, has absorbed *La Haine* (1995) as much as Hugo in making this assured first feature, a neorealist exposé that begins and ends in rioting.

A slum kid named Issa (Issa Perica) steals a lion cub from a traveling Romani circus, setting into motion a plot that moves through all the layers of power and control in his housing project. One of the three main cops in the movie, Gwada (Djebril Zonga), shoots Issa in the face with a flash-ball gun, a supposedly nonlethal weapon used to quell riots in France. A drone films this moment of police violence. Buzz (Al-Hassan Ly), the kid with the drone, also from the banlieue, is a budding De Palma in black-frame glasses who more often uses his drone to film girls undressing in windows. He becomes the object of the cops' chase, which they juggle with getting Issa medical help without taking him to a hospital because they don't want to report shooting him.

Ly wrote *Les Misérables* with Alexis Manenti and Giordano Gederlini, and it is Manenti who plays Chris, the main cop, known locally as "the Pink Pig." Damien Bonnard, a striking actor who has been in movies by filmmakers as disparate as Christopher Nolan, Nathan Silver, and Roman Polanski, plays a cop with a conscience whose good intentions don't matter by the end of the film. Bonnard was creeped-out and dazed in Alain Guiraudie's bizarre *Staying Vertical* (2016). In Ly's film, his distinctive look switches between Ratso Rizzo and handsome/sensitive, the key to his appeal. This new *Les Misérables* offers a panoply of contemporary French faces, all angry, from the unofficial mayor of the housing project (Steve Tientcheu), to the lion tamer (Raymond Lopez) who throws Issa into a cage with a full-grown lion, to the imposing ex-Muslim Brotherhood restaurateur (Almamy Kanoute) who is the philosophical center of the movie, the man whom Ly lets explain, while he makes a sandwich, that in Islam the lion is a majestic animal that embodies force and power. Inserted into all the grit and violence and naturalistic lower-depths acting, it's this kind of written, acted speech that often makes a neorealist film.

Cane River

Certain films go beyond neorealism into a place all their own. Horace B. Jenkins's lyrical, romantic, low-budget *Cane River* is one of those. Shot in rural Louisiana in the early 1980s, it was screened in New Orleans in 1982, but Jenkins died about a month later, at age 42, and his film was never shown nationally. Two years ago it was restored, played some festivals, and has now been released in theaters, thirty-eight years after it was ready.

Jenkins combines an Americana sensibility reminiscent of King Vidor's early 1930s films with a class consciousness unique in the film's setting: African American red-clay Louisiana, the once-French central part of the state where some light-skinned Black Creoles owned plantations and slaves. Peter Metoyer (Richard Romain) arrives there from college in the North, where he was a football player offered an NFL contract. He, however, has chosen to be a poet and to farm his family's land. He meets Maria Mathis (Tommye Myrick), a tour guide at a plantation who lives with her mother and brother but wants to leave home to attend college in the city. The two fall in love, despite Peter's status as a light-skinned Creole and a Catholic and hers as a dark-skinned Protestant.

Scenes set in their respective churches highlight the documentary feel of *Cane River*, in which local non-actors appear in most of the roles, except for possibly Romain, who though easy in his part has a stately bearing suited to reading not-so-great poetry. Myrick is friendly and persuasive as an average girl interested in the bigger world outside her small town. Her performance adds something rare to the film that I wouldn't call authenticity or naturalism. She brings it to life. I don't know if Jenkins shot *Cane River* in 16mm or 35mm, but its bleached images capture its time and place perfectly. The film has the faded-color look of a country and western album cover from a musical tradition lost in thrift store bins.

The Assistant

This compact, almost Bressonian narrative feature by Kitty Green, an Australian non-fiction filmmaker now in Brooklyn, has a dark, tense force it keeps in place through minimal dialogue in limited settings. *The Assistant* holds itself almost exclusively to the confines of the gray-blue outer offices of a film studio in Tribeca, where Jane

(Julia Garner) works as an office PA for a movie mogul based on Harvey Weinstein. Since this is a Kitty Green film, there has to be a gimmick: the Weinstein character appears as a voice only, difficult to make out, like the adults in a Charlie Brown special—sometimes on the phone, sometimes from the company's inner sanctum, barking orders other times, then cajoling and assuaging via email when his trespasses go too far. His half-heard voice tries to dominate the film, but Garner's subtle, understated performance centers it outside his field of view.

Garner is in every shot (or almost every one) so that Green can block-switch events to the periphery, where Jane works. Her long hours begin and end in darkness, and the company exists to keep the mogul's behavior quiet and hidden. Thus *The Assistant* is a film of sound design, which as usual gets obtrusive in Dolby—the clack of keystrokes is incessant. Jane has to stow her winter coat in her biggest desk drawer because the company is too cheap or unconcerned to provide a coat rack for its employees. The film briefly cuts to a black car's interior when Jane has to accompany a beautiful girl from Idaho (Kristine Froseth) to a hotel for an assignation with the mogul. Later, Jane has to put up with this model-like provincial as she occupies space in the office and explains that she wants to get into the film industry despite her lack of work experience. "My uncle's in craft services," she notes to Jane.

When Jane has had enough, she goes to Human Resources, always a risky idea in creative-class occupations. The HR guy (Matthew Macfadyen) persuades her to say nothing about their boss, explaining that there is a lot of competition for her job from other young people who went to better schools than she did. At the end of her work day, Jane emerges into the night with some senior employees who perch on the tailgates of company SUVs texting, oblivious to anything else, unable put their phones down and go home.

Jane, for her part, ends up on the phone, too, talking to her father as she sits at a counter in a bodega eating a muffin for dinner, hiding the facts of her work life in favor of silence about the man who signs her checks, the man who has, in effect, replaced her father. *The Assistant* is the only film in which I've seen the shame-filled, eating-in-a-Manhattan-bodega aspect of life in New York City portrayed so acutely, or at all.

The Traitor

Since the 1960s, the Italian director Marco Bellocchio has made about thirty feature films and many shorts and documentaries. The dozen or so I've seen were innovative and surprising, and they made me want to see the others. Radically anti-Church and a former Marxist, Bellocchio shows no sign of slowing down. He ran for Parliament in Italy in 2006 as a "Rose in the Fist" socialist. Older than Martin Scorsese by three years to the month, he made an epic mob history film last year too.

The Traitor starts in 1980, at the height of the Palermo heroin trade, and ends twenty years later, after many murders and court trials. It's a three-continent odyssey that includes torture in Brazil, Christmas shopping in New Hampshire, and a car crash in Italy like none I've ever witnessed in another movie. *The Traitor*'s first scene, set at a wedding, begins under the credits and is so eventful and unconventional that it almost overshadows the rest of the film. Dark, claustrophobic, with a big cast on the move in primo period formal wear, each character introduced with a supertitle, Bellocchio launches into the story by presenting interconnected members of what seems like a dozen Mafia families one after another in a way he defies the viewer to sort out.

Post-wedding, Bellocchio's Mafia is deglamorized, poorly dressed, and repellent. There is no young Al Pacino, no Paul Muni, no computer-aged De Niro in this group. Pierfrancesco Favino, who stars as the "honorable" mafia informer Tommaso Buscetta, looks like a cross between Fred Flintstone and Jerry Haleva. His cronies and enemies reminded me of possible Steve Buscemi cousins with crossed eyes, Cuomo relatives they'd lock in a basement, or Joe Piscopo in a new wig.

Parts of *The Traitor* take place in the United States. It's always great to see European films with American-set scenes that weren't shot here. Most of them were filmed in Germany, from what I could glean in the credits. Tommaso and his family go to a supermarket, shop in a mall, and eat in what is maybe supposed to be an Olive Garden. The supermarket stocks huge two-gallon containers of milk on the shelves in the regular, non-refrigerated aisles next to canned food; the New Hampshire mall looks more like The Grove in LA than anything in New England; and the Olive Garden features a grotty, beardless Santa wandering the dining room with a guitar, singing in Italian. (That last, of course, would be an improvement.) Nearing the end of his career, a paranoid, exhausted Tommaso fits right into US life, making himself comfortable on a rooftop in a Miami ghetto, perched there with an assault rifle like an anti-Scarface as he carefully observes stray dogs sniffing garbage.

Vitalina Varela

On the other end of the spectrum of radical narrative filmmakers in Europe, Portugal's Pedro Costa makes films far more austere and forbidding than Bellocchio's. Being from a generation after Bellocchio, he is less prolific. Costa has made seven narrative feature films since 1989, most of which create intimate, modernist portraits of the very poor in Lisbon, focusing, with great intensity, on Black immigrants from Cape Verde. Costa is dedicated to actual locations in the worst of slums and to the real people who live there. He casts the people in his films as versions of themselves, day laborers and drug addicts who have nothing and live on nothing in public housing, in crumbling concrete bunkers, or on the street.

Costa's cinema isn't neorealist. He fixes his actors in square-framed shots lit to resemble Golden Age Hollywood noirs or westerns, so they come to look like paintings by Old Masters. He pays close attention to natural sound, a very present but not obtrusive aspect of his films. His screenplays are oblique, repetitive, and glacially poetic tales of misfortune and exploitation. Surrounded by darkness, faces emerge in medium close-up only to suddenly drop out of frame, the way a trembling priest does at his makeshift pulpit in Costa's new film, *Vitalina Varela*.

Vitalina, the title character, plays herself, a Cape Verdean widow who arrives in Lisbon a few days after her husband's funeral, decades after they parted. Descending barefoot at night from the cargo hold of an airplane, baggage handlers and aircraft cleaners dissuade her from proceeding. Continuing on, her wanderings in the hellish landscape of her husband's former life approach science-fiction in Costa's mise-en-scène, which becomes otherworldly, post-apocalyptic in its darkness and rubble. The Costian night is sometimes pierced by the bright yellow of a blanket used as a coat, but not by much else, except occasionally in memories of Cape Verde.

Vitalina spends the film in black mourning. Costa pins her and the people she meets in place, so much so that in his constrained motions, the priest (Ventura) sometimes resembles the armless and legless Prince Randian from Tod Browning's *Freaks*, wriggling helplessly on a dirt floor, as much as he does Darby Jones in *I Walked with a Zombie*, his corollary that also links this film to Diop's *Atlantics*. There is a reason there are not many films like this. *Vitalina Varela* is so uncompromising and so concentrated that it threatens to absorb the projector beam, as if the projectionist's black cue mark could take over the whole frame from one corner.

Circumstantial Pleasures

The collage animator Lewis Klahr's new cycle of short films also presents a world on the wane, one even more depopulated and emptied than Costa's. No actors appear in the six films that make up

Circumstantial Pleasures, not even photos of them like Klahr has used in earlier works. These films are made out of the detritus of our existence, which is shot in stop-motion and made to blip on screen and then slide away. The inside of security envelopes, bubble wrap, blister packs, receipts, takeout salt and pepper packets, and laundry tickets for things nobody ever reclaimed—these scraps provide the motion and drama in the closed, tertiary worlds of Klahr's latest droplet-globule movies. Sometimes it's impossible in them to tell if something is a close-up of a Ritz cracker or the back of a sofa.

Made between 2016 and now, the films, with titles including *Ramification Lesions*, *Virulent Capital*, and *Ratchet the Margin*, take on a new significance today, when the stock market and Covid-19 are combining to create forms of virality outside the confines of the digital. Klahr's imagery is pared down—few of the romance-comic figures or the photos of products clipped from midcentury advertising that he used to use in his work appear in these films. His use of the interiors in layouts from home decor magazines is also mostly gone.

Instead, an occasional oil barrel pops up, or an industrial landscape of power stations will fill the background, with time clocks, cold pills, and piles of mattresses overlaid in the foreground. Later, these switch to men in hazmat suits and wheelchairs. Round red translucent bingo chips dot the screen as split-second, black-and-white news images of Donald Trump, Mark Zuckerberg, Jeff Bezos, or Mitch McConnell appear and disappear. Some of Klahr's abstractions resemble shoegaze album covers from the 1990s. Electronic neurofeedback music by David Rosenboom plays over much of this, and one film is scored to a Scott Walker piece from *Bish Bosch*, a parallel track telling a story that diverges from Klahr's images of sleep and money.

In a post-screening conversation with the film historian Tom Gunning at Light Industry in Brooklyn last Leap Day, Klahr said his new films are "codes without messages" that are "not poetic" and "have no language." He said he made them in a hurry starting after the 2016 presidential election and that the images he wanted to create were ones that would be "not deep, but very controlling." They reflect above all a toxic consumerism abetted by the internet, politicians, and businessmen. In these short semi-abstractions, Klahr peers through a microscope at the dregs of our civilization as they mutate and infect its survivors today.

Postscript

I finished writing the column above on March 8, and the next day, a Monday, I intended to go see Kelly Reichardt's new movie, *First Cow.* Already the coronavirus was spreading, and the fear of it I mentioned in my first paragraph was spreading too. Before I left the house to go to *First Cow,* I began to have second thoughts about it, about taking the subway and sitting in a movie theater. Movie theaters were still open then; they wouldn't be shut by the city of New York until March 17, which now seems like it was a very long time ago, but it has only been two weeks as I write this.

Instead of going to that movie or any other, I began composing post-coronavirus non-reviews in my head, for the movies I wanted to see but now thought it better not to. *First Cow*? I'll wait for *Second Cow. Sorry We Missed You*? Sorry I missed it. *The Whistlers*? Whistled past it for good luck. *Bacurau*? Back away. *Never Rarely Sometimes Always*? If those are the choices, I'm going to have to go with "never." *The Invisible Man*? You didn't see me there?

I have spent my whole life in movie theaters. First (and always) as a spectator, then working the concession stand and as ticket seller and Hoky-ing the auditoriums between shows at the Nickelodeon on Cummington Street in Boston, a movie theater that no longer exists because it was demolished in 2003. After that, I was a projectionist at the Brattle in Harvard Square. The Brattle has been in operation as a movie theater since 1953, in a building that opened in 1890 for stage productions, five years and two months before the Lumières first projected their movies before an audience, five years and ten months before a movie was ever screened for an audience that paid to see it. Of course, the Brattle is closed now because of the pandemic, as are the movie theaters in every state in the Union. At no time in our history has every movie theater in the country ever had to shut down before.

One thing I learned from Netflix is that the feeling I get staying home to watch a movie is like the feeling many other people get when they are asked to go out and see one. They literally can't get off the couch. I literally can't stay home and not go out. Now I have to. Now I feel like Josh Brolin in Spike Lee's remake of *Oldboy*, a movie that few people liked but that was actually good. Like Brolin, my apartment is my cell, food is brought in, I can do push-ups if I want, till I somehow get out to exact my revenge on the people who confined me. The people whose fault this is.

Thankfully, distributors have paired with arthouses across the country to stream movies, so I can see them and write about them that way. Now everyone is home streaming movies, so much so that in Europe, Netflix was forced to reduce the quality of its downloads to avoid crashing the internet. Alone in our houses and apartments, we stream content, removed from our old lives, or watch the DVDs we have been saving to watch when we had the time.

The movies now refer to another life, the one from before. In an interview that I can't find but that I recall from the time his movie *Film Socialisme* came out, Jean-Luc Godard says that DVDs are for the apocalypse—we save them for some ominous *later*. *Film Socialisme* is set on a cruise ship that, in real life, was wrecked at sea two years after the movie came out in 2010. Cruise ships, of course, are notorious incubators for viruses as well as symbols of capitalist excess. Right now, some cruise ships can't find any port. They're filled with passengers who have corona, and nobody wants them to unload, as Donald Trump initially didn't. Godard's film was a message to the future, but it was a future I didn't think would arrive quite so fast. Ten years after *Film Socialisme,* the sick shipwreck of capitalism is here.

It's easy to think of movies about isolation and plague, about quarantine and groups of survivors. Everyone right now is making their own lists to watch at home. Here are three double features for you. You might have already seen some of them by now. *The Shining* and *The Crazies, The Exterminating Angel* and *7 Women, The Thing* and *Quintet.* There are fewer novels about situations like this. Katherine Anne Porter, who also wrote *Ship of Fools,* wrote one of them: *Pale Horse, Pale Rider,* about lovers during the 1918 influenza pandemic, which Porter survived. Its last line is: "Now there would be time for everything."

ZERO HOUR CONTRACTS

CINEMA DOES NOT CURRENTLY EXIST, OR IF IT DOES EXIST, IT'S IN THE form of videos from the Black Lives Matter protests against police brutality, shot on smartphones and put on Twitter, which viewers can watch from anywhere. These videos, hundreds of them from all over the United States, record rioting police officers dressed in warzone military gear lashing out at peaceful protesters, beating them with batons, shooting them with rubber bullets, firing tear gas canisters in their faces, and plowing into them with police cars and trucks.

One video, a horrifying document that exposed a killer cop, precipitated this reactionary violence from the police, which has now, in turn, been documented by hundreds of citizens. That video captured the murder of George Floyd, who was Black, by a white cop in Minneapolis. The cop, Derek Chauvin, knelt on Floyd's neck for almost nine minutes as two other cops held him down. During the last three minutes of this state-sanctioned homicide in public, George Floyd was most likely already dead.

Floyd had been accused of spending a fake twenty-dollar bill, although no one has seen this phony bank note. "Public officials have been mum on the location of the alleged counterfeit," *USA Today* reported nine days after Floyd's murder. Witnesses filmed his extrajudicial execution as they shouted at the cops, imploring them to stop.

Had Floyd's murder not been disseminated on video, it would not have led to mass protests, calls for justice that spread to every state in the country, and then to cities abroad. While cinemas were shuttered, and film and television production halted, this one horrific motion picture has changed the course of history. The world witnessed a police station in Minneapolis torched by rioters and abandoned by cops, an unprecedented scene in America, and then the looting of ostentatious upscale shopping districts, including Soho in Manhattan, while cops stood by. Unlike the reality TV show *Cops*, which glorified the police and insulted the public continuously for thirty years, these videos are not department-approved. In June, the studio that makes *Cops* canceled the series and pulled it from streaming. At the same time, the Police Department in Austin, Texas, revealed that a similar reality TV show, *Live PD*, had filmed the arrest of Javier Ambler. Ambler, another Black man, in this case stopped for a traffic violation, was killed by cops as they held him on his stomach while he pleaded for his life.

The corrupt administration of President Donald Trump immediately exposed itself as fascist in reaction to the Black Lives Matter protests. The commander in chief cheered police violence against citizens, especially Black citizens, and demanded "domination" as "the president of law and order." He also suggested, in his typical half-assed way, that the US military might intervene by attacking Americans on American soil. Trump's staff, in response to the protests, made a short video of their boss propelling himself across the street from the White House to pose for a photograph as he held a Bible upside-down in front of an Episcopal church that did not want him there. It took teargassing protesters for Trump's thugs to get him to the boarded-up building for what has been universally derided as a photo op, an empty pseudo-event designed to produce a simple image for Trump's supporters.

The black square of Trump's Bible coincidentally predicted the black square with which many social media users flooded Instagram as a show of solidarity with Black Americans, as a call for justice for George Floyd, and as a plea for an end to unfettered brutality and killing by militarized police forces in the United States. This digital blackout was criticized by some for being lame, a gesture from people who otherwise never contemplate injustice nor act against it, and by others for being disinformation, a way to remove images of injustice and protest from social media. But there it was: a series of black frames, like black leader before or after a movie. A blank film strip had taken over the timelines.

AS I WRITE THIS, IT HAS BEEN one hundred days since I have been inside a movie theater. Since then, the AMC cineplex chain "warned," as Reuters had it, that they might never reopen. A week later AMC did a complete one-eighty, claiming they would be open worldwide by July 17. Earlier in the Covid lockdown, AMC consulted with bankruptcy lawyers, then tried to sue the studio that made the movie *Trolls World Tour* for releasing the cartoon sequel straight to video-on-demand, even though AMC theaters were closed, and they couldn't show it anyway. This is an industry in free fall, caught totally unprepared for the consequences of a worldwide pandemic, resorting to legal tricks, obsessed with a now nonexistent "window"—the length of time that used to exist between theatrical release and streaming.

While independent theaters came up with ways to share art-house movies among themselves so filmgoers could stream them via virtual theater portals, the Hollywood exhibition industry all but disappeared, leaving empty their hulking fortresses with their big glass doors, some now covered in plywood. The studios have pushed back their release schedules to Christmas and beyond, though they still believe that Christopher Nolan's *Tenet* will be the one movie that comes out in July and saves the summer box office.

Shot over many months in 2019, in many countries, for about $225 million, *Tenet* is expected to cost about $350 million to finish and market. Whatever it makes, whenever it emerges, Nolan reportedly gets 20 percent of the first-dollar gross. The film is about a time-traveling secret agent stopping World War III, not the former CIA director George Tenet, who lied about torturing Iraqi prisoners of war. The name appealed to Nolan because it is a palindrome. It may also be the last blockbuster, the last huge waste of money at the end of an era defined by a wealth gap depicted on charts like a big backwards letter L.

In truth, the yoga instructors, hairstylists, and personal chefs of Hollywood, who immediately turned to YouTube to disseminate how-to videos for audiences in quarantine, were more prepared for the Covid pandemic than the studio executives who make a lot more money than they do. In 1995, Wolfgang Petersen's action movie *Outbreak*, about a pandemic that starts in a California movie theater, made close to $200 million on movie screens. In 2011, Steven Soderbergh's *Contagion* cleaned up, too, even though it was not an action movie and was better than *Outbreak*. *Contagion* displaced *The Help* at the box office and took home $136 million in its first few weeks.

Despite these two stories of deadly illness spreading through the population and killing loved ones willy-nilly, both of which suggested fairly realistic plans for how to act in a pandemic, Hollywood was as blind as the Trump administration. In the 21st century, no industry has institutional memory. *Outbreak* and *Contagion* meant no more in the socio-cultural history of Hollywood filmmaking than a *Harry Potter* movie. Those two didn't even have sequels. Now we face a series of crises, one after another, a franchise in which each entry gets longer, more expensive, and suckier, Hollywood-style.

IN NEW YORK, MOVIE THEATERS like the Metrograph have opened as way stations for protesters. That's an idea hatched by the group of film programmers who created the Cinema Workers Solidarity Fund to raise money for theater workers unemployed because of the Covid lockdown. The lockdown officially began in New York City on March 16, weeks later than it should have. The last movie I saw in a theater was *The Conversation*, at a 10 AM press screening on March 4. Francis Ford Coppola's 1974 conspiracy thriller was set to be rereleased at Film Forum on March 20 in a new 35mm print. Soon after I saw it, I began to live like Gene Hackman's Harry Caul at the end of Coppola's movie: alone, tearing at the interior of my apartment to make sure Covid wasn't there. I had recently hooked up a Roku box, and since then I have seen 115 movies by myself, streaming them every night.

Cinema became archival. It was clear homebound viewers were using movies in a new way, something Abel Ferrara, living in Roman exile, pointed out to The Film Stage. "It's obvious now movies are keeping people sane in a way. . . . Everybody's really hunkering down with the films." Meanwhile, in Hollywood, the aging nabobs of the industry were eager to hunker down in their mansions and leave theatrical exhibition behind for good. Peter Bart, the 87-year-old *Deadline* columnist and former *Variety* editor, spoke to 77-year-old John Bailey, the cinematographer and former president of the Academy, who shot *American Gigolo*, *Groundhog Day*, and *The Sisterhood of the Traveling Pants* (the trajectory of the business in three movies).

Bailey, Bart wrote, wanted "to become less dependent on the vicissitudes of exhibitors," so now he would "shift from his 60-inch home screen to a 4K 106-inch screen that will run classic films via The Criterion Channel." *Deadline* called the current situation a "doomsday scenario"—Hollywood's favorite kind. The previous month, Bart was worrying about "How To Build A Film Critic For The Post-Pandemic Age."

It's always interesting when Peter Bart starts to worry about film critics. It means the industry is in trouble. In 2007, as some critics refused to stop deriding blockbusters, he implied that movies should be reviewed only by people the same age as their intended audience, so if a film were aimed at 9-year-olds, that's who should write about it. Now he is looking for the next Roger Ebert, confessing he was late in "understanding [Ebert's] craftsmanship and his zeal for doing his homework."

Edgar Wright, the director of *Hot Fuzz* and *The World's End*, was bunkered down and digging in, too. In early May he wrote an open letter to the Criterion Collection, joking that because he had longed for a time when all he had to do in life was just watch movies at home, maybe somehow he had started the pandemic so he could do that. He was traveling the world, he wrote, without leaving his couch. "In Sweden, I've been on the existential odysseys of Ingmar Bergman (*Shame, Summer with Monika, Scenes from a Marriage, Cries and Whispers, Autumn Sonata*), then I went to France with the hard lessons of Robert Bresson (*Au hasard Balthazar, L'argent*)." As his Grand Tour continued to Japan and Italy, I wondered when he'd get to the hard lessons of Germany, but he took a detour into Tarkovsky's Zone (*Stalker*) before he decided to see how his "fellow countrymen dealt with previous crises with David Lean (*This Happy Breed*) and Powell & Pressburger's wartime films (*The Small Back Room, 49th Parallel*)." Close to twenty thousand people had died of the coronavirus in New York, according to official statistics, by the time Wright published his letter. Maybe watching *The Seventh Seal*, the Bergman film that takes place during a medieval plague that Wright left off his list, would have dampened his trip.

Whatever films are being made now, whether they are in the mode of the films Jafar Panahi has made since the Iranian authorities put him under house arrest in 2010, or like the Twitch event the New York avant-garde maestro Ken Jacobs (who is the same age as Peter Bart and hasn't given up) did with Anthology Film Archives and Screen Slate, somewhere films are still being made, even if I haven't seen them yet.

Jacobs's is called *Movie That Invites Pausing* and is now available on Vimeo, but I haven't seen it because I was too stupid to figure out Twitch when it happened in late May. A filmmaker in Oslo named Jakob Rørvik did send me a short he made called *Apocalypse Norway*, about a group of teens trapped at a beach house during a deadly pandemic. Rørvik was ahead of his time. He shot the film in 2018, and it was supposed to play in festivals this year.

A few days before George Floyd was murdered, I read an article on Medium that stated the post-pandemic movie houses of the future would resemble Apple stores, but with Whole Foods-branded concession stands run by Amazon. As streaming brands begin to vertically integrate and run their own theater chains, Paramount Consent Decrees of 1948 be damned, the writer of this piece, Eric Ravenscraft, believes that is inevitable. He welcomes it.

Against the backdrop of this dystopic corporate vision, watching the movies at home that I had missed right before quarantine did not seem so bad, though it still didn't strike me as the whimsical voyage Edgar Wright was enjoying wherever he lives. I just couldn't picture Wright wiping down a box of Cheez-Its with a paper towel soaked in rubbing alcohol. Unlike in *The Seventh Seal*, today we are not all playing at the same chessboard. Reading Wright's letter, I remembered something I learned from Bergman's movie. Terrible things are going on, yes. We may all be standing at the edge of life and facing darkness. But in this last minute I could still feel the immense triumph of rolling my eyes.

Bacurau

Secrecy pervades this Brazilian acid western set in the sertão, "west of Pernambuco," in a tiny, self-sufficient town imperiled by unseen forces. In June it was announced that the government of Brazil would no longer release Covid death statistics to its people, so the way that local pol Tony Junior (Thardelly Lima) neglects to tell the residents of Bacurau that he has rented them as targets for foreigners to hunt isn't all that odd. The government has also cut off the town's water supply, so the film begins with the arrival of a water truck, carrying with it a young native of Bacurau (Bárbara Colen) returning with medical supplies.

Cowriter/directors Kleber Mendonça Filho and Juliano Dornelles mix styles here, which they casually signal with music. The score, by Mateus Alves and Tomaz Alves Souza, replicates the sound of Carpenter and Howarth but alternates it with plaintive Tropicália and bossa nova songs. The town hides criminals, who become heroes as the plot unfolds. One, Pacote (Thomas Aquino), a hit man, is internet-famous because of surveillance videos of his assassinations. The other, Lunga (Silvero Pereira), is a warlord whose gang hides out near the dam, like the Dancin' Kid's gang in *Johnny Guitar*. Pereira plays Lunga as a dangerous queer icon. He wears black nail polish and lots of silver jewelry, plucks his eyebrows, has the most extreme mullet ever in movies, and dresses in jams without a shirt. Lunga has a back story in the town that we never learn. "You were a good writer, Lunga," someone tells him before he goes to sharpen knives and dig graves for the American hunters.

Bacurau's loping pace disguises how much is packed into it. The film's two directors masterfully move the story from Tony Junior's video-screen truck, so out of place in the arid landscape, to UFO drones, piles of caskets along the roadside, wild horses, naked gardeners with shotguns, and severed heads. The dialogue in this socialist western is worthy of Cinema Novo and spaghetti westerns: "A man is judged by the bad he does, not the good"; "Whores vote too"; "We have taken a powerful psychotropic drug and you are going to die."

The Hunt

As pulp trash it has its moments, but it's too Hollywood, so its gleeful gore comes off slick and unearned. *The Hunt*'s release was delayed from early last fall because its subject matter coincided with two mass shootings in the United States, and then it displeased Donald Trump when he heard it existed. Like *Bacurau*, it's about wealthy people who hunt human beings for sport. In this case the victims are self-avowed Red State deplorables. As in the Brazilian film, this update of *The Most Dangerous Game* raises class issues, but class here is primarily a matter of taste, always a funny subject to Hollywood. The deplorables are not presented as poor, just stupid, and the odious wealthy liberals are also stupid, but smarmy instead of loudmouthed. Into this fathead conflict Betty Gilpin mistakenly strides, playing a blonde superwoman, an Afghan-war vet who now works a car rental desk in Mississippi. Gilpin brings it like crazy, accent and all, committing to this sophomoric material because she has finally gotten the star turn she deserves.

The Hunt, trying to be clever, ends up forgetting not to hide the main emotion of Hollywood: the embarrassment of trying to be all things to all people. Providing several messages for the price of one, none of which quite make sense, the film lathers the soundtrack with girl power in the form of The Raincoats, Dusty Springfield, and Bobbie Gentry. The real mass shooting at the Walmart in El Paso last summer was carried out by a lunatic white nationalist; the murder of Ahmaud Arbery in February was an actual racist hunt. Yet here elitists, not racists, are the armed madmen. Which is not to say such people are not trying to kill the poor. Notably, however, since they are liberals, in this movie they are not trying to kill Black people, who—fortunately for everyone—are not represented at all in *The Hunt*. The final girlfight between Gilpin and her nemesis, brunette executive Hilary Swank, ribs the lean-in crowd, leaning in hard on how it is necessary for women to kill each other to get ahead. While Gilpin ends the film on a non-serious note of sisterhood, sharing caviar with a flight attendant (Hannah Alline) on a private jet, just two working-class white gals and a bottle of champagne, it is hard not to see (hear?) her victory as some kind of dog whistle.

Capital in the Twenty-First Century

Watching new movies at home means getting press links from publicists. Sometimes they come with conditions: you can only watch the movie twice, the link is only good for a few days, there is a giant company logo over the top of the frame throughout the entire film. They call that a watermark, but it is not transparent, and it blocks the top fifth of the screen all the way across. If a documentary is anti-capitalist, this practice is particularly egregious. If it starts with the logos of seven different production companies, which are then repeated as text in the opening credits, it gets really annoying. Then, at the very end of the end credits, they reappear. How is all this branding anti-capitalist? That is how capitalist ideology works. It asks you to pretend you don't notice it.

It is possible to agree with everything in a film and still understand that the film is bad. So it is with *Capital in the Twenty-First Century*, a documentary based on Thomas Piketty's 2013 book, by a filmmaker from New Zealand named Justin Pemberton. Piketty appears throughout the film in interviews, along with a large number of other economists and political theorists, including Francis Fukuyama. If the film had limited itself to presenting them expressing their ideas, it would have been something.

Instead, it is a montage-orgy of historical clips cobbled together to do the good work of exposing the wealth gap and explaining the society-destroying effects of inherited riches. So when we get to the 1990s, we see fast sequences of the "Smells Like Teen Spirit" cheerleaders and Britney Spears. At least I think it was them; it all went by so fast, like in one of those CNN documentaries about a specific decade.

Often it is clips from recent British movies, which are identified by name and director but not year (*Pride and Prejudice* Dir. Joe Wright; *Les Misérables* Dir. Tom Hooper). I should not have to see those again in a documentary about the ill effects of unrestrained capitalism, unless their existence is supposed to illustrate that more than their content.

Meanwhile, the clip cascade neglects to identify *Gold Diggers of 1933*, a song from which is used in conjunction with colorized footage of flappers in the 1920s doing the Charleston. *The Grapes of Wrath* is only identified as a film after Pemberton implies one scene from it is documentary footage. Silent movies are not identified at all. They are just "history." Eventually, films are replaced by clips from *The Simpsons* and *Family Guy*, the lowest-grade way of explaining anything to anyone, which probably cost some real money to include.

France Against the Robots

Jean-Marie Straub's new short is the exact opposite of Pemberton's film, but it is about the same thing. *France Against the Robots* repeats the same one-shot-long scene twice, the first time at twilight, the second time during the day, I think early in the morning. In the scene, a man (Christophe Clavert), seen in a three-quarters view from behind, walks along a lake shore reciting a text from Georges Bernanos, the author of *Under the Sun of Satan*. The text is about capitalism, fascism, and technology, subtitled in English by Ted Fendt. It is "against the entire current system," which is unreformable. It describes "a fatal evolution toward the dictatorship of money, race, class, or the nation," concluding that "a world gained for technology is lost for liberty."

Everything the documentary of *Capital in the Twenty-First Century* tries to do at feature length, this film does in under ten minutes. The difference is that it is not a crowd pleaser. It doesn't talk down to its viewers in any way or even accommodate them, which is especially interesting in this case because the film premiered on the Kino Slang blog and then on YouTube, subtitled in various languages. This film, by an 87-year-old director, took advantage of the current crisis to completely bypass everything: festivals, arthouses, museums, VOD. *France Against the Robots* is anti-technology and therefore a paradox: Straub almost beamed it into our eyes.

Heimat Is a Space in Time

Thomas Heise's new documentary, by further contrast, is three hours and forty minutes long, told in five sections, and nearly as off-putting as *France Against the Robots*. Fortunately, it is equally original and accomplished. It begins in a forest, in color, by showing metal cutouts that crudely depict the story of Little Red Riding Hood. A sign reads, "According to legend here stood grandmother's house." *Heimat Is a Place in Time* then switches with no warning into the mode it will hold to throughout. Heise himself reads letters and other documents written by members of his family and their acquaintances (one is the novelist Christa Wolf) dating back to 1912, before World War I, when his grandfather was a schoolboy. The first text we hear condemns murder and war, but places them in the context of German patriotism and symbolism—mountains and mist. We see photos from the same period, then black-and-white footage of a train creaking through the night.

This mix of these three elements make up the entire film. Heise's family history during wartime Germany, then the divided Germany of the communist GDR where he grew up, then the Stasi and their constant spying, then reunification and post-reunification—they come by in huge blocks, indicting more than a century of state authoritarianism in various guises. We see photos, hear the text, and view elegant, forbidding tracking shots through the landscapes where the events of his family's life took place: railway and subway stations, half-dismantled forced labor camps, forests, large empty fields. Trains speeding by carrying new automobiles to the West contrast with long lists of Jews relocated and killed by the Nazis in the Holocaust. There is no score, but watching the film reminded me of listening to ambient techno by Wolfgang Voigt's Gas while simultaneously reading Uwe Johnson's *Anniversaries: From a Year in the Life of Gesine Cresspahl*. In other words, it was very German and nearly impossible to do at all, much less get through.

That was not Heise's fault. Watching *Heimat Is a Place in Time* at home took me two nights and eight hours. The first was the night Trump made his Rose Garden speech in response to the Black Lives Matter protests, which I paused the film to watch on Twitter. The speech was sniffy and angry, purely authoritarian and weird. Trump had trouble saying the word "assaults," which came out of his mouth as "uh-sauls." It fit in with Heise's documentary too well. "Being German is the last illusion of identity," Heise reads at one point.

At almost the same time, the 7 PM neighborhood cheering for essential workers began outside my window, competing with the omnipresent ambulance sirens I still had not gotten used to and which went on and on both nights I watched *Heimat Is a Space in Time*. Life was merging with Heise's movie, but instead of family letters I read texts and DMs from friends. I looked from my phone to the TV to see a black-and white shot of a huge pile of cord wood or to read subtitles that said, "Should we meet again, look for a room with soundproof walls," or that described "an hour of silence in the crocodile house." By myself, in my own apartment, I was devolving, the sole audience member in a blurred space where I'd become a movie-theater texter while the world erupted outside, without me.

Jenny Perlin Bunker Films

The previous month I had seen three of the New York avant-garde animator and documentarian Jenny Perlin's bunker films online, part of an ongoing series she is making. The performance space The Kitchen was hosting them in the Video Viewing Room on their website. These short films are portraits of men who have decided to live in bunkers either underground or at abandoned military facilities, a fitting subject now that Trump is going down in history for retreating to the White House bunker and turning out the front lights. I've thought all along that Trump's only response to the coronavirus was to try to get us to all to live like he already does: sleep odd hours, watch TV all day and night, go to meetings he doesn't want to go to, talk on the phone to old cronies, address the world through social media.

Perlin's films deglamorize the prepper lifestyle, presenting it as threadbare and emotionally bereft. The first, *Doublewide*, introduces the series and details the construction of a commercial bunker in the middle of nowhere that an unknown buyer could move into when the government collapses, the world is ending, or maybe never. The bunker was large and austere, with a low ceiling, like a submerged ranch house. It did not look inviting. Its prime feature was its secret location. Contractors put it together, made sure the generators and air filters were functional, and talked about more normal things while they worked.

In *Milton of Vivos*, a fairly young man who'd led a life of hardship and abuse detailed his upbringing on the streets with a single mother. His bunker was one of a series of many others in South Dakota that look like mini-airplane hangars in a field. Milton's belongings were scattered about in big piles, giving the windowless undivided space the feel of a hoarder house yet to be filled, as if Milton had moved from his car into a warehouse and now had plenty of room for storage. A bed was in there, somewhere. Milton had decided to get away from everyone else. Now he lived like a homeless person, but in a military shelter where he'd scraped up enough money for a 99-year sublease. Offering subleases does not speak of a firm belief in the apocalypse on the part of his landlord, the Vivos Group. Milton's bunker could house two dozen other people. He did not seem like a prepper so much as a lost soul.

The third of the bunker films Perlin has made so far presented *Ed of Subterra*, an old hippie in a nuclear missile silo in Kansas, whose wife had left him after living there for a couple of decades. Ed had transformed the silo, built to withstand nuclear blasts, into a castle, but it was really a hippie house with lots of junk in it. The contrast between the monolithic industrial look of the bare interiors and the crunchy-crusty knickknacks Ed had filled it with was like something from a 1970s science-fiction novel brought to sad, quotidian life. Ed, a Gandalf in decline, wasn't doing too well. He'd had a stroke and walked with difficulty. Inside, he'd stocked lots of vitamins and medicine, including his medical marijuana, an exercise bike, a copy of the book *Sex at Dawn*. A novelty clock on the wall had jumbled numbers made to look like they were falling. Spelled out above them, in pewter letters: WHO CARES.

The Trip to Greece

If becoming a hermit in a bunker is limiting, the antidote, now closed off to most of us, is foreign travel. Unless perhaps you are Steve Coogan and Rob Brydon, who have done this three times before, each time under the direction of Michael Winterbottom. *The Trip to Greece* cannibalizes not just the three previous *Trip*s but also Winterbottom's *Greed*, which came out in March. Here Coogan meets one of the actors (Kareem Alkabbani) who played a Syrian refugee in that film, which was also shot in Greece. Alkabbani is a real refugee, so Coogan and Brydon visit the camp where he lives. Coogan can't get his name right. This type of cringe humor is now reflexive and no longer quite reads as comedy. Coogan is too good at it and can refer to it now without fully embodying it, so that its function in the dire circumstances of the lives of displaced people is just a gentle reminder about a contrasting existence, in this case a wealthy celebrity's.

Coogan and Brydon's al fresco meals, their discussions of Aristotle, their appointments at Delphi or at the amphitheater where drama was born, are scored for melancholy with Nyman and Glass music. The air of wistfulness that pervades their journey indicates closing time for this cynical Quixote and his Sancho Panza. Death intrudes, and once again we see Steve as a lonely, aging rake and Rob as a well-adjusted family man. Along the way, Coogan reveals his uncanny ability to imitate the dialogue of actors in dubbed movies, and the two men do the Bee Gees in funny voices. The film reminded me of Astra Taylor's recent documentary *What Is Democracy?*, which starts in Greece, but here with sophisticated, world-weary *MST3K* types guiding us through it. They talk over the scenery instead of Taylor and Silvia Federici, who, while they couldn't perform dueling Arnold Schwarzenegger and Werner Herzog impressions, had more to offer.

Tommaso

Abel Ferrara, as prolific as Winterbottom but able to vary heavy and light with greater fluidity even though he is not a comedy director, presents *Tommaso* as a meta-movie on the road to his next film, *Siberia*, which is about to come out any minute, the way *The Trip to Greece* followed *Greed*.

Willem Dafoe plays a version of Ferrara the way Coogan and Brydon play versions of themselves. Dafoe/Tommaso/Ferrara, an American film director living in Rome with his young wife (Cristina Chiriac, Ferrara's real wife) and little daughter (Anna Ferrara, his actual kid), works on his screenplay, takes Italian lessons, teaches attractive drama students, and spends a lot of time at NA meetings with English-speaking addicts in recovery. They look and sound like Robert Quine and Mary Gaitskill, as if Ferrara had imported the Lower East Side of the 1980s and 1990s to Rome.

The film is a trip through Ferrara's tortured soul as much as a voyage in Italy. It begins as a story of domestic bliss with just a few cracks letting the darkness in, then moves through Fellini-isms and self-conscious borrowings from Scorsese to get to a violent, paranoid ending that is both sick fantasy and meta-commentary on Italian-American relations. This denouement has room for homicide, a crucifixion, and a clip of Sophia Loren singing "Tu vuo fa l'americano." Like the screen personas of Ferrara and Dafoe themselves, *Tommaso* draws you in with a kind of cool friendliness that verges on the distrustful or psychotic. Every moment in it is charged with possible failure. The night photography by Peter Zeitlinger is strikingly glowy, yet clear. It places the film in a unique time and place but still made me think of the New York streets I temporarily wasn't visiting any more than I was the alleys of Rome.

Irm Hermann

More than any other actress, especially the most glamorous ones, the plain Irm Hermann exemplified Fassbinder's cinema. She died May 26 in Berlin, age 77, after a "short respiratory illness." In addition to appearing in significant roles—but never starring—in twenty movies Fassbinder made, Hermann was his confidante, secretary, sidekick, and, at some point, lover. She acted in about half the total output of his sixteen-year career. She said *auf Wiedersehen* to him in the mid-1970s, and one can only imagine all the things she had to put up with while they were associates. Obviously, she did not shy away from trouble. But she came back into the fold in 1980 to appear in *Berlin Alexanderplatz*.

No one else in the movies looked like Irm Hermann. No matter who she was playing, she was instantly recognizable and welcome. Part of Fassbinder's brilliance was to meet her, realize no one looked like that, and to insist she be in movies, almost as if he had started making films for that reason. When Irm Hermann showed up in a Fassbinder film, it indicated that this was going to be one of the good ones. Of course, they are all good in varying degrees, but the presence of Irm added something, even if she played a mute, like in *The Bitter Tears of Petra von Kant*.

Her small, baleful eyes looked at the world with disappointment, hatred, and sometimes ignorance because even though the people around Fassbinder were probably each pretty interesting and great in their way, he had no compunction about making them look petty, cruel, or wrong—always wrong, people who had never been right about anything. Hermann played a great unsympathetic idiot, whether long-suffering wife or heinous busybody sister-in-law.

In the Fassbinder ensemble, there had to be a point to roles, which is the opposite of how most directors' stock companies work now. It's the opposite of, say, Judd Apatow, who casts comics he likes, knowing they are messed-up or unhappy, then has them play people who are just really nice in the end. Irm Hermann was never just nice in a Fassbinder movie. He knew that was too much to ask.

Netflix movies

Because I am stuck at home and movie theaters are closed, I am still trying to get my head around the cheesiness of Netflix films. *Uncorked* is a tepid drama of Black family life in Memphis centered on a barbecue joint run by a couple played by Courtney Vance and Niecy Nash. Their son, Elijah (Mamoudou Athie), wants to be a sommelier instead of working at Papa's Kitchen, a very on-the-nose restaurant name. In thinking about it now, Prentice Penny's film mainly brings to mind David McAtee, a Black man in Louisville who ran a barbecue takeout place called YaYa's and was shot and killed by the cops or the National Guard during the protests in Louisville, after they pepper-sprayed him and his family. *Uncorked* portrays the possibilities of Black middle-class life that are constantly subverted by deadly incidents like that one, kept offscreen in this mild film.

The Platform is a dystopic horror film from Spain that I watched dubbed but also with the English subtitles on because of the sirens outside. It is a disgusting, cruel film that seems written by a smart eighth-grader. A pallet of Michelin-star restaurant food descends through hundreds of floors of a prison, one floor at a time, in this reactionary microcosm of class relations. Prisoners fight over scraps with no concern for those below them. Director Galder Gaztelu-Urrutia is so nihilistic he will undoubtedly make the leap to Hollywood, especially since his cynical banquet leaves room for religiosity as the last course. Spoiler alert: the dog dies.

The Wrong Missy is a throwaway comedy with an emasculated David Spade in a bad haircut and dye job, less than one-one-hundredth as funny as he was doing monologues on Instagram after his talk show couldn't be televised with a studio audience anymore. Spade is forced to confront the nimble-faced Lauren Lapkus as a former date-from-hell during a Hawaiian work getaway in this *Bringing Up Baby* for sports-bar TV screens. One shot of Lapkus summarizes pre-Covid American life and should be preserved by the Library of Congress. Puking over a shark cage on an excursion boat, Lapkus looks up and spies a shark fin slicing through the water, getting closer. With vomit running down her chin, she tilts her head toward the horizon and yells, "Let's fucking party!"

Blow the Man Down

In an attempt to be fair to giant entertainment conglomerates who are ruining the world, I also watched an Amazon movie. Like *Bacurau*, *Blow the Man Down* was written and directed by two people, in this case Danielle Krudy and Bridget Savage Cole. It takes place in a small remote town, this one in Maine, which is the opposite of Brazil. Music is used in a unique way in this violent murder mystery, with the action interrupted by beefy Gorton's Fisherman types who perform a cappella sea shanties while working on the docks. The ominous shanties were adapted by David Coffin but the eerie score is by Brian McOmber and Jordan Dykstra. As with *Bacurau*, just hearing the music makes the film worth seeing.

Also like *Bacurau*, the film begins with the funeral of a powerful woman in the town who was a good presence and whose absence reveals secrets. This is a feminist genre film, about two sisters

(Morgan Saylor, Sophie Lowe) and some senior citizens (Annette O'Toole, June Squibb, Marceline Hugot) who free their town from the grip of an evil madam (Margo Martindale) so local women won't have to work for her as prostitutes. It takes place in winter and in the snow; there's a lot of knife and harpoon work in it; it is not about comical accents in a cold state. *Blow the Man Down* is swift but not choppy, with Martindale silencing people merely by appearing in doorways. The local nice-guy cop (Will Brittain), who has a crush on Lowe's character, thinks he's figured things out, but Lowe rejects him in the end, and no one tells him anything.

Never Rarely Sometimes Always

The first thing we see in Eliza Hittman's feature is a desultory high-school variety show with a 1950s theme—strangely, kind of a corollary to the opening of *Mulholland Drive.* One act in the show is a young woman, Autumn (Sidney Flanigan), playing a guitar and singing, who gets heckled by a boy (Brian Altemus) in the audience trying to humiliate her. At a pizza place with her parents after the show, she argues with her stepfather (Ryan Eggold), then leaves the table, stopping on her way out of the restaurant to throw a glass of water in the heckler's face.

Later, in a Planned Parenthood office in New York City, far from her home in Northumberland County, Pennsylvania, a social worker (Kelly Chapman) asks Autumn a long series of questions about her sex life before she is allowed to go through with her abortion. Hittman films this interview in one shot, holding on Autumn, and we watch as she tries not to break down. Hittman, with great subtlety, draws our attention to Flanigan as a performer without violating the naturalism of her documentary-like film. The focus is on Autumn and the realization that she has been abused. By whom we never learn—the heckler? her stepfather?—another aspect of Hittman's unwillingness to provide pat answers. Earlier in the film, another long take concentrated on Flanigan piercing her nose in a bathroom mirror.

Autumn and her cousin Skylar (Talia Ryder) steal from the supermarket where they work and leave on a bus for New York City. They dress in dark hoodies and work clothes with a camo layer, and wear black nail polish—the national uniform of not wanting to be seen. Autumn's abortion turns into a two-day process, for which the girls don't have enough cash. To get more, they end up going bowling near the Port Authority bus station with a slightly older boy who has money (Théodore Pellerin) while he tries to woo Skylar and while Autumn is in pain from her dilation. Then they have to listen to him sing karaoke to a Flock of Seagulls song.

Even in these scenes, Hittman maintains the film's tone of harsh reality. *Never Rarely Sometimes Always* is a serious film about the difficulties young women face in getting an abortion in America, but its asperity is such that it also becomes a documentary on the indignities faced by anyone who has ever had to travel through Penn Station.

Sorry We Missed You

Hittman is a Ken Loach-style director of social realism, and it is a testament to the days we are in that her work seems more hard-edged than even Loach's unflinching examinations of working-class problems. Which is not to say he is diminished. Loach has been at it since the mid-1960s, and nothing has kept him away. If he has ever had a real break in his output, I'm not aware of it. The three years between *Sorry We Missed You*, his new film, and *I, Daniel Blake*, the one before, was the longest gap he's had between releasing films since the era when the Tim Burton *Batman* was new.

Loach's latest film, not to be confused with *Sorry to Bother You*, takes place in Newcastle upon Tyne, in Northern England. It follows a family through their work and school days after the father, Ricky

(Kris Hitchen), gets a job as a delivery driver working on a zero hour contract, which means he only gets paid per delivery. His wife, Abbie (Debbie Honeywood), gets paid the same way in her work as a visiting health aid for the elderly and infirm, and she has an equally grueling schedule of home visits, which she gets to by city bus. They have no time for anything but work, which their two children, Seb and Liza Jane (Rhys Stone, Katie Proctor) can see. Their lives are too difficult and too unrewarding; their kids know it and don't understand why people who work so hard don't get to have decent lives.

Seb, a graffiti writer who tags local billboards with his crew, begins to lose respect for his father and acts out, spray painting black X's over the family photos on the walls in their house. Ricky wants to spend more time with the younger Liza Jane, but the delivery company does not allow her in the van even though Ricky owns it himself. Every person Ricky delivers to is an asshole. Have things in England really made people so horrible? And everyone Abbie visits is incoherent and needy, except one ex-union organizer who can't walk and pisses herself in her chair.

Pissing is a theme in *Sorry We Missed You*. Ricky has to urinate in a bottle in his van because he doesn't have time for bathroom breaks. When he is mugged at work one day, the muggers grab the piss bottle and dump it on him. No matter what happens, he goes back to his deliveries. "I have got no choice," he tells his family. As essential workers, Ricky and Abbie would no doubt be working through Covid and trying to figure out how to homeschool Seb and Liza Jane. This is what going back to work means for most people, except for one person in this film, a teenage friend of Seb's named Roz (Natalia Stonebanks) who finds Newcastle too mean, splits for Blackpool, and gives a remarkably self-effacing, Linda Manz-ish performance in her few brief scenes. Is she a professional actor or someone who was just hanging around? Everyone does a seamless job here, especially the family and the belligerent delivery boss, a frightening guard-dog of a human (Ross Brewster). But this odd girl who left town stuck in my mind.

THE OLD BAMBOO

BAMBOOZLED AND *CROUCHING TIGER, HIDDEN DRAGON* TWENTY YEARS LATER

IN APRIL 2006, SPIKE LEE APPEARED ON NATIONAL PUBLIC RADIO'S Weekend Edition Saturday to promote his new film, *Inside Man*, the heist thriller starring Denzel Washington. Early in the interview, Scott Simon, *Weekend Edition*'s host, did something I thought was strange and that I still remember fourteen years later. He switched the conversation away from *Inside Man* to ask Spike Lee about his fellow film director, Ang Lee, because they have the same last name.

A month before, Ang Lee had won the Best Director Oscar for *Brokeback Mountain*, his film about a secret love affair between two cowboys. The film was a critical and box office success, and proved groundbreaking and controversial. Spike Lee explained that he and Ang Lee had gone to college together, and that Ang had worked on an early short of his. He said he was happy his colleague had won an Oscar. Simon then pointed out that Ang Lee had "done well for himself since he worked for you." "Yes, he has," Spike agreed, adding that he and Ang were "the two Lees."

Here Simon, who is white, became jocular. "Oh my gosh, you guys aren't related, are you?" he asked. Lee audibly side-eyed the conversation: "He's Chinese. I'm African American." Simon didn't take the hint. "Well, in some other ways, though, you know, a blended family, I think is what we, is what we call it these days," the radio host continued, awkwardly.

Simon didn't ask a lot about *Inside Man*, beyond pointing out that it was made with a bigger budget than Lee's first feature, *She's Gotta Have It*, from 1986. He seems to have brought up *She's Gotta Have It* to ask Lee about its rape scene, a part of the film that Lee had, over the years, expressed remorse for including. Lee mentions he thinks the scene was a mistake, but that filmmakers shouldn't excise material they later regret. He brings up Judy Garland and Mickey Rooney's appearances in blackface in *Babes on Broadway*, and Rooney in yellowface in *Breakfast at Tiffany's* as Mr. Yunioshi. These scenes are now historical facts, Lee is indicating. Trying to cover-up the past is a form of lying.

What did NPR listeners get from this interview? They learned there was a new movie out with a big star in it. They learned that Spike Lee, a Black man who once made a movie with a rape scene, now gets to work with more money. And they learned he shares a last name with one of his contemporaries, a Chinese director who started out working for him but who had recently surpassed him. Listeners, therefore, from what was only supposed to be a puff piece, got a miniature history of race relations in America. One group is pitted against another; an Asian man is held up to a Black man as a model of achievement that betters his own, based on a pretext that was odd to mention at all.

WHAT NEITHER SPIKE LEE nor Scott Simon brought up in that interview was Lee's movie *Bamboozled*, his scathing satire of blackface minstrelsy in American entertainment, which came out in 2000. Blackface did come up in their conversation, but Simon sees it as an opportunity for a quip: Mickey Rooney's got a lot to answer for. *Bamboozled* was left unmentioned then, but now the film is celebrating its twentieth anniversary. So is *Crouching Tiger, Hidden Dragon*, Ang Lee's epic tale of love and swordplay in 18th-century China. Twenty years later, let's look at the two films together.

Crouching Tiger, Hidden Dragon briefly made wuxia mainstream in the US, dazzling audiences with its beauty. The film was so exceptional that American audiences didn't complain about its subtitles. Spike Lee's movie had a different effect. *Bamboozled* confounded audiences. Its intent was to wake them from a racist stupor that had allowed the continued degradation of Black people in American media. It was received as an ugly polemic the America of Bill Clinton had outgrown, some kind of foreign object the country didn't need.

Bamboozled did not do well with critics or at the box office, which is no doubt why Lee did not want to call attention to it on NPR. Today it is understood to be a milestone in the cinematic analysis of racism in American culture, and has gained a cult following and a deluxe Criterion Collection release. *Crouching Tiger, Hidden Dragon,* on the other hand, was a massive worldwide hit and the highest-grossing foreign-language film ever released in the US. Nominated for ten Academy Awards, including Best Picture, it won the Oscar for best foreign-language film and prizes in three other categories. Perhaps its initial success has prevented *Crouching Tiger, Hidden Dragon* from attaining the status it deserves. While it is no doubt still making money, it has not gotten a fancy treatment on DVD or Blu-Ray. Streaming in high-def, it looks a little punched-up, in a cursory way, as if Sony Pictures doesn't consider it a classic. The termite audacity of *Bamboozled* now speaks directly to a society marked by continuing racial injustice and the efforts of the Black Lives Matter movement to change that. Ang Lee's feminist legend, however, has sunk into the stream of entertainment at the same time as the Hong Kong film industry has declined under mainland Chinese rule.

A belated Netflix sequel, produced by Harvey Weinstein in 2016, didn't help. Although *Crouching Tiger, Hidden Dragon: Sword of Destiny* was directed by the original film's renowned stunt coordinator, Yuen Woo-ping, the sequel relied on computer effects to remedy bad scripting. Michelle Yeoh's return as fighting legend Yu

Shu Lien didn't much help. Without Ang Lee's depth or acuity, it felt more like Weinstein's dreary Marco Polo Netflix series, which over twenty episodes never employed an Asian director.

Considered together, *Crouching Tiger, Hidden Dragon* and *Bamboozled* point to a brief time in mainstream cinema when Black filmmakers and performers were on the rise and American audiences were open to Asian stars and genres. After the debacle of the Bush-Gore election and the subsequent war on terror post-9/11, that began to change. Retrenchment set in. American film audiences marched into cineplexes dominated by superheroes, transatlantic children's movies, and TV remakes. In the first decade of the new century, eight *Harry Potter* movies, three *Lord of the Rings* movies, and two Batmans made about a billion dollars each. As the global market grew between 2001 and 2011—especially in China—Hollywood produced movies for export that were loudly, almost parodistically white. By mid-decade, a big-screen version of the '70s good ol' boy TV show *The Dukes of Hazzard* was the number one movie in America.

BAMBOOZLED'S PROTAGONIST, Pierre Delacroix (Damon Wayans, in a performance of great originality and daring) is the lone Black writer at a broadcast-television network. Sick of his white boss (Michael Rapaport) telling him he's not Black enough, he creates and airs a purposefully racist primetime variety revue, called *Mantan: The New Millennium Minstrel Show*, so that he will be fired without losing his bonus package. The show stars two tap-dancing street performers, Manray and Womack (Savion Glover and Tommy Davidson). Hungry for success, they agree to Delacroix's plan for the show: filmed on stage before a live audience, Black performers in blackface will shuck and jive in a watermelon patch to the music of the Alabama Porch Monkeys, a band dressed in prison stripes (played by The Roots). Lee's joke—or more accurately, his contention—is that this old-timey hootenanny will be an immediate ratings success. Returned to its *Hee Haw* baseline, the vast audience of American TV viewers won't be able to get enough of Delacroix's blatant, racist extravaganza.

Put at ease by Manray and Womack's talent, the predominantly white live audience's initial apprehension turns quickly into admiration, then to joy. Soon they are at ease in this setting, laughing along with the retrograde comedy routines, fully embracing a form of entertainment that Lee insists has not been consigned to history. Glover and Davidson's virtuosity in bringing this once-popular material back to life is uncanny and disturbing—a séance as agitprop.

Lee did not tell the studio audience what they were in for when they signed up to be extras. As the show gets more and more popular, he has the entire audience appear in blackface and white gloves, a sea of mini-Jolsons. A white man in the audience (Al Palagonia) shows up ready to rap: "No matter what color / No matter what race / You know you're cold chillin' / When you're in blackface." The effect is shocking. It exposes something ever-present in American culture that we are encouraged to ignore: white people like to clown as Black. Not only do they want Black people to tell them that's OK, they want them to re-enact these stereotypes as outlandishly as possible, and to confirm them as real and true.

The film programmer Ashley Clark, who has written a book on *Bamboozled*, observes in an essay on the film that "while the arc of the moral universe is long, it bends toward spiritual abjection and comprehensive mental collapse." In twisting Martin Luther King Jr.'s words that way, Clark points to something that our culture was only beginning to understand in the '60s, before King was assassinated: that by the end of the 20th century all perceptions of race would be created in the media and maintained there. That is the subject of *Bamboozled*: there is only this mediation. When it breaks away from TV into real life, it has moral and spiritual consequences that can turn deadly.

The video of the murder of George Floyd by a cop in Minneapolis is the latest example of the way Black deaths are disseminated and televised, something Lee predicted in *Bamboozled*. When Manray quits the show on the air, he is kidnapped and later executed live on the internet by a radical rap act called the Mau Maus, who are in turn gunned down by the police, live on the news (except for their sole white member, who complains he was spared).

In *The Original Kings of Comedy,* the concert tour film Lee made right before *Bamboozled,* Bernie Mac insists, as part of his stand-up act, that "there are no Black terrorists," because they would immediately get arrested if they tried to buy dynamite. In *Bamboozled,* there are Black terrorists, almost as if the film is responding to the comedy in the previous film. The presence in *Bamboozled* of Junebug (Paul Mooney), an embittered comic on the Chitlin Circuit, implies as much. Lee turns the comedy from his previous film inside out, bringing it to bear on the network employees who staff Delacroix's show, a large group of white comedy writers whose knowledge of Black life in America comes from sitcoms like *The Jeffersons* and nothing else.

Now, in the age of digital blackface, anyone can use a gif of a Black person to get a quick laugh. And in the twenty years since *Bamboozled* came out, old-school blackface has not gone away. Instances of blackface spiral in on each other, implicating one white TV personality or politician after another. One of the *Real Housewives of New York* goes to a party made up as Diana Ross in blackface and an afro wig, then claims that was OK because the makeup she used was just her usual bronzer. Andy Cohen rebukes her on his show not for being racist, but because in his mind Diana Ross wasn't known for having an afro. In response, conservative anchor Megyn Kelly bamboozles herself out of a job by announcing on TV that costume-party blackface is fine with her.

The cluelessness of the American news media revealed itself again in October 2018, in a surprising way. Responding to Kelly's dismissal, *CBS This Morning* did a segment on blackface with host Maurice DuBois, a man who will immediately remind anyone who has seen *Bamboozled* of Pierre Delacroix. While writer and critic Margo Jefferson was telling DuBois that blackface is still in the culture, the show's producers put up an image of Tommy Davidson and Savion Glover from *Bamboozled* to illustrate Jefferson's point, blindly implicating Spike Lee's film in the racist tradition it was made to oppose. FEED THE IDIOT BOX, as the sign reads over Delacroix's TV in his luxury condo.

Similarly, in Lee's film, a white media consultant (Dina Pearlman) instructs Delacroix and his bosses on how the network should counter the inevitable accusations of racism their minstrel show will face. If things get bad, "wear kente cloth," she tells the network execs. Wearing kente cloth is exactly what Nancy Pelosi, Chuck Schumer, and other members of the US Senate did last June while taking a knee to show solidarity with African Americans after the murder of George Floyd. As Doreen St. Félix pointed out in the *New Yorker*, by staging this photo op for the media, these members of Congress "only made themselves models of obtuseness." Chuck Schumer lives in Brooklyn just a short walk from the offices of 40 Acres and a Mule Filmworks, but that doesn't mean he saw *Bamboozled*.

TOMMY DAVIDSON EXPLAINED *Bamboozled*'s invocation of blackface comedy by saying that "laughter is the reflex of pain." Michelle Yeoh, in explaining *Crouching Tiger, Hidden Dragon*'s approach to both its genre and its women characters, noted that "fighting is the exhilaration of repression." The swift grace of Ang Lee's film exists in images of conflict. Women representing three different generations seek to master the same fighting skills as Chow Yun-fat's Master Li Mu Bai, an adept of the Wudang Mountain school (from which the Wu-Tang Clan takes its name). Li is also the star-crossed love of Yu Shu Lien, the swordswoman played by Yeoh.

Set during the Qing Dynasty, the film has a fragile yet resilient quality befitting a period in which women were assigned specific roles and not expected to question them. A teacup nudged off a table by Shu, and silently caught by Jen (Zhang Ziyi), a rich heiress, before it can break, is a key image from early in the film. Jen trains in secret as a ninja with Jade Fox (Cheng Pei-pei), the discarded concubine of the master of the Wudang, who trained Li. Both Jen and Jade harbor a hatred of the Wudang. Jen calls it a whorehouse when rejecting Li's offer to make her his disciple.

Li and Jen's fight in the bamboo forest is justly remembered as the film's high point: an unexpected scene of lyrical, floating beauty, so impossible-seeming that it had to have convinced wuxia purists skeptical of an American coproduction. In fact, while it may be the coincidence of the word bamboo that unites *Crouching Tiger, Hidden Dragon* and *Bamboozled*, what is apparent is how "the two Lees" understand an important secret of the cinema: Dance scenes should be shot in full frame, so that actors are visible head-to-toe.

Ang Lee's film is a ballet of movement the same way the tap-dancing in *Bamboozled* splashes primary colors into the drabness of the rest of the film's handycam-video look. Both films rely on the fluidity of motion and music to lift their characters above the repression they face. Both films are spectacles and both are fantasies. *Bamboozled* satirizes the destructive fantasy of white oppression, which turns Black people into servile, smiling caricatures. *Crouching Tiger, Hidden Dragon*'s fantasy is a positive one, kept aloft by Tan Dun's percussive score.

Jen's callow actions earlier in the film lead to Li's death, robbing Shu of the possibility of happiness. Ang Lee has referred to this wealthy, spoiled girl from the ruling class as being "in some ways the villain of the movie." She's an ambivalent character, too self-centered to understand the fragility of the relationships between the people around her, and how quickly they can come apart.

Jen finally frees herself of her resentments, and breaks the boundaries of her arranged marriage in favor of true love with Lo (Chang Chen), a desert bandit from Xinjiang, yet she ends the film fantasizing about flying away, alone, into the foggy void around Wudang Mountain, the way Master Li disappeared years before.

The romance between Jen and Lo transpires as a captivity narrative, barely more modern than *The Sheik*, with Rudolph Valentino, from 1921. A high-born, feisty girl in pants fends off a desert chieftain but submits to his love. Lo implores Jen to "come with me to the desert," as if he is speaking to her in silent-movie intertitles. In the context of a Chinese-American coproduction from the year 2000, one that brought together star actors from Hong Kong, Malaysia, Taiwan, and the People's Republic, the film now seems like a wishful moment of Chinese unity, a dream of harmony possible only in the cinema.

Lo, like Valentino, is presumably a Muslim. *Crouching Tiger, Hidden Dragon* is partially set in Xinjiang, where the current Chinese government is actively oppressing the Muslim Uyghur population, rounding-up hundreds of thousands of people in concentration camps. The Uyghurs have a tradition of separatism dating back to Mao, and Xinjiang, an autonomous region of some 640,000 square miles, wasn't part of China until the second half of the 18th century, the years in the Qing Dynasty during which the film takes place.

Crouching Tiger, Hidden Dragon was shot all over the mainland with a Hong Kong crew, at a time when the Hong Kong film industry was still its own kind of autonomous entity. Now it is being squelched and subsumed, like Hong Kong itself, into an oppressive system run from Beijing.

ANG LEE, AS A TAIWANESE and as an American film director, understands the evils of national division. The film he made before *Crouching Tiger, Hidden Dragon*, 1999's *Ride with the Devil*, told the story of Bushwhackers in Missouri, Confederate irregulars fighting the Union Army on the Kansas border in the 1860s during the Civil War. One of them is a freed slave (Jeffrey Wright) committed, as the film begins, to the wrong side of history. The film failed at the box office as big as *Crouching Tiger, Hidden Dragon* succeeded, too tragic and unheroic for the kind of massive popular audience *Crouching Tiger, Hidden Dragon* attracted.

The power of Ang Lee's cinema comes from the way each scene is potentially heartbreaking, filled with subtle emotion, but combustible just the same. He achieved that in film after film, almost imperceptibly, for twenty years. Now Lee devotes himself to a more esoteric challenge: combining mise-en-scène with very expensive technological innovation. Both *Billy Lynn's Long Halftime Walk*, a war drama from 2016, and 2019's *Gemini Man*, a sci-fi thriller with Will Smith, were shot in 3D at a super-high frame rate few theaters could show. I don't think anyone fully understands why Lee, the director of *The Ice Storm*, *Sense and Sensibility*, and *Lust, Caution* is devoting himself to this kind of specialized work. *Crouching Tiger, Hidden Dragon*'s achievement was that it was made with no digital effects. Or only one: Lee digitally erased the wires that allowed the actors to move so freely, climbing walls, darting across rooftops, and balancing on tree branches.

At the beginning of this century, recut Jackie Chan films were still coming out in American cineplexes. The combo of Asian and African American stars was good for business. Chan's pairing with Chris Tucker reached its box office height in *Rush Hour 2*. Jet Li, who had supposedly turned down Chow Yun-fat's role in *Crouching Tiger, Hidden Dragon*, got together with Aaliyah in *Romeo Must Die*, her film debut, which topped the box office in the months before she died in a plane crash. By 2002 these crossover films had disappeared. Spike Lee's new film, *Da 5 Bloods*, set in Vietnam, provides a link. Veronica Ngô—a screen star in Vietnam who appears in *Star Wars: The Last Jedi*—plays a fighter in *Crouching Tiger, Hidden Dragon: Sword of Destiny* and has the plum role of Hanoi Hannah in *Da 5 Bloods*, where she implores American soldiers to give up and go home. "Black G.I., your soul sisters and soul brothers are enraged in over 122 cities," she announces over the radio while describing the riots in the US after the assassination of Martin Luther King. "They kill them while you fight against us."

Postscript

After this piece went to press but before it went online, I saw in the news that Thomas Jefferson Byrd, who plays Honeycutt in *Bamboozled*, had died in Atlanta, age 70. He was shot several times in the back, at 1:45 AM on October 3rd. The police investigating his murder say they don't have any suspects.

Honeycutt is the emcee in *Bamboozled*, a tall, gaunt figure who Delacroix and his staff discover during auditions for *Mantan: The New Millennium Minstrel Show*. His audition consists of delivering part of the "to be or not to be" speech from *Hamlet*, then explaining a scene in the play, and then going into an a cappella rap on the theme of "niggas is a beautiful thing." He appears in the Da Bomb malt liquor ads in the film and, most importantly, he is the pre-show warm-up act who appears as a blackface Uncle Sam and a blackface Abraham Lincoln, exhorting the live studio audience to shout racist epithets.

There really should be an oral history of the making of those scenes. In them, Lee and Byrd reproduced the reality and squirmy discomfort of racist complicity in the American TV audience, something that had never been done before, by pulling an elaborate practical joke on the extras in the film. Byrd acted in a number of other Spike Lee joints and in other directors' films, too, and he was a distinguished stage actor who knew his Shakespeare. His performance as Honeycutt is a unique creation that links the Hollywood cowboy actor Arthur Hunnicutt to the sooty woodsman in *Twin Peaks: The Return*, through a strange portal of 19th-century Americana, like the racist toys Lee features in the movie.

Byrd shows great verve in his difficult role as a performer in the film, doing a white person's version of a Black person while playing white people in blackface as a Black man. He shows how certain Black performers had to, as the late critic Stanley Crouch noted, "reinforce the bars of the cage they were in, through their talent."

ALL-CONSUMING HORROR

IN JOHN CARPENTER'S *THEY LIVE* (1988), AN UNEMPLOYED CONSTRUCTION worker enters a Los Angeles bank wearing sunglasses and carrying a shotgun. Called Nada in the film's credits, he is played by the professional wrestler "Rowdy" Roddy Piper.

Backing in through the glass doors, Nada turns toward the bank's employees and customers, many of whom are revealed through his sunglasses to be metal-skulled aliens. These aliens maintain and control the human race as a herd of passive consumers, conformists who are unaware of the authoritarian nature of the society they're part of. Nada, however, knows the truth.

"I have come here to chew bubblegum and kick ass. And I'm all out of bubblegum," he announces, shotgun in hand. Then he begins firing into the crowd, killing the aliens and sparing the humans among them.

This line of preposterous dialogue, now almost as well-known as the OBEY signs Nada's sunglasses reveal on billboards in *They Live*, is unexpected, out of place. It both heightens and relieves the violence of the scene, moving it away from the reality he is trying to expose. After all, from the outside, Nada's actions look like the kind of random mass shooting we have increasingly come to expect in the US since this movie came out near the end of the Reagan era.

Carpenter, always careful not to slip over to the side of authority, yet always on the brink of madness, knew that something ridiculous, even confounding, was called for here.

To express it by mentioning bubblegum right at the beginning of the scene all but reduces its mayhem to a childish level. But that is where consumerism begins, with children wanting gum. Nada is announcing that he is through with this kind of naivete, done with the false consciousness of the consumer who believes that his wants and desires, his tastes and preferences, are authentic. He is *all out* of it. He is placing himself outside that system of gullibility.

Bubblegum is the exact product to best express this. The chewer doesn't finish gum; it is never fully consumed. You don't finish it, you finish *with* it and then spit it out. You are not supposed to swallow it. If gum is the first consumer product people choose, its lesson is never really learned.

As Nada learns, to consciously divorce yourself from the tyranny of consumerism is a pathological act. It separates you from others. To conform may be normal but wrong, but to revolt is suicidal, doomed. And maybe, in any case, Nada's view of the truth is just a phantasm, something no one else sees and wouldn't believe if they could.

THERE IS NO SPACE OUTSIDE of consumerism. That is the principal lesson of a group of American horror and sci-fi films that began to emerge after George A. Romero's *Night of the Living Dead* came out in 1968. This kind of movie, never quite a fully-formed subgenre, peaked in the second half of the 1980s and all but disappeared after 1990. It flourished in the margins of Hollywood production like a Day-Glo mold growing where the wall meets the ceiling, erupting into a splatter of exploding heads, limbs, and organs. It was a kind of polychrome spin-art that accompanied the growth of American retail into shopping centers, and into the television commercials that advertised their stores and products.

We can divide movies about the horror of consumption into three overlapping types, linked by their depictions of steps in the cycle of production and consumption. Some of these films are dour and grim, cynical and disgusted; others are poppy and neon, clever and facetious.

First, there are films of the factory, where goods are made, making their appearances in these movies just as the decline of American labor began. Second, there are films set in the sites of consumption, where the goods end up, primarily the supermarket and the mall. Finally, there are the films that show how consumers and product merge to the point where products take over human consciousness, then individual bodies, and then entire populations. In these, people serve the products, not the other way around. That's the scenario posited by Larry Cohen in *The Stuff* (1985), the most blatantly anti-consumerist of these films.

All of them seem to have come out of Romero's gruesome world of zombies-as-ordinary-people, and to have mixed his dark view of society with two popular movies of the early 1970s, weird films about production and consumption designed as mainstream entertainment: *Willy Wonka & the Chocolate Factory* (1971) and *Soylent Green* (1973). The dangerous factory tour Wonka conducts as a test of the child-consumers who have won his contest by purchasing chocolate bars gives way to a dystopian future in which corpses become the sole product feeding humanity and allowing it to survive. Both films depict factories and abhor overconsumption. Together, they expose capitalism as a destructive system that proceeds from the creation of desire to the transformation of humanity into a cannibalistic product of self-annihilation.

TED V. MIKELS'S *THE CORPSE GRINDERS*, from 1971, was an early warning of movies to come, connected to sleaze, sordid and very cheap. The consumer product here is cat food, made by a company that seems to operate out of a cellar room containing only a plywood grinding machine with an anus-like hole in it, through which the ground meat of human corpses emerges, shit-like, to be packed into cans. Eventually anyone and everyone goes into the grinder, rich and poor, beautiful and ugly. They go in fully clothed, in bras and panties or in business suits.

This ugly, inadequate atmosphere became artier and Europeanized as the decade progressed. *Messiah of Evil* (1973) is a low-budget seaside horror movie from Willard Huyck and Gloria Katz, who went on to make *Howard the Duck* (1986) and cowrite *American Graffiti* (1973) and *Indiana Jones and the Temple of Doom* (1984). At the same low level of production, Huyck and Katz transformed the genre into something that was as subtle and eerie as *Corpse Grinders* was banal and shabby. *Messiah of Evil* emphasizes empty spaces of commerce, seen at night and populated by isolated groups of proto-zombies who cry tears of blood.

Supermarket scenes have a special place in the cinema, almost as if the supermarket was constructed as the soundstage of consumerism. In a grocery store sequence rivaled only by the ones in Fassbinder's *Love Is Colder Than Death* (1969) or Godard and Gorin's *Tout va bien* (1972), the one in *Messiah of Evil* features ghouls dressed for office work gorging on raw meat from an open-top refrigerated display case. A woman looks on in disgust from the cheese aisle, trapped in the store and unable to protect herself when the ghouls finally turn on her. Throughout *Messiah of Evil*, retail spaces are depicted as empty, lit-up interiors. Furniture stores, car lots, gas stations, appliance stores, movie theaters—the typical shops on an average American small-town Main Street–become sites where commerce is halted for cannibalism.

Prominent toy factories in *Halloween III: Season of the Witch* (1982) and *Child's Play 2* (1990) bracket films that define this area of cinematic discourse. The factory in *Halloween III* manufactures deadly "Silver Shamrock" Halloween masks, which are advertised, with a peppy synth track, non-stop during children's TV shows. The factory in the second *Child's Play* movie becomes a production line for melding the evil doll Chucky's consciousness, and his eyes, into human beings. Chucky melts and explodes into a pile of multicolored goo, the ultimate fate of human-product brand synergy. The same fate befalls the melting winos in *Street Trash* (1987), who dissolved into garish, sputtering colors after they consume their discount bottles of Tenafly Viper fortified wine.

The explosions of consumer goods in certain earlier non-horror movies, such as Frank Tashlin's *The Disorderly Orderly* (1964) and Michelangelo Antonioni's *Zabriskie Point* (1970), had already linked American consumerism to destructive violence. *The Disorderly Orderly* ends with Jerry Lewis on a gurney being chased by ambulances through a supermarket, destroying stacks of canned goods and reducing the store to a kind of pop-art sculpture-painting. A balletic detonation of Wonder Bread and other grocery items closes Antonioni's anti-American art film in an unprecedented paroxysm of disgust made beautiful. If Tashlin and Antonioni could explode the supermarket, it would take horror filmmakers to place the violence within the shoppers themselves, now insensate and lumbering instead of frantic or neurotic like shoppers in 1960s films.

GEORGE A. ROMERO'S GORY analysis of American consumerism in *Dawn of the Dead* (1978) is more indelible than Antonioni's, precisely because it is a horror film. Its zombies are us, as the main characters in the film do not hesitate to point out. Where Antonioni, indicting a whole country and its way of life, destroyed a modernist house full of consumer goods, Romero dismantled a mall, transforming it into a battleground and a graveyard, turning its full stock of products, including guns and other weapons, against its former shoppers. Like many of these films, it traveled from a TV studio through sites of American poverty before arriving at the mall, which becomes a trap, an end point. In *Dawn of the Dead*, as in the later films set in malls, grocery carts, hand trucks, rolling racks, escalators, and glass elevators become opportunities for a mise-en-scène that utilizes the tools and architecture of real spaces designed for shopping.

The four main characters in *Dawn of the Dead* ensconce themselves in the mall like the members of a quarantine pod. They begin to enjoy lives of ease, sampling all the comforts the mall has to offer, everything from designer clothes to gourmet food, from cosmetics and perfume to stereos and sports equipment. Impervious to those other consumers outside (the living dead), these survivors now exist unshackled from commerce. When the class of citizens below them shows up, in the form of an invading gang of bikers, their empty, consumerist paradise is destroyed. It returns to its former chaotic state. Wandering zombies again groan their way past Florsheim Shoes and Waldenbooks in search of human flesh to eat. A benign consumerism was a mirage, a memory, in this post-apocalyptic atmosphere of gore and death.

THE 1980S MALL FILMS couldn't compete with Romero at that level of horror, metaphor, or allegory. Instead, Thom Eberhardt's *Night of the Comet* (1984) and Jim Wynorski's *Chopping Mall* (1986) added Southern Californian satire reminiscent of the contemporaneous *Repo Man* (1984). These two movies present the tropes of a more mildly subversive anti-consumerism in a teen movie setting. Here, the mall is a trap but also a funhouse. Overrun by criminal stock boys, killer robots, and evil scientists eager to steal the blood of Gen X teenagers so that their elders may become immortal, the mall becomes a space that has to be cleansed of threat so it can emerge as a shopper's paradise, where no one has to earn money or carry ID to buy things.

In *Chopping Mall*, guys who work in a furniture store party after hours with girls from the food court pizza place. "You smell like pepperoni," one randy dude says to his girlfriend, associating her with a food product as they make out on a couch in the store. A matter-of-fact dream quality takes over, like in a Buñuel film, when she wanders the mall in her underwear, without the ID that protects her from robot security guards.

Night of the Comet, an underrated film that happily combines some of the more outré elements of 1980s teen and pop sci-fi, presents the post-apocalyptic mall as a party space for clothes shopping montages, with "teenage comet zombies" freed from the obligations of adolescence and economics. Most of Los Angeles was already "an absolute monument to consumerism" for these teens before the comet emancipated them from supervision. It also turns them into prey for adult survivors who weren't vaporized into orange dust when the comet arrived.

THE CREAMY WHITE DESSERT product known as *The Stuff* is one part Blob, one part satire. It is a natural resource, like oil or coal, and a drug, like cocaine or heroin, that is refined in factories, like it is white sugar or Marshmallow Fluff (its obvious inspiration). Consumers of The Stuff become so eager to eat it that all-night Dairy Queen–style restaurants open in the suburbs to dispense it, and pushcarts selling it appear on the streets of New York. Supermarkets devote entire aisles to it, and families serve it in crystal bowls as the main and only entree for dinner at home.

The Stuff is also a jizz-like monster-substance that attacks lovers in bed. Viscous spurts form out of consumers' mouths, pinning people to walls post-coitus, filling motel rooms. Once The Stuff completely takes over people's minds and bodies, and they become "Stuffies," they die in a rictus of consumption, mouths wide open, trapped at the point of confusion between consumer and product consumed. The movie targets fads as much as lifestyle addiction and societal breakdown. It makes room for a blithe consumerism, with TV commercials featuring the Wendy's "Where's the beef?" lady asking sitcom character-actor Abe Vigoda, "Where's The Stuff?"

The films-within-the-film we see in David Cronenberg's *Videodrome* (1983) are not as cute. The brain-tumor-inducing signal embedded in these sadomasochistic TV transmissions begs Cronenberg's explicit question: "But why would anyone watch?" Videodrome, the product of a corporation that also makes eyeglasses for third world countries and missile guidance systems for NATO, exploits flaws in the human nervous system by exposing people to images of violence. This film positions itself as post-consumerist horror, in which television exists to change the nature of humanity by melding with it. There is no factory, no real product. Viewer research is the product, and exposure to this non-product is eventually fatal.

Videodrome connects people to the irreality of televised discourse and turns that experience into a new organ in the body, part of "the new flesh," just as "television is part of the eye." The Videodrome signal is a form of fascism that can be consumed at trade shows, on TV, through VR helmets—anywhere a signal can be broadcast. It somehow works best through images of realistic "torture and murder," with "no plot, no characters." As in many of these films, including *They Live* and *Street Trash*, the first victims are the homeless, who in *Videodrome* are the subjects of experimentation at "the Cathode Ray Mission," a church where they watch TV in makeshift cubicles for hours, so they can "patch back into the world's mixing board."

THIS CONNECTION TO THE LIVES of winos links many films about the horror of consumption to a harrowing 1956 documentary on alcoholism, *On the Bowery*, while the alignment of surrealism and poverty connects them to Luis Buñuel's neo(sur)realist *Los Olvidados* (1950). *Videodrome* was a McLuhanesque transition from a cinema that abhorred consumerism and TV into a new kind of horror in the 1990s and 2000s. "Body horror" replaced the analysis of consumption, substituting objectification and self-loathing for mind control and institutional power. Moving abjection from external to internal, body horror maintained the gore but moved the emphasis, made it more passive. Before that, as one of the characters says in *Dawn of the Dead*, they were "working on the whole phenomenon from the point of view of a viral disease."

Today, brick-and-mortar retail and broadcast television are becoming things of the past. Internet shopping and prestige TV on streaming services have sucked consumers into the realm of the digital, fooling them into thinking they have escaped the regime of the hidden persuaders who turn them into zombie shoppers and other kinds of ghouls. A recent essay called "Dead Mall Dream" by the music writer Chris Richards eulogized the mall for the Covid era. Richards returns to the mall of his youth, Marley's Station in Glen Burnie, Maryland, after he dreams he has visited it one night. The mall is closed because of the pandemic, its parking lot empty except for delivery trucks ominously coming and going from an open section of the building that's now an Amazon warehouse. When Richards gets home he theorizes, perhaps prompted by the mall's ghostly Dickensian name, that "Whenever people think they're seeing ghosts, what if they're actually seeing the spirits of living people who happen to be dreaming about that particular physical location?"

Indeed, maybe today's housebound shoppers, instead of taking instructions from TV, are using their computers to will themselves into the now-empty spaces they know from our collective past. Maybe now, as a character muses in *Dawn of the Dead* about the zombie shoppers, they are relying on "memory, instinct, what they used to do."

"This was an important place in their lives," a place that in Romero's film referred to the mall but now also means the cinema itself. In their heyday, malls and cineplexes were often joined together in one place. Cinema was already depicting the mall to eulogize mankind by mocking a form of sub-humanity that had lost itself to buying things it didn't need. A new era of insomniac zombie shopping online is now here, and with it a new kind of consumerist horror. It is situated outside the old spaces of consumerism, and outside television, too.

This era is just as alienated, but even lonelier, having internalized consumerism through ever-smaller screens. Special sunglasses won't expose the truth of this new condition. Just another blank surface, now they will only reflect the tiny new screens back into their lenses.

SLIME REGAINED

BARRY SONNENFELD

AT THE END OF MAY 2011 I WAS STANDING AT THE CORNER OF UNION AND Court Streets in Brooklyn with a man in his late seventies named Bobby Russo, who was born in the apartment where I live. Bobby and I were stopped there because the street was blocked off so that Columbia Pictures could shoot *Men in Black 3*, a sci-fi action-comedy starring Will Smith and Tommy Lee Jones, directed by Barry Sonnenfeld.

The street had been dressed to look like it might have in 1969, with Peter Max–style advertising in place of the usual signs outside bodegas. As we watched a scene featuring vintage cars and a bus being filmed with an elaborate camera rig, Bobby turned to me and said, "You see all this and you understand how they spend one million, two million dollars on a picture."

In fact the total production budget of *Men in Black 3* was $250 million. Columbia spared no expense to make it. That spring, Will Smith's pair of fifty-three-foot-long, pop-out, two-story trailers—which housed a full-size kitchen, a bedroom, a lounge bar, a screening room, an office, a meeting room, and a full gym—had been rousing the ire of New Yorkers. It wasn't just the amount of parking the trailers took up in the neighborhoods where the film was being shot. It was also the smells emanating from them when their bathrooms were emptied by Teamsters. Those trailers cost the production of

Men in Black 3 close to a million dollars to rent, maintain, and staff. That didn't matter. When it came out in 2012, *Men in Black 3* made $625 million worldwide in first run, of which Will Smith pocketed $100 million himself. Critics called the movie "amiable" and "reasonably entertaining."

While Bobby and I watched the vintage cars slide by, he told me that in the very cold winter of 1954 he had witnessed another movie being shot in our neighborhood, *On the Waterfront*, with Marlon Brando. The total budget for Elia Kazan's classic was $910,000, including Brando's salary. The cinematic journey of my neighborhood as a shooting location, from *On the Waterfront* to *Men in Black 3*, has encompassed the span of Bobby Russo's life, along with the history of Hollywood filmmaking from black-and-white neorealist drama to huge-budget action spectacle—from movies about the kind of people who had lived here and worked as longshoremen unloading ships, to movies about aliens from outer space. If Sonnenfeld's *Men in Black* movies began as contemporary allegories about immigrants in New York, in the end they became stories obsessed with the past, filmed by armies occupying gentrified neighborhoods.

IN *BARRY SONNENFELD, CALL YOUR MOTHER*, Sonnenfeld's recent autobiography, there is another connection between *On the Waterfront* and *Men in Black 3*. Roberta Hodes, who was the script supervisor on Kazan's movie with Marlon Brando, was one of Sonnenfeld's film professors at NYU about twenty years later, in the 1970s. Sonnenfeld is unkind to her, as he is to almost every older woman we meet in his book, starting with its costar, his mother. He calls Hodes vindictive, frustrated, and eager to imply that she'd had an affair with Brando while they were making *On the Waterfront*, which began shooting the year Sonnenfeld was born. Hodes was unimpressed with the fledgling efforts of Sonnenfeld and his film-school classmates—who included Spike Lee, Susan Seidelman, and Jim Jarmusch—barking at them, with a cigarette pasted to her lower lip, "What is this? A comedy? . . . Who cares about these people? Have any of you jerks led a life?"

Sonnenfeld's book succeeds in proving that he has led one, and that it has in fact been a comedy. *Barry Sonnenfeld, Call Your Mother* is a tale of Jewish family dysfunction in the tradition of Neil Simon and Philip Roth (in that order), with a self-involved narrator who, despite his mother's best efforts to pulverize his psyche, finds himself a great and unexpected success. The book begins at a Jimi Hendrix concert in Madison Square Garden and winds its way through Sonnenfeld's eventful life, pausing now and then on his deck in Telluride, Colorado, so he can sip a martini, surrounded by his large, happy family. Sonnenfeld views all of it through the neuroticized lens of baby-boomer privilege, which distorts his blemishes, in a flattering way.

It's a wide-angle lens, in other words, the kind Sonnenfeld brought to the movies he filmed as the Coen brothers' first cinematographer, and then the ones he shot for the ex-spouses Penny Marshall and Rob Reiner, before becoming a director himself. That lens, the 21mm, was his whole secret, the post-blockbuster indie innovation that made his career. "I have always framed the images I photograph with very wide-angle lenses and dead-center framing," Sonnenfeld explains more than once in his book. "I could be as close as five feet away from someone and yet see most of their body and with just a three-foot push in on the dolly be in an extreme close-up."

His other moment of truth came to him, in gimmick form, almost at the same time. It happened in an editing room, after he had shot the now-famous bar-top tracking sequence in the Coens' first film, *Blood Simple* (1984), with its infamous camera-hop over a passed-out boozehound. This simple bump over a drunk was a shock to viewers when the film came out. Initially, Joel and Ethan Coen wanted to cut it, worried it was "too self-conscious." The man who shot it convinced them otherwise. Laughing at their concerns, Sonnenfeld pointed out to them that their whole film was "nothing *but* self-conscious shots." The brothers, already their own editors, left it in, creating a whole school of hyper-self-aware postmodern cinema that has delighted and/or annoyed moviegoers for close to forty years.

Sonnenfeld continued in this style as a director in the 1990s, applying it to his *Addams Family* and *Men in Black* movies, Hollywood franchise films he oomphed with arty 1980s-style New York energy for a younger generation of viewers already too sophisticated for Spielberg and Lucas. His main competition in this field, narrow thematically but big at the box office, was Tim Burton, whose West Coast gothic sensibility lacked Sonnenfeld's pizzazz and devil-may-care goofiness.

Raul Julia and Christina Ricci—as Gomez Addams and his daughter, Wednesday—inhabit that energy in Sonnenfeld's films, perhaps even more than the toned-down and cool Will Smith and Tommy Lee Jones. Where Julia is deranged and full of joie de vivre, Ricci is as serious as an undiagnosable illness. Only she and Sonnenfeld could have brought to life the monstrous grammar-school and day-camp plays in the two *Addams Family* movies, in which Ricci's Wednesday obliterates her classmates, using Grand Guignol and arson in the service of anticolonial history. It is no wonder children raised on those films grew up to tear down statues and to despise any fathers less entertaining, understanding, and faithful than Julia's Gomez.

SONNENFELD'S PARENTS, IT SEEMS, were as grotesque and negligent as the Addamses, but with none of their romance or charm. If Angelica Huston's Morticia is too spectral a presence in the *Addams Family* movies, Sonnenfeld's own mother, Kelly, is an ever-present lady ogre in his book, oppressing young Barry with her stinky breath, her unfeminine looks, and her incessant demands that he not stray from her side—unless she leaves him to be babysat by her cousin Mike, a pedophile who eventually tried to molest him. "Back then child molesting didn't have the stigma it has now," Kelly explains.

Like the mother in Woody Allen's *Oedipus Wrecks*, Kelly hovers over Sonnenfeld's New York skyline, blotting out the son. She was even a teacher at the public school he attended. Sonnenfeld is like Spalding Gray in the monologue film *And Everything Is Going Fine*, in which Gray says one of his great psychological epiphanies was realizing he'd dated only his mother until he was 23 years old. Perhaps not unrelatedly, Sonnenfeld took baths in a bathing suit until he was in high school "in order not to see [himself] entirely naked."

In revenge, Kelly is dragged through this book by her hair. When not reminding us of the liquor bottles she would hide around their Washington Heights apartment, Sonnenfeld brings up his mother's resemblance to the stocky, loud character actor Vincent Gardenia, to George Washington, and to the film critic Roger Ebert. He goaded both David Letterman and Billy Crystal into mocking her looks in public. Crystal, meeting Kelly on the set of *When Harry Met Sally*, informs Sonnenfeld that his mother is a lesbian. Sonnenfeld once slammed the door of a Pontiac on her leg.

In this psychodrama, it may come as no surprise that Sonnenfeld married a woman several years older than him, one who also worked for his first boss. Susan Ringo, called Sweetie, a Texas beauty queen, was married to the photographer and cameraman Elliott Erwitt when Sonnenfeld met her. He worked for Erwitt for about ten years while getting to know his future spouse. As his friendship with Sweetie progressed, Erwitt began to mockingly refer to Sonnenfeld as "Susan's hairdresser." Erwitt seems to have been more angry and jealous about *Blood Simple*'s success—reviews mentioned its cinematographer by name—than he was about losing his wife.

MOST OF SONNENFELD'S BOSSES were similarly cruel. After Penny Marshall's *Big* became a massive success, due in no small part to his cinematography, Marshall told Sonnenfeld, "I never thought you were a good cameraman. But you picked a good film stock"—surely one of the meanest, dumbest, and funniest things a director has ever said to a cinematographer. In turn, Sonnenfeld points out that Marshall could not start a day's work until she'd had "a dozen White

Castle hamburgers and a carton of Marlboros" delivered to her on set. The Coens, however, a pair of matched obsessives who treated Sonnenfeld as a younger brother, emerge fairly unbruised. They shared Sonnenfeld's sense of humor and invented new movie-production terms with him, such as "Clinkscales," the "Larry Kasdan Panty Insert," "giving someone a cake," and "Greenberging"—readers interested in definitions can consult the book. The Coens were equally hapless, early on. While making *Raising Arizona* in Scottsdale, Joel got a ticket for driving too slow.

Will Smith once told Sonnenfeld he wanted to take him to public schools in Philadelphia to give kids hope—if this guy could make it big as a Hollywood director, anyone could succeed in life. The book's most abject incident permeates Sonnenfeld's work, and watching Sonnenfeld's movies in order, it also comes to explain a lot about Hollywood blockbuster filmmaking, and about America in the 21st century. Early in his career, before *Blood Simple*, Sonnenfeld worked as a cameraman on porn films. During one particularly arduous and lengthy shoot, an actress lost control of her bowels and shit all over him while he was filming her from below, using his other favorite lens, the ultra-wide-angle 10mm. It happened on his birthday, which happens to be April 1, April Fools' Day.

Sonnenfeld's chapter on his porn period is presented as hilarious and traumatic. It is also his birth scene, his origin story that explains so much about his life and work. He extricated himself from this placenta of diarrhea to become a top-notch director of photography, but he never mentions that a river of fundament runs through his solo work. The way the G-men played by Smith and Tommy Lee Jones are slimed by aliens again and again in the *Men in Black* movies, shot with the same lenses, replicates this primordial scene of viscous secretion in pursuit of a paycheck.

This reaches its apotheosis in Sonnenfeld's late-period movie *RV*, in which the family man played by Robin Williams unleashes a literal geyser of shit at a desert trailer park while he is trying to repair his huge camper's waste-removal system. I watched *RV* after

I read Sonnenfeld's book, and I could not help being reminded of the porn incident. Seeing *RV* also reminded me it was a film that came out at the height of the war in Iraq, in April of 2006. Recreational vehicles like the one in the movie get about four miles a gallon, and the fecal fountain in the movie, explicitly compared to an oil strike, in retrospect seemed like a sick reminder of how Middle Eastern oil still supports our way of life, which includes blockbuster movies made for the whole family. Look at them too closely and you can see what they're coated with. In *RV*, Williams's dad character keeps telling his family, "I have to get to that meeting or I lose my job and we lose a lifestyle."

The erasure of memory becomes a theme in Sonnenfeld's films, with various characters forced to forget traumatic incidents that happened to them during slimy alien encounters. In the second *Men in Black* movie, released the summer after 9/11, the Statue of Liberty becomes a monumental alien device that "neuralyzes" the populace, making them forget aliens live among us. Sonnenfeld describes a prank he plays on Will Smith in which he hides a threatening, mewling note inside a package of Tucks Medicated Comfort Pads, a product both men evidently prefer to regular toilet paper. This is something no one needed to know and that I wish I could be neuralyzed into forgetting I read.

SONNENFELD'S MOST BELOVED FILM may be *Get Shorty*, a 1995 Elmore Leonard adaptation starring John Travolta. The film deals explicitly in memory, specifically cinematic memory. The reason Chili Palmer, the loan shark played by Travolta, can succeed in Hollywood is because he is a classic-movie buff and has a better understanding of screenplay structure and plot devices than the lowlifes he's shaking down. One of them, a B-movie producer played by Gene Hackman, is the auteur of a movie called *Slime Creatures 3*.

Sonnenfeld tells a number of funny stories about the making of *Get Shorty*, involving various levels of getting slimed. In one, Warren Beatty, interested in the lead role, drags Sonnenfeld from New York to the Hotel Bel-Air just to ask him, "Why would someone who looks like me be so far down the mob pecking order at the beginning of the movie?"

The two men ponder this question in the Bel-Air's restaurant before Sonnenfeld slips out and goes back home. Later, he meets John Travolta in the restaurant at the Scientology Celebrity Centre in Los Angeles, a three-hundred-table ballroom where, at the only other table with diners, sits Luciano Pavarotti. Sonnenfeld, Danny DeVito, and screenwriter Scott Frank try to convince Travolta to take the excellent lead role in *Get Shorty*, but they get nowhere. Travolta seems not to understand the screenplay, and passes on the film. Later, Quentin Tarantino explains it to him and he says yes. At another restaurant he meets a waitstaff still traumatized by a visit from Robin Williams twelve years before. Sonnenfeld spends a lot of time in restaurants, and carries in his wallet a laminated photo of a steak to show how he wants it done.

He gave himself willingly to the Hollywood blockbuster, and now that the Hollywood blockbuster is becoming historical, like the Pyramids, it is interesting to note the differences between him and the Coen brothers, whose films his sometimes superficially resemble. Sonnenfeld makes it a point in the book to mention, more than once, that unlike the Coens, and unlike Chili Palmer, he is not a film buff. Sonnenfeld scaled the heights of Hollywood success, even surviving the failure of 1999's *Wild Wild West*, the reboot starring Will Smith that was, at the time, the most expensive film ever made, and which flopped with critics and audiences. But since *Men in Black 3*, his career as a film director has sputtered. His last film, 2016's *Nine Lives*, a talking-cat movie starring Kevin Spacey, was a French-Chinese coproduction. The Coens, meanwhile, have made less expensive, more ambitious films year after year, with other cinematographers. Sonnenfeld told Joel Coen he was writing his autobiography, and Coen told him to call it *Asleep at the Eyepiece*.

IN THREE YEARS WE CAN QUIT CHICKEN SEXING

OSCAR MOVIES 2021

Another Round

If you can accept Mads Mikkelsen as a depressed high school history teacher in the suburbs, maybe you will also believe that his beautiful doctor wife (Maria Bonnevie) would take him back after he makes drinking on the job the guiding principle of his life. Thomas Vinterberg's *Another Round* is a semi-Dogme film called *Druk* in Danish, which means "binge drinking," not "drunk." I would rather see a film called *Binge Drinking* than *Another Round*, but I guess the film's US distributor thought binge drinking had negative connotations. In Denmark, as in much of the world, it's just a way of life.

Danes, we learn, were once Vikings, ancient chieftains who didn't have to teach high school kids about Hitler (teetotaler), Franklin Delano Roosevelt (martini lover), and Winston Churchill (full-on degenerate boozebag). The point is, we know who won World War II. After this lesson, Mads and three of his teacher colleagues dance to "Cissy Strut," a step on their way to "the ultimate catharsis, total oblivion," something that often comes to Europeans when they listen to music from America by Black people. Later, in fact at the end of the movie, after a funeral and after his students graduate, Mads breaks into an exuberant drunken dance performance on a pier.

Ending films with dance scenes has not been a new or surprising idea for a while but, you know, now is the time in the movie when we dance.

Borat Subsequent Moviefilm

Agitprop that doesn't convince, comedy that isn't very funny, *Borat Subsequent Moviefilm* is notable for introducing the world to Maria Bakalova, the film's Cinderella, a young Bulgarian actress who Sacha Baron Cohen locks in a cage and has perform a crazy dance at a debutante ball that involves exposing herself during menstruation. He also puts her alone in a hotel bedroom with Rudolph Giuliani, "America's Mayor"—the personal lawyer to Donald Trump and a man who once held a press conference in the parking lot of a landscaping company in Philadelphia by mistake. Giuliani, a total lying mess as usual, a pathetic weirdie whose brain is long gone, lies back on a bed in Bakalova's presence to adjust whatever's in his pants, then skedaddles when he realizes something ain't right. Because of that one moment, the main reviewer in the *New York Times* called *Borat Subsequent Moviefilm* the best film of 2020, an instant credibility killer that I hope haunts him for years.

The Father

Anthony Hopkins, unlike Rudy Giuliani, has found a way to bring dementia to a new level of flawlessness. He runs the gamut from cantankerous, insistent patriarch who is obviously confused and wrong to mewling, needy, infantile shell of his former self. Presented by Florian Zeller, a first-time director known (not to me) as a playwright and novelist in France, *The Father* unloads a lot of temporal tricks that involve unexpected cuts in its apartment set, so that we, like Hopkins, are confused as to what time it is and where we are. The film's actors, including Olivia Colman, achieve the kind of acting perfection that is so good it makes movies bad. The effort here is so apparent, and yet so fully achieved, that the film becomes a total virtuosic work of art, so that anyone can recognize it as such and then move on.

The Father has a very precise Resnais quality. But it excises all humanity from a story that is at the same time aiming for the ultra-human, the sickly relatable, and the tragic-but-ordinary. That's because acting is both a special effect and the reason for the existence of this scenario about memory and family. At the same time, almost in another reality, the reality of dementia, the film is a batty chamber piece about a man who doesn't remember where he put his watch. He mentions it again and again because he's old and running out of metaphors.

Sound of Metal

In the first half of Darius Marder's *Sound of Metal*, a rock drummer, Ruben (Riz Ahmed), on tour with the two-person noise band he's in with his guitarist girlfriend, Lou (Olivia Cooke), realizes he has gone deaf. He rebels against his new condition and tries to continue the tour, but can't. Then eyebrow-less Lou leaves him to a rehab facility that helps recovering addicts cope with hearing loss.

This bucolic grouping of New England farmhouse dorms and schoolrooms is run by a deaf Vietnam vet played by Paul Raci, who in real life is not deaf but may be the wrinkle-faced hound dog he is in this film. His performance, along with the deaf actress Lauren Ridloff's, makes *Sound of Metal* work, placing it beyond Ruben's individual condition and his harsh reactions to it with Lou, where we saw the literalization of the way men talk and yell but do not hear.

Marder glides the film into a loping turn in its last third, after Ruben flees to Belgium to reclaim Lou, now revealed as the rich-girl daughter of a famous songwriter. This Belgian tunesmith is played by Mathieu Amalric, a great star actor who suddenly appears out of nowhere, the opposite of Paul Raci in many ways, yet somehow endearing on the same level. In this part of the movie we learn, inadvertently, that deafness is a class position and that class mobility is not possible. We'd learned, earlier in the film, that health insurance in the United States does not cover surgery for hearing problems. That is what I choose to take away from this movie—a shocking reveal equal to finding out Lou was a dilettante fleeing daddy issues by pounding a guitar back in the USA.

The White Tiger

A tale of capitalism run amok, *The White Tiger* is too long, too talky, has too much music in it, too many touristy shots of India that pad the film inexcusably, too much extraneous narration, smells of Netflix as much as Delhi, and is Ramin Bahrani's best film to date. Finally, after years of austere, punishing neorealism in New York and the American South, he has found his voice as a pop maximalist man of the people on the other side of the world. All it took to get him there was Priyanka Chopra Jonas, an emissary from the beau monde if ever there was one, here playing a woman from Jackson Heights who has married into a wealthy, corrupt family in India. Her character in this movie is Bahrani's last link to the Willets Point of *Chop Shop*.

Because it's the adaptation of a novel, this rags-to-riches story about escaping the caste system has a shameless literary framing device—the protagonist, Balram (Adarsh Gourav), is reading aloud a letter he is writing to Wen Jiabao, premier of China at the time the action takes place. Fortunately Balram's story is absorbing enough to make you forget this epistolary nonsense. His education in Indian hyper-capitalism takes over the film, especially after the sleazy family he works for as a chauffeur forces him to take the fall when his boss's wife (Chopra) kills a pedestrian in a hit-and-run.

As an Indian *Parasite* that should have come out in 2019, the film succeeds without any of Bong Joon ho's gift for surprise, instead relying on Scorsesean drive and a strict literalism. When a white tiger appears, it's in CGI, like the zoo animals in *Mank*, fake as hell and unnecessary, but in this case the film wouldn't be complete without it. Like the letter to Wen, I wish it wasn't there, but I can't just wish these things away, same as with capitalism.

Balram strives for escape, but his only recourse is success. He puts what he's learned from the bourgeoisie to good use because he knows you can get away with killing people on lonely roads at night. Rajkummar Rao, as Balram's boss, a rich boy and a liberal modernizer who wants to do good in the world as long as it doesn't cost him anything, is excellent in the most thankless role of the year. When he meets his fate at the wrong end of a broken bottle of Johnnie Walker Blue, we learn *The White Tiger*'s main lesson: kill your masters with no guilt but don't forget to turn misfortune into a fleet of slick limos.

Hillbilly Elegy

This rote filmization of J. D. Vance's bootstraps memoir, by Ron Howard, does not have things straight. You can either worry about what everybody at Yale Law thinks of you while you are being taught by the Tiger Mom and meeting people like Brett Kavanaugh and sucking up to power, or you can demand that people there respect your smart, dope-addict mom (Amy Adams) and your tough, cranky grandma (Glenn Close) when you get dewy-eyed about them in conversation at fancy banquets. Another thing about this movie is that no hillbillies were harmed or even elegized in making it. They are barely even depicted. Amy Adams, once an unerring actor who appeared in good movies, here melds with Bev, the character she plays, because both continue to make self-defeating choices for reasons no one can understand. *Hillbilly Elegy* is whiny and teary, and if J. D. Vance runs his inevitable Senate campaign the same way, it will be a more enjoyable spectacle than this film.

Nomadland

On the one hand, I'm glad *Nomadland* exists, because it exposes the precarity under which so many Americans live, whether they are vandwellers, migrant workers, retirees, or Amazon employees at other studios. On the other hand, the film is a beautiful valentine to Amazon's CamperForce and the warehouses in which the 'Force works. The main character, Fern (Frances McDormand), decides she wants to live a life of freedom even though it's clear that it's not a decision she has really made on her own, nor is it one that most out-of-work, homeless 63-year-old women would make on their own. *Nomadland* wants to honor her decision and let her completely own it, but . . . is that my door buzzer? Wait a second, my Searchlight Pictures giant crate of *Nomadland* promotional food items has arrived.

God, look at this stuff. Stuff that I, as the editor of a website focusing on comic book movies, totally deserve to get, and that, as I eat it, will not influence my coverage of *Nomadland* in any way. Nor will it remind me that millions of people in the United States do not have enough to eat and don't have access to organic food, which they couldn't afford anyway. Do you know how much a wheel of Cowgirl Creamery Mt. Tam cheese costs? Neither do I, because my comic-book-movie-covering website gets half a billion views a year, so I get this awesome shit for free.

OK, so *Nomadland* isn't a superhero movie, but . . . hold on. These dill pickles come already sliced? I appreciate that, let me tell you. I don't want to do any work like Fern has to do in the movie. Did you see those giant-ass rutabagas rocketing out of that chute? At dusk? No thanks.

So as I was saying, on the one hand, *Nomadland* is a beautiful work of art by one of our great new auteurs, Chloé Zhao, in which she even lets Frances McDormand recite some Shakespeare. And on the other, I don't know, it's pretty good and is that two canisters of organic wine?

That's going to help wash down this banana bread, not to mention this trail mix and that salami. Hey, are those cookies, for later? The organic figs, those I'm going to donate to a food pantry along with the grapes, cherry tomatoes, apricots, cucumbers, purple carrots, and mandarin oranges. Even though I already ate some of the grapes.

Second thought, I should eat the figs, too. And the oranges. They're good for me. What I'm trying to say is: *Nomadland*, important movie, should win awards, made by people who care. And I want to thank Searchlight Pictures, a division of the Walt Disney Company, for turning my say-so into a pie-eating contest.

Minari

This miracle of a film, about a Korean family that moves to Arkansas in the early 1980s to start their own farm, is small in scope but deserves to be seen on a big screen, all in one sitting. *Minari* has a lot of non-flashy, coiled-up power that builds to something bigger than it seems. Its conclusions about the American dream, and what it does to relationships, are strong stuff.

On the production line at a poultry farm, Jacob Yi (Steven Yeun) tells his wife, Monica (Han Ye-ri), that if things go well, "in three years we can quit chicken sexing" and devote their time to working their own land while they raise their two kids. Jacob adjusts to his grueling schedule, and to the United States in general, better than Monica. When she gets the chance to bring her mother (Youn Yuh-jung) over from Korea, Jacob balks but gives in for the sake of domestic harmony. Youn, a star in Korea who's been in a few Hong

Sangsoo films, plays the mother-in-law as a kind of terror, who both scares the Yis' Mountain Dew–loving children and gets them out of their shells.

Lee Isaac Chung directs the film in widescreen, a choice that makes sense here, given the land and the tornadoes, more than it did in the apartment in *The Father.* The elemental qualities of the film are the whole story. Earth, water, and fire equate to various states of strength and weakness or success and failure in *Minari,* which unfolds in what Monica calls "this hillbilly place" and which, unlike some other films, is able to take life there seriously enough not to just turn it into hysterical nonsense or pretty pictures of decay.

Judas and the Black Messiah

I don't trust movies that mention the Academy Awards in their dialogue. It's a little overweening, and it's thirsty. How is it that both movies from last year that involve the Black Panthers mention the Academy Awards, and both are nominated for Oscars?

In Shaka King's *Judas and the Black Messiah,* an FBI agent (Jesse Plemons) says about a snitch (LaKeith Stanfield), "Either this guy deserves an Academy Award, or he really believes this shit." He's saying it to Stanfield himself about the character he's playing, and Stanfield has been nominated for an Oscar. So has Daniel Kaluuya, who plays Fred Hampton.

In *The Trial of the Chicago 7,* Noah Robbins, playing Lee Weiner, gets to say "This is the Academy Awards of protests, and as far as I'm concerned it's an honor just to be nominated." Robbins, however, wasn't nominated. He plays one of the two least nominate-able of the Chicago Seven. But the film did get six Oscar nominations, which kind of works out to one for each of the other defendants.

After I saw *Judas and the Black Messiah,* I watched three clips of the real Fred Hampton on YouTube. Kaluuya is nothing like him. Actors will disagree, but I believe that if you are playing someone who exists in the historical record on film or video, you have some obligation to play that person as he existed, not just his ideals. If you're playing Jesus Christ or Judas Iscariot, you have a lot of leeway. Nobody who knew those guys is going to pop up and say, "uhn-uh, no way." For roles based on people we can observe on film, there has to be—as anathema as it may be for practitioners of the craft—some aspect of doing an impression.

Kaluuya is rousing as Hampton, for sure, but he is playing him so that even if your grandma is sitting in Row ZZ she will still get it drilled into her head that political power grows out of the barrel of a gun. Stanfield, though, is subtle, in control, doesn't veer from his usual brilliance, and still creates an accurate portrayal of William O'Neal, who we also see in the film from real life, in clips from a documentary made just before his suicide in 1990. This is the difference between these two types of acting. One is aimed at the balcony, the other designed for the screen.

One Night in Miami

The actor who plays Malcolm X in Regina King's *One Night in Miami* is doing an impression, but it's an impression of the wrong person. Kingsley Ben-Adir's Malcolm X sounds a lot like Barack Obama. There's a scene in this movie in which Malcolm forces Sam Cooke to listen to a Bob Dylan record. Maybe my imagination is constrained, but I just can't picture Malcolm X doing that. Later he lectures Cooke, Muhammad Ali, and Jim Brown on the meaning of the Beatles. And despite this scene and all its talk and explanation, I still cannot imagine the Malcolm X of February, 1964, bothering to have any thoughts on the Beatles beyond annoyance when "I Want to Hold Your Hand" comes on the radio. But I can easily imagine Barack Obama, king of the yearly music playlist, pontificating about it at length.

As Cooke, Ali, and Brown, Leslie Odom Jr., Eli Goree, and Aldis Hodge are all in the pocket. It's Hodge, though, who brings the most to his character while still recognizably playing Jim Brown. The scene where Brown visits a rich white benefactor and football fan (Beau Bridges) back home in Georgia seems like it was designed to open up the play the film is based on. It's an early scene in *One Night in Miami*, and it depicts casual, stinging racism in a startling way. But it sets up a different movie than this one.

Ma Rainey's Black Bottom

Malcolm X and Sam Cooke went theatrically on and on about how white musicians profit from Black musical innovation. *Ma Rainey's Black Bottom*, based on August Wilson's 1984 play about the state of jazz and the blues in 1927 Chicago, embodies the process in storybook fashion—a stark, deadly storybook, but an illustrated tale nonetheless. Viola Davis turns Ma Rainey into one of the great aging divas in American cinema, her face a mask that makes her a star attraction and protects her from white exploitation. With silver teeth, spidery false eyelashes, plucked eyebrows, heavy rouge, and a penumbra of smoky luminescent kohl that makes her look like she's been punched in both eyes, she presents herself on stage and in the recording studio with the highest of drama, grandiloquent but low-down and annoyed. Even the way she drinks a bottle of Coke is played for maximum fuck you.

The late Chadwick Boseman, as Levee, a trumpet player and composer, becomes the focus of Ma's annoyance. Boseman vamps around her, more than credible with his horn, a genius showboat. But when he pounds on the door of life and kicks it open, it leads to a coffin-like airshaft. If Ma's lesson is that life is difficult, plodding, a rip-off, and unfair, Levee's lesson is more explicitly spelled out: "Death will kick your ass and make you wish you never been born." Levee's life ends after a spasm of unforgivable violence that he directs at a fellow musician. Boseman's last performance is a marvel of enthusiasm and detailed invention, with Levee's final outburst the polar opposite of this actor's generosity. Though he worked hard for it, stardom always seemed thrust on Boseman, something extraneous and beside the point of what he was trying to do.

Mank

Gary Oldman is the opposite of Chadwick Boseman. Where Boseman is subtle and often unexpectedly buoyant, as if his acting decisions were sudden discoveries, Oldman is a showboat stuck in a canal. Whatever he finds himself in is too small. He doesn't appear in movies, he gets lodged in them.

David Fincher is not up to the task of propelling Oldman forward. In *Mank*, Fincher allows Oldman every leeway, to the point where his performance as Herman J. Mankiewicz, Hollywood screenwriter, alcoholic, and wit, creates a logjam. *Mank* is heavy and unmoving, with too much plot. The black-and-white 1930s and early 1940s Hollywood depicted here seems to be occurring inside a computer where Oldman is narrating a 1960s TV Christmas special—the voice he is doing is generated from somewhere, but can we ever know exactly where? Maybe it's Burgess Meredith?

Fincher resuscitates *Mank*'s historical inaccuracies—many of them leftovers from Pauline Kael disproven long ago—because they help him diagram our present era of fake news and streaming content. Yes, these flubs and inventions are an insult to Orson Welles, but that seems so minor to Fincher, who is doing the important work of demonstrating how images can be manipulated for political gain. Which is what *Citizen Kane* also did in 1941, in twelve fewer minutes.

The fake authenticity on display in *Mank* is a form of cutesiness. The black circles of fake projectionist cues are added to the upper right-hand corner of the screen every twenty minutes or so, just as they appeared when movies where shown on reels of 35mm film with a changeover between projectors about every two thousand feet.

Fincher, this master of digital technology, is obsessed with these cues, mentioning them prominently in the projectionist scenes in *Fight Club*. There's something fetishy about this. It's a fixation of his. The first place cues appear in *Mank* is fifteen and a half minutes in, during a scene in a writers room—which did not exist as such in 1930s Hollywood—that also features, equally dubiously, a topless stenographer. Furthermore, the cues appear as an actor says the word "cue" in the dialogue, and after a quarter has fallen to the floor, an old projectionist's trick to remember that a reel change was coming up. The cues also mimic the pasties the stenographer is wearing, which may be why she's in the scene.

Fincher also has an actress play the girl on the ferry that Mr. Bernstein (Everett Sloane) describes in *Citizen Kane*. The point of Bernstein's anecdote is that the girl exists only in his memory. She cannot be seen by the person Bernstein is talking with, or by anyone watching the film. Cinema, in a way, brings back the dead and restores memory. But Welles made a decision not to show that girl. Some things are beyond reach.

Not for Fincher, who insists that digital technology has special powers that allow him to praise film without using it, so that we can have cinema absent all the things that made it work. We can do away with the things we love and pretend they're still there by digitally adding effects that call them to mind. They are cues in yet another sense of the word. *Mank* also advocates for wealth redistribution without revolution and asks us to believe that the 33-year-old actress who plays Mank's wife has been married to him for twenty years.

The United States vs. Billie Holiday

Lee Daniels is an auteur trapped in an industry trying to do away with them, and it is his struggle that is often the most interesting thing in his movies. In *The United States vs. Billie Holiday*, the beauty of his images, the tone and feeling he sets up, and the people he casts are all at odds with the blunt writing in Suzan-Lori Parks's screenplay. It's almost like watching Terence Davies forced to make a movie from a script by Samuel Fuller. I'd like to say this antagonistic relationship between form and content reflects the struggle of Billie Holiday to bring beauty and truth into a hostile, racist world with her voice, her presence, and the lyrics to "Strange Fruit." But I can't ignore that there is a scene of Billie and Lester Young doing calisthenics in Billie's home office.

Tyler James Williams's Lester Young reflects a lack of interest on Daniels's part in the man who reinvented sax playing and who invented his own slang vocabulary so he could confuse and avoid white people. Andra Day's Billie Holiday, however, is intensely studied by Daniels and by cinematographer Andrew Dunn. Day meets the challenge of their scrutiny, creating a Holiday with a debilitating intensity and glamour, and with a sweet gravelly voice that is her own and also the original's. And it was impossible to predict the scene where she gets her ass tongued in silhouette, an encapsulation of Daniels's vision staged, inevitably, in a cheap motel room.

The Trial of the Chicago 7

The mediocrity of *The Trial of the Chicago 7* is its own form of tawdriness. The film is as useless as a cable-television special about the '60s, and has the same point: last-ditch nostalgia.

With the notable exceptions of Michael Keaton and John Carroll Lynch, who show up at key points in futile attempts to get things on track, everybody in this vapid history lesson is terrible. Especially Eddie Redmayne and Sacha Baron Cohen, who are horribly miscast as Tom Hayden and Abbie Hoffman. I do not know what the strange voice Baron Cohen is doing is supposed to be, but he does not sound like someone who has ever even seen Worcester, Massachusetts on a map. Whatever he has as a provocateur, Daniel Day-Lewis he is not. The Abbie Hoffman stand-up lecture routines he is forced to deliver are flat and unfunny. These clumsy attempts by writer-director Aaron Sorkin to re-narrate events in the film, events which are gone over again and again, threaten to make *The Trial of the Chicago 7* go on for twenty-one weeks like the real trial did in 1969 and 1970.

Redmayne is totally lost here, playing someone from Michigan who has to say the word "Chicago" far too many times. He looks like he's about to cry whenever he opens his mouth. Mark Rylance plays William Kunstler like a scarecrow on a broomstick being thrust up from the counsel table by a hippie protester. He wears a too-big suit and wig, like he's in disguise. Frank Langella's judge is bombastic, written to annoy and grate in his many, many senile outbursts from the bench. There is an odd phenomenon in American culture in which someone not very good at their job becomes known to everybody as its best practitioner. In his line of work, that person is Aaron Sorkin. *The Trial of the Chicago 7* is the worst film of the 21st century so far.

Pieces of a Woman

I thought that until I saw *Pieces of a Woman.* This film's back story is too hard to untangle, but evidently it is based on a play by married Hungarian writer-director team Kornél Mundruczó and Kata Wéber that was a hit in Warsaw. Somehow Martin Scorsese and Sam Levinson (*Malcolm & Marie*) ended up as executive producers of the film version, along with the eighteen other people credited as producers, and it became a Netflix movie.

That makes sense, because like Cuarón's *Roma* it features the death of a baby during a protracted birth scene, filmed in one long take. The baby's mother, played by Vanessa Kirby, required two dialogue coaches to sound American, and the film takes place, for some reason, in Boston, though it was shot in Montreal and I think also maybe in

Norway and Budapest. In addition to Kirby, *Pieces of a Woman* stars Shia LaBeouf and Benny Safdie as her husband and brother-in-law, and Ellen Burstyn as her mother, who is a Holocaust survivor.

For me, the highlight of this overbearing mess was an awkward scene in which LaBeouf and Safdie had to improvise a lengthy conversation about the White Stripes. The film ends, long after the death of the baby, with Kirby's character getting everything she wants and deserves from life. That part, because it was more embarrassing than the rest of the movie, was all done in either a crane shot or a drone shot, I couldn't tell which, under the end credits, in what appeared to be an apple orchard with a garage. Apples and seeds are a thing in this movie, but I don't want to go into it.

Promising Young Woman

A major feminist statement in the form of a pop movie that looks and acts like it was made the same year *Death Proof* came out, Emerald Fennell's *Promising Young Woman* takes place in Anywhere, USA, in a town referred to as "the city," which is so obviously Los Angeles I don't understand why Fennell bothered with this aesthetic abstraction.

The first half of the movie places Carey Mulligan in a series of dicey situations with predatory-yet-average young men who want to take advantage of her while she's pretending she's drunk. The dude played by Christopher Mintz-Plasse, for instance, is clearly no good because he reads David Foster Wallace novels and has a *Satyricon* poster on his wall.

What Mulligan's Cassandra is doing is practicing to take revenge on the frat boys who raped her best friend in college. The setup is novel and interesting, and it extends to punishing a college dean played by Connie Britton, and a girl from college who looked the other way, now a peppy wine enthusiast played by Alison Brie. It is not just a few amoral male slimeballs who are under attack here, but the entire system that allows young men to get away with rape.

In the end *Promising Young Woman* turns into the very old and very misogynist waking-up-in-bed-with-a-dead-hooker joke. Then the film and Mulligan's corpse get tossed around by male comedy actors, including Max Greenfield from *New Girl*, the Zooey Deschanel sitcom that also took place in LA and somehow survived on the air for seven seasons. These guys take over the film because Mulligan's character is, after all, dead.

She has her revenge from beyond the grave, but despite Fennell's clever plotting, Mulligan's absence lessens the film's impact. Those who did not see the plot twist involving Bo Burnham's nice-guy character coming down La Cienega Boulevard will hopefully see more movies one day, and also visit Los Angeles, but not necessarily just because they are posh British people trying to collect Oscars.

POSTCARD FROM HOME

JUNE 2021

EARLY IN THE PANDEMIC, SOON AFTER THE LOCKDOWN STARTED HERE IN New York, I decided I would only watch movies on my TV using Roku. For news I would go to my phone and laptop. It was important to me to keep these two spaces separate, to make a distinction between kinds of televisual experience. While it became clear that news was replacing cinema, at least for the time being, I still had to maintain my sanity. I did not want the Covid death count and the murder of George Floyd to come at me the same way movies did, through the flatscreen. And I wanted to maintain some semblance of the theatrical experience when watching movies while theaters were closed.

Though I hate to admit it, it was the apps of commercial entities the Criterion Channel, MUBI, and Tubi that kept me sane. And I read everything I could about the flu pandemic of 1918–1920 and watched three plague films: Roger Corman's *The Masque of the Red Death*, with Vincent Price; *The Seventh Seal*, with Max von Sydow, who died right as lockdown began (no cause of death was given), and *Death in Venice*, with Dirk Bogarde. I contend that if every American had watched those three films last March, things would have gone differently in this country. But try to get 330 million people to watch a Visconti film. They watched *Contagion* on Netflix instead, and look what happened.

A particular type of cinema has got me through this. One marked by being unassimilable into the regime of TV, that doesn't work well when cut into chunks, and makes little narrative sense when interrupted at regular intervals. This kind of film, that can't be divided into neat episodes of a half hour or an hour, it turns out, is often very long or very weird.

The first long film that opened my eyes to the form of viewing I was going to endure and thrive under for a year (and counting) was *Peterloo*, the Mike Leigh film about the Corn Laws of the 1810s. I'd read it was boring, but it was not the least bit boring, especially under the circumstances. It was deeply involving, and it changed my idea of time spent at home. Then, *La Flor*, over its fourteen (or was it fifteen?) hours, became an endless dream, a film that stretched out across a month, with those four actresses trading parts over the many days it took me to watch the whole thing.

I realized only films that had strong elements of insanity and an unpredictable sense of narrative drive would put me in the proper state for the long haul. Which ones would burn themselves into my skull was impossible to predict. These did that, however (in the order I saw them): Melville's *Two Men in Manhattan*, with its black-and-white existential Brooklyn, now denied to me; *Runaway Train*, relentless, crazed in its acting; *A Boring Afternoon*, the best short film ever made; *Carving Magic*, a Herschell Gordon Lewis industrial about serving meat at dinner parties; *The Night of Counting the Years*, the silence of the tomb amid thievery and corruption; *All My Good Countrymen*, communism as a haunted-rainbow Day-of-the-Dead miasma; Sara Driver's *You Are Not I*, a black-and-white American miniature from beyond the grave; *The Railway Children*, vivid socialist-bohemian utopia of British childhood, directed by an actor; *Bulworth*, a screwed-up satire of American politics and race relations, with absurd rhymes; *Malina*, Isabelle Huppert on fire in the closed, interior world of Bachmann-Jelinek; *Inferno*, Dario Argento's lunatic

New York gothic; *Queen of Diamonds,* a flat evocation of a deadened Las Vegas, starring the director's sister; and last, *The Forbidden Room,* in which Guy Maddin and company broke down narrative form into a paroxysm of stained-glass shards that mirrored my deteriorating consciousness.

THE BITTER WITH THE SOUR

BILLY WILDER

IN AUGUST 1945, THREE MONTHS AFTER ADOLF HITLER'S SUICIDE IN THE bunker and the Allied victory in Europe, the Hollywood film director Billy Wilder arrived in Berlin. Wilder's film *Double Indemnity*, that pinnacle of film noir, had come out the previous summer to great acclaim and box office success. *The Lost Weekend*, Wilder's next film, equally dark and also a future classic, was being readied for fall release at Paramount. Now Wilder had been enlisted by the US Office of War Information to return to the city he'd fled in 1933, when he was forced out of screenwriting because he was a Jew. The OWI wanted him to make and oversee films that would help "recivilize" the German population as they were de-Nazified by the Allies.

Double Indemnity had been shut out at the Academy Awards the previous March, in the first Oscars ceremony that was broadcast nationally. (It only took seventy minutes.) Wilder was annoyed that his film lost to *Going My Way*, which starred Bing Crosby as a priest, so he tripped the film's director, Leo McCarey, on his way to the podium to get his award. But that was just Hollywood clowning. Oscar or not, no one could deny that Billy Wilder was sitting on top of the world. Chased out by Hitler, he returned to Berlin with a conquering army, eleven years after arriving in America with only eleven dollars in his pocket.

Had an artist of Wilder's caliber ever been in a situation like that before? Certainly no film director had. Wilder's Hollywood mentor, Ernst Lubitsch, for whom he had cowritten *Ninotchka* in 1939, had last visited Berlin, his birthplace, in the winter of 1932. A key figure in the German cinema, Lubitsch had gone to Hollywood in the silent era, and went on to invent the romantic comedy and then the musical. He was also Jewish, famous in the film world since the 1910s, initially as an actor for his comic portrayals of cosmopolitan Jewish strivers, and therefore a special target for German anti-Semites. "Nothing good is going to happen here for a long time," Lubitsch told the local press about their country that December in 1932. "The sun shines every day in Hollywood," he added.

BILLY WILDER WAS BORN Samuel Wilder on June 22, 1906, in the Galician town of Sucha, now in Poland but then part of Austria-Hungary, a vast empire that ceased to exist when Wilder was 12 years old. His mother called him "Billie," because he was a rambunctious kid and she had seen Buffalo Bill's Wild West show during a brief period living in New York. In Hollywood, Wilder would modify his name to "Billy" with a *y* when he realized that Billie with an *ie* was considered a girl's name in the US, a fact that plays into his lifelong fascination, as a writer and director, with cross-dressing and gender roles.

Wilder's father was the manager of a string of railroad cafés and moved the family to Kraków to run a hotel, and from there to Vienna. He died when Wilder was 22. Wilder disliked school and by 18 he was writing for newspapers in Vienna, starting in the crossword puzzle department and working his way into movie reviews and feuilletons. He got his first job after writing to an Austrian paper asking to be their American correspondent. They laughed at that but Wilder showed up at their offices unannounced, he later claimed, and caught either the editor or the drama critic in flagrante with a secretary on the office couch, a very Wilderian situation that also echoes a 1914 German short, *The Pride of the Firm*, which Ernst Lubitsch appeared in but did not direct, and which Wilder had probably seen. *Why should I hire you?* the editor-or-critic supposedly asked Wilder. *Because I am a keen observer,* he said. He got the job.

Covering the American bandleader Paul Whiteman's 1926 tour of Europe for a Vienna newspaper, Wilder, a jazz fan, followed Whiteman and his musicians to Berlin, and stayed. There, he captured in print, for low pay, the fads and celebrities of the Weimar Republic in bloom. Wilder's prose improved under the guidance of Berlin newspapermen and cabaret sketch writers. He became a café-dwelling Berlin hipster who wore snap-brims to cover his red hair. Soon he started ghosting screenplays, then writing his own.

In 1929 he wrote *People on Sunday* (1930), a groundbreaking film of the *Neue Sachlichkeit* ("New Objectivity"), the style, or movement, that was replacing the German Expressionism of the 1920s defined by *The Cabinet of Dr. Caligari* (1920) and the films of F. W. Murnau and Fritz Lang. The New Objectivity favored sociological naturalism and a cold eye on real life, a kind of modernism in opposition to Expressionism's intense angularity and stark chiaroscuro, its psychology of horror and crime. Made in the capital of the German film world but away from the studios by a group that included future émigré directors Robert Siodmak, Edgar G. Ulmer, and Fred Zinnemann, *People on Sunday,* a Strassenfilm ("street film"), predicted Italian neorealism and the French New Wave.

The lessons of *People on Sunday* stayed with Wilder. He used a hidden camera on the streets of New York for *The Lost Weekend.* In *Sunset Boulevard* (1950), he ferried the darkness of the silent era into the noir of postwar Hollywood, making the film a *Neue Sachlichkeit* commentary on German Expressionism, on how one era looked to another, melting in the California sun.

WILDER'S MOTHER, HIS STEPFATHER, and his grandmother were all missing when Wilder got to Berlin at the end of World War II. He suspected that they had been shipped to concentration camps, though he did not know for sure. It was not until later that he was told that his stepfather and grandmother had been killed at Auschwitz in 1941 (evidence later proved that his stepfather died at the Belzec death camp and his grandmother in Kraków). Wilder never learned his mother's fate; in fact she was killed in the Kraków-Płaszów slave labor camp in 1943. In any case, Wilder had seen hours of abhorrent film footage from the camps, sent to London as Buchenwald, Bergen-Belsen, and Dachau were liberated by the Allies, watching in hope that he might spot one of his relatives. Working on that footage for the OWI, the same footage Alfred Hitchcock had assembled for the British into another documentary, *German Concentration Camps Factual Survey*, Wilder put together a twenty-two-minute film called *Death Mills*. It was his goal to make it mandatory viewing. He suggested that every German seeking a ration card should be required to watch it. "After all, it was only a short walk from any German city to the nearest concentration camp," as the film's narration has it. Now you can see *Death Mills* on YouTube, though not many people have watched it in the six years it's been up.

The summer of 1945 was hotter than usual in Berlin. Bodies were still buried in the rubble of the city and it stunk. As Wilder drove around in a jeep with American soldiers to interview his former colleagues from the German film industry, he could not believe the devastation the war had brought. The Eighth Air Force and the Red Army had devastated the Kurfürstendamm, Berlin's Broadway. The city of *People on Sunday* was destroyed.

Fifteen years before, Wilder had been sitting at cafés, writing films and interviewing celebrities for newspapers. One vaudeville performer he wrote about was Omikron, a novelty act billed as "the human gasometer." "He gulps in enough gas to send off a couple of people into the hereafter with some to spare. He uses this gas to light lamps, heat an iron, cook a fried egg. You wind up with a bitter taste in your mouth, but you're amazed by this fellow, and how!" Wilder raved in the May 10, 1927, edition of the *Berliner Börsen–Courier*. In 1945, people he had written about and worked for were sucking up to him. Those who stayed behind and did nothing when his name was removed from the credits of films he'd written were asking him to believe they had not been Nazis. The whole situation was tragic, horrible, and petty.

Of course it gave Wilder an idea for a movie. Two years later, he returned to Berlin to shoot *A Foreign Affair*, with Jean Arthur and Marlene Dietrich. Bankrolled by Hollywood, he was finally able to direct his own movie in the place his film career began. The difference was that now he had to move from street film to Trümmerfilm ("rubble film").

"WHO ELSE BUT WILDER would make a romantic comedy set in the post-war ruins of Berlin?" asks Joseph McBride, the prolific film historian, critic, and screenwriter whose weighty book, *Billy Wilder: Dancing on the Edge*, has just come out alongside two slimmer volumes of Wilderiana. Those are *Billy Wilder on Assignment: Dispatches from Weimar Berlin and Interwar Vienna*, a collection of Wilder's newspaper pieces edited by Noah Isenberg and translated by Shelley Frisch, and *Mr Wilder and Me*, a beautifully elegiac novel by Jonathan Coe, the author of the Brexit novel *Middle England* and books on Humphrey Bogart and James Stewart.

Coe's novel follows Wilder as he shoots *Fedora*, his troubled swan song to the cinema, a film he made on another return to Germany, in 1977. *Mr Wilder and Me* has not been published in the US. It should be. One of the best movie-set novels, it sticks closely to the facts but turns them into an elegant, melancholy reflection on Wilder's escape from Germany, his return to Berlin, and the troubled production of his late-career film maudit. All three books are excellent reminders of a German complaint published in the *Berliner Zeitung* when Wilder's breakneck cold war spoof *One, Two, Three* came out in 1961, right before the construction of the Berlin Wall: "What breaks our heart, Billy Wilder finds funny."

There have been many books on Billy Wilder published over the years, including Ed Sikov's excellent 1998 biography, *On Sunset Boulevard: The Life and Times of Billy Wilder*. These three new ones each add something vital. Though Leo A. Lensing, in the *Times Literary Supplement*, has noted that Isenberg's collection is missing important pieces, and that the book seems organized more for film buffs than scholarship, the opportunity to read Wilder's journalism in English is welcome.

Wilder also writes about figures he knew personally, not just celebrities of the day. The one-named writer Klabund got Wilder to report his first important piece, a multipart series on Wilder's experience as a taxi dancer in a hotel, working as a kind of Weimar gigolo. Klabund died young, of tuberculosis, in 1928. Wilder's piece on him, "Klabund Died a Year Ago," shows an unexpectedly tender side to the director of *Some Like It Hot*. This 1929 essay—a concise three pages, subtle, witty, mournful, dry—looks back on 1926 like it was an eon ago. Such is youth.

His piece on Erich von Stroheim is perceptive and resonant, especially for cinephiles. In it Wilder reminds the readers of a Berlin magazine in 1929 that Stroheim's *Greed* was "five years ahead of us." This stayed with Wilder—Stroheim, with his love of screen-crowding detail and sexual kink, is his other great influence. When he met him for the first time on the Paramount lot after casting Stroheim as the Nazi field marshal Rommel in *Five Graves to Cairo* in 1943, Wilder told the director-actor that he had been "ten years ahead of his time." "Twenty," Stroheim replied, thereby increasing Wilder's original assessment by a factor of four.

What's particularly impressive, even slightly eerie, is how many times this young film buff and Americanophile wrote about people he would later work with in Hollywood. Of course Wilder could not have known that someday, in California, he would write screenplays for Lubitsch and employ Stroheim and Gloria Swanson as actors in his own films. In Vienna and Berlin, he was a young nobody filing stories on short deadlines. Wilder's secret was that he never forgot anything. McBride notices that hand gestures Wilder had witnessed in films he wrote about and even in *Death Mills* show up in his own movies, years later.

McBride met and interviewed Wilder several times before Wilder's death in 2002. That adds depth and insight to his book, and McBride doesn't let us forget they met. At this point in McBride's long career, however, he's earned this kind of autobiographical tallying-up. He's written, cowritten, or edited more than twenty books, not just on film, also memoir and books on baseball and the assassination of John F. Kennedy. He had a stint at *Daily Variety* as their film critic and he cowrote the screenplay for *Rock 'n' Roll High School* (1979), starring the Ramones. His other accomplishments include acting in Orson Welles's *The Other Side of the Wind* (2018) and shepherding its long journey to the screen.

Sometimes all this trips him up. McBride reveals that when he interviewed Nancy Olson, who plays a fledgling screenwriter in *Sunset Boulevard*, he explained to her that the character she played in the film was his dating ideal. "I'm very sorry to hear that," Olson says to him. "I am still puzzling over that remark," McBride writes. While inadvertently funny asides like that slow down his otherwise brilliant exegesis of Wilder's life and work, they also prevent him from replicating the straight narrative approach of Sikov's biography and other Wilder books. McBride divides his thematically, grouping Wilder's films with the events in his life—Wilder's, not McBride's. His approach works well, illuminating Wilder's themes and obsessions across the entire span of a lifetime, and therefore across almost the entire 20th century, since Wilder lived to be 95.

WILDER OUTLIVED LUBITSCH by fifty-five years but always kept a sign in his writing office that read: HOW WOULD LUBITSCH DO IT? (Saul Steinberg painted it for him.) Wilder and his two principal co-scenarists, first Charles Brackett, then I. A. L. Diamond, spent their working hours figuring out the Lubitsch touch—how to tell the audience without telling them. "How do we do that, without doing that?" Lubitsch would ask his writers. Later in life, a favorite restaurant in LA, Mr. Chow, put a plaque over Wilder's table: *Make subtlety obvious.*

When Wilder cowrote the language-besotted *Ball of Fire* with Brackett in 1941, he made sure to watch as Howard Hawks directed it. Wilder had been outraged by a change director Mitchell Leisen and actor Charles Boyer made to his and Brackett's previous script, the elimination of dialogue delivered to a cockroach crawling on the wall of a cheap hotel room in *Hold Back the Dawn*. After that, he knew he had to start directing his work himself. Wilder was part of the screenwriter-to-director class of the early 1940s that also included John Huston, Preston Sturges, and, in his way, Welles. Sturges turned to directing because he too became frustrated with Leisen's changes.

Brackett's diaries, which have been published, reveal that he and Wilder thought Sturges was a nut, but Sturges made the end-run around Leisen first, in 1940. Wilder's Hollywood directorial debut, *The Major and the Minor*, with Ginger Rogers fleeing New York by impersonating a 12-year-old girl so she could buy a cheaper train ticket, came out in 1942. Naughty but commercial, the film was a hit. Wilder learned a lesson with it: you could get away with a lot if you didn't back down to the studio heads, and they would be happy if everybody made money. In a film he wrote in Germany, *Scampolo* (1932), a character explains the most important words in various languages. The two most important words in English? *The money*. His pithiest line of dialogue proved he understood Hollywood before he got there.

For nine years, Wilder turned out risky hits for Paramount. They got darker and weirder and angered producers at other studios for their acid depictions of the film industry and of America. "I portray Americans as beasts," Wilder confessed. *Ace in the Hole* (1951) proved it. Audiences stayed away from this cynical, angry exposé of news media ethics and the voyeuristic stupidity of crowds.

Movies like that were getting risky in another way. The blacklist was now in full swing. Wilder, an outspoken leftist, avoided it because he worked with the old-school Republican Brackett and openly mocked other writers. Of the "unfriendly witnesses" of the Hollywood

Ten, called to testify before the House Un-American Activities Committee, Wilder said, "Only two of them have talent. The rest are just unfriendly." *Stalag 17* (1953), Wilder's most underrated film, the story of an informer in a Nazi prison camp (it's a comedy), excoriates groupthink and holds up a wrongfully accused con man (William Holden) as sane in a fascist environment. Paramount wanted him to change the informer character from German to Polish for the German dubbing, so as not to offend this newly opened market. The Polish Jew Wilder refused, quit Paramount, and never returned.

He reached his apotheosis in 1959 and 1960, a great period in cinema history in which Wilder, usually ahead of his time, found himself, in an unexpected way, in line with developments like the French New Wave. *Some Like It Hot* and *The Apartment,* Wilder's frank, funny appraisals of sex and romance in black-and white, succeeded with audiences and the industry and allowed him the same kind of freedom he had after *Sunset Boulevard*'s success a decade before—the freedom to offend the public all over again. He made *Kiss Me, Stupid,* with Dean Martin and Kim Novak, and everyone hated it except, of all people, Joan Didion. "The Wilder world is one seen at dawn through a hangover," she wrote at the time. "A world of cheap double entendre and stale smoke and drinks in which the ice has melted: the true country of despair. *Kiss Me, Stupid* is, in fact, suffused with the despair of an America many of us prefer not to know."

WILDER WAS NOT A FAVORITE of serious American film critics while he was making films. He had the rare distinction of being disliked by opposite schools. Andrew Sarris thought he was too cynical; Pauline Kael found him contemptuous. And Peter Bogdanovich thought he was just plain mean. Wilder was aware of this and didn't like it. What could he do but try to make the films he wanted to make? In *Fedora,* William Holden's character, a film producer looking to revive his career by bringing a star actress out of retirement, quoted Samuel Goldwyn, the Hollywood producer and malaprop master, about the proper attitude toward such things: "In life you have to take the bitter with the sour."

By the early 1970s, after what was supposed to be Wilder's chef d'oeuvre, the big-budget *Private Life of Sherlock Holmes*, was mutilated by Wilder's producers and released to general indifference amid the turmoil of its era, Wilder began to resent the New Hollywood, "the kids with beards," as he called them. A portrait by David Hockney from 1982, a Polaroid composite, depicts Wilder photographing the artist as Audrey Wilder smiles at her husband in profile. Wilder, who wrote a piece in 1927 called "Film Terror," about how he didn't like to be photographed or filmed, was captured there by Hockney at almost the exact moment of the end of his career, right after the release of *Buddy Buddy*, his final movie. McBride describes it as "not funny in the slightest," quoting the critic Dennis Cozzalio, who wrote that the film is "an aging director's defiant 'fuck you' to the system he could sense was about to toss him to the curb, a last blast of venom disguised as a tired formula comedy."

Wilder spent the last twenty years of his life going to his office to write, even after Diamond died. He tried to get many new films off the ground, most of them weird in brand-new ways. One was to be called *Naked in a Volkswagen*; one was about a former child star, based on Shirley Temple, who moves into an old folks home where no one can stand her; another was going to cast Cary Grant as a medieval locksmith specializing in chastity belts. The strangest of all was a biopic about the turn-of-the-century French vaudeville performer, Le Pétomane, whose act, according to McBride, "consisted of creative variations on farting, including playing 'O Sole Mio' and 'La Marseillaise' through his ass." Some of Wilder's best films were set in the insurance industry (*Double Indemnity, The Apartment*), but in the end part of the problem was that Wilder was considered too old to insure, a Wilderian irony in real life.

Wilder had been a collector of modern art since his Berlin days. His and Audrey's condo in Westwood was stuffed with it, the walls filled with works by Picasso, Miró, Klee, Matisse, Dufy, Chagall,

Kandinsky, and Grosz. One of the pleasures of documentaries made about Wilder while he was alive is seeing all this art in his living room, and in his office and beach house in Trancas, as he unspools anecdotes about Hollywood and theories about screenwriting. He had so much art that a lot of it was stacked on the floor, leaning against walls, because he had run out of wall space. In 1989, he decided to sell almost all of it. A Picasso he'd bought for $5,000 sold for $4.8 million at auction in New York, and the rest went for close to $30 million dollars—more money than he had made in his entire career as a film director.

It's not *the money* that's important here, however. It's something unspoken anywhere in his biography: his collection to a large extent replicated the artists in the Nazi "Degenerate Art" exhibition of 1937. Here he'd triumphed over the Nazis once again. Just as he brought the sensibility of Berlin to Hollywood, he surrounded himself with its art in California, inadvertently saving it from Hitler as he collected it one piece at a time in the US.

As *Fedora* says, as Norma Desmond knew, "Endings are very important. That's what people remember—the last exit, the final close-up." And endings are hard. *Some Like It Hot* famously ends with Jack Lemmon revealing he's not a woman to the millionaire (Joe E. Brown) he has somehow become engaged to marry. "Well, nobody's perfect," Brown says, and THE END appears onscreen, accompanied by jazzy musical stings.

Maybe the card-playing Shirley MacLaine's final line to Lemmon in *The Apartment* is better, and should have been the one on Wilder's gravestone. It summed it all up, the whole ninety-five years, from Poland to Vienna, from Berlin to the long sunny days in Los Angeles, including the nights he had to sleep in the Chateau Marmont ladies' room because he was broke. "Shut up and deal," she says.

TIME IS A RABID DOG

AT THE PALACE THEATRE IN LAKE PLACID, NEW YORK, THERE IS A SIGN with white plastic letters at the ticket window. It lists the admission prices—one for matinees, one for regular shows—and at the bottom it says PLEASE STATE WHICH MOVIE. So when I got to the cashier, I handed her the money, looked her in the eye, and said "*Old*."

The title of M. Night Shyamalan's new film fit the situation that afternoon last July. The other three movies playing at the Palace were aimed at people too young for a driver's license. But those movies were old, too. *Jungle Cruise* was based on a theme-park ride that opened to the public in 1955, *Snake Eyes: G.I. Joe Origins* on a doll that was first sold in 1964, the same year the title character in *Black Widow* debuted in a comic book. My friend and I chose to see *Old* because it looked the least like kiddie fare, but it was really the newest film playing. Shyamalan adapted it from a graphic novel published in 2010. *Old* was contemporary, not a nostalgia item shoved down the throat of the summer.

Old was the first movie I'd been to see at a movie theater in seventeen months. And Lake Placid was the first place I'd been outside New York City since February 2020. The pandemic appeared to be subsiding. The town was filled with tourists from all over the country, judging by the license plates on the SUVs in the crowded municipal parking lot. Main Street was busy and there was a line at the Palace.

In the theater, my friend and I sat in the first section, face masks on, as people filed in behind us to see Vicky Krieps and Gael García Bernal trapped on a beach that caused them and their kids to prematurely age. They grew old before our eyes, inching closer to death, unable to figure out what was going on or how to stop it. Shyamalan's movie was too timely, an obvious and exact mirror of pandemic life over the previous year and a half.

His metaphor included an added frisson for the vaccine-hesitant: the leisure class, it turns out, are lab rats, there to test new medicines. Abbey Lee, playing a trophy wife with a calcium deficiency, hides herself in a cave in *Old*, embarrassed to be seen as she deteriorates. Her Botox fades and her bones get brittle, causing them to break and then heal at an accelerated rate. This quick, repetitive cycle of damage and repair turns her into a twisted mass of fused dislocations, her joints and vertebrae permanently misaligned along with her chakras. Gazing at this monster of female vanity, the teens in *Old* gasp in horror. She's "healed in the wrong position!" one shouts, summarizing what happened last summer when we thought the pandemic was ending.

The Palace Theatre was built as a one-screen in 1926. It features a large, impressive marquee with its name in incandescent lights. Inside, there is a tall fireplace behind the concession stand. When I was there, a concessionaire in a black T-shirt and a rosewood-colored face mask stood between the fireplace and the glass counter selling *Black Widow* popcorn tubs with black plastic logo lids from on top of the mantle, ten dollars each, more than the price of the movie. Shyamalan shot *Old* on 35mm film, but the Palace was showing it digitally. In the lobby, the theater had put on display one of their decommissioned 35mm Simplex projectors, with a Xenex lamp house. At least they'd saved it.

The digital projection didn't bother me that day. I was glad to be back in a movie theater. The early shots of beaches and nature, of people on vacation, were emanations from a past life. The screen-size was overwhelming. Even so, seeing a movie with a mask on, my glasses fogging up, added a level of anxiety disguised as mere discomfort. Every way to see a movie now, in a theater or at home, subtracts something from it.

Annette

In some quarters it was the most anticipated movie of the summer, and it arrived as something of a miracle just by existing: Leos Carax had made a movie in English for Amazon. But a movie that could use less Adam Driver and Marion Cotillard and more wooden puppet-baby and Simon Helberg can't be judged wholly a success. *Annette* begins with the pure delight of seeing Sparks in the studio and then with the cast in the street. After this exhilarating musical opening, *Annette* jerks into Comedy Night at the Orpheum and tries hard to be convincing as *Adam Driver: Raw.* Later, the film gathers its green-hued darkness around the light of baby Annette, international singing sensation, but right away Carax wants the audience, wherever they are, to understand that the film is going to be a 140-minute endurance test.

Annette has things in common with Carax's *Lovers on the Bridge* beyond musical numbers, street scenes, the battle of the sexes, plunges into water, and the ever-present threat of death. But now Carax sets his drama in the post-*Holy Motors* world of money and power, of fame and limousines, not street drunks chugging from clear plastic jugs of cheap red wine. As usual with Carax, obscure autobiographical elements mix with deconstructions of storytelling and cinema. *Annette* describes and witnesses the way comedy and tragedy become outrage and sentiment under commercial pressure. The film is self-consciously an anti-entertainment product for the streaming-content age.

Teetering on the edge of an abyss it keeps mentioning, *Annette* posits the height of expression as a masculine obsession intimately connected to murder and exploitation. That's the family drama of high art on hand here, male jealousy, anger, and self-pity that Carax sets in opposition to Cotillard's and baby Annette's cathartic, ethereal trilling. The film's terrifying qualities are insistent and demanding, forcing a second viewing so that its indictments of gossip news and halftime shows disappear in the rearview mirror with the California wildfires. To have the child of a comedian announce at a stadium concert that "Daddy kills people" is taking a pun to the bitter end, where Chris Rock and Bill Burr are thanked in the credits.

The Worst Person in the World

The Norwegian auteur Joachim Trier is the opposite of Leos Carax. He doesn't aim high enough, and he still never hits his target. Every movie he makes unspools like an assignment, though paradoxically he also seems to work in total freedom. He's like an MFA in fiction writing who wakes up one morning and realizes that now he actually has to write a novel. Trier is professional, he's accredited, and his work is dutiful. The new thing in his new movie, *The Worst Person in the World*, is that now he's trying to please a larger crowd.

This is Trier's fifth feature, and it's the rom-com version of elevated horror. It's time for him to get it together, just like the protagonist in this film should have. Julie (Renate Reinsve) is a floundering twentysomething who starts out serious and ambitious, then bumbles through work and romance for over two hours, unable to commit to anything. So, yes, she's relatable. Trier, however, tells her story with banal gimmicks. When Julie runs to her new lover (Herbert Nordrum) at the café where he works, the people she passes freeze in place, like something from a 10-year-old TV commercial for phone service. Julie wants life to be magical and fully charged, like a phone, and she finds it isn't. Maybe Trier is trying to depict cruel optimism.

The main love of Julie's life, the graphic novelist Aksel (Anders Danielsen Lie), a man a little older than she is, gets sick and complains about analog vs. digital at a picnic table on the grounds of a hospital. Also relatable. But also not a good thing here, anymore than it is with Julie. More productively, the film showed, quite by accident, that if Julie had stuck with medical school, she could have operated on Aksel and maybe saved his life, the way Rock Hudson becomes a surgeon in *Magnificent Obsession* and cures Jane Wyman's blindness.

Instead, Julie has to listen as Aksel goes on and on about how much he loved vinyl records and how much the world he is leaving has changed because there is less stuff in it, even though Julie works surrounded by books in a bookstore. Having to listen to this is where not thinking ahead got Julie, and also where it gets Joachim Trier. At the end of *An Affair to Remember,* Deborah Kerr said to Cary Grant, "If you can paint, I can walk. Anything can happen." Maybe it's not that way anymore, even in Norway and the movies. But that makes this movie an affair to forget.

Wheel of Fortune and Fantasy

Ryusuke Hamaguchi's *Drive My Car* will go down as one of the great films of its era, but to me there was something unsatisfying about it. It was too long, so by the time it got to the confession at the collapsed house in the snow, I wanted Hamaguchi to wrap it up. There was also something comically perfunctory about the way the homicidal actor was eliminated from the film. Was it supposed to be funny? It was to me. Finally, there was the Covid-era supermarket parking lot coda, which I didn't quite get. I loved it while I was watching it, but the more I thought about it, the less it held together.

The film's tough love for its characters, Hamaguchi's ability to put the process of acting and directing into the film through the Chekhov play at the center of it, the rehearsal tape on the car stereo, the credits that come forty minutes in: I was moved or surprised by these things, one at a time. Yet at a certain point the film was like a too-long bass solo. It was all warm feeling and cold technique. All I could think was: End it.

Not so with Hamaguchi's other masterpiece this year, *Wheel of Fortune and Fantasy*, with its longer title and shorter running time. In an hour less, it tells three separate stories, each of which was odd, compact, and more mind-bending then *Drive My Car*. Notably, these are original screenplays by Hamaguchi. *Drive My Car* is based on a Murakami story.

The three segments center on women, whereas *Drive My Car*'s wheels turn around a man. The story of his adulterous screenwriter wife, Oto (Reika Kirishima), and the sound of her recorded voice were the film's engine, but Hamaguchi's attitude toward this complex, slightly menacing character was never quite clear to me. He put a whole lot of ambiguity into *Drive My Car*.

The contradictory impulses and thorny emotional lives of the women in *Wheel of Fortune and Fantasy* make each story sharp and focused while subtracting none of the characters' complexity. The first story sets up a cute fashion model (Kotone Furukawa) as pleasant and supportive, then leads her into jealousy and possible violence, her initial unthreatening manner giving way to rage. In the second, a lazy student (Katsuki Mori) having an affair with a callow wannabe (Shouma Kai) is led by him to honey-trap their professor (Kiyohiko Shibukawa), who has won the Akutagawa Prize for his latest novel. In the third, a woman in town for a class reunion (Aoba Kawai) mistakes someone on an escalator (Fusako Urabe) for her high school love, a girl who rejected her. The passerby goes along with it and takes her home.

The anguish of misunderstanding that revolves around love and sex in ordinary lives has become weirder in these two Hamaguchi films, edgier than it was in his earlier features. Hamaguchi is a Rohmer for a time when nothing makes sense, things don't work out, and everybody is in some kind of mental anguish that they suspect won't interest other people. His matter-of-fact coldness, with its conflicted humanism and acceptance of change, now places his work in the forefront of contemporary cinema.

The French Dispatch

I don't trust a magazine without a film critic, especially one in a movie based on the *New Yorker* directed by someone who famously courted Pauline Kael's approval. Maybe the director himself is the missing film critic. Certainly, *The French Dispatch* is an amalgam of dozens of other movies, which Wes Anderson went so far as to list in a press release. On that list are some of my favorite films, so I guess I have to admit that Anderson and I share a sensibility. But that is the problem. I don't want to be roped in. I'd prefer his film convince me.

The French Dispatch, like Hamaguchi's *Wheel*, is made of three stories, plus some other stuff. In the first one, Benicio del Toro is a mad painter in a high-security prison, watched over and encouraged by a guard (Léa Seydoux) who is also his nude life model, which is something of a joke on the viewer since del Toro's character is an abstract expressionist. Adrien Brody and Tilda Swinton are at their best in this beautiful segment, with its gray prison walls in black-and-white and the explosive color of its Seydoux-inspired bas-reliefs. It could have been the whole movie. It's the best thing Anderson has done in a long time, maybe since *Rushmore*.

The moment in this story when del Toro switches places with Tony Revolori as the young version of himself, going from promising if troubled youth to incipient breakdown and madness, was a touching key to this film that the other two stories struggled to reach, though they try. Jeffrey Wright in particular came close as an erudite food writer interviewed by a wry Liev Schreiber on a period-specific talk show set. What period exactly I do not know. Sometime in the mid-1960s to early-1970s.

The thing I have never understood about Anderson's movies appears in that last story: the lame chase scene that goes nowhere.

Here it is animated, *Tintin*-style, and is self-consciously pointless, ending where it began. Anderson's movies often credit multiple screenwriters. I don't get how it takes four people to come up with those chase scenes, and not one writer points out that they don't work. Maybe that person is always outvoted.

As for the middle story, about the student revolt, it reminded me less of *La Chinoise* or *Masculine Feminine* and more of something from Tess Slesinger's 1934 novel, *The Unpossessed*, which is about a group of radicals trying to start a magazine. One of them is a shiftless, married dilettante communist who pictures himself as an editor at the nonexistent magazine's French office. His co-editor eventually has to admit something.

About starting their magazine he says, "Oh, we don't really, we just pretend to." "There are no Magazines, there are no revolutions," he explains, finishing with "and now it's time for growing boys to get their sleep."

El Planeta

Amalia Ulman has an almost expressionless quality that is fully reflected in the deadpan brilliance of her debut feature, *El Planeta*. She stars in the film with her mother, Ale Ulman. They're a pair who Spanish neoliberalism has turned into a *Grey Gardens* duo in training. Or they could be, if they can keep their apartment, and if María (Ale), who shoplifts in a mink coat and charges restaurant meals to a local politician, can avoid arrest and a jail cell.

Returned from London to Gijón against her will, Leonor (Amalia), a fashion student, wanders the streets in couture, with little to do but browse shops. Looking for a source of income, she Skypes with art directors and considers sex work. We meet Leonor meeting a man (Nacho Vigalondo, the director of *Colossal*) who wants to pay her to urinate on him, at a discount rate not much better than the "exposure" an art director offers her to work on a celebrity fashion shoot. Leonor goes on a date with a dude her own age (Zhou Chen) who she meets in a shop. He seems nice, intelligent, an artiste like her, but he doesn't treat her much better than her two potential employers.

María's reliance on magic spells mirrors her belief in a fictional economy where women like her and Leonor can lead decent lives, where their cat isn't dead, where they have reliable companions. Instead, they are surrounded by the trappings of a consumerism to which they are addicted and which is growing out of their reach. At the end, Ulman's film pops into color from black-and-white like *The French Dispatch* does throughout.

Here, however, it is to show that this mother and daughter are spectators in the street with hundreds of others as Martin Scorsese arrives in their town to be given an award, like the ending of *The Life Aquatic. El Planeta* also brings to mind early Jarmusch, but its self-aware position in the economy of image production goes beyond comparison to earlier films. Ulman's directing is as strange and demure as its two main characters. Too polite to cause trouble, they would rather just wander out of frame. But the movie itself doesn't fizzle. I have not seen as sly and hard-hitting a debut in a long time.

Zola

Zola is the most audacious of the films in the category *Sex Workers of 2021*, especially considering it started as a Twitter thread and was originally a James Franco project. Janicza Bravo and her co-scenarist Jeremy O. Harris removed it from a trash fire and turned it into a stunning work, a savage, comic B-movie about a sane woman (Taylour Paige) in a hard world, embroiled in a triangle of exploitation across state lines.

Paige's Zola, a Black Hooters waitress, meets Stefani (Riley Keough), a white customer at one of her tables, and soon the two are on a road trip to work a strip club. With them are Stefani's boyfriend, Derrek (Nicholas Braun), maybe the stupidest man ever depicted in a movie, and X (Colman Domingo), Stefani's manager and, as it turns out, pimp. When Zola realizes the truth of the situation, which she cleverly narrates in retrospect, it falls to her to set things right. Effectively X's prisoner, she has to negotiate her escape, avoid prostituting herself, and raise the duplicitous Stefani's price and self-esteem.

The film's dick montage is a new moment in the cinematic depiction of johns, an unexpected interruption amid the film's beautiful 16mm color cinematography (by Ari Wegner, who also shot *The Power of the Dog*). The degradation of Florida is really proving itself to be a continuing source of innovation in movie photography. It lends an eerie atmosphere to the film's chaos, a feeling that any bad thing could happen, from the most trivial to the most final, and receive the same eye roll from Paige.

Red Rocket

The former MTV VJ Simon Rex has had a convoluted career in the mid-level trenches of Hollywood. In Sean Baker's new film, *Red Rocket*, he's mixed in with a cast of mostly non-professionals who Baker assembled near Texas City, Texas, a Gulf Coast town that has seen better days. Rex plays Mikey Davies, a.k.a. Mikey Saber, an immature, middle-aged, failed porn star who returns from LA to his ex-wife (Bree Elrod). Lexi is also an ex-porn star, a sometime crack smoker now living a precarious existence with her mother (Brenda Deiss), and turning the occasional trick via Craigslist.

Mikey is the true worst person in the world, but with plenty of sleazy charm and a terrifying, destructive lust for life. He immediately and without hesitation proceeds to mess up every person he meets, including a hapless neighbor who lies about his military service (Ethan Darbone), some hard-bitten drug dealers he goes to work for (Judy Hill and Brittney Rodriguez), and an underage donut-shop counter-girl who calls herself Strawberry (Suzanna Son). He rogues his way through, until he's stripped of everything, including his clothes, making everybody's lives worse for having met him.

Rex and Son give two of the best performances of the year, finding a cruel joy in the series of bad decisions they make or succumb to. The film's ending is ambiguous, playing into the sordid fantasy of the contemporary American dream, which Baker and his cinematographer, Drew Daniels, shoot in a full-color 16mm that rivals *Zola*'s. *Red Rocket* takes place in 2016, during Trump's campaign, which hums low in the background while Mikey clamors among the poor in Texas City. His last act is as ominous as President Trump's was, and portends disagreeable, unlucky things for all concerned.

Bad Luck Banging or Loony Porn

Radu Jude's *Bad Luck Banging or Loony Porn* is a film of ideas, so to make sure that anyone who doesn't like ideas doesn't stay to watch it, he starts it with an explicit homemade video of an ordinary couple having real sex. This video is also the film's founding document. When it's uploaded to the internet, Emi (Katia Pascariu), the video's costar, is put on trial at the school where she teaches, and faces losing her job.

Jude films Emi documentary-style on various errands in the Covid-era streets of Bucharest before her trial at the school. This is the first film I've seen that is in full pandemic mode. People in lines in shops wear masks improperly and argue about it. During Emi's trial at the school, her colleagues grapple with their various styles of mask, pulling them down, then fixing them, taking them off, forgetting about them, being scolded for not having them on.

After Emi's tortuous, long-lens walk through downtown Bucharest, which Jude presents as unfriendly and garish, with patriotic Romanian messages everywhere, he interrupts the film for a slide show of definitions, which appear as aphorisms drawn from Romanian writers, including E. M. Cioran, but from many other sources, too. (Over a shot of a sliver of pond with apartment towers in the distance: "Nature: Alexander Blok, journal entry, April 15, 1912: 'Yesterday, I took great joy in the wreck of the *Titanic*. So there is still an ocean.'")

These systematically dismantle ideology and serve as a prelude and introduction for Emi's outdoor trial, which takes place at night on the school grounds, and which Jude lights in garish magentas and oranges in a mise-en-scène reminiscent of the cover of Hüsker Dü's *Warehouse* album or a Michael Bilandic film shot by Sean Price Williams.

Emi's fellow teachers are normal people, vindictive monsters with a couple of thoughtful outliers dotted in. The film's shock ending, the best of the year, was far better than, for instance, *Black Widow*'s, which also took place in Eastern Europe. Forcefully pro-woman, *Bad Luck Banging* places violence in a realm of fantasy far more satisfying than that movie's. It's more honest because Jude understands that's where it will stay, and it's even more ridiculous.

Bergman Island

A filmmaker (Vicky Krieps) and her older husband (Tim Roth), also a filmmaker, get a dual residency on Fårö, the Swedish island where Ingmar Bergman lived and worked during the second half of his life. While Roth doodles S&M sketches in his notebook, Krieps conceives a somewhat boring film about a young woman (Mia Wasikowska) attending a wedding on the island and reconnecting with a lost love (Anders Danielsen Lie, Scandinavia's official ex-boyfriend, who looks something like the younger Bergman).

The meta aspects of *Bergman Island* are bland and convoluted, requiring careful attention, which doesn't pay off. The film is more a testament to how the complacent international creative class can no longer make films like Bergman did, or doesn't want to, because Bergman was a bad husband who acted on his artistic impulses, then flayed them on the screen, instead of a loving family man who drew dirty sketches and hid them. Mia Hansen-Løve is too comfortable with her film's mediocrity, which she presents as an irrefutable condition of contemporary existence. It would be better to watch the other *Bergman Island*, Marie Nyreröd's 2004 documentary featuring Bergman near the end of his life, or Dheeraj Akolkar's documentary *Liv & Ingmar*, from 2012. Both are sensitive, unsparing, and emotional films that do justice to Bergman and his complicated relationships, especially his working life with Ullmann, who speaks of him with love but without illusion.

The Souvenir, Part II

Joanna Hogg's *The Souvenir* was maybe the best film of 2019. The disappointing follow-up includes what may be the worst scene of 2021: young filmmaker Julie (Honor Swinton Byrne) sobbing in front of her TV in 1989, deeply moved as she watches the Berlin Wall come down. It so easily could have been cut.

Unfortunately, it encapsulates the solipsism of the whole enterprise, in which Julie completes her thesis film, all the odds in her favor as a human being on this Earth, those odds improved by a large cash outlay from mother (Tilda Swinton, as excellent as she was in the first one).

The Souvenir, Part II is the exact opposite of the other daughter-mother films of 2021, sublimely unaware of its good luck (because still reeling from boyfriend death) as it pursues the film-within-a-film, which we see and which is maybe supposed to show Derek Jarman's influence on Hogg in the 1980s. It reminded me more of Kenneth Anger's *Rabbit's Moon*, and it would have benefitted from being sped up like that film was. As in the first *Souvenir*, but more so, Richard Ayoade's performance as an ambitious rival filmmaker who is maybe based on Isaac Julien puzzled me with its pompous Wildean *non-mots*. He's not funny, he's annoying, he's right about things?

France

Shot in eye-pounding high-def, to bring out the sparkly whiteness of Léa Seydoux's dazzling, erotic teeth, *France* creates a unique digital anxiety in the viewer that demands full attention. Seydoux plays France de Meurs, a popular and successful TV news anchor with no scruples. At the start, the film appears to be a satire of twenty-four-hour television news media, focusing on a terrible blonde who is gossipy and ruthless at work, cold to her husband (Benjamin Biolay) and son (Gaëtan Amiel) at home, both of whom, like her, kind of suck as human beings.

The film then takes a deceptive turn into Haneke territory when a distracted France hits an immigrant deliveryman (Jawad Zemmar) with her car. Her sense of guilt precipitates a breakdown, and the film kicks into high-gear, best represented by another car accident, one of the most jaw-dropping in any film. It's much longer than car crashes usually are in movies, rolling and tumbling with great violence on and on. Bruno Dumont wants the audience to feel it, recoil from it—a cycle the film reproduces in many scenes.

France has space for someone to play Angela Merkel (Marina Tamássy), glimpsed outdoors at a mountain sanatorium, and for a digitally snipped-in Emmanuel Macron to take gotcha questions at a press conference. France's journey is not one to enlightenment or redemption. Her job drills something into her, and her confrontation with it makes life seem mysterious and threatening. The film has one of the great non-endings, an enigmatic scene of nothingness that epitomizes and transcends the European art film, maybe because it's another ruse from the ever-cunning Dumont.

Whirlybird

Bob Tur and Marika Gerrard were a husband-and-wife news-reporting team in Los Angeles who, starting in the late 1970s, realized that television news coverage in LA County would benefit from twenty-four-hour air surveillance. Using a helicopter would allow them to get to crime scenes faster, while filming from above would provide television news with unique, all-encompassing views that added great drama to breaking stories at active crime scenes, fires, and other big disturbances. They learned to fly, invested in a helicopter, and flew it to dubious glory during the 1980s and 1990s, the key inventors of a new form of television. It worked hand-in-hand with police surveillance to contribute to the degeneration of journalism as it became hypnotic, appalling entertainment.

Matt Yoka's documentary, *Whirlybird*, tells this story, including the effect it had on Tur and Gerrard, who narrate their work life, a history of Los Angeles that coincides with Tur's increasing belligerence and hostility as the job takes over their lives. Tur's meltdown ends the marriage and then their business. Before it's over, they have filmed, from the air, the Rodney King riots, including the beating of trucker Reginald Denny, and the low-speed white Ford Bronco chase as a brigade of cop cars followed O. J. Simpson for over an hour on the freeway and then up to the door of his house, where he surrendered forty-five minutes later. Close to a hundred million people watched that live. *Whirlybird* is an invaluable document on how it happened.

Bob (now Zoey) came out as transgender in 2013 and moved to the woods. She and Marika are the parents of Katy Tur, the MSNBC television news journalist who Donald Trump publicly excoriated throughout his 2016 campaign, about which she wrote a book. Katy is interviewed in *Whirlybird*, where she explains her estrangement from Zoey, who put a microphone in her hand when she was a toddler and had her reporting in the helicopter by the time she was in elementary school. (We see the home videos.) She has since reconciled with Zoey, and now she's married a TV news reporter. Maybe France de Meurs had the same kind of parents.

The Card Counter

When Barack Obama put Paul Schrader's film *The Card Counter* on his list of his favorite films of 2021, *Variety* noted that he also liked the movie *Quo Vadis, Aida,* which the trade paper called "a 2020 Bosnian war film." *Variety* described Schrader's film as "an edgy character study," neglecting to mention that the former president was giving his thumbs-up to a movie about the illegal torture of prisoners by American soldiers in Abu Ghraib during the war in Iraq, a subject covered in the Senate report that Obama, bowing to CIA pressure, refused to fully declassify.

Schrader, ever the productive irritant, does not let his characters off for the CIA Detention and Interrogation Program administered under George W. Bush. His protagonist, a former Abu Ghraib guard turned professional gambler, played broodingly by Oscar Isaac, has served time for this crime but can't shake his guilt. He goes by the name William Tell, *tell* being a funny word for a professional card player to pick. Tell was at least punished for torturing prisoners, unlike the people who ordered him to do it. We see his training and the lead-up to his crimes in ugly, harrowing flashbacks, filmed by Schrader and his cinematographer, Alexander Dynan, as loud, wide-angle nightmares.

Schrader is deep in the *Pickpocket* here, his predominating late-period Bressonianism now applied to non-Vegas casinos, cheap restaurants, highway driving, and American prisons. Isaac is cool and intense in the film, as is his handler, played by Tiffany Haddish, while Tye Sheridan, his apprentice, and Willem Dafoe, a veteran turned military contractor, are secretive and bizarre. Schrader leaves the grueling denouement of the movie offscreen, playing it as sounds from another room, a refusal on the film's part to indulge in the same things the CIA did. *The Card Counter* is a subtle exorcism of national crimes eighteen years old, an unusual, serious genre film unafraid to hold its protagonist to account. It tries hard to keep in mind Romans 12:19. Vengeance is mine, saith the Lord. Avenge not yourself.

Project Space 13

Michael M. Bilandic's new gem, an airtight chamber comedy ripped from Covid-era headlines during the Soho looting scare of summer 2020, takes place in a locked-down art gallery. There, two rent-a-cops (Theodore Bouloukos and Hunter Zimny) protect the investment of a gallery owner (Jason Grisell) in an artist (Keith Poulson) and his work, an elaborate, junky assemblage where he lives in a cage, fed bugs by a small, annoying robot. Every idea in *Project Space 13* is exceedingly stupid and beautiful. Bilandic cuts it all to the quick so that nothing is wasted in this film where paradoxically nothing is necessary.

Poulson, as mouthy and abject as he was in Bilandic's *Hellaware*, plays the artist as a pretentious regular guy, while Bouloukos and Zimny's increased nervousness as the film proceeds gives them opportunities for dumb monologues that place them in a history of downtown failure. As usual Grisell steals every scene he is cut into, delivering instructions from the back of an SUV or rambling about Woody Woodpecker's popularity in Brazil as he wanders a gray beach out of town. Whoever did his wardrobe deserves an Independent Spirit Award presented by Judy Tenuta. What may be the film's best performance, however, comes from a club kid (Kyle Brown) in frameless palm-leaf sunglasses and a fuzzy pink fur jacket. He crawls under the gallery's closed grate and faces the drawn guns of the two security guards. Then he crawls back out without having said a word, a concise encapsulation of downtown's early 2020s vibe.

The Scary of Sixty-First

Bilandic and Grisell have absurd cameos in *The Scary of Sixty-First*, actor-podcaster Dasha Nekrasova's directorial debut, also an exemplary low-budget wonder ripped from today's headlines and shot on 16mm. It doesn't scale the Bilandician heights of ludicrous astonishment because it's a horror movie about Jeffrey Epstein, an ambitious concept for anyone's first film. But it gets close enough in this second year of blighted pandemic cinema. The increasing hysteria of the film's three co-leads (Madeline Quinn, Betsey Brown, Nekrasova) progresses insidiously as their obsession with the absent Epstein's sex crimes takes over their lives, or possesses their souls, or whatever's going on.

The film presents itself in the guise of travesty, and ends with a film-history joke, having nowhere to go because it has backed itself into a corner. Quite literally—it is Nekrasova's final girl who ends up in a basement in blood and black boots. Yet as an actual work of horror-exploitation, *The Scary of Sixty-First* is only posing as irony. Its ambitions are impressive, though the whole movie keeps going up to the line of naughtiness, a strategy guaranteed to draw in the film's built-in reply-guy audience.

As with the glimpse of Angela Merkel in *France*, in *The Scary of Sixty-First* we get a quick sighting of someone (Anna Khachiyan) who might be the now-convicted Ghislaine Maxwell, Epstein's familiar. Seeing this film during Maxwell's trial was a reminder of the slipperiness of the entire class she represents and worked for. There should be more cheap movies made this quickly about current events, so that the whole area isn't ceded to streaming services and Oscar hopefuls.

Spencer

The first half has a horror movie feel, with Jonny Greenwood's "Diana Runs the Voodoo Down" score working with Kristen Stewart's Porsche driving to create a sense of confusion and menace. The second half is a Lady Antebellum video brought to you by Kentucky Fried Chicken. In between, the walk-in dessert fridge and the holiday weighing ritual performed their magick, but to no avail. In this world of high-toned entertainment, you can flee from the Windsors like Diana Spencer did, and you should.

Social Hygiene

In the forests and meadows of Quebec, or maybe in a city park, a feckless vagabond revolutionary (Maxim Gaudette) is criticized, berated, and implored by his sister (Larissa Corriveau), his wife (Évelyne Rompré), his mistress (Ève Duranceau), a tax collector (Kathleen Fortin), and a woman who he has robbed (Éléonore Loiselle)—all from at least six feet away.

Denis Côté's *Social Hygiene* is classical French theater, stripped down via Straub-Huillet, and then presented with Covid-era social-distance rules in place. Set in the present, the characters act and speak as though they inhabit a previous century. Dressed like they've been asked to pose for Manet and didn't have time to put the right outfit together, they declaim their dialogue in the manner of Jean-Pierre Léaud playing Saint-Just in *Weekend*.

Each scene in this excellent, amusing, and unexpected film is one shot long, with the actors placed a little too far from the camera, figures in a landscape. The film works because of how it looks. It's only seventy-six minutes long and beats *Malmkrog* at its own game, almost a parody of the Puiu film. But could either of these films have known the other existed? They occupy separate bubbles of oddball philosophical discourse.

Côté has made over a dozen low-budget, semi-conceptual films in Canada since 2005 and shows no sign of letting up. Each of his movies is a bracing delight designed to perk up an audience by asking it to see and listen in some new way. Antonin (Gaudette), an irresponsible male id figure like in *Red Rocket*, has just as many self-justifications as Mikey Saber, though his are of a higher order. And he's fully clothed. Asked by his wife where he's been for two weeks, he tells her, "Time is a rabid dog." She replies that they need more structure in their lives. *Social Hygiene* has plenty of that. Filled with birdsong on the soundtrack, stitched together with fast tracking shots and whip pans, it's beautiful, too.

The Matrix Resurrections

The suicide bots near the end are a brilliant new metaphor. With them, Lana Wachowski and her screenwriters David Mitchell and Aleksandar Hemon have created a frightening and visually arresting new version of the self-victimization of pod life. Keanu Reeves's and Carrie-Anne Moss's Gen X romance in the Simulatte coffee shop, and their acceptance that they "can't beat time," was moving and glorious, while Lambert Wilson's and Christina Ricci's cameos as, respectively, the anti-sequel, bile-spewing Merovingian and a stylish video game marketing professional were delightful, welcome, and gone too soon. Everything in the middle had a contemporary TV feel, in which old IP was rebooted for a Riverdale-in-Captain-Nemo's-submarine effect that struck me as counter to the aims of the film but was also just being nice to kids.

Days

Tsai Ming-liang's films are test cases of cinema. They require projection on large screens in dark auditoriums, even demand it, but quietly.

Goodbye, Dragon Inn takes that as its subject, that the contemplation of life inside a movie theater is a necessary and important thing to do, no matter the condition of the film industry in the 21st century. And that takes a certain amount of time—the uninterrupted running time of the film.

Increasingly in Tsai's films this form of contemplation is his most important and maybe his only subject. So to watch his most recent movie, *Days*, in my apartment became an exercise in how not do it. As the now middle-aged Lee Kang-sheng sat on a couch, staring ahead, trying to ignore his neck pain, so I stared at him, also immobile, a shadow on the wall. Eating dinner alone watching Lee get an erotic full body message in a hotel room from the other guy in *Days* (Anong Houngheuangsy) brought it home: this is not how I expected I would be living at this point in my life. And after they leave the hotel, they go to a restaurant.

Don't Look Up

The next time capitalism and climate change force the employees of a candle factory in Kentucky to have to work through a deadly tornado, they'll be able to say Adam McKay got it. He understood. He knew. And then when they get home from one of their coworker's funerals, they'll be able to once again watch *Don't Look Up* on Netflix and say thanks for the laughs.

McKay is a filmmaker who has learned nothing. After *Vice*, his tepid anti-Dick Cheney biopic from 2018, he might have reexamined the effectiveness of mild comedy and failed satire on the issues of the day. No, he is running a big production company, and he is busy with TV shows, websites, and basketball podcasts. One has to be a mogul in Hollywood just to survive. Only a mogul could wrangle such big stars and so much B-roll into one giant movie, the *It's a Mad, Mad, Mad, Mad World* for the end of the world, minus the *Melancholia*.

To do something else besides that, something that required actual thought and concentration, such as making a good movie, is too time-consuming for someone like McKay. Here's a quick-and-easy lesson for the next time: if the end credits sequence is sixteen minutes long, the movie is part of the problem, not the solution. Leonardo DiCaprio, the only person pulling his weight in the rest of the movie, wasn't even in that part of the film.

Lamb

Lamb, Pig, Cow. Old MacDonald had a boutique film studio. Nicolas Cage in *Pig* was better than anything in *Lamb.* Both start off seeming like they are going to be genre films, *Pig* a vigilante action drama, *Lamb* just more elevated horror. *Pig* gets mixed with a vague neorealism—*Bicycle Thieves* or *Umberto D.* in Portland, Oregon—while *Lamb* becomes a quietist farming story with adulterous undertones, like a Dreyer silent.

Lamb ends in very unexpected way, really out there, but it's too much too late. *Pig* succeeds because it keeps undercutting the potential for Cagian craziness, even during a stupid *Fight Club*-style underground semi-bumfight, in which the overripe Cage is repeatedly punched in the face by a busboy. *Lamb* is an Icelandic movie cowritten by the novelist Sjón, who played with the Sugarcubes, but it is best summarized by a different 1980s band, Duran Duran: "I'm on the hunt, I'm after ewe." *Cow* I didn't see. I heard it was a grim documentary about the repetitive drudgery of life in captivity, and I've had it with domestic drama.

INSIDE THE SPECIAL PEOPLE CLUB

WELCOME TO THE DOLLHOUSE

EVERY YEAR THE FILMS OF TODD SOLONDZ GET BETTER. THAT'S BECAUSE, of all the American indie directors of the 1990s, his vision of American life has proved to be the most accurate. His deadpan worldview is one of total dismay at the banality of everyday tragedy, pushed to a point where jokes become terminal. No one can deny, unless they are living in a dream world, that this is a valid account of 21st-century America and its current state of flailing, immiserated despair. In the 1990s maybe Solondz's point of view seemed a little harsh, maybe too peculiar. The times have caught up. Solondz was right.

If Solondz has been the most accurate, it is partly because he has compromised the least, or is the most pure, undiluted. This leanness is reflected in his films, in his style, where nothing is wasted, nothing overelaborated. And there are no Solondz TV miniseries, no TV commercials, no concert films, no studio assignments that went wrong or changed the trajectory of his career by reorienting it toward Hollywood.

The misery of his first feature, *Fear Anxiety and Depression* (1989), which was seized from him by its producers and finished without his involvement, had already taken care of all that. Solondz realized early that there was no sense in giving in, that it would only lead him as a writer and director into the worlds of mental anguish and artistic mediocrity his films describe with such precision. We can see that in the artist's worlds of certain novelist, poet, screenwriter, and documentary-filmmaker characters in his movies. Their emotional messiness and their unhappiness come from having expectations of how their careers should go, even if they are sometimes, to all outward appearances, successful.

So for Solondz there are only the seven features he has made since 1989 (and, in addition to his three early shorts, high-quality juvenilia, there's also his one sly, hilarious later short, *3013*, made for the Venice Film Festival in 2013, which encapsulates all the bleakness of his work in three minutes, without actors or mise-en-scène, and is in Chinese). Because there are only those seven films, Solondz now occupies a space in the American cinema similar to the one Robert Bresson held in the French cinema when he was alive. Except, unlike in Bresson films, in the work of Todd Solondz humans are without divine assistance. They are without grace and unacknowledged, no matter how much they know they should change.

It all started with *Welcome to the Dollhouse*, his second feature, in 1996. *Welcome to the Dollhouse* won the Grand Jury Prize at Sundance that year, a big shock to everyone involved. "I showed it to some sales people and they didn't even finish watching it," Solondz said in one interview. Sony Pictures Classics released it in the US soon after, and it was surprise hit in theaters and later on home video. The story of seventh-grader Dawn Wiener's awkward and embarrassing suburban life, her bitterness and defiance and her loneliness, became as much of a touchstone for Gen X as Richard Linklater's *Dazed and Confused* (1993) was, except that *Welcome to the Dollhouse* was set in an inescapable present, with no golden weed-smoke 1970s mystique. *Welcome to the Dollhouse* was comfortless, like the light in a New Jersey mall.

SOLONDZ HAS LONG BEEN understood as an auteur of discomfort and moral disorientation, though he describes himself as a filmmaker who deals in sorrow and ambiguity, presenting a world where the worst things that can happen to people become funny, if only for a moment. Both interpretations often meet in what at first can seem like cruelty. For *Welcome to the Dollhouse* is cruel to Dawn (Heather Matarazzo), or more accurately everyone in the movie is cruel to her—parents, siblings, teachers, fellow students, everyone save Ralphy (Dimitri Iervolino), her one friend, and the only other member of her "Special People Club."

Of course, since abuse runs downhill, eventually she abandons him, and their club is destroyed. It is wrecked three times over. First, when her parents insist she dismantle the clubhouse so they can celebrate their wedding anniversary in their yard; second, when Dawn is told that "special" is a euphemism for "retarded"; and third, when Dawn succumbs to dominant ideas of popularity and rejects Ralphy for being a "faggot."

The cruelty here is free-floating and mixed with shame. *Welcome to the Dollhouse* is an emanation from the history of adolescence before *cringe*, when awkwardness was a social death sentence, too obvious to be discussed or given a name. Dawn's main question for the world is "Why do you hate me?" The answer comes back, without hesitation, "Because you're ugly." Ugliness is the film's subject, something Solondz identifies at the core of American life, the same way H. L. Mencken did when he wrote "The Libido for the Ugly" in 1926. What Mencken saw in the manufactured landscape on a train ride through Pennsylvania, Solondz discovers in the behavior of human beings in neighboring New Jersey.

It's a scene "so intolerably bleak and forlorn that it reduced the whole aspiration of man to a macabre and depressing joke." That's what Mencken would have discovered if he had taken a ride on New Jersey Transit in 1995 and got off in West Caldwell, where *Welcome to the Dollhouse* was shot. What Mencken describes as "the lust to make the world intolerable" is what Dawn finds all around her, in every interaction she has with her fellow suburbanites.

It is only in fantasy, when Dawn escapes to New York City to look for her kidnapped little sister Missy (Daria Kalinina) and to plaster Manhattan with MISSING posters, that anyone says "I love you" to her. As with Missy, her name comes to seem charged. "Dawn," we realize, indicates a creeping realization more than any kind of new day.

The constant Solondzian questions, with their childish, mean-spirited, and socially unacceptable vocabulary, are all first introduced in this film. Who is a lesbian, a faggot, a retard? Who is a pedophile? What is rape? This focus on the sexuality of outsiders, from a time before it was common to refer to oneself as "queer," turns on the people asking them. "Normal" in *Welcome to the Dollhouse* indicates meanness, a sensibility of accusation and punishment.

The single family suburban house is a locus of neglect and rejection in *Welcome to the Dollhouse*, but it is junior high where punishment and violence find their true home, where the ideas that congeal in the family become activated. Solondz's film is an anti–*Zero for Conduct* (1933). Here, the lives of schoolchildren are repressed and cruel, not anarchic and free. The typical locations of adolescent spite become vicious in *Welcome to the Dollhouse*. The cafeteria, of course, plays a role right off, but the girls' bathroom and the area out back, behind the school by the dumpster, are the settings for a kind of malevolence that goes beyond the cattiness in later films like *Mean Girls* (2004) into brutality.

Bullying in this film makes up Dawn's whole life. She says nothing about it to her family, remaining silent about what she faces at school every day. Why would she tell them anything? Solondz makes it clear that they are where the problems started. Their idea of advice is to ask "Whoever told you to fight back?" Family is no help. Dawn is alone. These are the people who tear down the Special People Club, and enlist her siblings to help. Saying anything would be saying too much in this tight, compact, and abrupt movie where nothing is wasted by the filmmaker. Even at the end, on the school bus, when Dawn has finally acquiesced, Solondz shows her isolation as simply and quickly as possible, in a model movie ending that permanently burns itself into memory.

HEATHER MATARAZZO WAS 11 and a half when she played Dawn Wiener in *Welcome to the Dollhouse.* She so inhabits her role in the film that her identification with it probably hurt her career as an actor. Though she's had major roles since, in big-budget Hollywood movies, in the *Princess Diary* films in the early 2000s, and as a regular in various popular TV series, it is as Dawn that we will remember her.

Casting her was wise, but Solondz's choice to move away from casting himself as the lead in his own films was wiser. In his first feature and in his witty and accomplished early student shorts he had cast himself as the loser lead, a kind of No Wave Woody Allen. The failure of that first film got him out of his own head for the belated comeback of *Welcome to the Dollhouse.* Solondz's move from concentrating on himself by switching to a girl in seventh grade is what made him the filmmaker he is. He had to get outside of himself.

Yet at the same time he is Dawn and she is him, and this has obscured something about Matarazzo as an actress. The identification between director and actor here is very complete, which is perhaps why he started his fourth film, *Storytelling* (2001) with Dawn's funeral, because Matarazzo didn't want to play her again, and then brought Dawn back, played by another actor (Greta Gerwig), for *Wiener-Dog* (2016).

But it's Matarazzo's Dawn who is indelible. No other actor could have brought dignity to the outfits she wears in the film—the pink tops, the Schlitzie dresses, the red heart-shaped earrings for the party scene, with that blue polka-dotted, ruffled half-shirt and lime-green stretch pants. She is often dressed like a refugee from John Waters's Baltimore or like an American girl who for some reason had to audition for a role in an Almodóvar movie.

Despite those undignified looks, it is as a middle child alone at the dinner table in semi-darkness that Matarazzo is more memorable, even more than when she is smashing a VHS tape with a hammer. In the film's now-iconic shot of Dawn cross-legged on a car hood, bopping from the waist up and smiling along to Jill Wisoff's excellent title song, with its dirty lyrics that are inappropriate for an

11-year-old ("I got a blow-up doll and she looks like you, little girl"), Matarazzo and Solondz reached a 1990s cinematic apotheosis.

STARTING RIGHT AWAY, with *Happiness* (1998), name actors began to populate Solondz's subsequent films. They knew a good thing when they saw one, though critics did not always get it. By the time of *Life During Wartime* (2009) even British actors wanted to play his dysfunctional, suburban New Jerseyites.

Welcome to the Dollhouse was one of the American indie films, perhaps *the* American indie film, that moved feature filmmaking in America away from the Tarantino-inspired, tough-guys boy's club of the mid-1990s into a more deviant and perverse, less binary realm. In 1995, on one side there were movies like *Seven, Heat, Casino, The Usual Suspects, Braveheart, The Basketball Diaries, Get Shorty,* and *Things to Do in Denver When You're Dead.* On the other side, pretty much only *Clueless.* Several transitional films pointed in a new direction that year—*Safe, Kids, The Doom Generation, To Die For, The Addiction*—all made by men but indicative of a desire for something beyond *Pulp Fiction* and beyond Hal Hartley (Solondz is a kind of anti-Hartley), whose *Flirt* that year seemed like the end of a run.

In a period where the investigation of the New Jersey suburbs instigated by Susan Seidelman in the 1980s with *Smithereens* (1982) and *Desperately Seeking Susan* (1985) had been pushed aside, *Welcome to the Dollhouse* indicated there was unfinished business there. As a locker-room jock in Solondz's *Storytelling* reminds us, "They make fun of New Jersey all the time. But I don't care. 'Cause they're just snobs. 'Cause Jersey's where America's at."

Between 1995 and 1996 there was a transition that we could call the movement from *Kicking and Screaming* to *Walking and Talking,* from early Baumbach to the promise of Nicole Holofcener. *Welcome to the Dollhouse* was the signal movie in a group—the oddest, the least expected—that included *Fargo, Citizen Ruth, Sling Blade, Paradise Lost, Breaking the Waves, The Watermelon Woman, Trees Lounge,* Cronenberg's *Crash, The Daytrippers, Flirting with Disaster,*

Foxfire, The Craft, and *I Shot Andy Warhol.* Though 1996 was also the advent of the Andersons, with *Bottle Rocket* and *Hard Eight* both debuting, it was also a year with more women directors, weirder stories that investigated sexuality and shame, and a movement into the suburbs. Tellingly, Richard Linklater had moved to *SubUrbia* that year, too.

By the end of the decade that all collapsed into *American Beauty.* The kind of films *Welcome to the Dollhouse* heralded became Hollywood shamesploitation in the first decade of the 21st century—*Happy Endings* (2005), *Little Children* (2006)—then blinked out of existence or went downscale in mumblecore. Solondz struggled to get new films made as American movies changed into something very different from what they had been during the high-water mark years of American indie cinema. Bloated, CGI-heavy fantasy blockbusters reigned.

Exactly twenty years after *Welcome to the Dollhouse* came out, in the semi-sequel, *Wiener-Dog,* the non-Matarazzo Gerwig Dawn Weiner asks some traveling mariachis from Mexico, "Do you like it here in America?" "America is so lonely," one of them answers. "Sad," says another. "Depressing," adds a third. "Like a big fat elephant drowning in a sea of despair. Sometimes it's just too hard to lose weight. And you give up."

Dawn doesn't argue with them. Like Joy (Jane Addams) in *Happiness,* she had already learned what the proper response to "I love you" is. When a Russian immigrant tells Joy he loves her, she knows what he really means. "You don't love me," she tells him. "You love New Jersey."

CINEMA IS NEVER ON TIME

SERGE DANEY

SERGE DANEY HAS EXISTED IN ENGLISH MOSTLY IN A KIND OF SAMIZDAT, translated and published online by dedicated cinephiles with blogs, whose valiant work for two decades has tried to remedy this essential critic's absence. While a short hybrid interview book, *Postcards from the Cinema*, did appear in 2007, in Paul Douglas Grant's excellent translation, the majority of Daney's writing has been unavailable in English in book form.

As Grant points out in his introduction to *Postcards from the Cinema*, by that year a "proper introduction" to Daney was already "so overdue that the very mention of this deficiency is itself becoming something of a cliché." That was and is the case, that it is long overdue. It had been the case since before Daney's death in 1992, from complications resulting from AIDS.

Grant traces "The History of an Absence" in the *Postcards* introduction, explaining why the work of this important French critic and editor has been so resistant to publication in English. Or, I mean, it's the other way around. Before Semiotext(e), no US publisher dared to do it. It's a known fact that American publishers consider books of film criticism non-sellers, despite evidence to the contrary that there are many dedicated readers. The cinephiles who translated Daney and put him online knew that, first among them Laurent Kretzschmar and Andy Rector.

Parallel to that, it also sometimes seems as if everyone who has translated Daney into English, even just to quote him in an article, a review, or an essay, at some point left the United States to go live someplace else. Some of them came back, some move back and forth, but they have been wise enough, unlike those of us who can't translate from the French, to understand how on some level an engagement with Daney means a rejection of America and its hollow film reviewing sector. Better to watch all that devolve across an ocean.

At this point we are so distant from Daney that mentioning his absence can no longer be called a cliché. Bill Krohn and Jonathan Rosenbaum have kept Daney's name alive in English for two generations, but the cinephiles of the new Letterboxd era didn't learn they were supposed to miss him. Daney's prescient, fundamental engagement with the same issues facing us now can therefore come as news.

Christine Pichini took on a monumental task in her extraordinary translation of *La Maison cinéma et le monde I: Le temps des Cahiers (1962–1981)* into *The Cinema House and the World: The* Cahiers du Cinéma *Years, 1962–1981,* the first volume of Daney's collected work, and not just because the book is six hundred pages long. Daney loved the American cinema but he resisted where it comes from. He inscribed that resistance into everything he wrote. His resistance as a writer is also a resistance to translation.

That's true right on the cover. Daney's title refers to Bengali cinema, specifically to Satyajit Ray's late masterpiece, *Ghare Baire,* from Rabindranath Tagore's 1916 novel of the same name. Ray's film came out in the United States in the summer of 1985 as *The Home and the World* and in France as *La Maison et le monde,* the same way the Tagore's novel had appeared in the late 1910s.

In the movie, Bimala (Swatilekha Sengupta) must choose between her husband, Nikhilesh (Victor Banerjee), and a revolutionary, Sandip, played by Ray's great actor, Soumitra Chatterjee, from *Apur Sansar* (1959, originally called *The World of Apu* in the United States).

Bimala's choice is in some ways one between Western culture and her own, and between the radical and the commercial, just as Daney's was a choice between the West and the third world (as the Global South was called while Daney was writing), between the radical and bourgeois, between Satyajit Ray and his film and Nicholas Ray's *We Can't Go Home Again* (1976), the last pairing mentioned by Patrice Rollet in his original preface.

But to call this book *The Cinema Home and the World* risked proving American publishers right. Though that is the more literal title, it is also awkward in English, and we already have the term "movie house" to describe the place that was Daney's true home. If the new title renders Daney homeless, such is the fate of the film critic in the age of streaming and the pandemic. Being forced out of his real home and relocated in front of the TV screen or computer was a trajectory Daney knew well, long before the existence of Netflix.

In 1988 Daney published his collected newspaper columns about watching television as a book called *Le Salaire du zappeur*, another hard-to-translate title based on a movie, in this case a pun combining Henri-Georges Clouzot's *The Wages of Fear* (*Le Salaire de la peur*, 1953) with a French word for someone clicking between TV channels using a remote control, "zapping" between them. The device and the person using it are the same thing, a "zapper."

In addition to everything else he accomplished as a writer, Daney was the best and earliest film critic to describe the differences between film and television. He knew that to understand the second required full knowledge of the first. He had a politics of television, something television critics do not seem to have in this new age of peak TV, which thinks it has performed the magic act of making the medium disappear.

Wherever and however this full knowledge began, it took form in 1962, as you will discover in *The Cinema House and the World*, in a zine that lasted two issues, *Visages du cinéma*, where the equally original and equally neglected-in-English Louis Skorecki was the publisher, editor, and only other writer. Daney's first pieces were on films by Howard Hawks and Otto Preminger, Hollywood giants from overlapping eras of film history, one all-American, the other an émigré, a refugee from Hitler.

Daney and Skorecki then went to Hollywood to interview other American auteurs, including Leo McCarey, Jacques Tourneur, George Cukor, Samuel Fuller, and Jerry Lewis. There they experienced what Daney called "the cruelty of Hollywood," witnessing McCarey's bitter senility and Cukor's contemptuous dismissal of Nicholas Ray. (Lewis and Fuller treated them nice.) These encounters with "madmen" directors, Daney wrote, explained how he was "able to learn to breathe outside polluted France in American cinema, and at the same time I had no problem being furious in the 1970s with American imperialism."

Daney became a world traveler on the cheap, covering film festivals in the third world and behind the Iron Curtain as a contributor to *Cahiers du cinéma* in Paris. By 1973 he and the other Serge, Serge Toubiana, became the editors of the magazine. They evolved it from its revolutionary, Marxist-Lacanian phase of the late 1960s and early 1970s, returning it to more regular film coverage without sacrificing its political orientation.

Daney was perhaps the magazine's last great editor. While he was there, *Cahiers* maintained its opposition to commercial cinema without abandoning its analysis of it. Feminism and nascent queer theory came to the surface in his work along with anticolonialism, already present in *Cahiers* at the time. There was a difference with Daney, maybe because he was gay, maybe because he was also a popularizer, maybe because he was used to corralling so many other writers as an editor. He put it all together like no one else.

That led to a gig at Sartre's post-1968 leftist newspaper *Libération*. Daney comes to us as a critic who wrote more than his peers but who never dropped his standards or changed his interests for bigger publications or for his TV and radio appearances. He died too young, at 48, in 1992, the year Éric Rohmer's *Tale of Winter* came out. To put that in perspective, Rohmer had been an editor at *Cahiers*, too, was twenty-eight years older than Daney, and outlived him by almost twenty years. A year before he died, Daney founded a new film journal, *Trafic*, that promised a return to committed film writing without commercial considerations. It was the beginning of a new period in the history of cinema, different than the televisual era he had described so well in the 1980s, with a different look and feel, defined elsewhere: Iran, Taiwan, *D'Est*, David Lynch, *Basic Instinct*. . . . He did write a startling piece on *The Elephant Man*, collected in Semiotext(e)'s volume.

Here and Elsewhere (1976) seems to be the most important of Jean-Luc Godard's films for Daney. He mentions it many times, even more often than Mizoguchi's *Taira Clan Saga* (1955). He makes sure to emphasize the *and* in the title. Godard and Anne-Marie Miéville's difficult attempt to analyze Godard's failure to join filmmaking in the West with revolutionary struggle in Palestine opened a door for Daney. A door we can walk through now.

The question is whether Daney in translation comes to us too late. Finally having him in English in this form must not lead us to believe something has been fixed or repaired, even though it has at last appeared. Because it is so late, like this piece I'm writing, it cannot be a validation. Daney must remain an open question. "Cinema is never on time," he writes in one piece, then answers later that when it is good that doesn't matter, because then it is both "very slow and incredibly fast."

Daney is the same way. He was fortunate to arrive on the scene in the 1960s, but not too early in the 1960s, at the twilight of the classic auteurs, when they were still making films but they were their last films. Their kind of cinema was dissolving, what appeared then in the low tide of the 1970s, when everything left behind was revealed and the cinema was "skidding toward a new world."

So much, then, in Daney's search for a new world, was not good enough for him—not Joseph Losey, Jiří Menzel, Glauber Rocha. He found the future in spaghetti westerns instead. He despised Louis Malle, Elia Kazan's *The Visitors* (he should have seen *Wanda*), *The Night Porter*, and *The Mad Adventures of Rabbi Jacob*. Like many at *Cahiers* at the time, he couldn't really accept the American and German film directors (the new Hollywood and the new German Cinema) who were his peers, though he was blown away by Francis Ford Coppola, so much so that he compared *Apocalypse Now* to *Wind Across the Everglades*. Ditto Hans-Jürgen Syberberg, perhaps the German filmmaker most like Coppola, whose work was equally controversial. Daney admitted there were people who didn't like Warren Beatty, predicted Paul Schrader's interest in porn, and identified Diane Keaton as the co-creator of *Annie Hall*.

He did all this while keeping one of his eyes (he identifies four) on the *militant*, stopping along the way at various stations that certain American readers, no matter how young, may recognize from grad school: the *carnivalesque*, the *cloacal*, *potluck*, *the territory and the map*, and *hic et nunc* (like in Gide's *Marshlands*, the product of another French scene).

Some stations only Daney knew about. Those ones are called *aesthetic minimum wage*, *desquamation*, and my favorite: *blobbing*. Let's stop at that one ourselves. It comes from Daney's short 1976 review of a forgotten horror movie called *Beware! The Blob*, a too-late sequel to the original *Blob* from 1958. This belated follow-up came out in the US in 1972, reached Paris in 1976, and was directed by Larry Hagman, the star of TV's *I Dream of Jeannie* and *Dallas*. Daney calls it "the anti-*Jaws*" and describes the end of each scene, in which characters are eliminated by the lumpy globule, with the phrase "they are blobbed."

Here is a key. Months later, at a film festival in Tunisia, Daney sees a documentary he doesn't much like. The film is normalizing certain political issues that should be dealt with by the cinema in a more meaningful and complex way. "French cinema is starting to 'blob' immigration," he writes, "to 'naturalize' it, to make it a theme like any other." Apart from what may have been a reference to

Godard and Jean-Pierre Gorin's 1968 Dziga Vertov group *A Film Like Any Other* (*Un Film comme les autres*), here we see Daney opening the door. He is showing us the *and*. From *Beware! The Blob* Daney takes something he can use, directly from an image, and applies it in a political context to another, totally different kind of film.

There are many filmmakers and films to discover in *The Cinema House and the World* that have not yet been blobbed (Criterionized). Not translating Daney in book form has heretofore saved them from that fate. Since the only worthwhile things are the ones that no one cares about, let's try not to blob them. I won't even name them. They are inside. Daney let them in.

THE WORLD WAS JUST AN ADDRESS

OSCAR MOVIES 2022

BROADCAST TELEVISION IS TANKING SO BADLY THAT ABC, THE TELEVISION network that airs the Oscars, has insisted to the Academy of Motion Picture Arts and Sciences that eight categories be cut from the annual awards telecast, including Film Editing, Production Design, Sound, Original Score, and Hair and Makeup.

Worried about ratings and therefore ad dollars, ABC (a division of the Walt Disney Company), is willing to ignore the essential crafts of Hollywood filmmaking, from editing to hairdos, in favor of the rancid Best Original Song category. That way the aging broadcast TV audience won't miss out on seeing performances by such contemporary crowd pleasers as former country-and-western sitcom star Reba McEntire, and maybe even overmodest, ubiquitous Lin-Manuel Miranda.

Miranda also directed an Oscar-nominated film this year, so if he were to sing his song, it would be like if Alfred Hitchcock had also written "Que Sera, Sera" for *The Man Who Knew Too Much* (1956) and had to perform it onstage at the Oscars instead of Doris Day. Or, since Miranda has nominations for two movies, only one of which he directed, if Hitchcock had written a song in *The King and I*. This is what a film director is to ABC-Disney, Netflix, Warner Bros.-HBO Max. What film directing has become in Hollywood is a team-building exercise with lots of group hugs and a public-facing mascot from the generic world of show biz. The mascot could be anyone camera-friendly. Being a director is now something of an honorary position at that level, like being the Grand Marshal of the Hollywood Christmas Parade.

ABC has lost faith in the films themselves, swallowing the right-wing notion that the nominees do not reflect popular taste. Therefore the less time spent on them the better. Give the people what we think they want: Beyoncé and Billie Eilish. Anything but actors from these movies. Olivia Colman? Where are the three Spider-Men? Where is The Batman?

The atmosphere in which the highest honors in filmdom are now broadcast to the masses is more like an episode of *Wheel of Fortune* in which the contestants can't solve the puzzle, no matter how many vowels they've bought. The audience on social media engages in Frustration Discourse as they watch loser-winners grapple with their moments of professional glory on live TV, all so ABC can continue to exist in a world that has left it behind. It's also a world in which actual movies have become marginal, especially during the Oscars.

Every moment is confused, all of it a ritual no one in the film industry believes in anymore but enacts to ward off demons of their future: simultaneous release in theaters and on streaming, no back end, no residuals, voice-over work in animation and video games, shrinking foreign markets, foreign markets where film releases are moral quandaries, a series of bad decisions like the ones that led to *The Suicide Squad*, Cameo, and the final, furthest away specter: a world without an In Memoriam reel.

As I watched this year's Oscar films, a cargo ship called the *Felicity Ace* burned in the North Atlantic. Massive and packed with luxury automobiles bound for the US, it was on fire and adrift, abandoned by its crew, its shipment of expensive cars doomed. Life at the beginning of the pandemic reminded me of the *Costa Concordia*, the luxury cruise ship in Jean-Luc Godard's *Film Socialisme* that later sank, a metaphor for the shipwreck of capitalism that Godard guided into reality in 2010. Now this new *Titanic* appeared without people, only machines, floating aimlessly and aflame as the pandemic moved into a new phase, possibly its end phase but probably not.

The *Felicity Ace* sank on the first day of March after two weeks burning at sea. "The American industry rules cinema the world over. There is nothing much to add to this statement of fact," Godard wrote in the press book for his film *La Chinoise* in 1967. The *Titanic* model of American cinema remains in place, it still rules the waves, but these days each Oscar movie is like a Porsche, a Lamborghini, or a Bentley on that cargo ship, packed and streaming, going down without a crew, part of a semi-automated supply chain that has issues getting its pricey goods to the public. The Oscars are the abandoned auto show of that industry.

CODA

Sign language was prominent in cinema this year. It is an important part of the play in *Drive My Car*, and Clint Eastwood used it with a little girl in *Cry Macho*. If last year's Oscar-nominated musical drama of deafness, *Sound of Metal*, was too edgy for you, with its noise duo, drug addiction, and shock Mathieu Amalric appearance, this year's *CODA* (which stands for Child of Deaf Adults) cleans up the act. It's an all-American family affair, suitable for the wholesome executives at Apple TV, who released it, though the protagonist, a high school singer (Emilia Jones), does somehow own a Shaggs album. I don't think anyone expected a discussion of the Shaggs in a movie about a deaf family, who in this case really don't know what they're missing.

CODA admirably focuses on the working life of a Gloucester fisherman family in which the father (Troy Kotsur), mother (Marlee Matlin), and son (Daniel Durant) are deaf (and played by deaf actors), and the daughter is not. Their struggles with the hearing world and with unfair labor practices, and their plan to collectivize the docks, are the backdrop for daughter Ruby's conflicted desire to get away from the sea and go to the Berklee College of Music. The deaf characters are easy to relate to in this pleasant, unmemorable movie. For instance, even though I can hear, I would have the same confused, impatient reactions were I forced to attend a high school musical. Presented with a group of teens singing David Bowie's "Starman," I would watch in silent frustration, too. The issue is that for me it would be easier to forget.

Dune

The self-conscious boredom and fascism of Denis Villeneuve's films, along with their sandy-inky beige-taupe-gray-black-brown-orange color palette, make them look different than other blockbusters. They are in fact post-blockbusters, and Villeneuve's unnecessary new version of the first part of *Dune* shows how a depressed attitude that has given in to all that is wrong with current Hollywood filmmaking, and has also given in to all that is wrong with the world, might appear to be new. Especially to a director who believes mankind still tells stories around the fire at dusk, or after dinner, or before watching *Euphoria*, which Zendaya is also in, but more often. After all, as Flaubert said about writing *Salammbô*, "Few will guess how depressed one had to be to undertake the resuscitation of Carthage!" Same with the resuscitation of *Dune*, which already exists as a movie, a TV miniseries, and a documentary about a movie version that didn't happen and should have.

The futility and pointlessness of Villeneuve's secondhand white-savior epic comes through as laziness. To understand that, we need only compare one scene from the 1984 David Lynch version to the same scene in the new one. In Villeneuve's hand-in-the-painbox scene, nothing is charged with hidden meaning, and nothing seems painful to Timothée Chalamet's Paul. It is not much of a trial for him, and all the work in the scene is done by Charlotte Rampling's Bruce

Conner *Couch* costume. We know Chalamet will not have a problem. It's already clear he is "The One."

In Lynch's version, which incidentally occurs in a movie that is not that great but is at least very weird throughout, Kyle MacLachlan's Paul seems genuinely frightened by being forced to put his hand deep inside a woman's box. The viewer does not yet understand Paul's status in this world, and there is no way to know what will happen when he places his hand in this trap.

Where Lynch is hallucinatory, intense, and Freudian (or, in a word, hysterical), Villeneuve is dull and literal, and his scene is simply a test that allows the lead character to move up a level, like in a video game or a YA novel, which we knew he was going to do. Later in the movie, the idea that Chalamet could just speak in a certain tone of voice and other people would do exactly what he wanted them to do reminded me of Brooklyn teens ordering in restaurants.

Lynch's penile sandworms, pre-CGI, were better realized and more menacing, and the Harkonnens, whose name is now pronounced differently, were more disgusting in 1984. This *Dune* toys with the idea of genocide, but it's mostly a movie for people who like to memorize things. All these stupid names, one after another. Frank Herbert was trying too hard. So is Villeneuve. This basic *Lawrence of Arabia* tribalism and its jihad-mongering, with its conflicted son and dangled possibility of revolution, were also aspects of Villeneuve's equally ponderous *Blade Runner* sequel. Since these notions have already appeared in so many other 21st-century blockbusters, it is hard to ascribe them to Villeneuve-as-auteur, despite all the black water he dips them in before rolling them in the sand.

Belfast

Jackie Wilson said the Troubles were a wee bit of fun now, weren't they? In our little house on our little street, which were fine for us when they were being bombed, we had perfect TV reception, and

Pap (Ciarán Hinds) was twenty years younger than Granny (Judi Dench), who loved nothing more than winning acting awards. Pa (Jamie Dornan) was handsome and good, when he was around, and in perfect shape from those *Fifty Shades of Grey* sessions, and Ma (Caitríona Balfe) was such a put-upon knockout mommy like she was in *Ford v Ferrari* that she should have been in this a lot more, instead of it being such a Balfe fast. Our director, Kenneth Branagh, he loves Shakespeare and Agatha Christie and, yes, even Thor, which he reminds us of with a shot of a comic book, but in black-and-white, unlike the splashy Marvel comics in *West Side Story*, which is also set around the same time, has a lot of music in it, and is about two sides fighting a turf war.

Belfast is in black-and-white so Branagh can separate it from his hack work, because it's a personal story from his childhood, and because documentaries about the past are in black-and-white (or "monochrome," as Netflix calls it now when promoting films like *Passing*), and *Belfast* takes place in the past and it's about real things that happened. 2021 was a big year for b&w, and this movie falls in line with one of its current uses: telling stories for dads. Branagh's explosion of treacle, with Jude Hill as a cuddly blond toddler, was the most popular. Mike Mills's *C'mon C'mon*, with Joaquin Phoenix as a public radio producer shepherding a neurotic little kid (Woody Norman), was enervating to the point of narcolepsy, the opposite of what Branagh's doing in *Belfast*. It was unlovable.

The best of these films, and therefore the most ignored, was Alexandre Rockwell's *Sweet Thing*, in which his own daughter and son (Lana Rockwell and Nico Rockwell) are menaced by an alcoholic father, who Will Patton plays with every stop pulled out, a performance of total fucked-up-edness, a man trying to be nice before he loses it completely and swirls down the drain. Rockwell's film also featured Van Morrison music like *Belfast*, but not in the same celebratory, uninhibited way. *Sweet Thing* is set in a kind of fairy tale, skid-row present and shot in New Bedford, Massachusetts, without any cute Irishness, even though there's no doubt some could have been located in the area.

Sweet Thing confronted American racism and child abuse and cops shooting Black kids, none of which were presented as fun like the Troubles in *Belfast*, though Rockwell placed them in a beautiful film where his use of black-and-white was justified and worked. It made *Sweet Thing* more immediate, not less. It was clearly a Gen X movie about childhood, in which Rockwell's memories of freedom and neglect were poured into a constricted, dangerous present. *Sweet Thing* was also unlike Mills's film, which took place coast-to-coast in Dullsville, USA, and catered to and indulged kids while recapitulating white parental self-regard instead of exposing it like Rockwell did in his film. *C'mon C'mon* (terrible title) attempted to do that through documentary scenes with Black parents and their children that struck me as well-intentioned cop-outs. It therefore made sense that Phoenix worked for NPR in it, but I don't think that was the idea.

Being the Ricardos

Nicole Kidman and Javier Bardem are post-life versions of Lucille Ball and Desi Arnaz in *Being the Ricardos*, spruced up and perfected by computers and surgeons to exist as animatronic forms whose ability to handle drama and comedy surpasses anything humans could do back in the 1950s. Creating these androids on his keyboard and in the studio must have been so difficult for Aaron Sorkin that he dropped his own mask and finally admitted it was entertainment, not politics, that has interested him all along.

What else could explain the outright fabrications in this movie, which include a phone call from J. Edgar Hoover, in front of a live studio audience, that washes away Lucille Ball's 1930s membership in the Communist Party and makes everyone cheer? This right-wing appeal to Hoover and the FBI is the opposite of Clint Eastwood's in

J. Edgar (2011), where Eastwood and Leonardo DiCaprio carefully outlined how a police state was created in the US.

That Sorkin glosses the McCarthy Era like this and places himself to the right of Eastwood is surprising. But it makes sense, because no one in Hollywood is more aligned with the entertainment/tech industry/Washington politics nexus than the power-loving, success-worshipping, union-hating Sorkin. Somehow this extended to slighting Karl Freund, the German cinematographer of *I Love Lucy*, who invented the three-camera sitcom setup that's still in use seventy years later. Why Sorkin chose to do that is also telling: it made Desi Arnaz look smarter, Sorkin's goal with all his protagonists.

The Eyes of Tammy Faye

Jessica Chastain's performance as Tammy Faye Bakker, disgraced televangelist wife and singer, borders on the monstrous. By the end it almost crosses over into a kind of American Fellini. It doesn't, though, because *The Eyes of Tammy Faye* is a whitewash of this con artist's life. Like her husband, Jim Bakker (Andrew Garfield), Tammy Faye was a grifter who preyed on the homebound via broadcast TV, convincing them to send money so that their souls would be saved and they would go to Heaven. The Bakkers of course lived in luxury and built a Christian theme park with that money. No one at any time seems to have brought up that they were turning Jesus Christ into Mickey Mouse.

Chastain and her screenwriter and director want us to believe Tammy Faye was an ambitious but God-fearing Christian puppeteer desperate to get out of her Minnesota hometown. The film excuses her, insisting her Christianity was deeper than that of her televangelist competitors—Jerry Falwell, Pat Robertson, and their ilk. Though it is clear Tammy Faye empathized with gay men stricken with AIDS and tried to convince her followers to treat them as human beings, not as the pariahs the Reagan Right wanted them to be, this fact doesn't exonerate her. As a Christian, it was the least she could do. Her second husband, a church builder and developer played in the film by Sam Jaeger, ran afoul of the law just like her first. The film, however, shows Tammy Faye alone at the end, toughing it out in a crap condo, not married to conman number two.

The fun here is supposed to be in watching Chastain transform from a cute, peppy, and horny Bible-college student in the late 1950s into the full-on, Divine-in-a-John-Waters-movie look of Tammy Faye's infamy thirty years later. While she is never not a chipper cornball high on her own supply, she is never tragic, either, because like a Trump wife, she shits in a gold toilet. Garfield's Jim is a closeted, prissy fake, yes, but Tammy Faye is a grotesque with a Betty-Boop-meets-Sarah-Palin voice, unhappy because she's blinkered to reality. Through it all, the Bakkers' audience of twenty million kept sending them money whenever Tammy asked. Though she did live in a life-size dollhouse, her fate was to become a national joke, not the heroine of an Ibsen play.

King Richard

King Richard demonstrates, step by step, the value of sticking to your plan, even if some folks think you're crazy. I don't mean Richard Williams's plan to turn his daughters Venus and Serena into tennis champs. I mean Will Smith's plan to win an Oscar. Williams, like the actor who plays him, knew the value of finely tuning a capitalist product and introducing it into the marketplace as a brand. This is a business movie, which reaches its height not when Venus Williams (Saniyya Sidney) almost wins her second professional match and reveals her talent and grace to the world, but when the Williams family decides to hold out for a better sneaker deal. "Nine months later," we read on screen at the end of the movie, "Venus signed a contract with Reebok for twelve million dollars." I don't mind being nudged to cry as the Williams sisters' reach for the stars in Compton.

But I call "out" when I am asked to weep with joy over their first professional product endorsement.

Drive My Car

I did not quite get why the theater director protagonist (Hidetoshi Nishijima) in *Drive My Car* was not allowed by the theater company to drive himself to work every day. The idea that it would have been an insurance liability seemed odd. In any case, his 1987 red Saab 900 becomes essential to Hamaguchi's film, and without it the rehearsals of *Uncle Vanya* that make up much of the rest of the drama would have been stifling. Not that the film is necessarily opened up by the driving, since a lot of that is interior: a man inside a car listening to the voice of his dead wife (Reika Kirishima) on tape while another woman (Tōko Miura) drives him around.

Cars attained a strange new level of prominence in movies in 2021, an indicator of our changing relationship to the automotive as cars helped destroy the planet, became unaffordable as the pandemic continued, and sometimes burned and sank into the ocean. I don't mean in *F9*, the latest *Fast & Furious* movie, in which a car travels into outer space, driven by Tyrese Gibson and Ludacris. *F9*, a truly stupid movie, wastes resources, just burns through them to make money, and part of its stupidity is that it makes room for Helen Mirren and Cardi B before explicitly comparing the idea of "family" to a 1970 Dodge Charger. That's not it, Vin. Not at all.

But it is not too far off from Julia Ducournau's staggering *Titane*, a French film in which a woman (Agathe Rousselle) has sex with a Cadillac (baby, you can fuck my car), gets pregnant, and gives birth to a hybrid. As in *Spencer* and *France*, these films explored women's relationships with their automobiles, putting them in the driver's seat instead of men. *Titane* took this to an extreme that was maybe too much for car-centric North American viewers. It didn't meet with the same outrage as David Cronenberg's 1996 adaptation of

J. G. Ballard's *Crash* only because it came out during the pandemic, and the few people who saw it were rendered speechless. It was my favorite film of last year. Cars develop consciousness in these films. The way the voice of the wife returned, speaking through the Saab's tape player in *Drive My Car*, pointed in that direction—the direction of getting over grief and loss as we try to return to life.

It is a trend that began in art films with the talking limos in the garage at night that ended Leos Carax's *Holy Motors* in 2012. In the recent *King Car*, an underseen Brazilian movie that is almost as good as *Bacurau* and has a lot in common with *Titane*, director Renata Pinheiro creates a revolutionary situation in Pernambuco, prompted by a talking car in a junkyard. Sex with vehicles ensues. "From this evolution there is no return," *King Car* explains. Through intercourse with machines, in this contaminated environment, "we discover our true values. It's where we face our ghosts."

Drive My Car, *Titane*, and *King Car* are the products of different cultures with different film traditions, but there is a direct line connecting the ghosts in each. Car accidents were way up in the US last year. College students strapped for cash began living in their cars inside university parking garages, and reality TV shows staged deadly airborne car stunts. A show at the Museum of Modern Art called *Automania* put cars on display like in a showroom, parked safely away from the road. It was evident on movie screens, however, that the evolution of the automobile as a sexy, dangerous vehicle continues in new directions, and they are not driverless ones. Cars exert a different kind of control than that and have a tight hold on us, driving mankind.

Licorice Pizza

The in-reverse, out-of-gas moving-truck scene in Paul Thomas Anderson's *Licorice Pizza* approaches driving from the opposite direction. It's an anti-chase that glides backwards without a roar.

Alana Haim guides the truck expertly, younger men nattering at her, threatening to choke her. The film becomes obsessed with the 1973 oil crisis, which is maybe why it's so frenetic and high-energy. Characters are in motion and running—Haim runs so much in the film that it becomes like a parody of *The Worst Person in the World*. The adult men in *Licorice Pizza* are automotive maniacs, poor players strutting their hour in the movie, actors and directors playing actors and directors.

Defined by nostalgia for 1970s California, *Licorice Pizza* is to 2021 what *American Graffiti* was to 1973, but from the other side of the mirror. Anderson's 1970s beats George Lucas's 1950s because Anderson is expressing a minority opinion, not celebrating a majority culture. *American Graffiti* existed as something it knew everyone who saw it would agree on. *Licorice Pizza* turns the camera around and speaks to the few. Thus, everything is backwards and wrong in *Licorice Pizza*, as it was in the 1970s when compared to now: children raise themselves, adults date teens, teens start businesses, restaurants alienate customers, and getting work is an audition for something else, with hidden, sexual motivations barely under the surface erupting as stupid jokes. It is impossible to know whether things are based on skill or luck as the world slips backwards into the future. Everything is temporary and can be snuffed in an instant, like the waterbed sales that reverse supply and demand overnight.

The effect is that *Licorice Pizza* can never be central to the culture it is part of. That is its strength. It exists on the edge of Hollywood and is written in the margins of the film industry, adjacent to it, with an address in the Valley. This movie seems like a transitional film for Anderson, a stopgap, like so many things that emerged during the pandemic. And like the pandemic, it goes on too long but time flies.

Parallel Mothers

The melodrama in Pedro Almodóvar's latest film is deceptively muted, though the film's plot is brazenly manipulative. The director of *All About My Mother* makes it easy to guess how this story of thwarted motherhood will unfold as soon as Janis (Penélope Cruz) and Ana (Milena Smit), both pregnant, end up in the same hospital room. This concentration on the present-day mechanics of the plot buries the film's parallel story, about mass killings in fascist Spain in the 1930s during the Franco regime. *Parallel Mothers* is a film of corpses and skeletons as much as it is about babies and children. Almodóvar leads the viewer to an excavation the same way Janis leads Ana to understand the history of her country. Unlike the story of what happened at the hospital, it should not come as a surprise to her.

Almodóvar has always dug up whatever is buried in the subconscious of his characters. As they fall into comas, we find they have been raised in caves or that their family history is hidden below the surface in a mass grave. From film to film, his characters' psychological states come more and more to resemble the political history of Spain. At the same time, his filmmaking, like Penélope Cruz, does not age. He seems more contemporary the more he becomes an outlier to the mainstream of commercial cinema.

Billy Wilder told Almodóvar there was one thing he should never do, and that was to give in to the temptation to make a film in Hollywood. Almodóvar has made twenty-two films since his first in 1980, and now we learn he is on the verge of making his first feature in English, with Cate Blanchett. Either it is time for him to show us how it's done, or this is a bad idea. Over forty years, we've learned from his films that things usually don't go so well, but it's foolish not to be optimistic. As things fall apart, at least they can look great.

The Lost Daughter

That is a lesson Maggie Gyllenhaal did not keep in mind as she adapted Elena Ferrante's novel *The Lost Daughter* for the big screen (Netflix). In Almodóvar's *Julieta*, two actresses played the same woman twenty or so years apart, as Olivia Colman and Jessie Buckley do here. Where Almodóvar dressed his seaside tale in 1980s New Wave colors and Hitchcockian ambiance, Gyllenhaal's beach melodrama is a new kind of arthouse film for home viewing, in which seriousness of intent must be signaled at all times.

It could be that the difference is that *Julieta*, which is not Almodóvar's greatest film in any case (though it was also based on literature—Alice Munro), was the twentieth film he directed, and this is Gyllenhaal's first. But I think it's that Netflix believes this is what serious, award-winning films are: not fun, never fun, and not very nice to look at.

Through flashbacks, Gyllenhaal makes the bizarre or mysterious elements of the film too clear, right up to the end, when everything goes haywire in the opposite direction, and it becomes hard to understand what's happening. Colman phones her daughter and bleeds into the tide with an orange in her hand, a stew of symbols assembled from previous scenes.

The problem is the flashbacks. We see Buckley as the young Colman, an English professor and a harried mother and wife embarking on an affair with a colleague who is supposed to be brilliant. Played by Peter Sarsgaard to resemble late-period Michael Stipe, this sensitive, bearded academic cracks jokes about Pierre Bourdieu and Paul Ricœur (a first for Netflix). It is therefore obvious in a second why the middle-aged Colman feels such guilt for abandoning her family. Still discombobulated years later, she vacations in Greece next to a sketchy, semi-Mafia family like the one that lives across the street from me. She finds herself dancing to "Livin' on a Prayer" by night and translating Dante into English by day, two strange activities we didn't expect from her or anyone this year. The film follows the

Chekhov gun rule, but with a hatpin Colman gives to shady, unstable Dakota Johnson. It was only a matter of time before Johnson returned it.

Nightmare Alley

The movies force us to ask questions. Seeing *The Eyes of Tammy Faye* right after *Nightmare Alley* prompted a brain teaser, since the two films share a scene: Would you rather see Jessica Chastain give Andrew Garfield a hand job in a bathtub, or see Toni Collette do the same to Bradley Cooper? That was the old-timey con-woman convincer move, as far as Hollywood was concerned last year.

Guillermo del Toro's remake of *Nightmare Alley* corrupts an evil story. William Lindsay Gresham's terrifying and singular 1946 novel was itself a tale of corruption and the great sui generis work of hardboiled American fiction. Its plot did not need to be tampered with, but del Toro and Kim Morgan's screenplay cheapens something that purposefully dealt in tawdriness. Since this film comes close to being del Toro's best, it is too bad he had to throw out the penultimate sections of the book. I mark it down to his essential torturer's mentality. His flaw as a screenwriter-director-producer it that he thinks of himself as a great liberal and friend of the common man, but he can't not revel in the infliction of pain and suffering on his villains.

So instead of just making the millionaire industrialist Grindle (Richard Jenkins) a vindictive and deluded mark for Cooper's fake mentalist, Stan, del Toro has to turn Grindle into a serial killer who must be beaten to death, and then have Grindle's bodyguard (Holt McCallany) run over by a car, in graphic detail. In Gresham's novel, Grindle becomes Stan's Javert, the figure who hunts him, turning him into a drunk, a hobo, and finally the thing he most fears becoming, a carnival circus geek. Here I must indulge in psychoanalysis, like Cate Blanchett's character does in the movie. In fact, I suspect on some level del Toro wants the viewer to. I put his cruelty down to his subconscious identification with Grindle more than Stan. At some level, del Toro recognizes himself in this wealthy sociopath, an aspect of his personality he wants to punish and kill, harshly. There is no mercy there.

That kind of unnecessary cruelty continues to mar his serious work, as it did in *The Shape of Water.* Otherwise, del Toro's *Nightmare Alley* is a model of atmosphere and production design, with beautiful, committed performances from character actors who were given great roles, most of all Collette, Jenkins, McCallany, David Strathairn, Willem Dafoe, Mary Steenburgen, and Tim Blake Nelson, though if Nelson and Dafoe had swapped roles, the film would have ended with an extra dash of evil, turning it more hardboiled and more *Detour*-esque, a tale of fate more than gore. With the menacing Dafoe as the guy doing Stan the worst favor at the end, and Nelson the creep who got him into it in the first place, the balance would have tilted in the direction of eternity, or at least hell, where del Toro thrives, poking away with his pitchfork.

West Side Story

In all the film industry talk about how *Nightmare Alley* and Steven Spielberg's new version of *West Side Story* underperformed at the box office, and how that proves audiences are uninterested in seeing non-franchise films by high-end directors in theaters, no one seems to have considered that both remakes are period pieces, and that the original films, when they came out, were not. They took place in the present of the time they were made. So maybe it is something else the audience has rejected.

Furthermore, picture yourself sitting down in a movie theater in front a huge screen and settling in to watch a big, colorful, Hollywood musical with songs you love, shot on location in New York City. The trailers end, the lights dim, and on the black screen the first thing you see, in gigantic white letters, is CONTAINS TOBACCO DEPICTIONS. Who needs it? Being treated like an idiot right off the bat ruins the movie.

Cigarettes aside, Spielberg's film is marvelous, an improvement on Robert Wise's 1961 film version of the Bernstein-Sondheim musical. That one was distinguished by Daniel Fapp's stunning, Tashlinesque color cinematography as much as by the music. Unfortunately, there was not much Fapp could do with the brownface the actors playing the Sharks and their girls were forced to wear by the producers.

Though it is better than that, and maybe Spielberg's second or third best movie, it nonetheless feels academic somehow, the large cast a jobs program for theater kids, the gentrification theme something I don't believe Spielberg cares about in the least or has any experience with. Tony Kushner's rewrite of Arthur Laurents's original book for the show is quite convincing, however, as Spielberg goes bravura immediately, with a *Kane*-esque crane shot (computerized) through the ruins of the neighborhood that became Lincoln Center. This shot links the opening to so much in Spielberg's previous work. It is a set piece from a war film, reminiscent of *Saving Private Ryan*, *Schindler's List*, and of course, *Lincoln*, since a sign enters the frame that says LINCOLN in huge letters. Once again, all history is the same to Spielberg, a teenage gang war in Manhattan the equivalent of World War II, 1961 the same as *1941*.

Doing midcentury modern and crime jazz, Spielberg remains obvious. After an astonishing overhead shot of mounds of salt in a municipal salt shed as gang members approach in shadows from both sides, Spielberg has to have one of the gang members shout, "It's salt! For when the streets ice up!" Because after all these years he still thinks his audience is not the brightest, and all the world is the mass audience to him. As the song "Tonight" has it in the movie, "The world was just an address," a lyric that never sounded so fatalistic to me until I heard it in a Spielberg movie in 2022, with the wealth gap widening and pushing all but the richest people out of this city.

Spielberg moves “Gee, Officer Krupke” indoors, to a police station waiting room, which works better and makes more sense than the nighttime storefront in Wise’s film. More importantly, every decision Spielberg has made to open the film into the city streets works magnificently in this last-gasp movie of joyous urban life, all of it perfectly executed and choreographed with great verve and beauty. His Maria (Rachel Zegler) is more soulful than Natalie Wood was in the earlier film. With her Barbara Steele or Soledad Miranda looks, she fits into this film without a happy ending, adding to the sense that things will not work out, that the lovers are doomed along with the freedom their access to the city promised. There was always a bit of 1960s horror in this operatic tragedy. Then, it was the predictive horror of youth in revolt. Somehow the director of *Jaws* found it on location, in some small way, like he did in Martha’s Vineyard half a lifetime ago. He gives in to it. There is no future for these lovers, no way to fight against what is happening to them and their neighborhood.

Tick, Tick . . . Boom!

Jonathan Larson’s life was tragic. Cut short by an aortic dissection in 1996 just as his musical, *Rent*, was about to open to great success on Broadway, he’d written *Tick, Tick . . . Boom!* in 1991, but it was only performed twice in his lifetime. Now Lin-Manuel Miranda has turned this autobiographical musical into a Netflix movie starring Andrew Garfield as Larson. As in *CODA*, we hear “Happy Birthday” performed, because these films are about the birth of artists in their quest for musical theater acclaim. Both films have a desperate, fleeing quality, which posits that seeking artistic success is difficult and punishing, too hard on others around you, and a race against time.

As *Rent* was an updated bohemia for the 1990s, *Tick, Tick . . . Boom!* moves Larson’s vision into the present for theater kids raised on *Glee*. Here, the romance of sharing an apartment on the Lower

East Side with the bathtub in the kitchen is a kind of 1980s utopia, with fun, touchy-feely parties, a Jackson Pollock couch, and the threat of AIDS instead of Covid slowing down success.

In the hands of Miranda and Garfield, this becomes a form of desperation in which every song is forced out as a last-ditch effort. Near the end, when Michael (Robin de Jesús), Larson's best friend and roommate, discovers he has AIDS and sings, on the verge of tears, "Is this real life?," the answer is yeah, but no. That's because show biz dreams swamp social reality every time, even in scenes that pit them against each other.

Part of Larson's story is that in the late '80s he wrote an elaborate sci-fi musical called *Superbia* that was excellent but too complex to be staged. In Miranda's movie we see a bare-bones preview of it performed for critics, investors, and Stephen Sondheim (Bradley Whitford). In the context of 2021 and Netflix, Larson-Garfield's description of *Superbia* in this performance takes on an added resonance. *Superbia*, he explains, "is a satire set in the future on a poisoned planet Earth, where the vast majority of humanity spend their entire lives just staring at the screens of their media transmitters, watching the tiny elite of the rich and powerful who film their own fabulous lives like TV shows."

Including this can be read as either a pitch for Netflix to make another Larson movie or an example of how capitalism and spectacle absorb everything. Rest assured, however, that if Netflix did make it, they would probably hire Ben Wheatley to direct it, which would prevent anyone from enjoying and absorbing it.

The Power of the Dog

What we have here is the kind of movie André Bazin called a "superwestern," which is "a western that would be ashamed to be just itself, and looks for some additional interest to justify its existence—an aesthetic, sociological, moral, psychological, political, or erotic interest, in short some quality extrinsic to the genre and which is supposed to enrich it." Doubly true in this case, because in Jane Campion's *Power of the Dog*, her lead character (Benedict Cumberbatch), the ruthless cowboy with the non-ruthless name "Phil," is exactly that—ashamed to be just himself. Phil is a repressed gay man in a macho profession, needling his weaker brother (Jesse Plemons), who has married a woman (Kirsten Dunst) Phil considers a slattern.

Dunst's greenhorn son (Kodi Smit-McPhee) notices this and contrives to eliminate Phil from the ranch. Here it's the opposite of the situation in the superwestern *Shane* (1953). Instead of "Shane, come back, my mother wants you," its "Phil, go away, my mother *doesn't* want you." As a Netflix art film, a perfect breeding ground for a movie like this, it is also super-serious, like *The Lost Daughter.* Similarly, the film's ambition leads to confusion. Again, the ending is murky. A lasso soaked in anthrax is something new in a western, it has to be admitted, but getting to that point was a slog, a slow crawl to the Oscars.

In a non-superwestern, somebody on the ranch would have smacked Phil in the mouth in the first scene. Though he is threatening and mean-eyed, he is no Liberty Valance, and his needling of the other characters is intolerable and obvious. The way he keeps talking about "Bronco Henry," his absent mentor who we are led to believe was also his lover, is repetitive and tiresome. On the ranch it would have become a source of humor. Phil's banjo duel with Dunst's poor piano playing, in fact, is more like something from *Blazing Saddles* than *Unforgiven*. Most damningly for this film that is so subtly concerned with right and wrong, Campion's use of New Zealand in place of Montana and a British actor for a ranch boss is the moral equivalent of computer-generated imagery.

That brings it back to Bazin, where it should end. Ultimately, Campion's portrait of a repressed cowboy, I think, flatters Hollywood. Varmints like Phil may or may not have tamed the West, but for sure they continued on to Los Angeles to found talent agencies and direct superhero movies.

The Tragedy of Macbeth

Joel Coen's black-and-white film of the Scottish play is not made for an age when the TV remote and the smartphone are pointed toward your hand. More like a silent movie by Lang or Dreyer, this Apple TV production overwhelms Shakespeare with monolithic sets, powerful compositions, and piercing cries. Frances McDormand as Lady M. and Denzel Washington in the title role struggle to keep up with the mise-en-scène, while Kathryn Hunter, an amazing actor I do not remember seeing before, plays all three witches and the Old Man in tour-de-force performances that minimize digital trickery but still get lost in Coen's frames.

It was inevitable that this version would be compared to Orson Welles's. His cheapo 1948 *Macbeth* for Republic Studios is better because it isn't as distant as Coen's, despite being seventy-three years older, but it's more awesome, with more cold terror and high drama. Welles goes for it, as usual, while Coen's film is something of an exercise. As for being the first film from a brother act minus one, even with Shakespeare writing the screenplay, this movie certifies Ethan's value. When the best thing in a Coen film is a long sword fight, something is missing, and *The Tragedy of Macbeth* is a movie where we can pinpoint what it was.

THE CAPTAIN'S DINNER IS COMING UP

TRIANGLE OF SADNESS

THE ONLY THREE THINGS RICH PEOPLE TALK ABOUT ANYMORE ARE THE houses they own, how to avoid permanent residency so they won't have to pay taxes, and the exotic vacations they take to get away from it all. These are people on the move, settling nowhere, staying one step ahead of the rest of society, which gets sicker of them every day.

If you live in New York City, you are surrounded by their conversations, because in New York there are two things no one can avoid: seeing wealthy people and hearing strangers talk. Sitting in a restaurant in Brooklyn not long ago, I overheard from the booth behind me a foursome loudly discussing their recent trip to the Norwegian fjords. I could tell they'd had a great time because they were laughing so much. Of course they made me think of the ski vacation in Ruben Östlund's movie *Force Majeure* (2014), even though that's in the Alps. Along with *fjord,* another word kept leaping out at me as they laughed: *McKinsey,* the name of their employer, the management-consulting behemoth known for its work with authoritarian regimes and opioid manufacturers.

These four weren't laughing for any particular reason, not really. Their cackling reminded me of something the comedian Don Rickles once said about Merv Griffin, the sleek talk-show host and media mogul. While Griffin was chuckling over one of the comic's signature put-downs, Rickles turned to the audience and said, "Merv's laughing because he's so rich."

Will anything ever make this kind of laughter stick in rich people's throats? Does their merriment come with any cost they will ever notice? Plenty of streaming content addresses these questions, engaging with the cruelties of the widening wealth gap and the audience's need to see it undermined and fractured. Recent movies like *Glass Onion* and series like *The White Lotus,* however, mock the wealthy while also indulging viewers' desire to participate in the splendor of high-end travel and luxury living. These fantasy projections create mixed emotions of resentment and enjoyment. They are not destructive. And after a round of Twitter commentary, they fade from memory.

Östlund has a special knack for cutting through this thorny problem. He writes and directs movies that complicate things, making them pricklier and more troublesome, impossible to forget. In his films, the bad-faith arguments of his well-off characters, their irresponsibility, their selfishness, and their wrong decisions are shocking because they are so automatic, so reflexive. In *Force Majeure, The Square* (2017), and now *Triangle of Sadness* (2022), what Östlund calls a "trilogy of masculinity," he has taken elements from generic entertainment—the family vacation, the workplace comedy, lovers on a desert island—and treated them sociologically, with a clear logic, in presentations that discomfort by leaving nothing out, and then holding on a little too long.

His cold eye is what separates his work from that of other filmmakers, something the Cannes Film Festival has noticed. *Force Majeure* won a Jury Prize there. Three years later, *The Square* won the Palme d'Or, the festival's top award, and in 2022 *Triangle of Sadness* took the Palme again. Though it is not unprecedented for a director to win the Palme d'Or twice, there is something jolting about this provocateur's success at the most prestigious and fanciest of all film festivals. By singling out Östlund this way, it's like the jet set is trying to tell us something about itself.

STARTING AS IT DOES WITH scenes from the fashion industry, *Triangle of Sadness* comes haute out of the gate, but it's aiming lower. In its three acts, the movie mimics familiar reality television structures, getting beneath its subjects right away, like a mechanic sliding under a Rolls.

Part 1, "Carl & Yaya," traffics in the same fashion-biz world as *America's Next Top Model.* Part 2, "The Yacht," is like the various *Below Deck* series, which contrast the life of a superyacht crew with that of the passengers they serve. Part 3, "The Island," replicates the stalwart *Survivor* concept, in which people severed from their usual lives are trapped on an island and denied the resources of their class affiliations, so we can see them in a state of nature, and watch them fall or rise.

That trope goes back to 1719, when the first readers of Daniel Defoe's *Robinson Crusoe* assumed it was the true story of a shipwrecked man who befriends a native on a desert island, then makes him his slave. First, tragedy. Then—after colonialism and the robber barons and their conquest of the natural world during the Industrial Revolution—comedy. J. M. Barrie's 1902 play *The Admirable Crichton* provided the reverse template for stories of servants becoming masters when trapped in raw nature with their supposed betters. By the mid-1960s, the sitcom *Gilligan's Island* had banalized the various strains in these tales, with its crew and millionaire passengers stuck "on the shore of this uncharted desert isle," laugh track added.

In our era of climate crisis and obscene wealth, movies featuring cruise ships, troubled yachting excursions, and travelers stranded on the beach are newly relevant, and have popped up with some frequency. Jean-Luc Godard set the first part of his *Film Socialisme* (2010) aboard the doomed *Costa Concordia* cruise ship, which ran aground two years after that film's exposé of global capitalism. Its wreckage is visible in Paolo Sorrentino's film *The Great Beauty* (2013); two years later, it was scrapped. Martin Scorsese's *The Wolf of Wall Street* (2013) and *Annette* (2021), by Leos Carax, each trapped their wealthy characters on a superyacht in stormy seas, while M. Night Shyamalan's *Old* (2021) stranded resort guests on a beach.

Östlund acknowledges the familiarity of this setting. When the model Carl (Harris Dickinson) begins spending nights in the beached lifeboat with the former "toilet manager" Abigail (Dolly De Leon), the other men stranded on the island tease him by tracing the phrase LOVE BOAT on the side of the small vessel. Using a TV reference, they are mocking the privilege that Carl has garnered with the currency of his beauty—a reversal of his position with Yaya (Charlbi Dean) at the beginning of the film.

Yaya had claimed that her only future was as a trophy wife, and looked horrified in a taxi when Carl said he thought they should be equal partners in their relationship. After some nighttime working-class role-play in their cabin on the yacht, by the last act of the film Carl achieves this equality, but not in the way he expected. He becomes a trophy himself.

At the fashion show early in the film, a sign flashes on the runway: EVERYONE'S EQUAL NOW. Later, the wife (Sunnyi Melles) of a Russian oligarch exhorts the yacht's crew to join her in the pool. "We are all equal. . . . Everyone's equal," she tells them. "I want all the staff to go for a swim. . . . Let's reverse roles."

Triangle of Sadness plays the idea of equality in this unequal situation as an obvious joke. Östlund understands that, in an oligarchic society, the game is fixed. Equality is only a gesture performed by these tourists, who go on vacation to indulge themselves, including in their guilt, which becomes another luxury for them.

ACCORDING TO A PIECE BY Evan Osnos in the July 25, 2022, issue of the *New Yorker,* called "The Haves and the Have-Yachts," we are living through what one yacht broker calls the "greatest boom in the yacht business that's ever existed." In 2021, we learn, close to nine hundred superyachts were sold worldwide. Who buys them? Billionaires who keep their money in offshore tax havens. A superyacht can cost anywhere from about $75 million to $630 million, and on average its greenhouse gas emissions equal those of 1,500 passenger cars. Yet one ship designer tells Osnos that their villainous image is unfair, that "yachts have become synonymous with the bad guys in a James Bond movie."

Navigators, a 2022 documentary by Noah Teichner, is so named because the film traces the history of the ship on which Buster Keaton filmed *The Navigator,* his 1924 comedy. Five years before Keaton got ahold of the *Buford,* the US Department of Justice used it to deport Russian-born anarchists back to the Soviet Union. Emma Goldman, the labor activist and writer, was among them, with her lover, Alexander Berkman, who had spent fourteen years in prison for attempting to assassinate the financier-industrialist Henry Clay Frick during a union strike against Frick's Carnegie Steel Company. Just as Godard's use of the *Costa Concordia* turned out to be political in unexpected ways, so did Keaton's use of the *Buford.*

And so is Östlund's use of the *Christina O,* the three-hundred-foot superyacht formerly owned by Aristotle Onassis and named for his daughter. In World War II, the vessel was a Canadian antisubmarine frigate. Onassis bought it when the war ended, as his shipping empire boomed. He turned it into his private yacht, gutting, rebuilding, and redecorating it, right up to the leather made from the foreskins of whales that he used to cover the barstools.

The scale of sickness, confusion, and mayhem that Östlund rains down upon the superrich in *Triangle of Sadness,* a comedic anti-*Titanic* set in our present, is something you would have to have a gut of steel not to be moved by. If the film's class outrage doesn't stir something within you, on some level, somewhere in your soul, maybe you are too refined for movies.

Because, yes, it is the merciless puking in the Captain's Dinner scene that distinguishes Östlund's ship of fools from other cinematic sea voyages, even the other anticapitalist ones. Godard's harsh-looking HD video in *Film Socialisme* may be a form of digital retching, but Östlund gets literal.

"IF I'M GOING TO DO THIS, I have to go ten steps further than the audience expects," Östlund said in an interview with Deadline. The audience should be nervous, wondering, "Where is this going to take me?" He had to create onscreen the "authentic feeling of when the body is surprising you." Knowing he could not flood the actual yacht's corridors and stairways with vomitus and the overflow from lavatories, he and his crew stepped off the *Christina O* to shoot most of that scene over thirteen days in a re-creation of the yacht's dining area, using a gimbal on his camera to keep it steady so the set could rock twenty degrees.

Other Östlund films have hinted at how, when it really matters in today's society, no one is in charge. There's the driverless car going in circles in a parking lot, smashing into barriers, in his first feature, *The Guitar Mongoloid* (2004). In Östlund's second film, *Involuntary* (2008), a bus driver who refuses to drive nonetheless cites airline pilots as his inferiors because most of their work is automated. In *Force Majeure,* another bus driver can't quite make a turn on a mountain pass but keeps trying, endangering his passengers. When we meet the main character in *The Square,* museum director Christian (Claes Bang), he is asleep in his office when he should be preparing for an interview, which he then flubs.

In *Triangle of Sadness,* a type of canny casting new to Östlund's work is in play. Putting Woody Harrelson in the role of the ship's captain was a coup that finally brought this theme of the willful abdication of responsibility into the open, allowing Östlund to go further with it than he had before. Harrelson's Thomas Smith, an American Marxist and alcoholic, prefers drinking in his quarters to running the ship from the bridge. Faced with total destruction, his version of "Nearer My God to Thee" is drunkenly trading pointed anticapitalist quotations with an equally soused, Reagan-loving Russian oligarch. In their duel, they both get on the ship's intercom to berate the imperiled passengers about not paying their fair share in taxes, and then to lecture them about the lie of philanthropy.

The paunchy oligarch, Dimitry, is played by Zlatko Burić, whom fans of European crime films will recognize as the dope dealer Milo from Nicolas Winding Refn's Danish *Pusher* films—particularly *Pusher III* (2004), in which he stars as a mobster and murderer who gives his staff food poisoning with his cooking while he remains unaffected, just as Dimitry doesn't get sick in *Triangle of Sadness*. "Shit" is slang for drugs, and in Östlund's movie Burić is a man who has become wealthy selling agricultural fertilizer. "I sell shit," Dimitry keeps telling the other passengers.

Arvin Kananian plays the first mate, Darius, who refuses to say no to the situation at the pool that keeps the ship's kitchen staff from their duties and precipitates the disaster. In the dour Swedish science-fiction hit *Aniara* (2018), Kananian plays the lying commander of the massive spaceship that goes off course as it is headed to an exoplanet to save humanity. Even in devising some of the smallest parts, Östlund makes a point. The cabdriver who tells Carl to stand up to Yaya is Jiannis Moustos, the glowering hotel janitor from *Force Majeure* who looks down on that film's arguing couple whenever they go into the hall to discuss things away from their children. Vacations are rough. The staff can see you.

Regardless of Harrelson's unpredictable, enduring star power, Burić's wild-haired presence, or the nuanced, incisive performances of Harris Dickinson and Dolly De Leon, *Triangle of Sadness* will be best remembered for Charlbi Dean's costarring role as the manipulative fashion model Yaya. A unique beauty, Dean died tragically of sepsis at age 32, after *Triangle of Sadness* won at Cannes but before it came out in theaters.

Playing a character who could be seen as self-centered and testy, Dean instead brought wit and charm to this central role. The film ends with Yaya unable to picture Abigail as anything but an employee. ("Maybe you can come and work for me. You could be my assistant.") On the verge of rescue, she's poised to get her head crushed in with a rock, but her sense of entitlement will remain intact. Like Yaya, in this movie nothing lets up.

SOUND SLEEPER

MEMORIA

APICHATPONG WEERASETHAKUL BEGAN TO HEAR A LOUD BOOM IN HIS head while he was working in Colombia six years ago. One morning, gathering ideas for the film that would become *Memoria* (2021), he "was startled by the sound of an explosion. It was a bomb, at dawn, not from elsewhere but within my head. This, I later learned, is called Exploding Head Syndrome," he explains in the introduction to a book on the film.

Exploding head syndrome is real, even if the sound Weerasethakul heard was not. It's an auditory hallucination that occurs during sleep, usually near falling asleep or waking. It's loud and can be frightening to its hearer. Its cause is unknown, and the condition is untreatable. The hearer searches for the source of this booming sound, convinced of its authenticity. But it's all in his head—he just doesn't know it yet.

Strange phenomena are Weerasethakul's métier. Peculiar sensations, portents and apparitions make regular appearances in his work. They are presented as plain and real. The Sasquatch-like forest creatures in *Uncle Boonmee Who Can Recall His Past Lives* (2010) are maybe the most famous of these ghostly images, but it's the ending of that film, with the unexplained and casual doubling of its characters, that is most eerie. Instances of the otherworldly slowly take over Weerasethakul films, which are otherwise set in the recognizable daily reality of contemporary Thailand. One wouldn't necessarily call them attacks, but odd afflictions send his characters to doctors' offices in search of explanations and remedies. Things develop in a Weerasethakul film in calm, provocative uncertainty. Everything, visible or not, has a feeling of real presence.

In *Tropical Malady* (2004), a huge tree shimmers at night with radio voices and static, lit from behind with bright light. We hear it as much as we see it. Whether natural or man-made, these combinations of sound and image, unique to Weerasethakul, seem on the way to becoming something else, to revealing the true nature of their existence in just one more second. They hover between the world of the living and another dimension, one of dead voices and dark silhouettes.

This uncertainty is an effect of the cinema itself, a mechanical art which exists in the same space as these phenomena, a place where sleeping images, often of people no longer alive, are revived every time they are run through a projector. Weerasethakul has this reanimation, giving the dead another chance to appear and to speak, as his focal point. He brings a kind of liminal existence back to life at a time when spiritless digital images dominate movies around the world. He's made nine features so far, of which *Memoria* is the most recent.

It's his first film made outside of Thailand, but expatriation has not hurt his work. Weerasethakul has brought his cinema with him. The story may be specific to Colombia's violent political history, its geography and its weather, but as a character in *Memoria* puts it, "In this town there are many people with hallucinations."

In 2018 the actor Connor Jessup made a documentary called *A.W. A Portrait of Apichatpong Weerasethakul*. In it, Weerasethakul and Jessup, in a skiff on a river in Colombia, discuss the film that would become *Memoria*. Weerasethakul mentions how in dreams, you don't see your own face. This observation is key to the filmmaker's style, especially in *Memoria*, where the presence of an international star in the lead could have altered how he does things, as it has done with otherwise intractable directors, from Béla Tarr to Wong Kar-wai, when they have made movies with big names outside their home countries. But Tilda Swinton does not even get one close-up in this film. Instead, Weerasethakul makes novel use of her well-known capacity to seem in touch with aliens, to be *other*.

In *Memoria*, Swinton, as a Scottish botanist in Bogotá, is the one awakened by the booming sound Weerasethakul first heard in his own head. In the *Memoria* book, the director explains their twinned position. Like him, "For a second, she wonders if she is still in that film, lying in bed, opening her eyes from a dream."

Weerasethakul told Giovanni Marchini Camia, the co-author of the *Memoria* book, that the first conversations he and Swinton had were about what it meant to be an alien, "both in the most extreme sci-fi sense, and also in the most mundane, completely universal sense of feeling alienated by society, or feeling in some way isolated and solitary."

In a later interview with Camia in the *Metrograph Journal*, he explained that Swinton is also playing a ghost. "I think she realizes that she doesn't exist. She's an entity, she's a ghost, and she's cinema, you know? . . . She's the one who carries images and sounds."

Whatever she is, in the first two-thirds of *Memoria* she and Weerasethakul suggest that she is going crazy. At a neurological level, Swinton conveys a sense of being off, of being half there. When she and her sister discuss the "Uncontactable"—tribes of Indigenous people who live in willful isolation—she too seems like she is becoming one of the invisible people. Maybe that phrase also relates to her status as a middle-aged woman, but it's a term that applied to the "disappeared," citizens who have been forcibly vanished by government forces as a result of ongoing political protest in Colombia.

Weerasethakul subtly connects this to the situation in his own country, where resistance is quashed by the military, and the monarchy demands absolute obeisance. In the documentary he calls Thailand "a bullshit country" where he has been "lied to too much," describing it as an authoritarian gerontocracy defined by propaganda. Earlier he says the ghosts in his films are not actual ghosts, but "memories of ghosts."

Neon's release strategy for *Memoria* makes poetic sense in that regard. As the film's US distributor, the company decided, with Weerasethakul and Swinton, to release the film in cinemas on an eternal tour only "in theaters . . . forever." Like a ghost ship, *Memoria* will sail the seas, stopping at ports, but it will never be digitally stripped for parts on home video and streaming. (Not in the US, anyway.)

The sound in *Memoria* is, in any case, highly dependent on theatrical exhibition. The noise Swinton's Jessica keeps hearing has a booming fullness that catches audiences off-guard. In a theater, it's felt inside the body. A sound engineer in the film explains it to Jessica in his studio. "The bass depends on what you use to listen to the sound. On headphones, on a TV set, in a cinema, or with a sound system like this." He finds a sound-alike file in his system called *Stomach hit wearing hoodie* and plays it. "It's between sixty and a hundred hertz," he points out. (Everybody hertz.)

Jessica studies the fungi on orchids. A worker at a refrigerator factory that makes floral display coolers explains the way they preserve plant life: "In here, time stops." Anyone who has watched a Weerasethakul film at home has had the experience of pausing it, then coming back to the film and hitting Play, only to be unsure the film is actually moving again. *Memoria*'s key scene is exactly like that, with an older version of the sound engineer lying in the grass either asleep or dead, in a shot Weerasethakul holds for a minute and a half, then later repeats for thirty more seconds, ages of screen time that make the viewer wonder what the difference is between stillness and sleep, death or a dead battery in the remote.

Sound and stasis create empathy in Weerasethakul's films. As Jessica becomes more sleep-deprived, she consults a village doctor and asks for a Xanax prescription. The doctor won't give it to her. "It will make you lose empathy. You no longer will be moved by the beauty of this world. Or by the sadness of this world." Then she gives her a religious tract and tells her to look at the Dalí in the local church. Jessica gets her Xanax from another doctor.

Things being what they are in the worlds of independent cinema and international arthouse film production, Weerasethakul cannot survive as the writer-director of only feature films. He also makes lots of shorts and creates gallery installations. Lately he has dabbled in virtual reality, making something called *A Conversation with the Sun* (2022) in VR. He's come away from the experience seeing VR not just as a possible source of cinema's death, but also—if people become too dependent on it—as a threat to daily life. "VR cannot replicate this idea of [cinematic] point of view," he explains to Camia, "or even the idea of empathy."

We learn in their book that making *Memoria* cured Weerasethakul of his own exploding head syndrome. "In Bogotá and 300 km away in Pijao, as I was making *Memoria*, the morning 'bang' disappeared. With it the precious, murky, drifting realm was gone. For better or for worse, I could sleep for seven hours a night. This was another answer." Though at this point I have forgotten what the question was, it must have something to do with how to live in this world.

But that reminds me: In my own way, I can attest to this healing power of Weerasethakul's work. One of his films improved my health. In *Cemetery of Splendor* (2015), a character played by Weerasethakul's favorite actor, Jenjira Pongpas, suggests taking ginkgo to someone having memory problems. I started doing that after I saw that film, and it worked. Since then, my recall has improved. I'm like the sleeping/dying character who tells Jessica, "I remember everything. So I try to limit what I see. That's why I never watch movies or TV. . . . There are plenty of stories already."

The character goes on to say that he has never left his village, has no desire to go anywhere, and has realized that "experiences are harmful," so I'm not sure he's the exact right model for how to live in this world. "Our kind never dreams," he says. "What happens when you sleep?" Jessica asks. "Nothing," he tells her. If only the cinema could cure insomnia too, instead of just being an alternative to sleep.

RIDING THE ELEPHANT

OSCAR MOVIES 2023

Everything Everywhere All at Once

The film's simple message about the importance of family drew criticism for being predictable and a letdown after the elastic mayhem that led to it. But as much as I dislike rote wrap-ups shaded in warm Spielbergian glow, I would rather see the parent-child-hug ending with a working-class Asian family that owns a laundromat and has tax problems than in the usual mid-America, middle-class unit. The thing I didn't understand is how you lose money running a laundromat, especially if you own the building.

What makes *Everything Everywhere All at Once* work is the cast. Michelle Yeoh momentarily brought to earth, the return of Ke Huy Quan after lo these many years, the welcome antics of such disparate talents as Stephanie Hsu, James Hong, Tallie Medel, and Jenny Slate, even the pungency of nepo-granny Jamie Lee Curtis as an embittered IRS flunky—these add up to something new when set against the backdrop of franchise sequels, IP reboots, and the current mirthlessness of American filmmaking.

The humor, though, is silly and second-rate. The googly eyes, the talking raccoon, the pet rocks at sunset, the parody of *2001: A Space Odyssey*—all those work against the cast instead of with it. There should be a moratorium on *2001* parodies at this point, and writer-directors like Kwan and Scheinert should know that. In a film that is, in the end, really about adult regret, these juvenile ideas from sketch comedy and music videos one after another reveal themselves as distractions. If the multiverse needs that much flailing and tinkering to come out the same as it always does, then I don't believe in it and don't need it. The Ramones understood this universal truth better than the Daniels: "Second verse same as the first."

Aftersun

In contrast, Charlotte Wells's self-assured debut takes pains to be specific to its time and place. It is the late 1990s at a modest resort on the Turkish Riviera, where divorced Scottish father Calum (Paul Mescal) takes his 11-year-old daughter Sophie (Frankie Corio) on vacation. Like *Everything Everywhere All at Once*, *Aftersun* is a story of adult regret, but unlike the Daniels's movie, it is also a study in how patient, focused accumulation of detail can have devastating effect. This film has a true sense of lost possibility, the kind that can't be recovered in another universe but that can be recalled and recreated in a movie. Here, that feeling seeps outside the film's borders instead of exploding them.

Aftersun discovers non-cliché beauty in summer beach scenes. Against these, Calum struggles with a broken wrist to light his cigarettes and read paperbacks while Sophie videos him and kids him. A sleepy, delicate feeling pervades their interactions. When Calum mentions he can't picture himself at 40, his melancholy begins to take over the film, and Sophie seems stranded. When her father hangs her out to dry by making her karaoke "Losing My Religion" alone—a quintessential 1990s moment of awkwardness—we come to see how troubled and preoccupied he is.

I'm not sure I needed to meet the adult Sophie (Celia Rowlson-Hall), nor see Calum disappearing into the murk like a Scottish prole in *Under the Skin*. These scenes at the end gave Wells's otherwise remarkable film a confusing, student-film feel, just as closing with a

David Bowie song and a dance scene placed this beautiful film too much in the current of contemporary arthouse production (though Wells used "Under Pressure" quite well). That the movies can stand an infinite amount of Bowie and that all stories end in a dance are familiar cinematic notions a little out of place in this unembellished film defined by Wells's supernatural ability with her two actors. Sophie and Calum become guileless and real, as real as the Polaroid we see developing that someday has to fade.

The Whale

When heavyset Dom DeLuise was in *Fatso* in 1980, the only thing stopping him from finding love was that he ate too many "scraps." It says so right on the *Fatso* movie poster: "DO NOT EAT apple pie, baked beans, bologna" and so on alphabetically through "scraps," "spaghetti," and part of the word "sundaes." Now, after forty-two years of American hell, our movie fat man is Brendan Fraser in *The Whale*, six hundred pounds of prosthetics and CGI masturbating to gay porn on a greasy couch, pouring ranch dressing on pizzas, guzzling warm Pepsi out of two-liter bottles in bed at night, and never washing his hands after any of it.

Plus, he has conflicts over 19th-century American literature and loses his job as an English teacher. Why? Because of *honesty*. "Honest things" matter, he says. "Just write me something fucking *honest!*" he messages his students when he's not screaming at his estranged teenage daughter (Sadie Sink) to do the same. In one of his own fits of honesty, he describes the putrefaction of his blubber in detail, listing "the patches of mold between the flaps and the infected ulcers on my ass and the sack of fat on my back that turned brown last year."

Yes, sacks of fat, for he is the Whale, puking on his shirt, sobbing alone in his apartment in the green-brown murk of contemporary cinematography. And the whale is also Moby-Dick, and the whale is Herman Melville, too, who was using the metaphor of the whale to hide his own whaleness. Are we all the whale? I don't think so. Yet Darren Aronofsky's film of this joyless play was a hit, so I guess it touched something in the moviegoing public. It had to use a bodega claw to do it because it couldn't get off the couch, but it touched them.

Living

Skinny and impeccable, Bill Nighy in *Living* is the opposite of Brendan Fraser in *The Whale*, but he too is lonely and dying. This unnecessary remake of Akira Kurosawa's *Ikiru* (1952), scripted by the British-Japanese novelist Kazuo Ishiguro, retells the story of a quiet bureaucrat who learns he only has a few months to live. It takes place in the same early 1950s of the original film but is set in London and, like its protagonist, has little reason for existing. It seems structured solely to give Nighy a lead role he can get an award for. Nighy, now 73, always dashing, has been poorly served by movies, though he's done good work in several dozen since 1979, most of them disposable crowd-pleasers. Listing them would be more depressing than *Living*.

Britain and Japan have many things in common as class-bound, rule-bound island nations, so you would think this transposition would work. For a while it does. Then, when Nighy must go on a boozy and stripper-filled journey to the end of the night that will secretly turn him into someone who wants to do one good thing before he dies, *Living* becomes wan and unbelievable. Lacking the careless exhilaration of the same scenes in the Kurosawa film, Nighy performs his role as differently from Takashi Shimura's approach as possible, buttoned up and cadaverous, already dead.

Ten minutes before the movie ends, we see the completed playground the bureaucrat has been trying to get built in a slum. It looks ominous, with Nighy on a swing darkly singing a Scottish song to himself as a teary-eyed cop looks on, as if the scene were taking place at a gallows. *And in a way it is,* the film prods the audience to say to itself. Ultra-maudlin, grim, and ugly, the effect is to subvert the mature humanism of Kurosawa's sublime ending by making this into the exact kind of phony movie from which Nighy was trying to escape.

To Leslie

Equally British in its lust for American award season acknowledgment, *To Leslie* gives the English actress Andrea Riseborough an opportunity to mash her foot to the gas as an alcoholic hillbilly trying to get her life together after squandering a lottery jackpot. People keep saying of Leslie things like "I won't lie, she doesn't look good," and then we see her in longshot on a West Texas street looking glamorous, like a fashion editor or a publicist clomping down Madison Avenue. That forces Riseborough to imitate an ape in order to convey American dissolution, something her stunning profile works against at every moment in this film.

Michael Morris, a British TV director, works hard to counter that by making *To Leslie* look like a 1970s movie or *The Florida Project* but even more busted, or maybe something by Gus Van Sant. He wants that grainy feel of American realism in wide open spaces but also a happy ending where Leslie runs a little diner in Nowheresville that serves only one dish, "pasta fazool." Is that a joke? If it is, I don't get it. And I think pasta fazool was on the *Fatso* list of banned foods.

Causeway

So much puking in 2022 big-screen quality drama. Riseborough vomits when she's cleaning motel rooms and trying to lay off the sauce, and in *Causeway* an equally de-glamorized Jennifer Lawrence, as a shell-shocked veteran of the war in Afghanistan, throws up in a wastebasket while living in transitional homecare in Nebraska.

Back in her real home in New Orleans, she gets a job cleaning pools, showing us what successful movie actresses think they need to do to win Oscars in 2023: portray the immiserated working class puking and cleaning.

The first reel of *Causeway* is all Lawrence acting comatose in the snow. Back home, in warmer weather, she and the film start to come alive. Lynsey (Lawrence) meets a kindly auto mechanic, James (Brian Tyree Henry), who helps her with her car. He has a prosthetic leg and has experienced terrible trauma of his own, we gradually learn, and the two maybe start to fall in love a little, though Lynsey is gay. Henry plays James as entirely lovable, and the 1978 pistachio-green Mercedes he drives probably helps.

Lila Neugebauer directs the film as if were written by Kenneth Lonergan, which is to say she does an excellent job keeping everything low-key and natural. *Causeway*, however, is defeated by a clunky screenplay. The late introduction of Lynsey's deaf brother (Russell Harvard) in prison is there to explain so much about so little. The film gets better and better as it goes along, it's true, but then it just stops. The quick ending is an arty decision that reads as more of an evasion.

Elvis

If this is Baz Luhrmann's best film, it's because Elvis Presley forced him to become a better director. To tell Elvis's story it is necessary to show the full figure in the frame, head to toe, since Elvis's leg and hip moves on early television made him a star. That precluded *Moulin Rouge*-style seizure-inducing cuts. And Austin Butler's Tarantinofied performance as the King demanded a full view. Butler here is a co-auteur in a way usually closed to biopics in which the lead actors are more famous than Butler is, and so we never lose them in their roles as other famous people.

Apart from that, *Elvis* begins in didacticism, a popular mode these days, explaining the socioeconomic background of Elvis's life and the history of Black rhythm and blues in the South. This becomes like a series of PowerPoint slides featuring faces of actors posing for roles in Guy Maddin or John Waters films. Then Tom Hanks comes on in a fat suit (another newly popular device) and bloviates on his grating "snow job" theory of entertainment marketing, which he brings up again and again.

This is a non-normative use of the phrase *snow job*, which usually just describes a deception that conceals actual motives by flattery. Colonel Parker was Dutch, and Luhrmann is Australian, so who knows? It's not like anyone is going to consult Peter Guralnick to find out if that is really how Colonel Parker talked.

The film ends in tragedy, as it must, but it is a feel-good movie nonetheless, one that induces the summer fun Elvis movie musicals strained for. By definition it must ignore how, by the time he died in the summer of 1977, Elvis was already a moribund figure who was being used by punk for conceptual irony and rock 'n' roll autocritique. That fact of cultural history never comes up in these kinds of celebratory equations because it messes with the "Elvis is Everywhere" narrative that unites all races and leads to dancing in the streets, a mode Luhrmann's film, against the odds, actually achieves.

Blonde

Another Australian director, Andrew Dominik, took on another 1950s American icon, Marilyn Monroe, in *Blonde*, miscasting Ana de Armas as a Marilyn ripped from the pages of a Joyce Carol Oates novel. The film is like *Babylon* in the way it demeans and befouls everything it touches, but Dominik is meaner and more lowdown than anything Damien Chazelle has ever encountered, including Tobey Maguire.

Dominik's Hollywood, unlike Chazelle's, contains the pulsating viscera of surgery footage and has no love for the movies at all. That's because Dominik is dead certain he is a better filmmaker than anyone Marilyn Monroe ever worked with. *Blonde* is a brain-damaged movie but, unlike Chazelle's, it doesn't induce laughter or pity so much as miscarriage. If this film had been directed by Andrea Dworkin it would still have been easier on men and on humanity.

Specific dissections of "the blonde" are not new in the cinema. As out-there a director as Larry Buchanan made one (or was it two?) Monroe biopics, and there was an Australian actress in the 1970s named Linda Kerridge who specialized in Marilyn imitations and seems to have lived as if she were Marilyn herself. I saw her playing Richard Lewis's neighbor in an obscure movie called *Diary of a Young Comic* (1979) that I wouldn't mind seeing again.

From Warhol to Mailer to Madonna, Marilyn's body, her physical existence, and her corpse have been the subjects of the creepy, insistent fascination of weirdos. Dominik, with a Netflix budget, has outdone them all, without thinking he's one of them. He treats Marilyn by turns like she's Abel Gance's *Napoleon* and the Barbie whose head Dawn Wiener tries to saw off with a cleaver in *Welcome to the Dollhouse*.

In *Blonde*, Marilyn must suffer every kind of sexual predation and/or betrayal, from every man she meets. Dominik reduces each of them to a lowest common denominator of American 1950s manhood, making most of them look like Richard Nixon, including Joe DiMaggio (Bobby Cannavale), Arthur Miller (Adrien Brody), and Caspar Phillipson, brought back from *Jackie* (2017) to play JFK again. The film ends in a paroxysm of grubbiness, after many scenes of Marilyn puking and bleeding, with men waving at her, following her, their mouths distorted in vulgarity.

By then it is impossible to tell if the confused Dominik is attacking masculinity, Hollywood, and America, or if the film is a howl of revulsion at the existence of women. Paradoxically it is over the subway grate of his inevitable remake of the white skirt scene from *The*

Seven Year Itch that it becomes clear what's going on: he's blowing smoke up our panties.

Fire of Love

Katia and Maurice Krafft put together chic work outfits in their tireless quest to film erupting volcanoes. It is impossible to determine if these colorful ensembles are testaments to the radical seriousness of the Kraffts' life project or if it was just because they were French. Either way, we will never be able to ask them: this pair of married volcanologists died as they lived. Their commitment was so total that they met their end in Japan, obviously the most stylish place for French volcanologists to die. They perished in the 1991 explosion of Mount Unzen, disappearing in a cloud of smoke, ash, gas, and flying rocks.

Sara Dosa's mind-blowing documentary, *Fire of Love*, collects much of what there is to know about Maurice and Katia Krafft. Student radicals in the 1960s, they met at a Cinémathèque Française screening of a Haroun Tazieff volcano documentary, married, and honeymooned on the island of Stromboli so they could observe the ever-erupting volcano there, made famous by the 1950 Roberto Rossellini and Ingrid Bergman film, a product of their passion just as the Kraffts' filmmaking emerged from theirs.

Such was their dedication to their work that they began to camp on the edges of volcanoes, often sleeping in shifts so they could protect each other from the lava flows and rock blasts that come with the geologic territory of these formations from the Earth's crust. Romance to them was staring together into the magma, he an absent-minded Geoffrey Rush forever about to stick his foot in hot lava by accident, she a nerdy Lina Wertmüller searching for the best angle to film it.

It's hard to believe Devo had never seen them and that the look of Wes Anderson's *Life Aquatic* crew wasn't based on their red-beanie, light-blue-jumpsuit look. Even in head-to-toe silver fire suits and aluminum head-covering helmets with dark amber visors, the Kraffts brought savoir faire to that most philosophical and visually impressive of science experiments, the leap into the volcano, against a backdrop of molten orange.

Bardo

For some reason Alejandro González Iñárritu, after having directed six feature films in his career, decided it was time for him to make his *8½*. When Fellini did it in 1963, after having made seven features and one short, he did not lie by making his lead character a documentary filmmaker. The character Mastroianni played was based on Fellini (but handsomer), so he was a director like Fellini was.

In *Bardo*, Silverio (Daniel Giménez Cacho) is a filmmaker-journalist who has roused the ire of the authorities from the DF to DC. He lives with his family in LA as a kind of exiled Michael Moore (but more distinguished). On the verge of a stroke he does not see coming, he returns to Mexico to celebrate winning an award in the United States, thereby encountering the ghosts of his past and his home country's history.

Frailer and older than Iñárritu, Silverio is a deglamorized version of the director of *Babel* and *Birdman*, but also one who is much more politically engaged. Silverio has pissed people off, but they are angry at him because he's successful and can afford to live abroad, which he does because, as a rich person, members of his family are potential kidnap targets in Mexico.

As in *Birdman*, Iñárritu's real enemies are the critics. Luis (Francisco Rubio), an old friend who's now a sellout TV host, tells Silverio that his films "are oneiric to cover up for your mediocre writing." In response, Iñárritu turns off Luis's voice on the soundtrack so we see his mouth moving but no sounds come out. Silverio counters Luis by describing him as "rubbing elbows with the president, pushing faddish ideologies and idiocies." Is Iñárritu aware that this is also a description of the company that released *Bardo* (Netflix)? Later we learn that filmmakers are small men now, because "ideas ate the deities!"

Iñárritu shoots such self-justifications in elaborate crane shots through wide-angle lenses, exaggerating differences in scale. The film is much too big for the small screens of most Netflix users, making it hard to pick out the wealth of detail Iñárritu includes in his traveling shots and carefully composed frames. Throughout *Bardo* he appears to be congratulating himself for being experimental and for not presenting "a pasteurized reality." This approach, and this film, could be called *Wide Angle Mexican*. But it's only an experimental film if you are rich, and the reality he criticizes is the reality of other rich people not as self-consciously artistic as he is.

Babylon

This end-of-cinema epic starts by dramatizing the old joke about the man who cleans up elephant shit at least being in show biz, a literalization of *La La Land*'s contention that the audience likes crap, not jazz. Then *Babylon*'s musical score gives us so much fake jazz it's like the movie was made by the Squirrel Nut Zippers. The idea that we need Damien Chazelle to tell us that movies "meant something" and are not a "low art" is absurd, a sure sign of a disconnection from the reality of the lives of film fans across the world. Maybe Chazelle never meets any. Why would he? *Where* would he?

As a murky *Mad* magazine fold-out comedy, Chazelle's movie achieves a stupid grandeur in evoking a silent era that is half *Hollywood Babylon*, half *Everyone Poops*. It does this by directly imitating the work of filmmakers from the generation immediately before Chazelle's, lifting ideas and scenes from Quentin Tarantino, Guillermo del Toro, Baz Luhrmann, even movies as recent as *Licorice Pizza*.

But it pretends it's not doing this, claiming instead that *Singin' in the Rain* is its touchstone, going so far as to reproduce the predecessor

"Singin' in the Rain" musical number from *The Hollywood Revue of 1929*, as if that is some kind of deep research. *Babylon*'s sound-recording scene replicates *Singin' in the Rain*'s as something dire and unfunny and way too long. It's one of the movie's two lowest points, the other being Jean Smart's "Time! Marches On!" speech to Brad Pitt, a mean-spirited lecture because of course on top of everything else, *Babylon* is didactic.

Its real cohort is movies like *Zeroville* and *Under the Silver Lake*, disgruntled non-starters from 2019. Like *Babylon*, they are about the impossibility of achievement in Hollywood filmmaking, made by callow writer-directors who have tasted success and are afraid the supply is running out.

The Fabelmans

The defecating elephant from *Babylon* makes an appearance in Steven Spielberg's movie letter to his boyhood self, *The Fabelmans*. His Uncle Boris (Judd Hirsch) tells young Sammy Fabelman (Gabriel LaBelle) about his time working in the movies "the year of *The Jazz Singer*, that's when talkies started," the exact pivot point of the Chazelle film. Because Boris knows Sammy is like him, "meshuga for art," he understands that Sammy will be happy to "muck out the pachyderms" and that Sammy won't mind shoveling "until they say, 'OK, Sammy, now ride the goddamn elephant.'"

Like *Babylon*, *The Fabelmans* is a gross film of boogers, urine, puke, and bird shit in the face. I thought the last scene of *Babylon* was going to be a pigeon shitting on Manny's (Diego Calves's) head at the Paramount Gate. It wasn't, but in high school Sammy's "Ditch Day" movie, a jock gets it from a seagull. The way Sammy both sucks up to the superman jocks and subverts them reminded me of *Schindler's List* (1993), in which Spielberg makes Liam Neeson's and Ralph Fiennes's Nazis into attractive characters who he flatters in order to condemn.

Similarly, Sammy making his wayward mother watch his early movie efforts in his closet brings back E.T. and his hiding place behind the plushies. Michelle Williams's performance as mom does have an alien quality. She has a Dutch Boy Paint haircut and a marionette affect that makes her seem like June Allyson playing Howdy Doody. Before she becomes estranged from her family ("phone home!") she buys an evil, E.T.-looking monkey she names after her lover, Bennie (Seth Rogen), which she inflicts on her family because she needs a laugh. Unlike the killer chimp in *Nope*, it doesn't rip anyone's face off, but it looks like it could.

In the end, Sammy is anointed as the future of cinema by John Ford, played by David Lynch as shouting FBI Deputy Director Gordon Cole gone to seed. It was a good idea that Lynch makes no attempt to speak in Ford's Maine accent. Like Spielberg, Ford owned a yacht, the *Araner*, which became a financial drain on him. Near the end of his life, he sold it because he couldn't afford it anymore. It wasn't a superyacht like Spielberg's, which he sold recently for $150 million—not because he couldn't afford it, but to upgrade to one twice as long that costs almost twice as much. These computer guys, Bennie explains to Sammy in *The Fabelmans*, "they're gonna change the whole goddamn world." That's something young Steven absorbed more deeply than Ford's instructions about where to put the horizon.

All the Beauty and the Bloodshed

The family of a great Jewish-American artist is brought to life in Laura Poitras's latest documentary, her best film because its co-auteur is its subject, the photographer Nan Goldin. We meet her in 2018 at the Metropolitan Museum of Art protesting the Sackler family and Purdue Pharma for engineering the opioid crisis, and watch as her quixotic pursuit of these corporate capitalists becomes an unexpected triumph.

Poitras turns Goldin's photos, including her now immortal slideshow, *The Ballad of Sexual Dependency*, into actual cinema, preserving them in this medium they were already so close to. Goldin showed her photos—of her artist friends, drag queens, junkies, bohemians of all kinds—in grimy nightclubs at the height of New York's downtown scene, the early 1980s, accompanying them with music she selected. One song she used, as we hear in *All the Beauty and the Bloodshed*, was Screamin' Jay Hawkins's "I Put a Spell on You," which is where maybe Jim Jarmusch got the idea to use it in *Stranger Than Paradise* (1984).

Goldin's childhood in New England was hellish and she fled it as soon as possible, in an internal "running away from America" that led her to the drag demimonde of Cambridge and Boston, to Provincetown, where she met Cookie Mueller, Divine, and John Waters, and then to the Bowery and the Lower East Side, where she lived and worked on the margins in bars and strip joints. Drugs, sex, and an abusive boyfriend inflamed her art but threatened her life. Her work annoyed and confused the burgeoning world of collectible photography. Making her own life her subject was seen as an "outlier act," and she was told "this isn't photography," though what else it could have been was only implied.

Her abusive ex and her father both tried to stop *The Ballad* from being published in book form. Poitras follows Goldin's life through the AIDS plague that decimated her friends as the Moral Majority began its crackdown on arts funding in America. Goldin narrates all of it in a quiet, considered, uninflected voice, a writerly style stitching together distressing tableaux as they are turned into art.

Glass Onion

Rian Johnson's *Knives Out* (2019) was a delightful surprise, and now Netflix has thrown tons of money at a semi-sequel, and too much money has ruined the concept. *Glass Onion* is a locked-door mystery set in an island mansion—basically movie stars in a room together—and somehow it is all ugly CGI. Everything from a giant explosion to hot sauce running into Janelle Monáe's nose has a fake, effortful look. The all-star cast is upstaged by the many cameos in it. When Ethan Hawke comes on to do just one thing, he does it so handily that he upstages the stars assembled on a dock waiting for a superyacht to take them into the actual movie, which never quite seems to start.

Johnson's new takedown of the rich is paper-thin because he can't seem to concentrate on the actors and busies himself with stuff that doesn't matter, topical jokes and inserts of wacky products. This is not to say that Daniel Craig, Monáe, and Edward Norton are bad in it, or that the film isn't clever. They aren't and it is. But it had no aftereffect. It was as disposable as the fake *Mona Lisa* in the movie that was supposed to be the real thing.

Top Gun: Maverick

The film is pure ideology, pure militarism, generic, and like the first *Top Gun* in 1986, undemanding. The unseen enemy makes Tom Cruise and his Junior Tom Cruises look like they are fighting Daft Punk. This combination of bland and easy-to-follow plus pretty young people and a legit movie star made so much of the horror of recent years fade away when it was released to beleaguered cine-plexes last summer. The training film aspects of *Top Gun: Maverick* evaporate into the air of the movie's low altitudes. Val Kilmer is an awkward, living AI turning Ronald Reagan into Joe Biden before our eyes. I tried to turn away from that quasi-deepfake, but I couldn't.

Triangle of Sadness

The annoyance and rancor with which *Triangle of Sadness* has been greeted by certain cinephiles who consider themselves evolved has mystified me. It's worse than it was with *Titane*. I understand why the fake humanists and the rich socialists of the middlebrow press are against it; I understand why it bugs the Oscarologists who forced themselves to watch it. What I don't understand is the struggling writers who I have read on Twitter posting sarcastic non-reviews like "Newsflash: rich people are dumb and do dumb shit. Terrible, horrid movie." Then, when Ruben Östlund shows up in their feed after an interview, they wonder what he's so happy about and announce they are sick of seeing his stupid face, as if he is as inescapable as Harry Styles, which he is decidedly not.

I have a theory. Östlund's in a good mood because he lives in a country that isn't a total immiserated mess like the US or the UK, gets to make movies with great actors about whatever he wants to make them about instead of adapting idiotic IP crap, and keeps winning awards. And I'm confident someone will tell me if I'm wrong.

In 2021, people loved—unduly, in my opinion—a mediocre Scandinavian movie called *The Worst Person in the World* by a mediocre Scandinavian director who, in his film, did not show one original thing that anybody had not thought to themselves a thousand times before. This year a good Scandinavian director shows many things I have observed in real life but never once seen depicted onscreen and he gets castigated for it. It's not like the difference in reception between these two films is, let's say, pronounced. That doesn't matter in the utopian vision of Östlund's critics.

Another movie that a lot of smart people loved was *Top Gun: Maverick*. They reveled in it, they cheered, they buttonholed me to tell me how great it was. In *Triangle of Sadness*, a different well-established American movie star, Woody Harrelson, is the exact opposite of Tom Cruise in his movie: a drunken communist superyacht captain not in control of anything. He goes down with his $250 million yacht as his wealthy passengers are puking their guts out, shouting Chomsky at them through an intercom: "How people perceive themselves is nothing that interests me. There are very few who look in the mirror and say, 'The person I see is a savage monster.'

Instead, they make up some construction that justifies what they do." I wonder about people who disliked that.

All Quiet on the Western Front

What has happened to the German cinema? As an anti-war war movie, this tedious, inert remake has no dramatic force, with an air of distinct unreality best explained by the piles of corpses that litter the frames like so many garbage pixels. At least in *Bardo*, Iñárritu had the decency to show his pile of bodies coming back to life. Victims of colonialist murder, they were also actors, human beings, the current people of his country. Director Edward Berger's other big move is to paint his soldiers' faces with mud in various colors, for an arty effect of decay more appropriate to an Italian zombie movie.

Albrecht Schuch was quite good in this, as an illiterate soldier, and he was also excellent in another terrible German movie I saw last year, *Fabian: Going to the Dogs*, in which he played a failing intellectual. He was the only memorable actor in either film. *Fabian* was the exact opposite of *All Quiet on the Western Front* yet was somehow also unwatchable. It was based on a novel from the Weimar era. The trenches and fields of World War I, the cafés and brothels of Berlin, an actor like Schuch, these German directors can't do anything with them. I've got to go watch a Maren Ade movie so I can get these turkeys out of my mind.

Black Panther: Wakanda Forever

Letitia Wright, as T'Challa's younger sister, the government scientist Shuri, is now the Black Panther, as Chadwick Boseman's death is retrofitted to this saga. She has to lead her people to victory in a fight with an undersea race led by Namor, formerly the Sub-Mariner of Atlantis, now a Mayan god played by Tenoch Huerta with a convincing, wounded rage. He seems dangerous, while Wright seems like she'd balk at holding the elevator for someone. At one point she coyly tells Namor, "I'd love to see your nation."

Wakanda Forever is very long and needed an intermission. You know it's a Marvel movie because it's steeped in boredom, with every scene threatening to not end. Even when the end credits start, there are fifteen minutes left. Part of it takes place in Boston and Cambridge, on the Mass. Ave. Bridge, which was not damaged enough for my liking. Ryan Coogler brought something new to the first Black Panther movie, though now its importance has faded because these movies are never memorable. They exist to remind directors that they are wasting their lives. Remember when Sofia Coppola so wisely walked away from a Disney movie she had started? No one else does, either, but it happened. Other directors would be wise to look into it.

The Banshees of Inisherin

Shorter than *Wakanda Forever* by a whopping forty-seven minutes, *The Banshees of Inisherin* is also too long. Martin McDonagh, a writer always trying to be more of a director, insists on starting with drone shots because Ireland is beautiful, but drone shots are padding. When I see them at the beginning of a movie, I always expect there will be more. Introducing them early slows down later scenes because of that expectation. Drone shots also seem off to me in films that take place in the past, like this one, which is set in 1923.

They also detract from McDonagh's greatest strength, which is with actors. The ensemble here—Colin Farrell, Brendan Gleeson, Kerry Condon, and Barry Keoghan—are exceptional in the old Abbey Theatre way. This dark film plays on the enduring appeal of Irish music while teaching a hard lesson, which is that there is a difference between empathy and niceness. Colin Farrell is especially good as a stupid and boring but pleasant man driven to violence by his best friend's sudden coldness, which is also a form of violence.

McDonagh literalizes it through Gleeson's self-mutilation, the film's hook, the disturbing, awful thing that keeps it from being mere quality product. While Farrell works himself up like a Hibernian Jack Lemmon, and Gleeson gets steelier and gorier, it is Barry Keoghan who adds the most to the movie's truly unsettling vibe. Keoghan, one of the strangest actors working today, jerks his performances wildly between "this guy is the greatest actor I have ever seen" and "this kid is getting a little too weird." Playing a tragic figure in a film of tragic figures, Keoghan works against the padding, same as he did in *The Green Knight* and *The Killing of a Sacred Deer.* How long he can keep doing that before either insanity or stardom calls?

Tár

Movies set in the world of classical music often deal in difficult emotional states, as *Tár* does, but they usually present their turmoil against extreme stylization and great visual beauty, like in *The Red Shoes* (1948) and other Powell and Pressburger films, or in Ken Russell's crazed filmography. It is a testament to our time that this gray, controlled film is mostly meetings in offices and restaurants against a background of drab bureaucracy.

When the film opens up in its last act, set in some generic Asian country where Marlon Brando once shot a film, this other world is a revelation. Of course it makes Lydia Tár (Cate Blanchett) sick. She's been in Germany too long, conducting the Berlin Philharmonic, threatening children, cheating on her wife, ignoring her colleagues unless she's interested in them romantically, etc.

Todd Field's canniness in turning *Tár* into a great success as a cultural moment and artifact was in making his main character what Nancy Mitford once called a "you-know-what-bian." A number of prominent men in classical music have been outed for sexual harassment, so a gender switch here could be, and has been, seen as inherently misguided and sexist. Yet it is her queerness that makes

Lydia Tár the Woman You Love to Hate and dress up as. The world has been waiting for such a figure, a Daniel Plainview that 2022, with all its gender questioning, could call its own. A straight white man wasn't going to work. Voilà, Lydia Tár.

Field frontloads his film with material that made me suspicious of what was to come. All the credits right off, the onstage interview with LT by Adam Gopnik playing himself at the *New Yorker* Festival. Right away the film said: abandon hope. Plus the title, an anagram of "art" and "rat." By the time we see Lydia working out an anagram of someone else's name, the suspicion that she is a fraud begins to grow, and then it becomes clear we are witnessing the enjoyable spectacle of a *New Yorker* Festival participant's downfall, the comeuppance of the kind of person who calls other people robots and tells them what to order at lunch.

"You're all going to hell," she sings, drunkenly, with her low-class accordion, as we witness her breakdown and her return to her roots in Staten Island. She's a crocodile, though, and as she learns in Asia, "they survive." Prepare for *Tár II*, or *Lydia Tár XXL*.

Avatar: The Way of Water

The Na'vi aren't blue, they're turquoise, because they're fake tribal shit being sold to tourists in the post-cinematic equivalent of Taos, New Mexico. Cameron throws you off because turquoise is from the desert, and this is *The Way of Water.* You can put coffee in a blue Kokopelli coffee mug and stare at the Flying Toasters screen saver on your Macintosh Classic and get the same rush. It is bad juju to see these movies. I've got enough problems without exposing myself to the second one after I saw the first one fourteen years ago. By the time Cameron finishes these things he'll be a form of consciousness uploaded to the Cloud, married to a hologram of Mia Goth.

Women Talking

I recently moved to what can only be described as a remote area, and one aspect of living in the tundra is that I now live near several Mennonite and Amish families. I don't know any of them. I only see them on the road when I'm driving by their houses and barns, or when one of their black horse-drawn buggies appears out of nowhere on the state highway at twilight, like an apparition from a silent movie, *The Phantom Carriage* or *Nosferatu.*

There are three movie theaters nearby, but none of them was showing *Women Talking*, so I asked the film's publicists for a screener. After three weeks of frustrating haggling by email, they finally provided a link that was only viewable on my iPhone, which is the same as having no link at all. All of a sudden I was in the same position as my Mennonite and Amish neighbors. There was a movie out about them, one that indicted half of them as utter, depraved monsters, the worst possible human beings, and none of us was allowed to see it. They because they aren't supposed to see movies, me because God forbid MGM/UA should send me a screener that I might pirate.

Not to be defeated by today's technology, I drove to a movie theater across the Canadian border and saw *Women Talking* in a giant cineplex in a mall where many of the shops and restaurants are out of business. The film tells the story of a Mennonite colony in which for years the men have been systematically drugging the women and girls with a cattle anesthetic then raping them in their sleep. It's a true story that happened in a Mennonite colony in Bolivia and was the basis for a novel, though the film takes place in North America. A group of the women gets together to decide whether they should stay and forgive their husbands, brothers, and sons, or if they should leave the colony, abandoning the only life they have ever known to go live in a world they consider ungodly.

The film is structured like *12 Angry Men*, dramatizing competing opinions about what to do, though guilt here has already been firmly established. Eventually they leave, as they should—and the movie would not have been made if they'd stayed—and we see them in an *O Pioneers!* wagon train shot that was filmed by drone, which, as I've mentioned, doesn't work as drama and ruins films. I was surprised Sarah Polley included it.

Women Talking, which stars Rooney Mara, Claire Foy, Jessie Buckley, Frances McDormand as a character called Scarface Janz, and one adult man, Ben Whishaw, as their scribe, was obviously not made by Mennonite or Amish people. Since movies were at one time a purely optical and hand-cranked mechanical medium that required no electricity, I suppose the Amish could make a movie using old equipment if they for some reason wanted to, the same way they use a horse-drawn plow instead of a tractor with an engine—they plow snow that way, too, I've learned. If a group of Amish women did make a movie, would it be a joyless and punishing, desaturated conversation piece about mass rape in which all men except Ben Whishaw are predatory abusive criminals of the very worst kind?

This movie is the opposite of *All the Beauty and the Bloodshed* in the way it approaches both male-female relations and social justice issues. The work of Goldin and Poitras has real-world value and has effected actual change in society. I can't figure out what this movie was trying to do. But it's good those women left. In the real story, in Bolivia, the men were arrested, tried, and sentenced to prison. In the movie, the women just leave the men behind, telling poor Ben Whishaw to teach them to be better. I cannot imagine how that would go well.

Le Pupille

Alice Rohrwacher's *Le Pupille* is a film just under forty minutes long that also takes place in all-female environment, in this case a Catholic boarding school for young girls run by nuns. The school has become impoverished due to wartime privations—it's World War II in Italy. It's also Christmastime, when the people of the village visit the school to see the girls enact the Nativity and leave them small gifts of food, which they hope will curry favor with God. One rich woman, desperate for her cheating husband to come back, gives the nuns a zuppa inglese, a huge, gorgeous layer cake it takes dozens of eggs to make, and which is filled with chocolate and vanilla cream and soaked in something that turns it bright red.

The decadence of this confection angers the nuns while its mere existence obsesses the girls. The second half of the film shows what happens to the cake when the nuns deny it to their charges by telling them they are sinners who don't deserve it. Instead they will give it as a gift to a priest they are trying to curry favor with themselves. The unfairness of this plan is palpable, the outrage immediate and painful—this simple story about a dessert has more to say about what's wrong with humanity than *Women Talking.*

Rohrwacher's delightful movie is a Christmas miracle for several reasons. It was made under an abandoned plan by Disney to make live-action shorts. They made just this one. Shot on film, it uses every trick of editing and point-of-view to such great effect that it's one of those movies that proves again computer effects aren't needed. It is concise and wastes nothing. Furthermore, it is a semi-musical, with the girls singing directly to the camera, and it was nominated for a short-film Oscar. People, there is hope.

PERSISTENCE OF MISSION

MISSION: IMPOSSIBLE – DEAD RECKONING, PART ONE

AT THE END OF AUGUST 2020, TOM CRUISE WAS ON A MISSION TO PROVE IT was safe to go back to the movies. Donning a black mask over his nose and mouth, the actor sped off to see Christopher Nolan's *Tenet* as it opened in London. Such was the confusion of that summer in the film industry that even as *Tenet* debuted, *Access Hollywood*, the entertainment news TV show, pronounced the title of Nolan's film "ten-AY," to rhyme with *bidet*. "Back to the movies," Cruise said as he entered the theater by himself, very low-key. A hundred and fifty minutes later, exiting up the stairs, he quietly answered "I loved it" to someone in the audience who asked what he thought. A perfectly timed stealth mission: Cruise swooped in and out. Theatrical film exhibition would not die on his watch.

But as watchers of his *Mission: Impossible* movies know, every action has an equal and opposite reaction. Four months later, on the set of *Mission: Impossible – Dead Reckoning, Part One*, then called simply *Mission: Impossible 7*, Cruise was caught on tape berating his crew for violating Covid protocols. "We are not shutting this fucking movie down!" he yelled. "If I see you do it again, you're fucking gone. . . . No apologies. You can tell it to the people that are losing their fucking homes because our industry is shut down." The recording was leaked to a British tabloid; quickly social media pointed out that the old Tom Cruise, the one notorious for manic rants during which he did things like mansplain Brooke Shields's postpartum depression on the *Today Show*, was back.

Production on the new *Mission: Impossible* movie had been halted three times before Cruise's outburst, while the release of his *Top Gun* sequel, *Top Gun: Maverick*, completed in 2019, had been postponed again and again. He was on edge, but as it turned out there was nothing to worry about. In a career that has been defined by the greatest luck and hardest work, these delays worked to his advantage. Finally released last summer, *Maverick* was an enormous hit. It has made $1.5 billion to date, and is credited—*largely* credited, as they say—with saving Hollywood from ruin.

Mission: Impossible – Dead Reckoning, Part One, also delayed about two years, came out this summer and nearly performed the same feat as *Top Gun: Maverick* did. It raked it in at the box office after a full year of non–Tom Cruise movies like *The Flash* tanked—bad movies that are part of bad cycles that have gotten worse, and which no longer make money. The new *M:I* movie emerges into what is arguably a more perilous time for Hollywood than the pandemic, with studios threatening to use artificial intelligence to replace writers and actors, whose unions have called strikes. This potential new digital blight is coupled with the cheapness of the studio bosses in the streaming era, who goosed their studios' stock value during the pandemic and prefer to cut costs rather than share the wealth.

And yet nobody is going to thank Tom Cruise twice, not this year. As we wait until next summer or later for *Part Two* of Cruise's multimillion-dollar cliffhanger, production of which has been shut down by the Screen Actors Guild strike, mania for the binary of Greta Gerwig's *Barbie* and Nolan's *Oppenheimer* has gripped a world suddenly rich with quality non-superhero blockbuster success stories. Add to that the very unexpected smash breakout of another long-delayed movie, the right-wing action thriller *Sound of Freedom*, and suddenly the movies are back. They are so back it's almost like they have returned to a time before the superhero apocalypse—that computer-generated miasma instrumental in training AI to take over—ground them into digital dust. In that era, Cruise was the last man standing. Now all of a sudden he is underperforming, despite his movie taking in more than $400 million worldwide so far.

RECENTLY I SAW THE 1980 espionage thriller-comedy *Hopscotch*, starring Walter Matthau as a CIA agent fired for sticking to his old ways in an increasingly corporatized spy biz. Matthau was 60 when he made it, the same age as Tom Cruise when he was making *Dead Reckoning.* It goes without saying that these two quintessential American actor/movie stars have little in common. Cruise's Ethan Hunt is all action, his emotions hidden, his skills surprising, his loyalty to his team and their mission limitless. He is the master of every machine and gadget. We are meant to understand that he can do anything. Matthau, by contrast, chooses to do almost nothing. He shows no loyalty, wears his disgruntlement on his sleeve, and chews scenery. Always old before his time, Matthau lingers in cafés going over notes, scheming to make his bosses look dumb.

Hopscotch includes the things *Mission: Impossible* movies leave out. We see Matthau haggling over safe house rentals and forged passport prices, buying clothes for his disguises, walking around empty fields as he silently plans. As for gadgets, he uses a paperclip to short out the lights in a police station, the paperclip being the one device *Hopscotch* shares with *Dead Reckoning.* There, Hayley Atwell, playing a thief, uses one to free herself from handcuffs, then uses them to attach Cruise to the steering wheel of a Fiat 500, which is trapped in a tunnel where it is of course about to be hit by an oncoming train.

Cruise at 60 still does his own stunts, which appear more dangerous and extreme with each of these movies, especially since he has teamed with the director-screenwriter Christopher McQuarrie, starting with the fifth in the series, *Mission: Impossible – Rogue Nation* (2015). Legitimately thrilling, their set pieces are nonstop inventive in the manner of can-you-top-this American know-how, returned to ultra-professional glory from the dirtbag daring of the *Jackass* movies, their natural competition (rather than *The Flash*). Matthau at 60, on the other hand, knew one real test of cinematic greatness was the ability to sit there and do nothing and still hold the screen. We cannot picture Matthau at that age or at any age learning to hold his breath for nine minutes so he could do an underwater stunt in tactical gear holding a flashlight in his mouth.

It is hard to believe that when the first *Mission: Impossible* movie debuted in 1996, Cruise had already been a movie star for thirteen years. When Brian De Palma's film version of the TV series came out with Cruise and Jon Voight, the actors from the original 1960s show complained. The movie was nihilistic, there were double agents in it, it wasn't patriotic. These were strange objections from the stars of a series that featured extrajudicial assassinations, unofficial regime change, and state-sanctioned kidnappings.

In fact, the movie, post–cold war, kept the best parts of the show: the lifelike masks characters use to impersonate each other, allowing actors to play two parts with the same face, and the idea that espionage was a series of short or long cons more like theater acting and stage magic than diplomacy by other means.

De Palma also linked the franchise to cinema history in a way Cruise and McQuarrie have maintained, bringing the mise-en-scène and the mood all the way back through Hitchcock to German Expressionism via the silent crime and spy movies Fritz Lang made in the 1920s, *Dr. Mabuse, the Gambler* and *Spione*. Right away, in the first scene of De Palma's film, a tense interrogation is deconstructed before our eyes as the walls of the set are moved aside or flattened to reveal an empty warehouse—the soundstage itself—while the actors peel off their faces, revealing nothing beneath them but the faces of other actors.

As in *Hopscotch*, but not in the TV series, the enemy in the *Mission: Impossible* movies is within. It is always a competing government spy agency that is stopping Cruise and his team from accomplishing the mission they have chosen to accept. Beneath the deep state is a deeper state still. Fittingly, as on the TV show, the news of these missions comes from a tape recorder that self-destructs, as if Cruise has found a stray Nagra on the set that instead of being used to record dialogue has been rigged to emit smoke before the editor cuts away from it and the theme music starts to play. That music, by Lalo Schifrin, is the prime intellectual property in this series of films, in itself a reason to keep making them, and in its dot-dash intensity a spur to make them good.

CRUISE'S EMPLOYERS ARE ALWAYS disavowing him in these movies. He returns to work like Charlie Brown coming back to kick the nuclear football while Lucy holds it for him again. *Dead Reckoning*, despite its setbacks, has the lucky perspicacity to appear to be seeing into the future. The overarching conspiracy here has to do with a killer AI set to take over the world's entire OS, forever blurring the line between reality and illusion, truth and lie. More than ever, the *M:I* films are about the nature of the film industry itself, and the way stories are told by actors—actors who seem to act as writers, writing the movie as they go along.

The AI, therefore, can take over spy systems and imitate a familiar voice (Simon Pegg's), then say into Cruise's earpiece, "Go left! No, go right! No, go left!" as he chases an assassin, in imitation of the directions in a screenplay or those given by a director on set. Of course the AI paints him into a corner—it exists to ruin his performance. In *Dead Reckoning*, both Cruise and the entire US surveillance apparatus have to go fully analog to fight their AI enemy, a narrative turn that both reaffirms the movie's dedication to filming real stunts in front of the camera and presciently combats the studio bosses' insistence on a new filmmaking world of computer-generated screenplays and performances along with special effects.

One of the most admirable lines in the movie comes after Atwell's character asks Cruise and his team why they are willing to help her, since they don't even know her. "What difference does that make?" he asks, a fading echo of Hawksian professionalism and humanism in this globalized landscape, part of this film series' (and Cruise's) anti-psychological approach, where backstory always struggles to be buried and forgotten, and usually is. It's the opposite of the maudlin nonsense about family in the *Fast & Furious* movies.

It is hard to ignore that Cruise has looked a little tired during the extensive, international press tour for *Dead Reckoning.* Visibly older than when he went to see *Tenet* in London three years ago, he nonetheless exudes a kind of perplexed, patient bonhomie as he travels the world to sell his film, his slightly disconnected, mechanized mien and tense bearing now newly patient, an aura that envelops the entire category "movie star." In cinemas, before the film starts, a very short clip of Cruise and McQuarrie plays in which the star-producer and writer-director thank the audience for seeing their movie in a theater, where they made it to be seen. McQuarrie, gray-haired and gray-bearded, gets to look his age; Cruise is locked in, in more ways than one.

With the temporary shutdown of *Dead Reckoning, Part Two,* Cruise is once again stuck in the quagmire of 21st-century studio filmmaking, where every crisis resolves in stasis. Will there come a time for him when that kind of entropy beats his luck and hard work? So much went wrong in making *Part One.* When the young British actor Nicholas Hoult, slated to play the film's principal villain, dropped out, Cruise and McQuarrie or someone got the idea to replace him with the journeyman trouper Esai Morales. What luck that the most calm, cool, and collected character in the movie, and the best-looking and most evil, just happens to be a man for today—a pro-union Puerto Rican TV actor from Brooklyn the exact same age as Cruise. On such accidental genius the Hollywood cinema survives another year.

OBJECTS IN SPACE AT A MOMENT IN TIME

FERRARI

MICHAEL MANN'S ATTACHMENT TO FERRARIS IS WELL KNOWN. IN HIS 1980s television series *Miami Vice,* Don Johnson played Sonny Crockett, an undercover narcotics agent who drove Ferraris that the Metro-Dade Police Department had seized from drug dealers. In Mann's 2006 film version of the show, Crockett, now played by Colin Farrell, drove a dark gray Ferrari F430 Spider, a $175,000 convertible that goes from zero to sixty in under four seconds and at the time had a resale value of around $35,000, less if a cop had frigged it.

It's ironic, then, that the quintessential American cop car, the lowly but powerful Ford Crown Victoria, had, until now, the most screen time in any of Mann's films. In *Collateral* (2004), he deploys the Crown Vic not as a police cruiser but in its other standard role, as a taxi. Jamie Foxx chauffeurs hit man Tom Cruise through the Los Angeles night as Cruise picks off witnesses in a drug case—a West Coast *Miami Vice* in reverse.

This taxicab aside, Ferraris will always define Mann in both the popular and the cinephile imagination. The association is solidified, almost carved in stone, in his latest film, a biopic starring Adam Driver as Enzo Ferrari, the former race car driver who founded Ferrari S.p.A in 1939. Vintage Ferraris, not the 1980s models, will ensure Mann's legacy as a film director, the same way some men who get to a certain level of wealth start to fill their garages with them. The difference is that Mann has done it in art, not in life, putting *Ferrari* on the marquee above his oeuvre. Soon to turn 81, Mann is as busy as ever. Last June he published the novel *Heat 2*, cowritten with Meg Gardiner, a sequel to his signature crime film. He also plans to bring it to the screen. But in *Ferrari*, Mann's fixation on death, on the cemetery and the tomb, positions this melodrama as a consecration and summation of his life's work.

FERRARI IS DEATH-HAUNTED, even for a Mann film, even for a film set in Italy. Early in the film, before he visits a cemetery to pay a morning visit to his son Dino's tomb, Enzo mentions a "perpetual twilight" in connection with his losing soccer team. This crepuscular sense of loss, present as he starts his day, hangs over the entire film. "We all know death is nearby," an engineer tells Enzo much later in *Ferrari*, long after that has become clear to everyone in his life, to everyone in the Italy of 1957, and to everyone in the audience.

As played with great subtlety and control by Driver, Enzo Ferrari is a demonic but cool and collected presence. Driver's icy nonchalance here contrasts greatly with his off-kilter performance in 2022's *White Noise*—a tribute to Mann as a director of actors, not just automobiles. Whether playing Enzo in the guise of industrial designer (a craftsman of the old school), scuderia owner (a sportsman obsessed with winning but a gentleman all the same), husband (an adulterer), or grieving or loving father, the actor, like his director, is sly but guileless. He never quite allows us to understand Enzo's true degree of self-knowledge, except when he's scamming the Italian press.

Enzo thinks he's in control because he understands that at the bottom of his success is the inevitability of death. To live so close to it is not normal, but it is exciting, and lucrative. Yet fate, and his wife, Laura (Penélope Cruz), are always a step ahead. During the film's first visit to the Ferrari test track, Enzo tells a young driver he doesn't need another racer on his team. Then the film's first crash happens, hurling a red Ferrari through the air, killing the driver. The eager replacement just happens to be standing right next to him. A typical morning for Enzo, who has already been shot at by Laura.

Cruz embodies the Mannian woman in a new way. She plays Laura as a smoldering life force and great business mind who, like her husband, plays things close to the vest. She is the first woman in Mann's films whose husband listens to her and follows her advice. When Khalilah Ali (Nona Gaye) explained to her husband Muhammad (Will Smith) that he was being exploited in Mann's other biopic, *Ali* (2001), he paid her no mind and left her. Here, Enzo understands that he isn't and can't be free. At his factory a pigeon is kept in a cage with an open door. The pigeon chooses not to leave. "Freedom for that pigeon is pigeon pie," he explains.

SPEED IS RELIGION IN *FERRARI*, as shown in a scene set in church during morning Mass. The church is near Maserati's test track, and the Ferrari executives and workers in the pews can hear the cars revving and shifting into high gear under the priest's invocations. As a group, they bring out stopwatches to time the test runs of the new Maseratis they will be competing against in the upcoming 1957 Mille Miglia, a race described this way by the sportswriter Brock Yates, in his 1991 biography of Enzo Ferrari, *The Man and the Machine*, which is the basis of Mann's film:

> The notion of fast cars racing on real roads, around twisting mountain hairpins and through narrow city streets, was the embodiment of every man's fantasy to charge down an open road flat out, unencumbered by laws or moral and social impediments of any kind. For all its insanity, the Mille Miglia . . . [encompassed] "an entire lifetime condensed into a few hours." . . . To have [competed in it] meant that a man had faced down the specter of violent death for half a day over some of the most difficult and unforgiving roadways in the entire world.

It is this fatal mindset that Fellini mocked in the "Toby Dammit" section of *Spirits of the Dead* (1968), in which Terence Stamp races through the nighttime streets of Rome in a prize Ferrari until a wire stretched across the road decapitates him.

Ferrari's journey to the screen was not so fast. The film's screenwriter, Troy Kennedy Martin, died in 2009. Christian Bale was supposed to play Enzo; instead he ended up in a different Formula One movie, James Mangold's *Ford v Ferrari* (2019), playing the race car driver Ken Miles. Then it was supposed to be Hugh Jackman. Creating the illusion of speed can be a slow process. It took patience.

At times in *Ferrari* serenity takes over. A scene of Enzo showing his surviving son engine plans and explaining the utilitarian aspects of beauty to him becomes the film's calm center. "When a thing works better usually it is more beautiful to the eye," he says, underlining Mann's approach in this burnished film of bright red and yellow cars set against green and pale blue landscapes and gray-brown factory interiors.

Racing movies have always had a special place in the cinema, going back at least to Howard Hawks's *The Crowd Roars* in 1932. Hawks updated the genre for color (and product branding) in 1965 for *Red Line 7000*. In the late 1960s and early 1970s big-star auto racing vehicles followed, with James Garner, Paul Newman, Steve McQueen. Cars on a track replicate the motion of the cinema itself—reels going round like wheels, the film strip a ribbon of road, a circular motion that keeps going and indicates an infinite replaceability, an anonymity of actors hard to tell apart in helmets and goggles, just part of the machinery.

What interrupts this flow is the paradoxical reason for the existence of these movies: the car crash. Mann, in this regard, does not disappoint. The fatal accident at the test track early in *Ferrari* is a shocking moment, but brief, quickly integrated into the course of things, and all but forgotten by the time the infamous crash of the 1957 Mille Miglia has to—inevitably—be recreated. Mann does not balk. He presents the crash as a harrowing "holy shit!" moment involving a child. It is a new Odesa Steps sequence of deadly, wasteful capitalist excess, ending with nine spectators dead.

The driver, Alfonso de Portago (Gabriel Leone), lies on the road cut in two, his Ferrari a compacted John Chamberlain sculpture. The traveling shot in this scene becomes a grotesque response to Enzo's lecture to his scuderia at a team luncheon earlier in the film, one that also underlined his status as a man with two families, one hidden—"Two objects cannot occupy the same point in space at the same moment in time."

IN 1909 THE ITALIAN PROTOFASCIST poet Filippo Tommaso Marinetti published his *Futurist Manifesto*, a bizarre, hysterical, racist-sexist celebration of speed and machinery that welcomed the new 20th century as an epoch of violence and rejected past notions of how to live. He demanded glorious deaths in car crashes, and lauded war and destruction. "Time and space died yesterday!" Marinetti screamed. "We declare that the splendor of the world has been enriched by a new beauty: the beauty of speed. A racing automobile with its bonnet adorned with great tubes like serpents with explosive breath . . . a roaring motor car which seems to run on machine-gun fire"—this was his example of the new beauty that would replace the natural world.

One of the many things Marinetti opposed was museums. He identified them with cemeteries. "Museums, cemeteries!" he shouted. "Truly identical in their sinister juxtaposition of bodies that do not know each other." Seventy or so years later, after two world wars, Paul Virilio, the anti-speed cultural theorist, proposed a "Museum of Accidents" that could keep us from becoming habituated to the terror and violence created by new technologies. Virilio studied what he called *speed-space*, which he linked to the compression of time under capitalism. He theorized that each new advance in technology and its accompanying mechanical inventions came with disaster built in, and each would eventually uncover its own new brand of catastrophe.

These two strains—the mausoleum and machinery—compete against each other in *Ferrari*. Enzo's drivers become canned sardines packaged for the great maw, while he and Laura make their morning pilgrimages to their son's tomb. Enzo speaks to Dino through the marble, saying that he and Laura seem like ghosts now that Dino is no longer with them. This scene is reminiscent of gothic Italian horror, much like Toby Dammit's crash, which Fellini links with Mario Bava's *Kill, Baby, . . . Kill!* (1966) by the presence of a spectral girl along the sports car's route and at the scene of the final accident.

This strange aspect of Mann's film is heightened for viewers who are also racing fans. Many of them will know what happened at the 1957 Mille Miglia. The accident was preceded by an infamous "kiss of death," which Mann also includes. Portago was dating the movie actress Linda Christian at the time of the race (she's played by Sarah Gadon in the film), and Ferrari had warned him about having an actress at the track. "Actresses. I have admiration, but keep them away from the paddock," he tells Portago. "They distract photographers whose attention I want on my cars." Christian showed up at a pit stop during the Mille Miglia, and Portago took her in his arms, then rode off forever, like the motorcyclist boyfriend in the Shangri-Las' 1964 song "Leader of the Pack." *Look out, look out, look out!*

NEWSPAPERS AND NEWSPAPER headlines abound in *Ferrari* and *The Man and the Machine*. One reads, "The Mille Miglia, Cemetery of Babies and Men, Enough!" Another calls Enzo "An Industrial Saturn Devouring His Own Children." Like the newspaper clippings about motorcycle crashes in the homemade shrine in Kenneth Anger's *Scorpio Rising* (1963), these become collectible receipts that enhance the aura and therefore the value of the cars. Ferrari is so bent on winning the Mille Miglia not just for the sake of victory, but also to attract outside finance for his failing company, which in 1957, according to the film, was selling ninety-eight production cars a year to wealthy consumers, when it needed to be selling four hundred. One of those buyers, we see in the film, was King Hussein of Jordan

(Jonathan Burteaux). The tiny monarch complains that in his previous Ferrari his feet barely reached the pedals.

In his massive car collection, the current Sultan of Brunei is said to own as many as three hundred Ferraris, likely worth over $100 million. Or they were worth that much. It seems the cars, according to carsguide.com.au, have "fallen into disrepair after air conditioning in their storage garages was turned off many years ago." The most famous collectors of Ferraris are now comedians—Jerry Seinfeld and David Letterman own dozens of vintage Ferraris (and Porsches) between them. (Jay Leno, otherwise known as a preeminent vintage car collector, does not own a single Ferrari, in part because he "just never liked dealing with the dealers.") They are toys, like the toy race car Laura finds in Enzo's mistress's house, proving he has a child with her. Collectors seem to prize the red or white ones the most—rental car colors. In the movies, red will always be Ferrari's definitive color, as it is in Mann's film, though King Hussein's 335 S is yellow. Maybe the most well-known red Ferrari in the movies appears in a comedy, the 1961 250 GT California Spyder the teens in *Ferris Bueller's Day Off* (1986) take for a joy ride to the Art Institute of Chicago.

Beyond its status as a manufacturer of high-priced commodities and valuable collector's items, Ferrari exists today as a brand, licensed like Gucci and Hermès as a fashion logo for clothes and accessories. As Yates's daughter, the writer Stacy Bradley, points out in the epilogue to a new edition of *The Man and the Machine,* in today's marketplace "conceptual or hierarchical purity has no place." Ferrari now makes an SUV, the Purosangue, priced at $400,000. "Ferrari's value as a luxury brand is, in theory, limitless," writes Bradley. Ferrari is now so associated with the excess of luxury that there is a series of self-help books by a man who describes himself in print as "the monk who sold his Ferrari."

In Mann's film, Enzo poses for photographers at his factory with Portago and Linda Christian, leaning against one of his cars. He makes sure to slide Christian over to keep her butt from blocking the Ferrari "prancing horse" marque. The film ends with a reunited Enzo and Laura preparing to bribe the press so their factory will survive and someday manufacture those SUVs. It reminded me of a wealthy real estate developer in the 1968 Saul Bellow story "The Old System," who briefly recalls the beauty of the luxury automobiles—"Hudsons, Auburns, Bearcats"—that once filled the parking lot of a country club he has razed and replaced with a shopping mall. The cars were beauties, sure, but they were "only machinery. Nothing to get nostalgic about."

BEYOND THE VISIBLE

ABOUT DRY GRASSES

THE SOUNDS OF HARSH WEATHER OVER A BLACK SCREEN, THEN A SNOWY landscape in long shot. A white van drives into the frame, the red triangle of a yield sign the one note of color here, and a man gets out. He walks alone toward the camera. As *About Dry Grasses* begins, the only clear thing is that we are in the land of Nuri Bilge Ceylan, the Turkish filmmaker who, over the course of nine films, has carved this particular terrain out of rural stagnation and urban anomie.

Long, dense, and elliptical, Ceylan's films are thorny and difficult, and rousing in their starkness. There is a great pleasure in seeing them, despite their bitter stories of failure and regret. Each one, from *The Small Town* (1997) to *The Wild Pear Tree* (2018), records something essential. On a basic level, Ceylan's movies are a place where, in the future, we will see snow photographed in color once there isn't any snow (or only computer-generated snow in movies). They will be a way that we remember the reality of the world that once was.

Another example: *About Dry Grasses* ends with scenes shot in and around the ruins of the Karakuş Tumulus, a grand funerary monument featuring columns topped with sculptures—including a monolithic version of the statuette in *The Maltese Falcon*. In the short time since Ceylan shot those scenes, one of the pillars, over 2,000 years old, has collapsed—another casualty of the Turkey-Syria earthquakes that claimed tens of thousands of lives a year ago and that much of the world has already forgotten. Ceylan's films recognize this moment of ours, in which things fade from memory too quickly.

AT THE CENTER OF *About Dry Grasses* is the story of Samet (Deniz Celiloğlu), which Ceylan tells with a certain eternal gaze. At first Samet seems to be the kind of guy who gets along with everybody: He lives in a remote part of eastern Turkey—Ceylan country—where the government has assigned him his job as a middle-school art teacher. He's chummy with a wide range of characters: the local veterinarian, the military police sergeant who randomly checks people's IDs, even a wannabe Kurdish guerrilla. Samet has also become quite buddy-buddy with Sevim (Ece Bağcı), the prettiest, liveliest girl in his class, calling on her more than the other students and walking arm in arm with her down the school's corridor.

Here we have a problem, and not just with Samet's behavior. By the time his inappropriate conduct with Sevim blows up in his face, *About Dry Grasses* still has 150 minutes to go. Ceylan's last two films were also three hours and fifteen minutes long—this now seems to be his preferred length—and that is a lot of time for things to get worse for Samet, who, in the film's first forty-five minutes, has been slowly revealed as a disgruntled snob. Samet, we come to understand, exists in the ultimate condition of the Ceylan protagonist: He longs to be in Istanbul instead of living on the edge of nowhere, and his pining for the city is coupled with an unwillingness to commit to or even recognize anything that might help him get there.

But as we watch *About Dry Grasses*, we realize that the film's running time also opens it up in many other ways. In fact, its length allows Ceylan to keep changing the stakes. As Samet continues doing the wrong thing, Ceylan deepens the film's politics, subtly placing his story in the context of suicide bombings and Kurdish resistance, a world in which Samet's complaints about his lot in life are trivial and petty.

A non-feel-good movie, set in the present, about the impossibility of change and the opacity of human relations, *About Dry Grasses* is *The Holdovers* in reverse, its opposite in every way. It takes place right after winter break, not during, as if it were picking up where *The Holdovers* left off, and it's about a teacher who does not lose his job but probably should. It also comes last in a sequence of three recent movies about teachers and students; in between *The Holdovers* and *About Dry Grasses* was *The Teachers' Lounge*, an Oscar-nominated German film by a Turkish-German director, İlker Çatak, that shares a scene with Ceylan's, of students being unfairly searched in class by school administrators. It's almost as if the cinema were trying to get to *About Dry Grasses* but had to go through a metamorphosis first, arriving there in stages. As François Truffaut once noted, "If three films come out in Paris in the same month, and all are set in the same period—for example, the Occupation—or in the same place—Saint-Tropez—woe to the one that follows the first two, even if it is the best of the lot."

ABOUT DRY GRASSES IS THE BEST of the lot. I liked *The Holdovers* and thought *The Teachers' Lounge* was OK, but here we are dealing with the best the cinema can offer. It's a brutal fact that Truffaut was right: When it comes to the box office, the third time is not the charm. Few American moviegoers have even heard of *About Dry Grasses*. The time of "slow cinema" may be passing, and although Ceylan's films are not that—not quite—it is easy to conflate what he does with the kind of festival movie that values length over acting and screenwriting over drama.

And I do mean "drama." Ceylan's 2014 film *Winter Sleep* was built on Chekhov, and his other films often adhere to 19th-century dramatic and literary forms while remaining resolute in their cinematic modernity, much in the way that Ingmar Bergman's and Andrei Tarkovsky's films did. Those auteurs are two of Ceylan's avowed masters, and I think it's time to admit that he has equaled or surpassed them, even though saying so won't matter, or will seem perverse to the generation that came of age in Bergman's heyday and irrelevant to the current generation, split as it is between pseudo-obsessional pop culture and radical fragmentation.

Ceylan is out of step with popular culture in other ways too. His radicalism is subtle. One aspect of that is how Sevim's story eventually becomes a subplot in *About Dry Grasses* as Nuray (Merve Dizdar), a teacher with a prosthetic leg, takes over as the film's female lead. Nuray splits her time between Samet and his work colleague and roommate, Kenan (Musab Ekici), another man in that other constant Ceylanian state, bachelorhood. Dizdar won the Best Actress award at Cannes last year for her performance (to the revulsion of much of the Turkish establishment), probably because of the film's long centerpiece scene, a conversation between Nuray and Samet in her apartment that begins with her excoriating his politics and ends in one of the most caddish seductions in movies.

The scene has great emotional power, building menace in a slow burn, before breaking at the height of its tension when Samet leaves for the bathroom to pop a pill. At that point, Ceylan does something totally unexpected, and yet after that scene, which would end most movies, we still have forty-five minutes to go. Similarly, Ceylan has become so supple with what he does that in *About Dry Grasses* he can introduce a gun, in a shot with a great deal of force and implied future violence, and then let all that dissipate into mystery, violating the Chekhovian diktat on purpose.

About Dry Grasses becomes a *Jules and Jim* for the provinces far from the center of empire, as in a Kafka parable, and it's equally far from the golden age of the European art film. Ceylan is part of a generation of great filmmakers who do well at festivals and whose films get limited theatrical releases in the United States, but who, in their own time, are denied the status of their forebears. That's because the cinema itself is moving to the edges. The group that Ceylan is arguably a part of includes Jia Zhangke in China, with his similar focus on those lost on the periphery, Lucrecia Martel in Argentina, Lee Chang-dong in South Korea, Carlos Reygadas in Mexico, and all your major Romanians.

IN A PRESS STATEMENT, Ceylan mentioned that he wanted to show in *About Dry Grasses* three things that are, as the wannabe guerrilla says in the film, "beyond the visible"—an area hard to put on the screen. Those things are "how ideals can in time turn into disappointments"; "the burden of occupying a point in time"; and "the feeling of nothingness impossible to shake." The film's long coda, set in the summer, explains its title and brings those themes to the fore, introducing a voice-over narration from Samet for the first time.

Yet what is said is less important than what we see. As Samet, Nuray, and Kenan wander among the ruins, this film ends the way another French film, *Les Enfants Terribles*, began: with a snowball fight recalled in flashback and voice-over. In the Melville and Cocteau film, the schoolkids are interrupted by an adult—but here the adult is more of a participant than a voice of authority, and the schoolkids are girls, not boys. As Samet drones on about the hopelessness of his life, Sevim and the other girls are blissfully cut off from hearing him. They pelt him with snow, deaf to his misery as well as his earlier outbursts—including one in which he yelled at them that they could study art all they want but they would still end up being nothing but potato and beet farmers because "the show must go on."

"The puzzling incident deeply distressed the principal," Cocteau says in the narration during *Les Enfants Terribles*' schoolboy scene. In Ceylan's film, Samet, adrift in the crumbling remains of an ancient kingdom, becomes like the lost Odysseus: "The storm winds have snatched him away into obscurity. He is gone beyond sight, beyond knowledge." We are left to remember him by his dialogue earlier in the film, when he was trying to seduce Nuray, pretending to self-knowledge by implying that he had lied to Kenan to get her alone. "Have I been an asshole?" he asks, even though he knows the answer.

THIS GLASS, THIS DRINK, THIS COUNTERTOP, OUR BODIES

OSCAR MOVIES 2024

Anatomy of a Fall

Writers' lives as depicted in French films continue to be things of great mystery, and I don't mean murder mystery. In Justine Triet's *Anatomy of a Fall*, a married, middle-aged writer couple (Sandra Hüller and Samuel Theis) seems overly involved in rap fandom. Their dog is named Snoop and husband Samuel "often," according to wife Sandra, plays an instrumental steel-drum version of 50 Cent's "P.I.M.P." at full volume while doing home repairs on their massive A-frame in the French Alps. The day he falls out a window and dies—accidentally, a suicide, murdered by Sandra, who knows?—he's blaring it "on a loop."

The film will go on to pester us with this track five times during various flashbacks and trial scenes. It comes across as a weird joke or a prank Triet is playing that has some meaning for her but not for us. It's not mischievous like the repetition of "California Dreamin'" in *Chungking Express* because *Anatomy of a Fall* is otherwise po-faced. By the end, any sympathy we might have had for Samuel evaporates with these "P.I.M.P." needle drops. They make him into a ridiculous man, and after 152 minutes it's a great relief not that Sandra has been exonerated of his murder, but that we won't have to hear those steel drums again.

Triet's previous film, *Sibyl* (2019), was agile, witty, and original. This one is prosaic, as if an article from the *Cut* about the domestic lives of writers has been crossed with an episode of *Law & Order.* If only an expert like Ice-T had shown up in the courtroom scenes to push stop on "P.I.M.P." and explain things to the judge: "Somebody try to bust my eardrums, I'm gonna bust their ass."

Past Lives

The writer couple (Greta Lee and John Magaro) in Celine Song's debut feature, *Past Lives,* are younger, less established, and blander than the one in *Anatomy of a Fall.* Residents of a not-great apartment in the Lower East Side, they don't have much in the way of personality. Nora is Korean and a playwright, Arthur a white-guy novelist who has written a novel called *Boner.*

If Nora can be said to have a characteristic, it is her desire to win literary prizes. She has left her successful arty parents behind in South Korea "because Koreans don't win the Nobel Prize for Literature." She also dreams of winning a Pulitzer and a Tony. This seemed dated and contrived, since Koreans do win Oscars. Pretending Nora is not a screenwriter-director like her creator, or might become one, is a deflection after *Parasite*'s success in 2020.

The film is more literature than cinema, elevated mumblecore for graduate writing seminars, the opposite of, for instance, Hong Sangsoo, who makes low-budget films about writers and filmmakers without worrying about prizes, and whose films don't seem written at all. With its expensive-looking cinematography, Slowdive-sounding score, and fancy editing, *Past Lives* is designed to win awards, which it has. Like Nora, Celine Song made a conscious choice to leave one life behind and start another. Her film is the result of a series of other professional choices, too, and it shows.

American Fiction

It is hard to understand the decisions that went into Cord Jefferson's adaptation of Percival Everett's unique and startling novel *Erasure* but, with the exception of the cast, they were decisions that don't work. *American Fiction* is watered-down, unexciting, and nonabrasive. Its unclever title is an example of the film's basic strategy, which is to take material that might offend people, material that was in fact designed to offend people, and update it for a world that demands to not be offended. Though it's topped with an inconclusive series of postmodern codas, this is a family comedy with Hallmark touches. When the main character, Thelonious "Monk" Ellison (Jeffrey Wright), a beleaguered Black novelist, announces early in the movie that he doesn't believe in race, I didn't think that meant he wanted to be in *My Big Fat Greek Wedding*.

The twin worlds of publishing and Hollywood are mocked here, without ever looking or feeling anything like those worlds do in real life. The ersatz quality of it all extends to the music on the soundtrack. Why hire the great Patrice Rushen to play gentle jazz piano over everything, in a score she didn't write herself? An earlier meta-scene, in which we see Keith David and Okieriete Onaodowan as a stereotypical drunk father and gangbanger son acting out scenes in Ellison's deliberately bad novel, and arguing with him about how corny and exploitative they are, is a good idea, but it's truncated, maybe because it hits too close to what Jefferson is doing himself. The direct criticism of other movies in that scene and in other parts of *American Fiction* is dubious, too. Are we supposed to think *Boyz n the Hood* is a bad movie now? It's a thousand times better than this one.

The Holdovers

Jeffrey Wright seems held back in *American Fiction*. The same cannot be said of Paul Giamatti, who plays a lonely, bitter classics teacher at a New England prep school in Alexander Payne's *The Holdovers*. Fitted with one wall-eye contact lens, Giamatti stares at the corner of the room while fixing what's left of his gaze on his students, whom he considers recalcitrant philistines, "entitled little degenerates."

Giamatti's performance is a pleasure to watch. He is the presiding presence in the movie, and David Hemingson's erudite screenplay allows him free range to deliver long lines of invective. At the same time Giamatti is part of a Three Stooges act with Da'Vine Joy Randolph, as the taciturn manager of the school's cafeteria, and Dominic Sessa, the one student left behind at the school over Christmas. If this trio seems to shut out the rest of the world and to reduce the other characters in the film to walk-ons, it's because they are also doing that in their own lives, each trapped alone in various stages of grief.

The Holdovers is destined to be a Christmas classic precisely because it is not a feel-good movie. Randolph's son is a casualty of an unjust war, Sessa's father is a hopeless mental case with the official *Cuckoo's Nest* haircut of institutionalized madness, and Giamatti is denied a happy ending as he drives away from the school with a bottle of pilfered brandy pressed to his lips. Set in 1970, it is nostalgic, though. Payne and cinematographer Eigil Bryld have given *The Holdovers* a warm, old-school shot-on-film look that the viewer can slip into like a coma.

The Teachers' Lounge

Leonie Benesch gives a sensitive, lively performance in *The Teachers' Lounge* as Carla, a young seventh grade teacher in Hamburg. With her two big, functional eyes and her positive attitude, she's the opposite of Giamatti in *The Holdovers*. She shows love for her students and a great desire to help them, which she expresses with dance-like physicality in the gym classes she teaches along with her main job, teaching math, an arrangement that would be comic in an American film but in a German one is graceful and nurturing.

She's too good to be true, so of course director İlker Çatak is setting her up for a fall. A series of thefts at the school implicates minority students in the eyes of the other teachers, but Carla suspects one of her colleagues, thereby initiating a series of events that will embroil this place of learning in recriminations, ill will, and chaos. But it's a lite, low-stakes kind of chaos. The lesson here is that no good deed goes unpunished. The film is a mild version of a Haneke movie, seemingly made for the middle schoolers who populate it and who are presumably not yet ready for a full-strength *Piano Teacher*'s lounge.

Barbie

Barbie like no movie before it pushed the limit of what constitutes legitimate news versus what's free publicity for a pseudo-event designed to rake in money for a large corporation. Obviously *Barbie* came out ahead, making $1.5 billion worldwide, though even with that haul, *Barbie*'s parent company, Warner Bros. Discovery, somehow lost $3.1 billion in 2023. If their board of directors was on the ball, Margot Robbie and Greta Gerwig would be running the studio, not David Zaslav.

The push for *Barbie* was intense. Its only analogue was the right-wing media's obsession with Hunter Biden, the MAGA Barbie. CNN.com, which is also owned by Warner Bros. Discovery, published 128 separate news stories about the film. The *New York Times* published 84 pieces on *Barbie*, and mentioned Barbie in non-*Barbie*-related pieces over 450 times. Richard Brody of the *New Yorker* became *Barbie*'s number one fan among film critics, tweeting about *Barbie* or its principals some three dozen times, including one tweet in French and another that stated that *Barbie* was a better movie than *2001: A Space Odyssey*, "except for the unrivaled Stargate sequence." Brody had mentioned *Barbie* as early as February 2020, more than three years before the film came out, in a review of the Robbie-superhero-starrer *Birds of Prey*, in which he told readers he was "greatly looking forward to her performance in the title role of *Barbie*, the next film by Greta Gerwig, who, I suspect, will have an altogether more original view of Robbie's art." That is what you call *advance praise*.

One CNN.com piece, on how enraging it was to the author that Robbie and Gerwig were not nominated for a Best Actress and Best Director Oscars, stated that the only people who "*didn't* love" *Barbie* were "reactionary right-wing dorks." When Hillary Clinton weighed in with a punny tweet to console Robbie and Gerwig about the snub, it became clear that *Barbie* was a form of official art, an item of capitalist realism about which only one set of values should be expressed in public. It was supposed to matter that those values were feminist and not just consumerist.

This view and its proponents became clearer for me recently when a cinephile friend told me about how last July she had excused herself from a bachelorette party that included going to see *Barbie*. She thought she had dodged the pink bullet, but one day in January while she was out she got a couple of texts from her building's unofficial super, a man in his sixties. "Have you seen *Barbie*?" the first text asked. "If not, you should. It's quite clever and funny," said the second. "I left it on your stair just in case." When she got home and entered her building, there it was: a Blu-Ray of *Barbie* borrowed from the local library sitting on the steps to her door.

Poor Things

Yorgos Lanthimos is our leading auteur of half-baked ideas, but since he's begun working with screenwriter Tony McNamara on movies starring Emma Stone, things have started to gel and get moist. *Poor*

Things, a film of "sugar and violence," is a bizarro *Barbie*, a forceful, entertaining movie without smugness, featuring a kind of outré production design all its own. Every effect is thrown in: The film is in color and black-and-white, it pushes the use of wide-angle cinematography in new directions, hybrid animals wander about, and mad scientist Willem Dafoe belches floating orb-like bubbles—all this before the film gets to Emma Stone's Bella, a Victorian wild child chasing mysteries of the organism through an ocean liner's casino and a Parisian brothel.

Dafoe is a disfigured Frankenstein and Stone his messy, demanding monster, a creation that escapes his lab, moves on, and quickly takes over the action. Once she discovers the pleasures of sex ("furious jumping") with Mark Ruffalo's louche playboy, she leaves England for Lisbon, a world of fine dining and ballroom dancing where she gets to declare, immortally, "I must go punch that baby."

It was reported that *Poor Things* looks like a Tim Burton movie. It doesn't—it's more like an animated Karel Zeman movie come to life—though it does synthesize almost every Frankenstein movie that came before it. Instead, it's a film with a true Sadean quality, made for libertines, not Puritans, who will find many opportunities in it to be offended. It's about time something so wicked was made at such a high level.

The Color Purple

I'm troubled by writers who never ask themselves, "What if I didn't do this?" Some things should be passed over in silence. I felt that way last fall when *Taylor Swift: The Eras Tour* came out in theaters. When I noticed aging male film critics rushing to see this nearly three-hour concert film so they could write about it, I was embarrassed for them.

Another kind of movie is also like that to me: musicals based on movies that were not musicals but which became stage musicals, then movies again. I saw the musical version of *The Producers* when it came out in 2005 and it struck me as inert, laughless, and botched. Since then I have avoided musical versions of *Hairspray* and *Mean Girls*, and probably some others I've forgotten existed.

The new *Color Purple* movie musical is one of these. It starts well, with a pre-title song called "Huckleberry Pie" performed with delighted charm by Phylicia Pearl Mpasi and Halle Bailey as sisters, accompanied by Colman Domingo as a bluesman cowboy playing banjo on a horse. Set along the Georgia coast amid trees draped in Spanish moss, this number appeared to pay homage to *Daughters of the Dust* and was directed by Blitz Bazawule in a very up-to-the-minute CGI style that showed a certain flair, like maybe the movie was going to use its artifice to some new advantage other of these musicals had not. As an introductory interlude that evoked life in a rural Black community in 1909, it promised something that was not just hokum.

But then the rest of the film was just hokum, and there was a lot of it, with plenty of beatings, especially for poor Celie (Fantasia Barrino) at the hands of Mister (Domingo), who gets his comeuppance and is forgiven, and as an act of contrition decides to wear shimmery "fancy pants" to the big group hug at the end. He looked clownish but as punishments go he got off easy.

Killers of the Flower Moon

The brute fact of *Killers of the Flower Moon*'s three-and-a-half-hour existence is something to be reckoned with, but it also emphasizes how its story is hard to endure. Scorsese's film is truly novelistic, like a Dreiser novel—which is to say it also has the detail of a silent Stroheim film from the time in which most of it takes place, the late 1910s and 1920s, offering meticulous period set decoration, props, and wardrobe, down to the boots and driving goggles.

Once again, as he has been doing at least since *Goodfellas* in 1990 and up through the more recent *Silence* and *The Irishman*, Scorsese presents a mentor relationship in which an older man takes a younger one under his wing so that he can exploit him by making him do his dirty work. Here, this is pushed to its extreme, as it involves the murder of a race—the Osage on their reservation in Oklahoma—and the expropriation of their oil-rich land. DiCaprio and De Niro have lost almost all expressiveness at this point in this kind of story, both of them frowny-face masks riveted in place, with all the other white people, bastards with their hands out, looking like variations on the Pep Boys. Scorsese compares them to wolves, the same way the Chinese communists in *Kundun* were visually equated with vultures pecking at the bones of the dead.

The Osage are lost here, literally "vanishing Americans," a racist concept hammered home by De Niro's villain. In the film's criminal scheme, the performances of the Native actors are swamped by the white country and Americana musicians Scorsese has cast in small roles as various murderers, thieves, and creeps. William Belleau, by contrast, is tragic and difficult to watch as the hapless Henry Roan, the melancholic, suicidal, alcoholic Osage who is befriended and discarded, shot in the head and left in the road.

For the first time in a Scorsese film, however, a woman is at the center of the men's relationship. Lily Gladstone's Mollie, a wealthy, diabetic (she's "got too much sugar"), and unmarried Osage comes between DiCaprio's Ernest and De Niro's Hale after Hale subtly sets it up for Ernest to marry her. Gladstone's performance is unlike anything else in Scorsese's work. She's calm and smart, but taken in by Ernest even though she knows he's a kind of wolf, too—"coyote wants money." In the second half of the film, Gladstone must portray her as the martyr of the film's sickening, deglamorized violence. She lingers between life and death, unaware she's being poisoned by her husband as she grieves for her mother and sisters, dying one by one.

Ernest starts the film as a taxi driver, reminding us of Scorsese the modernist auteur of the 1970s, who here reasserts himself outside of this naturalistic movie in its coda, where the lie of entertainment mirrors the contemporary scenes of the cleaners in *The Zone of Interest*. In Europe there are museums for these horrors, their history expressed in piles of shoes and eyeglasses. In America it's called showbiz.

Nyad

"Yeah, well, fuck that. I'm gonna swim from Cuba to Florida" is probably the least relatable statement I've ever heard in a movie. Annette Bening, in the title role as Diana Nyad, however, convinces us that it's worth doing, no matter how many times she has to try. As Diana's ex-lover, best friend, and coach (Jodie Foster) says, "When she starts hallucinating, you go with it."

Nyad is a tribute to Diana's self-centered delusion, which the film eventually locates in her father's obsession with her destiny as a swimmer because he'd changed their last name to the goddess-like but fishy Nyad, and in the years of sexual abuse she suffered at the hands of a coach while she was a teenage Olympic swimmer in training. In the ocean she mentally escapes her past, using boomer pop hits like "The Sound of Silence" to measure her pace during these self-imposed, saltwater marathons. The film should come alive to these songs but it never quite does. A scene of a near shark attack is immediately followed by Diana just getting on with it, to the tune of Neil Young's "Heart of Gold"—she is crossing the ocean for one, you see. *Nyad* was directed by the sports doc couple who made *Free Solo*, and follows its story closely and faithfully, never rising much above sea level. Its one hallucinatory underwater scene looks too much like it's set at a fish-bowl castle. I couldn't tell if that was intentional or not.

Maestro

Bradley Cooper's ambitious Leonard Bernstein biopic starts out lively, presenting the world of midcentury classical music and life in the Carnegie Hall apartments as a fast-paced, same-sex romp, with Aaron Copland shouting advice from offscreen. It's in black-and-white, too, the same way the similar 1950s milieu of New York theater is presented in *Asteroid City*. Soon, though, it's in color and bisexual Lenny gets bogged down by a wife (Carey Mulligan) and a country house with a swimming pool, where, during the parties they throw, they also throw around adjectives like "big-ass" and "random" and phrases like "misread the room," which I'm certain no one was using in the Dakota or in Connecticut in the 1970s.

Mulligan's Felicia has to put up with a lot in Bernstein. She knows what he's like and what he needs to be happy and to do his work, and she gives up her career as an actress for him and their children, ignoring his male lovers as best she can while sliding inexorably into the lonely role of long-suffering wife. Bernstein exists parallel to her, and Cooper's performance is daring and convincing, but something doesn't add up. Since the film skips the 1960s, by the time we get to Felicia's cancer, Lenny and she have aged and now look like Evel Knievel and Nancy Reagan miscast in an unhappy marriage, a change-in-mood time leap commandeered from *Boogie Nights* and now standard in biopics that include cocaine. Gone are the late 1950s and all of the 1960s, when Bernstein went radical chic and was doing TV shows with Miles Davis and donating money to the Black Panthers at cocktail parties in his huge apartment with Otto Preminger and Richard Avedon by his side. That's a loss. If you have a chance to have somebody play Preminger in a movie, take it.

Oppenheimer

Robert Oppenheimer (Cillian Murphy) is closeted/not closeted, too, but his non-secret is left-wing politics and his parties are with the CPUSA. Around sexy fellow travelers he can't help mentioning he's read all three volumes of *Capital*, in German, making sure to add that Marx bored him. This tension also splits *Oppenheimer* into black-and-white and color. The color sections of Nolan's film concentrate on quantum physics and show the development of the atomic bomb at Los Alamos, the frenzy of the Trinity Test and its aftermath; the black-and-white parts follow the confirmation hearings of Lewis Strauss (Robert Downey Jr.), a former chair of the Atomic Energy Commission and Oppenheimer's stealth nemesis, who is up for a seat in Eisenhower's cabinet. Politics is for gray men; science is chromatic.

Murphy inhabits Oppenheimer so completely that at times he disappears into the background of his own biopic, making it easy to understand why his wife, Kitty (Emily Blunt), continually implores him to fight the politicos red-baiting him. Downey, freed from his iron suit and the MCU, is plunged into a hidden universe of waves and particles, where Oppenheimer casually dismisses him because he knows Strauss is in over his head. He doesn't realize he's paranoid, too. Downey's performance is one of subtlety and guile, right up to the last twist. I have never seen an actor so thoroughly redeemed by taking a hard, thankless role like this.

The film is cast like a Preminger movie, specifically like *Advise & Consent*, which it resembles in key ways: the backroom politics and endless meetings with the branches of the federal government and the panoply of stars in minor roles. *Advise & Consent* had Burgess Meredith and Betty White, this has Benny Safdie and Casey Affleck.

Nolan often cuts their dialog within an inch of its life, making his scenes less dynamic so that their words can emphasize how high the stakes are (ending World War II; nuclear holocaust). He does make room for the romance of radiation within the drama of security clearance. When Oppenheimer meets Kitty, we've already seen the firework bursts of color that play in his head when he's contemplating the motion of atoms in space, so there is an erotic charge when he explains physics to Kitty at a nighttime commie shindig in Pasadena. He looks almost into her eyes, touches hands with her, and describes the subatomic action in "this glass, this drink, this countertop, our bodies." Later he's part of a government group enumerating potential deaths when the A-bomb is dropped on Hiroshima, a corporate meeting that echoes similar conclaves in *The Zone of Interest*. These scenes of groups of men tallying mortality are an obscene cloud hovering over 2023 movies.

Rustin

The political activist Bayard Rustin, a contemporary of Oppenheimer and Leonard Bernstein who organized the March on Washington in 1963, was both gay and an ex-communist, so the struggles in his biopic are not going to be easy ones. Colman Domingo's portrayal of him in George C. Wolfe's *Rustin* is warm and involving, and this is a somber drama about a consequential time in our nation's history. Yet the film's perfunctory elements are enlivened by kitsch. Rustin mixing cocktails in his bachelor pad and playing the lute for his boyfriend was more than I expected.

The film, like *Oppenheimer*, offers a who's-who of its specific milieu, the Civil Rights Movement and its leaders. It's odd that Jeffrey Wright is so much stronger in *Rustin* than he is in *American Fiction*. Here he plays Adam Clayton Powell Jr. as a self-important raconteur with a cigarette holder, a man who doesn't know he's past his prime as a macher in national politics and race relations. The British guy who plays Martin Luther King Jr. (Aml Ameen), on the other hand, can't stand up to Domingo at all, or even to Chris Rock's Roy Wilkins. I'm convinced that hiring Brits to play MLK is a continuing conspiracy to undermine his message. Somehow the FBI has taken control of the casting.

The Branford Marsalis jazz score in *Rustin* is as tasteful as expected, the film less so. Rustin yelling "Cheese spoils! You should've known better!" at the movie's moment of truth came out of nowhere, like one of those loud, low blats Lester Young used to drop into solos.

The Wonderful Story of Henry Sugar

Wes Anderson released five movies in 2023. Four of them are his Roald Dahl adaptations, shorts, the longest of which is *The Wonderful Story of Henry Sugar*, at thirty-nine minutes. The others—*Poison, The Swan*, and *The Rat Catcher*—run seventeen minutes each. His feature film, *Asteroid City*, is a fleet 105 minutes, with no waste. That's 195 minutes of cinema, about the same length as *Killers of the Flower Moon* or *Oppenheimer*.

Bifurcated between black-and-white and color sequences, *Asteroid City* has a lot in common with *Oppenheimer* and *Maestro*. Its plot is clear enough, though it seemed to confuse some people, who somehow also found it thin. The film in color is a 1950s teleplay, the writing and production of which we see in black-and-white. In the play, a group of scientific whiz kids and their parents have gathered for an astronomy convention in a tiny town in the Southwest that's located near a nuclear test site. The kids are to be presented by a government agency with achievement awards for their various inventions. During the ceremony, an alien visits to retrieve an asteroid that fell thousands of years ago. Meanwhile, two of the parents—one a famous movie actress (Scarlett Johansson), the other a roving photojournalist (Jason Schwartzman), both actors in the play—briefly fall in love before going their separate ways.

Because of the sets, which were built on location, the film has an abstract quality. It draws on a rich history of midcentury drama and science, moves swiftly, nothing lingered on, it isn't a biopic, and it makes no concessions to emotionality. In *Asteroid City* and these Dahl shorts, through elaborate but simple onscreen stagecraft, Anderson presents an ever-changing world of plastic beauty that he creates from the ground up. The screenplays are hyper-literate. In an unprecedented total avoidance of cheese in commercial narrative filmmaking, the act of writing and the writers doing it appear in these movies, but Anderson refrains from showing their writing on the screen in superimposition.

Just by being cinema Anderson's work now seems to some viewers avant-garde and difficult, yet also something obvious they can parody on social media—another sign of the regression of the movies into content. In *Asteroid City,* Rupert Friend has a minor role as a singing cowboy in the teleplay who's later revealed to be a British actor as, of course, is Friend. That's another unprecedented thing, to reveal the Brit under the cowboy. Friend narrates and stars in *The Swan* in full British mode, as an adult version of the boy in the story who is set upon by two unseen, gun-toting bullies, whom he also brings to life just through they way he delivers their dialogue. Friend's also in *The Rat Catcher* as an auto mechanic with a shop next to a newspaper office. There was something so marvelous in seeing this actor in four roles, each of which he nailed, in these excellent films that did not get the recognition they deserved.

Society of the Snow

J. A. Bayona's *Society of the Snow* is this year's *All Quiet on the Western Front,* a mishandled European remake of an American film based on a grueling historical event and a best-selling book. Bayona has become a worse director since he made *The Impossible* in 2012, also a disaster movie but much more cinematic and enjoyable in the way it seemed to punish a tourist family for going on vacation in Thailand right before a tsunami. As CGI has become dominant, Bayona's work has suffered along with the cinema in general. Because of that we have to suffer, too.

The one fact everyone knows about the *Alive* disaster is that the Uruguayan rugby players who were trapped in the snow in the Andes after their plane crashed had to resort to cannibalism to survive. Netflix is touting *Society of the Snow* as a "much-needed celebration of the human spirit" and downplaying the cannibalism, which is now known as "survival anthropophagy," which doesn't sound much nicer and is still the movie's selling point. It's inhuman to deny that. Bayona ends the movie imitating Terrence Malick, because the boys had a religious experience, which is what having very little to eat in freezing temperatures for seventy-two straight days will do to you.

I have known about the *Alive* disaster almost my whole life. One summer afternoon when I was about 7, on a rainy day when I had to stay in, I was sitting in the living room with my grandmother in Alton Bay, New Hampshire, watching an afternoon talk show on TV. The survivors of the crash were the guests. I had never heard of cannibalism. It was a completely new concept to me, and at first I couldn't understand what these young men meant as they were discussing their plight with the host. When I began to get what had happened, I was horrified. I couldn't believe it. These guys had eaten human flesh? I turned to my grandmother and quietly asked her, "Grammy, if we were in a plane crash together and I died, would you eat my skin?" She answered without taking her eyes off the TV screen. "Sometimes in very bad situations," she said, "we have to do things we wouldn't do under other circumstances," ending our conversation right there.

May December

Natalie Portman plays an actress in Todd Haynes's *May December*, an alarming film with a poisonous view of drama. An equally brilliant companion piece to Haynes's *Safe*, from 1995, which also starred Julianne Moore, *May December* identifies and measures the new surfaces of banality that have emerged in our lives in the intervening twenty-eight years.

Moore is Gracie, a suburban housewife in Georgia in her fifties. Twenty-three years previously she'd had an affair with a 13-year-old seventh grader, Joe (Charles Melton), got arrested for it, became a tabloid media sensation, gave birth to Joe's son in prison, then married him when she got out. The story is in some ways similar to Gus Van Sant's *To Die For,* which came out the same year as *Safe,* and which was rooted in the Pamela Smart case the way *May December* comes out of the Mary Kay Letourneau story.

The present in *May December* is a goody-goody era in which sex crime and psychological complication have been swept under the rug. Portman arrives in Gracie and Joe's life in the form of legitimate fame—she's the star of a hit network-TV series called *Norah's Ark* who will play Grace in an indie movie—but she's also a duplicitous force who will rob them of their story and plunder Gracie's odd persona (odder than in the Bergman film) along with her slight lisp. The best acted film of the year, it compares people to all sorts of animals, including snakes and coyotes as in *Killers of the Flower Moon,* settling on butterflies and golden retrievers. These are associated with Joe, a nice-guy father of three, now in his thirties but stunted and kept babyish by Gracie, who makes him the provider and caretaker of her frilly, conventional life.

In showing Portman's Elizabeth concentrating on "the work," Haynes slowly reveals her as a self-centered Hollywood monster starting to understand that she's in the presence of a bigger monster. The film associates Moore's Gracie with pineapple upside-down cakes the way *Poor Things* associated Emma Stone's Bella with Portuguese custard tarts—pastries of excess and derangement.

Perfect Days

In my late teens I was obsessed with Wim Wenders, and I was fortunate because I got to see almost all the features and shorts he made between 1968 and 1982 before I saw *Paris, Texas* and *Wings of Desire* and began to doubt him. There were a lot of Wenders film series and revivals going on then, it seemed like *The American Friend* was always playing somewhere, and for a brief time in the early 1980s, Wenders was revered by young cinephiles more than Godard. In retrospect it is easy to see why. A cinephile director himself, dedicated to Nicholas Ray, Wenders made films of ennui and longing set in desolate landscapes in Germany and America that showed us what we saw through the windshields of our cars. His movies went directly to the heart of the kind of men who are in them: romantic, post-punk loners who can't express their feelings verbally and like the Kinks.

Now Wenders has entered his late period, so *Perfect Days* is a simple version—an excessively simple version—of all that. Wenders in a sense has come home. Not to Berlin but to Tokyo, and that's important in this context. In an interview with Wenders that I read back in that day, in a monograph published by New York Zoetrope, he discusses his love of Ozu's films and the people in them. It has stuck with me all these years. "I don't like American families at all," Wenders told interviewer Jan Dawson. He continued:

> In American films, I mean. And in reality. These Japanese families are so strong to me, even though I have nothing to do with them: I have nothing to do with the way they eat, or with the way they sleep, or with the way they get drunk all the time. It has nothing to do with me; and I feel so close to them that, if I had to choose, I'd rather sleep on the floor, and sit my whole life on the floor, and get drunk every day, and live in an Ozu family, than pass a single day as the son of Henry Fonda.

By obliquely referring to Peter Fonda, Wenders is slagging *Easy Rider* and the New Hollywood generation who loved John Ford movies as much as he did, and offering a differentiator. He knows about something they don't, and he is willing to be abject about it. All this seemed odd coming from a man who often dressed like he was auditioning for the lynch mob in *Johnny Guitar*, and it confused me, though it got me to watch Ozu films. I owe Wenders that.

I have a feeling Wenders has not slept on the floor very much since that interview almost fifty years ago. I saw some photographs of Wenders from the *Perfect Days* shoot in which he is dressed in the same Tokyo Toilet cleaning uniform Hirayama (Kôji Yakusho) wears in the movie. He's still abjecting himself. Now he's made a movie about it.

The meek Hirayama lives in a tiny apartment, sleeps on the floor, and listens to classic-rock cassette tapes in his van, which is outfitted for toilet cleaning the way the van in *Kings of the Road* was outfitted for fixing 35mm movie projectors. If it is raining out, Hirayama listens to a song that mentions rain ("Hey where did we go, / Days when the rains came?"); if the sun is coming up, he listens to a sunrise song ("There is a house in New Orleans / They call it the Rising Sun"). This is too on-the-nose, but like I said, simple. Here Wenders gives us a kind of pleasant neorealism about a man who has withdrawn from life but who literally has his shit together. I thought the film was going somewhere deep into tragic territory, but no, it turns out the quiet Hirayama has a rich father. Hirayama lives the way he lives because he has rejected his family's values—he's proving he's not Henry Fonda's son. A rock song that's not in the movie explains it: He wants to live like common people.

Io Capitano

Refugees from Africa who brave the Mediterranean to get to Europe are not doing it for personal glory like Diana Nyad. Matteo Garrone's *Io Capitano,* however, suggests that in some cases they are. Seydou and Moussa (Seydou Starr and Moustapha Fall) are 16-year-old cousins in Dakar who spend their free time making up songs to perform for their neighborhood pals. Though they are fatherless and dominated by their mothers and sisters, their lives are full, with school and part-time jobs in construction. Still, they dream of going to Italy to be music stars. "White people will be asking you for autographs," Moussa tells Seydou.

As in Garrone's remarkable, incisive movie *Reality,* about a man desperate to get on an unscripted television show (*Grande Fratello*) in his home country, Seydou and Moussa have to learn the hard way. An electronics repairman in the market (Oumar Diaw) tells them Europe is cold and crime-ridden, filled with homeless people. "You think Europe is better than Africa?" he asks them. "What you see on TV is not real."

They leave anyway, crossing the Sahara to get to Tripoli and a boat to Naples. Right away they are plunged into a precarious, dangerous world of human trafficking, violent militias, starvation, torture, and slave labor. Their journey, presented by Garrone as mythic, lyrical, and terrifying, ends with Seydou forced by Libyan gangsters to pilot the boat across the sea. Responsible for the lives of the other refugees onboard, Seydou rises to the occasion, because when you're 16 you can do anything.

Paolo Carnera's virtuosic, unhackneyed cinematography is the costar here. *Io Capitano* is an exquisitely shot film, with the warm colors of Senegal competing against the shifting tones of the desert and the rust of the boat at sea. I'm not sure if this is the most accurate version of the situation it's presenting, but it has got to be the most beautiful.

The Zone of Interest

More a report on the human condition than on the banality of evil, Jonathan Glazer's film of Nazi life next door to Auschwitz is also a Christmas card from a family of blonds in matching sweaters telling you what they've been doing all year. Seen as an exploitation film by people who have never seen an exploitation film, *The Zone of Interest* presents a series of distanced, precise tableaux, with father (Christian Friedel) going over the architectural plans of a crematorium at home in his stocking feet while mother (Sandra Hüller) tries on a fur coat upstairs and finds a used lipstick in its pocket, or tests desserts with the household staff.

Do flowers scream? The offscreen space of sound in *The Zone of Interest* is paralleled to the scale of the invisibility of the death camp, which we never see but hear in the background as Hedwig (Hüller) prepares for a garden party or goes about other activities in her family's domestic life. Here is a single-income family with a father the head of production at the factory next door. The insistent, harrowing chill the film produces is not relieved by the fairy-tale scenes of a girl hiding food around the perimeter of the camp so that the condemned Jewish prisoners will have something to eat while they work themselves to death. Glazer shoots those scenes in some combination of camera negative and infrared photography. In one, we hear the tale of Hansel and Gretel read over the image, the part about the witch being stuffed into the oven.

The story turns into one we know. Daddy is promoted and the family will have to move out of their dream house, spoiling their happy life. This is the same plot as Vincente Minnelli's Judy Garland musical *Meet Me in St. Louis*, filmed in Hollywood and released in American theaters during the exact same time frame in which *The Zone of Interest* takes place—1943 and 1944. In Minnelli's film, which takes place in 1903 and 1904, the father (Leon Ames) announces that he's taking a job in New York City and the family will have to leave their idyllic life in St. Louis. Things work out and they don't have to, which is also where *The Zone of Interest* ends, before its shock cut to cleaning women wiping the glass displays in the present-day Auschwitz-Birkenau State Museum.

Realizing this film's inadvertent connection to a nostalgic MGM musical as I watched the *The Zone of Interest* placed it in new, even more dire perspective. Glazer's film is a punk provocation, like the Sex Pistols' song "Holidays in the Sun," with Johnny Rotten singing about "the new Belsen" and "a cheap holiday in other people's misery" as he anticipates World War III. If this film is a work of banality, banal compared to what?

THE BUSINESS OF NOSTALGIA

UNFROSTED AND CORPORATE BRANDING MOVIES

JERRY SEINFELD'S MOVIE *UNFROSTED*, WHICH THE COMEDY SUPERSTAR cowrote, directed, and stars in, is an unauthorized, fictionalized account of the creation in 1963 of Kellogg's Pop-Tarts, the breakfast product officially described as "toaster pastries." The film was produced by Netflix and debuted on the streaming platform last week to mixed reviews. A business satire, *Unfrosted* has a certain energy and attitude in common with the films Jerry Lewis made in the early 1960s, or the ones Frank Tashlin made in the late 1950s.

Seinfeld has cast himself in the kind of role Tony Randall played in *Will Success Spoil Rock Hunter?*, a harried junior executive at Kellogg's looking for the next big thing. In this case, the next big thing is a handheld fruit-filled slab that will come in pairs, wrapped in silver foil, and will "split the atom of breakfast"—a real game changer. These first Pop-Tarts, of course, were unfrosted. The title is one of the movie's many winks. We are expected to know that later in the toaster pastry game, after Pop-Tarts became a big success, Kellogg's introduced a frosted variety.

The America of *Unfrosted* exists adjacent to the early 1960s world of *Mad Men*, so Jon Hamm and John Slattery have a cameo together in *Unfrosted*, reprising their hardboiled roles from the TV series to pitch Kellogg's an inappropriately sexy ad campaign. The joke is that Pop-Tarts is aimed at kids, not cigarette smokers and scotch drinkers.

Seinfeld revives the Lewis-Tashlin style in a vacuum—he and his cinematographer, William Pope, who shot the *Matrix* movies, defrost it like a TV dinner. As with that kind of food substitute, the film has a certain contempt for its concept and isn't trying very hard. Most of the jokes are as flat as turkey slices and the whole thing presupposes how predictable it will be.

We are supposed to know the product being created is silly and sugary—bad for you, but in a benign way, just a fad. In 21st-century moviemaking, however, the depiction of product development and branding has moved on from this kind of zany, joke-a-second comedy to something more reverent and worshipful. It's a new kind of business nostalgia, alien to companies with cartoon animal mascots like Tony the Tiger.

Unfrosted comes after a cycle of movies suffused with a deep love of capitalism, ones that look to the business world as a source of near-religious inspiration and worldly success. *The Founder*, in 2016, with Michael Keaton as Ray Kroc franchising McDonald's fast-food restaurants, was the prototype for these. The current cycle, by my count, includes five films, all from 2023: Ben Affleck's *Air*, about Nike's creation of the Air Jordan sneaker; *BlackBerry*, a rueful look at Research in Motion's development of their eponymous proto-smartphone; *Tetris*, a comedy-thriller on video-game licensing set in the Soviet Union as it's collapsing; *The Beanie Bubble*, Kristin Gore's cringey assessment of Ty's line of collectible stuffed animals; and *Flamin' Hot*, Eva Longoria's story of how a janitor at a Fritos factory came up with the idea that PepsiCo should market snack chips to Latinos by coating them in tongue-burning red dust.

These movies are defined by how self-importantly they treat their subjects, and how they show the desperation of the characters developing their products. All anyone wants in any of these films is riches and success, and not just any kind of success. The goal is the mega-riches, hundreds of millions of dollars in passive income.

Unfrosted, on the other hand, treats all this as a joke, which is strange because it was not made in response to the other films but alongside them. The film is an uncomfortable outlier in its genre.

It's Seinfeld's status as a dilettante director—he's said he doesn't want to make another film—that allows his throwback movie to provide a kind of meta-commentary on the other ones in its genre. And what adds to that is how he has become a current cultural annoyance, a humble-bragger popping in on *Saturday Night Live*, an aging man who goes out of his way to insult college students while giving backhanded compliments to his film crew for working too hard when he is so wealthy he doesn't have to work at all.

Seinfeld has said he wanted to make his film the opposite of *Barbie*, the biggest authorized product movie ever made. So besides being a film about nothing, the same way *Seinfeld* was a sitcom about nothing, with "no hugging, no learning," what is *Unfrosted*?

It's a movie that perfunctorily and even brutally catalogues and dismisses everything that was supposed to be good and true in movies like *Air*. It does what none of those movies could do in this time of precarity and gig work: It identifies clichés, using them to mock and dismiss the idea that any of this is worth anyone's time, including watching this movie. Product creation and marketing in *Unfrosted* are just an elaborate ruse masking the real work being done, which is, as Seinfeld's executive character says to his colleague in R&D (played by Melissa McCarthy), "jamming goo into tubes," coming up with a name for it, shipping it and selling it.

In contrast, how could so many clichés be packed into such a small group of films in just one year, all of which say the opposite of *Unfrosted*? Made separately by different producers for different studios, *Air*, et al., each cover the same ground the same way. Whether they end in success or failure, whether they have a satirical element or are earnest and sincere, they are all "hugging and learning" movies instructing viewers about how to succeed in business while trying very hard indeed.

Each of the five films cycles through the same kind of 1980s montage featuring MTV and the "Big Brother" Apple commercial, Ronald Reagan and the fall of the Berlin Wall. Songs by the Violent Femmes crop up in more than one of them, amid generous helpings of other better-known pop hits. Houses must be mortgaged in these movies, presentations fumbled in order to better speak from the heart without notes. Janitor carts roll through all-night work sessions, phones get smashed in anger, and little children, the wisest of all, finally offer that eureka moment of profound insight that unlocks the whole damn thing. Stats about market share and licensing income appear on screen at the end, telling us how many hundreds of millions Michael Jordan makes every year from the use of his name and image or that the Fritos janitor is now the director of marketing, how BlackBerry and Beanie Babies once commanded enormous percentages of their markets but now have zero.

Tetris is the best example, presenting the licensing of a video game as a subject of world-historical significance. International forces in Japan, the Soviet Union, and the UK are aligned against Henk Rogers (Taron Egerton), who immediately sees Tetris's potential in America when he discovers the game in 1988 at a booth at an electronics convention in Las Vegas.

Rescuing its creator from Russia as the country collapses and freeing Tetris to be sold overseas becomes a metaphor for the cold war and American success. *Tetris* is a movie of Heroic Capitalism—as a Russian character says in it, "Have you ever tried to say no to an American? It's impossible." Once we hear that, we know the entire Soviet system is doomed. Similarly, in *Unfrosted*, the old milk-and-cereal regime and its frowsy uniformed cock-a-doodle-doo mascots have no chance in the face of Pop-Tarts' inexorable success.

When the cereal mascots go on strike and attack Kellogg's headquarters, Seinfeld plays it as a parody of the invasion of the Capitol on January 6, 2021. The difference is that *Tetris* is ideologically, emotionally, and financially invested in that idea of regime change. For Seinfeld, it's just a funny illustration of futility in the face of breakfast's progress. He positions the mascots as labor only to also say yeah, but labor in silly costumes.

In one film, the triumph of capitalism is depicted as grand and moving. In the other, it's barely worth bringing up. The bigger picture is that, like *Tetris, Unfrosted* is a movie about marketing a product that's addictive, especially to children, but that *Unfrosted* is very clear on that and these other films are not. In those, getting the kiddies hooked is subtext. Henk plays Tetris for five minutes, then sees falling blocks in his dreams. Right away, he just knows, the same way Ray Kroc just knew.

Similarly, Air Jordan sneakers and Beanie Babies, products aimed at youngsters, become obsessional objects consumers will buy in multiples, including consumers outside the original demographic. The BlackBerry becomes known as the CrackBerry, and Flamin' Hot Cheetos are initially marketed by the film's janitor protagonist the same way drug dealers sell their wares in his neighborhood.

Pop-Tarts, of course, were explicitly made to appeal to children who wanted sugar for breakfast in a form they'd love because it was even easier to eat than a bowl of cereal. The movie portrays its first consumers, a pair of grubby tykes, as garbage pail kids so addicted to "the goo" (Pop-Tarts' fruit filling) that they will dumpster-dive to get it. This kind of open admission is what sets *Unfrosted* apart from the other films here—Seinfeld is saying here in this dumpster you will find your hopes and ideals.

Open business-world cynicism of that variety points up a hidden aspect of the product movies. The films are sold as nostalgic, but is anyone actually nostalgic for any of these things, or for the shameful addictions they engendered? If you lost money investing in Beanie Babies, or if you were inordinately sad when the BlackBerry disappeared, these are probably not feelings you want to revisit. In this uniquely unbearable moment in pop culture, in which Hollywood doesn't know what stories to tell because everything has been degraded by an addiction to the exploitation of intellectual property, turning to the drama of product naming and sales success is comforting most of all to studio executives. *Oppenheimer*, it should be noted, was the story of a product launch, too. It showed a group of men taking a risk on the biggest bomb in history.

The nostalgia factor is an optical illusion. It's not atomic destruction we are nostalgic for, nor addicting children to face-smearing goo, finger-coating dust, or Game Boys. It is massive success through licensing and franchising we love and want in on. The bourgeois-to-billionaire class that Jerry Seinfeld is part of doesn't even go to movies anymore, as he pointed out. To understand why these movies are made we must study the executives who greenlit them, because public taste is no longer reflected in the mass production of culture at this level. How did we get the masses to eat Pop-Tarts? Now there's a story. And in the case of *Unfrosted*, one that is not lying about being futzed with, rewritten, fudged, and made up.

In his recent book *Foreverism*, University of Georgia nostalgia scholar Grafton Tanner writes that movie studios have a different view of the past. The real strategy there, Tanner theorizes, is "to keep the past present so we aren't nostalgic for it anymore." "Nostalgia," he writes, "is experienced when one fondly aches for the past. Foreverism, on the other hand, will implore you to revive the past and save it from ever dying again," in order to maintain the current system of production in a way that disallows actual longing for anything better.

This being America, product development and naming has also become a religion that keeps the system in place. In *BlackBerry* we are reminded that it was "the Jesus phone," as the cult-object iPhone was nicknamed, that killed the handheld digital email assistant with the fruit-filled name. In *Unfrosted*, Seinfeld's character makes fun of the Quaker Oats guy behind his back for being both CEO and mascot in his black priestly garb. "Mixing religion and cereal. Why?" Seinfeld asks. By the end of the film, when Pop-Tarts is a success, he has seen the light. "These things are the greatest two rectangles since the Ten Commandments!" he shouts.

In *The Founder*, McDonald's CEO Ray Kroc's mantra was "crosses, flags, arches; flags, crosses, arches." He understood the fast food giant's golden arches were a new kind of business monolith that could stand on equal ground next to Church and State. In a stellar coincidence that may just be a frugal licensing consideration, *Unfrosted* brings things full circle by ending with the same song *The Founder* did: one-hit wonder Norman Greenbaum's "Spirit in the Sky," from 1969, an evocation of sinlessness, eternal life, and friendship with Jesus. Unsurprisingly, the song has also been used in TV commercials for Nike and for Kellogg's itself. "Spirit in the Sky" is a source of irony in *The Founder.* Kroc has cheated his way to the top and ruined several lives along the way. In *Unfrosted,* it's just another obvious joke rolling off the production line.

A YOUNG, HONEST GUY LIKE HIMSELF

REAL LIFE

ALBERT BROOKS'S FIRST FEATURE FILM, THE SHARP SATIRE *REAL LIFE,* IS laser-focused on what at the time of its release, in the spring of 1979, must have seemed an unlikely target: *An American Family,* the PBS documentary series that had premiered six years earlier. Regarded by some as the first reality television show, the series follows an upper-middle-class family, the Louds of Santa Barbara, California, through twelve hour-long episodes that were shot over seven months.

An American Family garnered a great deal of attention, not so much for its form as for the revelations of dysfunction in this enviable family who had been singled out for documentary scrutiny on TV. During its run, Pat Loud announced to her husband, Bill, that she wanted a divorce. One of their sons, 20-year-old Lance, was openly gay, a first for television.

More than ten million people a week watched the series. Brooks, then a young comedian, was one of them, and an article in *TV Guide* about the show, written by anthropologist Margaret Mead, caught his eye. *An American Family,* Mead wrote, was "as new and significant as the invention of drama or the novel . . . a new way in which people can learn to look at life, by seeing the real life of others interpreted by the camera." Reading her pronouncement caused something to click. Brooks includes the quote onscreen in his movie's precredits opening, where he also promises that *Real Life* will be "the next step" in this evolutionary process, by documenting not only a real family but also the people who have come to film them.

This opening scroll then gives way to a town-hall meeting in Phoenix with an "expensive buffet—*two grand*!" Here, Brooks—who stars in the film as a self-regarding comedian and fledgling documentary filmmaker who just happens to be named Albert Brooks—further explains, through the medium of song, his high-minded intentions, as a roomful of participants in his dubious project eagerly applaud him.

THE BEST SATIRE TRANSCENDS its time, replacing what it mocked with its own version. That is exactly what *Real Life* does. Brooks's movie effaces its origins as a parody and stands on its own, clear in its intentions even to viewers who have never seen the PBS series. The film, with which Brooks effectively invented the mockumentary as we know it, survives—thrives—as a unique comedy masterstroke. *Real Life* does to its source what Brooks, as a version of himself in the film, does to his version of the Louds, something between a steamrolling and a dissection.

The comedian onscreen playing himself does the steamrolling; the Albert Brooks behind the camera performs the dissection. As the former tells us from the campus of the National Institute of Human Behavior—a wholly invented research lab he has enlisted to oversee the production—he, too, could have been "a scientist or a doctor of some kind" if he had "been graded more fairly" in school. Two psychologists, Dr. Ted Cleary (J. A. Preston) and Dr. Howard Hill (Matthew Tobin), will guide his experiment in filmed sociology as he embeds with veterinarian Warren Yeager (Charles Grodin); his wife, Jeanette (Frances Lee McCain); and their two children, tween Lisa (Lisa Urette) and Eric (Robert Stirrat), a grade-schooler.

On the first night with the Yeagers, we witness their dynamic, which is prickly and bored and uncomfortable with the presence of Brooks and his camera crew. The film, with its muted 1970s domestic American color palette, has a believably lived-in look that makes their unease all the more palpable. Brooks's satire combines forms of documentary filmmaking from the previous two decades that had by then migrated to public television: the Direct Cinema of Richard Leacock and D. A. Pennebaker and the self-reflexive ethnological research associated with Jean Rouch and Chris Marker in France.

In fact, Brooks presents one sequence in *Real Life* as "a chance to show the French what a montage was all about." He films the Yeagers happily romping through a department store (Goldwater's—this is Arizona) and a local zoo, where he encourages Eric to toss a rock at a turtle, and has Warren and Jeanette kiss at the dry cleaner. These contrived scenes of ordinary happiness come at a point in *Real Life* when the onscreen Brooks knows his film has gone awry. Jeanette has developed a crush on him, which he has deflected by noting his charisma is misleadingly skin-deep, and he has offended one of the psychologists, who is Black, by noting that his equally skin-deep understanding of the Black experience "shouldn't stand in the way of this film."

After that, we are witness to one of the most daringly unsettling scenes in 1970s cinema: Warren's botched operation on a horse. That would be a risky scene even in a noncomedy, delicate to make work in any context. Here, it illustrates a Frederick Wiseman–esque but utterly misguided commitment to vérité. It brings the film to an *uh-oh* level we could not have guessed it would reach.

"I WAS DATING LINDA RONSTADT" sounds more like a bit than reality, but Brooks's relationship with the singer is where the story of the making of *Real Life* begins. As he explains to his lifelong friend Rob Reiner in Reiner's 2023 documentary *Albert Brooks: Defending My Life,* he and Ronstadt had been together for a little while when "one of her managers" introduced him to a cousin who was a part owner of the Chicago Bulls.

Jonathan Kovler, an investor and liquor heir the same age as Brooks who later signed Michael Jordan to the Bulls, fronted the comedian $500,000 for *Real Life.* The deal came with the stipulation that Brooks sign a letter of credit and not go a penny over budget. Brooks joked about the arrangement on one of his *Tonight Show* appearances, swearing on Johnny Carson's desk that he would pay Kovler back. His ambition is reflected backward in the funhouse mirror of the film, where the other Albert Brooks begins with a grand plan to shoot the Yeagers for a full year before his producers realize that things are not working out the way he pitched them.

A totally independent production, *Real Life* took three years from writing to completion, including seven months of editing. Kovler and his associates got back their investment when Brooks sold the film to Paramount. Studio executives knew Brooks had made a splash on TV, that he was a hip commodity, and they saw something in *Real Life.* They just weren't sure what. Paramount's resulting theatrical rollout was lackluster and commercially underwhelming. Critics did see *Real Life,* though, finding it nervy and original. For some of them, that was not a good thing. In her positive review in the *New York Times,* Janet Maslin worried that *Real Life*'s "manner is . . . so sly that some viewers may not find it comic at all."

THE SON OF RADIO COMEDIAN Harry Einstein, who performed under the name Parkyakarkus, young Albert Einstein was referred to as one of the two funniest people in America by Carl Reiner on *The Tonight Show* in 1963, the other being Reiner's former comedy partner, Mel Brooks. Who is this funny Albert Einstein? Johnny Carson wanted to know. Reiner explained that he was a high-school kid, a friend of his son's.

Since having the same name as the Nobel-laureate physicist would not work for a comedian, Albert tellingly risked comparison to that other genius: When he went pro, he chose Brooks as his last name. If Brooks's career seemed fated, the pressure must have been enormous. His shtick can be read as pitting low self-esteem and an innate desire for love against an insistent demand for stardom. This comes to the fore in *Real Life,* in which Brooks presents show business at its most needy and off-putting.

Getting to that point was a process of accumulation that started with his absurd, go-for-broke television variety- and talk-show appearances in the late 1960s. It continued through his polished stand-up act and his conceptual comedy albums. One of those, *Comedy Minus One,* from 1973, prefigured his interest in the subject of the average man. It positioned Brooks as half of a comedy team with you-the-listener, and came with a follow-along script inside and a mirror on the back cover.

Brooks's lean, ludicrous short films for *Saturday Night Live* (and one for PBS), in which no moment was wasted (despite Lorne Michaels's objections that they ran long), trained him in a kind of documentary economy, and included tropes and gags he would return to in *Real Life:* doctors, veterinarians, scientific experts in human behavior, TV news, eggs (always eggs or the word *egg* in his films), and the presence of "Jack from Cincinnati," a fictional Brooks fan.

But it's not just because *Real Life* is so trenchantly funny that the film still works so beautifully. Nor is it that it's the first full-length cinematic product of a high-level comic mind, one with a unique, even startling sensibility. It's also because, in 1979, Brooks was telling us something about a world of dubious entertainment yet to come, the world of ethically compromised reality "docuseries" that we inhabit today, in which cheap entertainment and sociological experiment have become entwined with and choke each other.

More than a quarter century after *Real Life,* a new kind of fake reality began to take over the televisual pop-culture landscape. Series including *17 Kids and Counting* and *Jon & Kate Plus 8* mixed documentary and sitcom to exploit voyeuristic interest in the bizarre dynamics of suburban families with large, growing broods. Celebrities inserted themselves into the genre when *The Osbournes* and *Keeping Up with the Kardashians* made the claim that name recognition gave the families of semi-famous people as much documentary interest as the Louds in 1973, but with added entertainment value. *Real Life* predicted this burgeoning new cheesiness, placing it at a crossroads where the "average" family meets a showbiz gargoyle.

The film is also a kind of comedic manifesto that sets up Brooks's further work. Not for nothing does *Defending Your Life,* his 1991 romantic comedy about what happens when you die, present the sum total of life as a movie that will be reviewed and judged after death. Supposedly, an early version of the screenplay brought things full circle in his oeuvre, ending with Brooks's character reincarnated as a farm animal.

YEARS AGO, A FRIEND OF MINE was working on a Hollywood movie set on location in a house in New Hampshire. The owners of the house had a pet monkey. Everything in the house seemed tidy and spotless, brand-new. She asked the owners how they kept things so neat, adding that the monkey must make that harder. It turned out the house *was* in fact new. The year before, a plumber had been working under the kitchen sink and had set a lit blowtorch down on the floor. The monkey rushed in, grabbed the blowtorch, and started a fire, burning the whole place down. The lesson is: don't invite a showbiz monkey into your house.

Real Life's ending also happens to involve a house going up in flames, as the desperate Brooks puts on a clown suit and resorts to arson after riffling through his memory for famous movie endings. One of the films that comes up is *Star Wars*—"How did it end?" "They blew up a planet!"—and, as it happens, many of the initial reviews of *Real Life* mention George Lucas's blockbuster. The onscreen camera operators in Brooks's film—in their white, one-eyed helmets—reminded critics of Stormtroopers or R2-D2 as they recorded the action in the Yeagers' house. The critics were referring to the fictional Ettinauer 226XL camera rigs, which come from Holland and, presciently, use "no film . . . All picture and sound information is recorded digitally, on . . . integrated circuit chips, some no larger than a child's fingernail." Why Holland? Why a child's fingernail? Because it's funny, that's why.

A couple of the younger comics in Reiner's documentary mention that Brooks struck them as very punk when they first saw him. *Punk* is not a term I would usually associate with a man whose alter ego introduces himself to the people of Phoenix by parodying a jazz standard ("When an irresistible town such as you / Meets a young, honest guy like myself"). But there is something undeniably anarchic, destructive, and brazen about Brooks's work, especially in *Real Life.*

There's also something hardcore about it, an unyielding attitude toward the material that disallows compromise even when selling out is its subject. When Brooks is confronted on speakerphone by his producer—who tells him he's not making a real movie and accuses him of just doing TV news, something people already get for free—Brooks goes into an epic downward spiral that concludes with him yelling, "I can do fake!" He then imposes a Hollywood ending on his film, which in turn descends into a chaos too real for most comedies. It suggests that, in this life, things can only end in tragedy, and that the best we can hope for is homeowner's insurance and a good lawyer.

The year before *Real Life* came out, the English postpunk band Magazine released its debut album, also called *Real Life,* the title taken from the lyrics of the opening song, "Definitive Gaze": "So this is real life / You're telling me?" It's the same question Brooks asks. His brilliant movie shows what happens when you try to reconcile the competing demands involved in translating "reality" to the screen. As the Albert Brooks in *Real Life* struggles to please everybody, from his producer to the social scientists to the Yeagers, the only person he winds up making a fool of is himself. "I shouldn't be allowed to do this!" he is shouting by the end. "Why did I pick reality? I don't know anything about it!"

TIME TO FACE REALITY

UNSCRIPTED TELEVISION

EMILY NUSSBAUM, THE PULITZER-WINNING TELEVISION CRITIC AND *New Yorker* staff writer, ends her well-researched, somewhat grueling book on the history of reality television, *Cue the Sun!*, with a reminder that critics have historically dismissed reality TV as a fad. Yet reality TV has not gone away. It's more than just a fad, she writes, because "in the end, all our faces got stuck that way."

It's a strange phrase to insert out of nowhere. Parents say it when their kids make funny faces—*keep it up and your face will get stuck that way.* The idea here, I guess, is that we-the-audience, all of us, including those critics who dismissed it, wear the childish face of reality TV because we participate in it as a matter of course, whether we want to or not. Reality TV is the air we breathe as well as the face we make. We and television are mutually stuck with the same idiotic expression, reflections of each other, in a metaphorical mirror like Groucho and Harpo in *Duck Soup*, unsure of who's imitating who. Now we all stream old episodes of *Survivor* and make TikToks, trapped in a televisual loop of mutually assured self-regard.

But in non-notional reality, most people aren't like that at all. And reality shows, a product of the broadcast-TV era, don't even make the top ten in the weekly Nielsen ratings anymore.

Nussbaum begins and ends at this same point of confusion. Her book starts with a quote from the French philosopher of disaster Paul Virilio—"When you invent the ship you also invent the shipwreck"—but a few pages later she insults people who take seriously the ideas of the French media theorist Jean Baudrillard, and people who might use those ideas to analyze TV. If you're a highbrow poser of that sort, you "clutch your pearls," Nussbaum says, and "won't stop yammering"; you are unable to "see the fun" at work in the study of reality TV. Like the critics in the book's epilogue, the scolds in the introduction also get it wrong about this rancid genre that has given us countless hours of stupid garbage. Fun people don't make that mistake.

NUSSBAUM IS A CRITIC and so am I, and I am here to tell you that my face did not get stuck that way, though it had every opportunity to freeze into a permanent rictus. For eight years I worked as a cultural analyst in an "omnicultural branding and insights" consultancy where the clients were television networks. During that period I estimate that I watched multiple episodes of nearly four hundred different reality series. I lost count early on, somewhere between the debut of *Undercover Boss* and season three of *Bait Car.*

In addition to watching all those shows, I had to give PowerPoint presentations to network bigwigs, explaining which direction my company's research found reality to be headed—both the genre of reality and actual reality itself, such as it was in the Obama years. Things heated up for us after we realized that the 2010 finale of MTV's reality series *Jersey Shore* had received the same Nielsen rating as *Hope for Haiti Now,* the star-studded charity telethon that was broadcast on MTV the day after.

Nussbaum does not include *Jersey Shore* in her book, but at the time its success signaled an apotheosis in reality TV programming—true trash had reached a pinnacle and crossed over. A bunch of no-talent, spray-tanned mooks had equaled George Clooney, Wyclef Jean, and Anderson Cooper, the telethon's hosts. The MTV audience came away celebrating Snooki, Pauly D, and The Situation, and forgot about the earthquake in Haiti and its victims.

After that my colleagues and I visited almost every network that made reality TV. We knew we had seen the immediate future of the genre. A process called mimetic isomorphism dictates what happens in television. Success inevitably, and quickly, leads to imitation, in a cycle of diminishing returns television networks refused to acknowledge in their pre-streaming spiral down the drain. Soon there would be *Jersey Shore* knockoffs on other networks. The subcultural strip mining of America had begun.

In one of the odder moments of my life, I sat in the offices of Mark Burnett Productions, the company behind *Survivor* and *The Apprentice*, discussing the future of television while clutching one of Burnett's Emmys. I think he'd won nine by then. I gave PowerPoint presentations at industry conclaves, including the Promax Conference, an annual gathering of television marketing professionals, which in February changed its name to the Global Entertainment Marketing Academy of Arts & Sciences, which should give you some insight into what people in television think of themselves.

At events like that and at the annual television upfronts, I ran into the stars of reality TV, finding myself in an elevator with feisty Jill Zarin from the original cast of *The Real Housewives of New York City*, or in a lobby with the hirsute family from *Duck Dynasty*, millionaire Christian fundamentalist bird-call manufacturers. Real Housewives were everywhere back then. One year, during a conference in Los Angeles, my company threw a happy-hour party for our clients on the terrace at Lisa Vanderpump's restaurant SUR ("Sexy Unique Restaurant"), which my boss had booked for the occasion. For some reason Vanderpump icily refused to speak to us, glaring from the dining room while we had fun knocking back artisanal cocktails, unaware a new algorithm-based form of television was breathing down our necks.

I have a record of that evening, smartphone photos of two of my colleagues, young women flanked by alcohol-infused Martin Genis, who is seated between them. Genis is wearing gray distressed jeans, a dark blazer, and a white shirt with the top four buttons undone. Who is Martin Genis? True fans of *The Real Housewives of Beverly Hills*, the real Real Housewife heads, will remember him as a slicked-back salt-and-pepper-headed hanger-on from Britain, a luxury real estate agent of some sort, who Vanderpump had set up on a blind date with her fellow Housewife Kim Richards early in the show's run.

Genis was hangering-on that night at SUR, but I was working, and I approached none of this as a fan. Knowing who these people were was part of my job, and if all this is a self-own, so be it. My job was valuable to me not just because it paid my bills but because of what I learned from it as a critic. Seeing the sausage get made at the C-suite level of television production, and then analyzing the fandom of the sausage, made me realize that every negative thing ever written about TV was true, the concurrent rise of quality television notwithstanding. Newton Minow's "vast wasteland" speech, Jerry Mander's *Four Arguments for the Elimination of Television*, Harlan Ellison's *The Glass Teat*, Neil Postman's *Amusing Ourselves to Death*—they were 100 percent correct.

Cue the Sun! puts this in a new perspective. Despite Nussbaum's gleeful fascination with the genre, she also exhaustively exposes how reality TV made producers wealthy while they exploited their casts and the people who worked on their shows, non-union labor all. The company I worked for was run the same way. What reality TV did was inscribe this system into a particular form of television, combining the way its workers were exploited with the way its cast members were taken advantage of on camera and off, and then after the shows were over. Reality TV has always been more about *reunions* than unions.

Throughout the book, Nussbaum brings up the way people on these series got temporarily famous without making much money, and how it led to "trauma-bonding" between them the same way it did between the lower-level employees behind the scenes. In Nussbaum's account, working on and being on *The Bachelor* in particular seemed pretty close to date rape. As with the traumatized, the lives of the people who appear on these shows tend not to go well later.

The lower reaches of entertainment news are still filled every day with their early deaths and suicides, their jail sentences and broken marriages, and the failing businesses they start in order to capitalize on what they thought was fame. Two of the cast members of *Vanderpump Rules* have just opened a sandwich shop, which on the ladder of success is a few rungs down from a sexy unique restaurant.

Mark Burnett, of course, got bigger and bigger until, along with Jeff Zucker and NBCUniversal, he got Donald Trump elected president. *Cue the Sun!* leaves the impression that had *The Apprentice* not happened, Nussbaum would have a sunnier view of reality TV, no matter how ethically challenged and morally suspect the rest of it was.

Even in the case of Trump, she lets television off the hook. We all had a hand in Trump's election, she concludes. "Everyone ignored the danger Trump posed to the country, because he was too good for business," Nussbaum writes, conflating the TV industry with its viewers. She lets us know that Random House, the publisher of *Cue the Sun!*, her own book, publishes *The Art of the Deal*, Trump's business memoir. If she and Random House are not innocent, who is?

It's absurd to conclude that everybody is and isn't to blame when it's Nussbaum's assumed audience of media mavens who are at fault. Television and publishing were the only businesses Trump had been good for, prior to those he helped once he was elected president: multinational oil companies, for-profit prisons, overpaid CEOs who wanted tax breaks, and the royal family of Saudi Arabia, who could be a reality show themselves if they would just loosen up and let the cameras in.

Bravo's series *The Real Housewives of Dubai* is geographically close to the House of Saud. It has just returned to television for a second season. A disclaimer on each episode tells viewers that the opinions expressed in the series do not "represent those of Emirati society as a whole," presumably because the series shows how much freedom its rich women stars have compared to other women in the Arab world. What the disclaimer is acknowledging is that, for the purposes of entertainment, the show is not sufficiently punitive. In *Cue the Sun!*, on the other hand, Nussbaum insists that in America it's the other way around. In the US, reality TV represents all of us, and we know it and kind of love it. My advice if you read this book is don't let your own face get stuck that way.

THE ANTEDILUVIAN HISTORY of reality TV is found in 1940s radio, traced by Nussbaum to shows like *Queen for a Day* and Allen Funt's pre–*Candid Camera* experiments with pranking the public on *Candid Microphone*. Both shows needed only minor adjustments to make the leap to television.

Queen for a Day had a tragic, *Miss Lonelyhearts* quality. Nussbaum calls the program an inadvertent "exposé of poverty dripping with luxury ads." One contestant, "a plain-faced waitress" named Viva, had a salesman husband who was bad at sales. Viva had lost her waitress gig after twenty-five years because she needed time off for leg surgery. Her greatest goal in life was to somehow obtain a wheelchair and a modified bicycle for her son with cerebral palsy. She won that episode, receiving the queen's crown and the wheelchair and the bike, along with a suite of kitchen appliances, dinner at the Brown Derby restaurant in Hollywood, and tickets to the opening night of the movie *Spartacus*.

Funt, for his part, was that rare thing, an actual visionary in his medium. *Candid Camera* innovated in early television as much as the comedian Ernie Kovacs had, but to different comic ends. It's with Funt that a certain kind of mean "fun" comes into nascent reality TV. Funt was a misogynist and a bully, and the first to see how television could be used *against* the public. His pranks were designed for everyman appeal in a burgeoning age of behavioral science. They manipulated people into going along to get along, but were often designed to flatter male desire. An early prank, for instance, consisted of a fake office manager asking a real locksmith to chain a fake secretary to her desk.

Reality TV, despite the best efforts of RuPaul, Tim Gunn, and *Queer Eye for the Straight Guy*, has from the beginning maintained a strict binary, as *Queen for a Day* and *Candid Camera* demonstrated. There are shows designed for men (*Ice Road Truckers*) and shows made for women (*What Not to Wear*) and they are shown on networks coded male and female—History (formerly the History Channel) is for the men's men and TLC (formerly The Learning Channel) is for the ladies. Nussbaum does not point this out, and when she identifies Fox's *Cops* and MTV's *The Real World* as the two starting points of contemporary reality TV, she doesn't acknowledge them as the daddy and mommy of the whole genre in its new but abidingly sexist form.

From the beginning *Cops* and *The Real World* combined the documentary with the staged. They were implanted with ringers in their casts, the action on screen was manipulated for entertainment value, and each episode was edited for dramatic impact, cut into acts that fit between ad breaks, then scored with pop music—the insistent, ubiquitous "Bad Boys" by the reggae group Inner Circle on *Cops*, a mixtape's worth of '80s and '90s MTV hits on *The Real World*, including "Welcome to the Jungle," played when a white girl from the South took a faked taxi ride through Harlem.

The phoniness and manipulation seem obvious now. At the time the differences between the real and the fake were not as apparent, though they were subjects of controversy, especially in their more racist forms. Today it is almost gauche to point out that things were not as real as they were meant to be seen. The fakeness of reality TV is a truism that supposedly only bothers the unsophisticated. Nussbaum's book works hard to make distinctions between the naive viewers of yore and the wised-up reality TV gluttons of today, enlightened superfans who know what's what and revel in artifice.

Cops has a bizarre history that combines the brutal policing of people of color with surveillance technology, embedding camera crews for ride-alongs in tours of poor neighborhoods as police officers/cast members make arrests. Unlike *The Real World*, which aired from 1992 to 2017 before MTV sold it to Facebook Watch, where it disappeared into the metaverse, probably with a "puff of smoke" sound effect, *Cops* is still on. It has moved from network to network for thirty-five years across close to 1,200 episodes, and is now back on Fox after a brief hiatus prompted by the murder of George Floyd and the ACAB defund-the-police period that looks like a blip on the screen as far as television is concerned. High-grade copaganda in its purest form, *Cops* has proved addicting to its public, its effects long-lasting in a society on the verge of re-electing a convicted felon. Note that there has never been a reality TV show called *Cops Gone Wild.*

John Langley, *Cops*'s creator, considered himself countercultural and his show a comedy. He was crazy about avant-garde filmmaking and drugs. An early version of *Cops, American Vice: The Doping of a Nation*, which Langley made in 1986 with Geraldo Rivera, existed to broadcast live drug busts as police raided homes. When Langley shot it, however, he was not yet in control of the meta elements of surveillance television. During one of the first live drug busts on *American Vice*, the Fort Lauderdale police found that their suspect, a corrupt, drug-dealing Bahamian former cop, was watching the show as they burst in to arrest him. Langley learned that a non-live version, sans Rivera, would work better because it would give him more control in making things look out of control.

Langley, like so many of the ex-hippie producers of the original wave of reality TV, came to question his achievement, ultimately deciding the problem with the series was that it was just too entertaining. By the time he told Nussbaum that in 2021, he was a very rich cigar aficionado, the owner of a vineyard in Argentina and several restaurants. He died soon after they spoke, suffering a heart attack at age 78 during an off-road race in Mexico. It seems fitting that he died recklessly doing something he hadn't thought through, though of course the boomer spin on it would be that he died doing something he loved, and what a way to go.

ONE OF THE ORIGINAL PRODUCERS of *The Real World*, Mary-Ellis Bunim, died of cancer in 2004. Her producing partner, Jonathan Murray, is, according to Nussbaum, proud of their legacy, has few regrets, and makes no apologies for his work, though he understands that "some people" will always see reality TV as "a dirty thing." Nussbaum introduces Bunim and Murray, famous names in the genre, in their small office in 1987, where "they worked together like Dorothy Parker and Robert Benchley, on either side of a shared table"—a curious comparison since neither of them were writers, and neither says, does, or creates anything witty or sophisticated in the *Real World* chapter of *Cue the Sun!* or, as far as I can tell, at any time in their subsequent careers.

In fact, they seem to have taken the concept for *The Real World* from a younger MTV producer named Lauren Corrao, a Brown semiotics major like several other reality TV producers in the 1990s and 2000s. (I was asked almost daily in my former career if I had been a Brown semiotics major—the answer is no.) After Corrao's nudge, Bunim and Murray refined her idea with one of their production coordinators, Danielle Faraldo, who'd been hired by Corrao at $300 a week. It was Faraldo, twenty-six at the time, who suggested that Bunim and Murray "put a few young artists together in a loft, then film them." She also came up with the title.

Faraldo is an interesting case study. Nussbaum tells us Faraldo was "a Gen X idealist who was deeply interested in the show's success" and that the show was intended to be "cinema verité for Gen X." But we have already learned by that point in the book that there is nothing Nussbaum has more disdain for than a Gen X idealist.

Her *Real World* chapter begins with a diss. "The heated battle over authenticity" was a "Gen X obsession, as obsolete as the Shakers." "The Gen X fetish for authenticity," we learn, "was long gone" by reality TV's 21st-century heyday, "as defunct as the desire for Zima," as if anyone had ever had a desire for Zima. The clear, proto–White Claw malt beverage, introduced by Coors in 1993, was universally reviled and mocked. Like reality TV, its exact legacy is how much it sucked.

Without ever copping to being a member of Gen X herself, just like she never admits to being a critic, Nussbaum takes every opportunity to bash her generational cohort. She's especially hard on Helen Childress, the screenwriter of the 1994 movie *Reality Bites*, whom she portrays as looking back with naive chagrin on the unfortunate way her anti-MTV screenplay was watered down, an attitude now rendered trivial by the realpolitik of the Bunims and Murrays of this world, the real one we all acknowledge. "It's almost endearing to think of what we were worried about," says Childress in a footnote, that "almost" a sub-note of minor tragedy Nussbaum doesn't seem to find particularly endearing at all.

I was reading *Cue the Sun!* the week Steve Albini died, so these digs of Nussbaum's at our shared generation stood out in high relief. Though he was exactly the type of purist who annoys Nussbaum the most, I suspect almost anyone would get more joy from the music he produced than from watching old episodes of *Survivor*, that activity Nussbaum believes so many people are engaged in. Or from anything Bunim and Murray produced. It's as clear as Zima who left the more lasting legacy, so I guess the question remains: What kind of people does Nussbaum mean? The finale of season forty-six of *Survivor* aired while I was writing this. Does anyone care who won it? Are all forty-six *Survivor* seasons worth one *Pod*, *In Utero*, *Surfer Rosa*, or *Rid of Me*? In the annals of culture, I think those are secure, while every episode of *Survivor* could be wiped by CBS tomorrow and probably not even Jeff Probst would care. He's made his money. His legacy is not what you would call artistic. Reality TV is by nature ephemeral; in that light, celebrating it is futile.

To do so, Nussbaum has to put down people with higher ambitions, and to ignore the way reality TV started as an experiment in exploiting Gen X in a war of all against all. That's what *The Real World* was, despite the warm fuzzies Nussbaum recalls around the death from AIDS of Pedro Zamora, the show's second gay cast member. It set the template for all the competition reality shows to come, even though it wasn't a competition show itself. The cast members, from their various backgrounds, were picked for prime conflict. It reminds me of a show I wanted to do called *Vegans in Wichita*, in which a group of diverse young people would have lived together in a house in the meat-eating-est city in the US, struggling to get enough protein while they pursued their dreams. Time and time again it is people's dreams that are quashed in *Cue the Sun!*'s stories. Practically everyone who worked on a reality show, we learn, started out admiring documentarians like Frederick Wiseman, hoping to get a toehold in the industry.

This relates to another proclivity of Nussbaum's. Every time the process of editing a reality TV show comes up, she reminds us how hard, how difficult and time-consuming, it was to edit any kind of documentary before Avid Technology developed nonlinear editing software in the 1990s. Truth be told, it wasn't that hard. Documentaries were shot, film editors cut them, they came out, and the best ones are still valued, watched, and studied. What Avid did do was make *this* crap simpler for underpaid video editors to cut on short schedules, which made it sloppier and more disposable. Nussbaum is sensitive to how everyone has been exploited by reality TV producers, except in this one area.

By contemporary editing standards, it was harder to make *An American Family* for PBS in 1972. Since Nussbaum presents that series as a voyeuristic nightmare experience for everyone involved, it's unclear why making things easier is an example of progress. The system of making reality TV reflected its content in that regard. Making a show became a beat-the-clock endeavor in which there wasn't enough time or money to get things right. Instead, suffering and tension were added to what should have been mundane work duties, the same way those elements were added into dating or cooking shows to ratchet up the conflict in areas that are supposed to be pleasurable, loving, or fun, not terrifying, hurtful, and vindictive.

To me, this in some indirect way relates to the title of Nussbaum's book, because it has to do with the difference between television and film, which is harder to make but survives longer. *Cue the Sun!* is not a phrase from reality TV. It's from the 1998 movie *The Truman Show*, a film about surveillance and how it stunts one man's life when the true nature of reality is hidden from him. The true nature of reality, of course, is that he is on a reality TV show and he is the only one who doesn't know it. In an essay on Albert Brooks's 1991 movie *Defending Your Life*, the film director Ari Aster brings up Brooks's 1979 movie *Real Life*, an early, prescient satire of reality TV, and praises Brooks for predicting what an "ethical hell-swamp" it would become. *The Truman Show* was about that, too, not about inventing anything but about how malign the whole set-up was.

I learned the hard way by watching so much reality TV that it was foolish to expect anything more from it. It was toxic, a Superfund site of collapsed morality. To slightly misread Nietzsche on the subject, "Hope in reality is the worst of all evils because it prolongs the torments of man." It was by quitting my job that I ended that particular torment. My hope that it would lead to a better life was one of those cruel optimisms you read about, and it mirrors the regret that almost every person Nussbaum spoke with feels about their time working in reality TV. If people hated working on it so much, what was it worth? Only Mark Burnett's and Jonathan Murray's accountants can tell us. Langley's and Bunim's are off the job.

I'm running out of space and I haven't even gotten to Andy Cohen, Bravo's oleaginous enabler of humanity's worst impulses and character defects, an employee of NBCUniversal, like Donald Trump used to be. Oh well, there's only room for so many visionaries in one piece. Instead, let's look at the fans. Reality TV is a curious genre because it has wrenched the willing suspension of disbelief into new forms. In order to enjoy it, you also have to pretend to enjoy it, and you have to celebrate your enjoyment, which may or may not be real, just as you have to acknowledge that what you're watching ("watch what happens live") isn't quite real.

At the same time—here comes the tricky part—you have to give yourself over to its unreality, which you then accept as another form of reality that is not dissimilar from what the producers wanted you to believe in the first place. I call this the double twist, in which self-awareness is enough of a pardon for wasting time and bad taste.

In the double twist, liking something you know is bad becomes smart if you think you know how it works. Here, the dated concept of the guilty pleasure is obviated by performative stanning, and we see once again how fandom pretends to elide all the market research, focus grouping, and brand analysis that goes into telling the superfans how smart they are for liking the latest iteration of whatever it is they already liked.

I've always believed that the antidote to this poptimistic self-delusion can be found in the worst gunk of reality TV itself. It's buried in the mud that I put my hands into every day for years in my old job. You will find it in the series not covered in *Cue the Sun!,* the ones too outré for a book like this—in *Hoarders,* for instance, and *Intervention,* in *The Swan, Naked and Afraid, Here Comes Honey Boo Boo, Teen Mom, Abby & Brittany, Storage Wars, Pawn Stars, Dog the Bounty Hunter,* in those shows with the Gosselins and the Duggars and their dozens and dozens of children, in *My 600-lb Life* and in *I Want to Work for Diddy.*

There's a reason Nussbaum ignores those series. They are the shows that make you turn your head away, that create the impression that you shouldn't be seeing them and they shouldn't be on TV. They are the shows in which people are literally soiling themselves and, by extension, the viewer. The better-known shows, the ones that make the covers of *People* and *Us,* might look different, but only because the networks that air them throw a few more dollars their way to make them shiny. Their slightly higher production values make them acceptable to decent human society, unlike the other ones, which make their appeal to the indecent. In the end, the glossier ones are not different than *Hoarders.* They are equally crass; both are about accumulation and sickness and how to flaunt them. It is in the lowest common denominator that we find the question Nussbaum's book doesn't answer: Would we be better off if *The Bachelor,* or *Cops,* or *The Apprentice* had never been made? The answer is yes.

VACUUM STUDIES

Deadpool & Wolverine

The summer's movie headlines were dominated by the box office success of *Deadpool & Wolverine*, with the Penske-owned trade magazines proclaiming that the superhero team-up had broken twenty-two distinct and individual records. That was a funny number to wave around, similar to inane superlatives like "biggest R-rated Tuesday ever at the domestic box office" and "second-highest opening weekend of all time for a third installment."

Along with the trades, semi-pro fanboy websites with aggressive names like Bam Smack Pow trumpeted how *Deadpool & Wolverine* "had done the unthinkable, managing to outperform none other than the face of the MCU franchise himself Iron Man. Yes, that's right; the 2024 movie has now out-grossed *Iron Man 3* at the box office, sailing past its impressive numbers," as if anyone knew *Iron Man 3*'s exact tally, or even remembered anything that happened in that movie from 2013.

Because *Deadpool & Wolverine* is a meta-lesson in industrial practices and their history, Deadpool (Ryan Reynolds) must get viewers up to speed right off: "Welcome to the MCU. You're joining at a bit of a low point." The actor then performs an expensive magic trick: With no gain in quality, he revitalizes the Marvel Cinematic Universe by treating Wolverine (Hugh Jackman) like an aging power hitter brought in late-season to get the franchise into the Series, justifying the stats that become the whole point.

The film also invents another sporty concept, the "anchor being." The notion there is that a piece of intellectual property (Wolverine, for instance) is essential to the survival of some random timeline in the Marvel multiverse. Already understood as characters who can't be killed because they have special regenerative powers, they have now been inducted into the multiverse, allowing them to be doubled, then tripled, quadrupled.

Wolverine's tiredness in the film makes sense in this repetitive regime of endlessness and its accompanying exhaustion of ideas. The lesson of the film is that things are not going to get better, only continue on. Reynolds/Deadpool jokes that the film is guaranteed to be such a success that Jackman will have to come back to play Wolverine again and again, doing it until he's 90. He doesn't joke about how eventually Jackman will just be replaced with some digital post-life version of himself, billed as Hugh Jackman in his complete absence.

Deadpool & Wolverine, by acknowledging this new low point, admits that as superhero movies decline, they should be seen as high-budget TV specials with lots of celebrity guest stars. Here, Jennifer Garner, Wesley Snipes, Channing Tatum, and Chris Evans ham it up like they're on an all-star roast of Kevin Feige. At last, the obvious burnout of this strategy has been exposed, flaunted by a zany, abusive jester-mascot-host. Now the MCU's core audience can enjoy it again, out in the open, with a sigh of relief.

The film is a business manual for boys, illustrated with cartoon violence. It teaches them how to crush the competition and then spit in its face. "Dishonoring memory" is an important part of that, so past Marvel failures are included in the fun. Instructions include how to be sarcastic in a job interview. As the human resources director Happy Hogan, Jon Favreau, once an important Marvel filmmaker, is now merely a functionary standing in the way of Deadpool's will to power.

The job interview scene exists at the intersection of the film's two levels of adolescent satire. The second belittles the fans themselves, who are portrayed as idiotic, tractable pornhounds jerking off to CGI violence. ("Get your special sock out, nerds. It's gonna get good!") The violence is scored to the left-behind pop music of their childhoods, which they are now self-aware enough to enjoy for its corny or melodramatic qualities. NSYNC, Madonna, Fergie, and Avril Lavigne are enlisted to deliver pleasure as items of ironic kitsch sentimentality, dated entertainment, the way the droog Alex performed "Singin' in the Rain" in *A Clockwork Orange*, minus any of Kubrick's analysis.

In this homosocial milieu, like in a prison, the biggest fears are rape and dying alone. Family has to be mentioned, but also kidded as ad hoc, a bunch of weirdos, not the mom and dad who are out of the picture now that we have our driver's license. The only real nuclear family here is Reynolds's own. He and his wife, cookie-cutter North Americans, are depicted in the media as the Tsar and Tsarina of 2024's new crap AI Hollywood, with Blake Lively represented in this movie by her voice and a big blonde ponytail stuck on the head of someone else's body. Their children are here, too, in superfluous cameos as tot Deadpools.

While Reynolds and Jackman are the Bob Hope and Bing Crosby of this particular *Road* movie, ribbing Marvel and Disney the way Hope and Crosby used to make fun of Paramount in the 1940s, their destination is not some exotic locale of colonial expansion, but a place called "the Void," an imaginary desert where old IP goes to die. The Void is a holding pen, a zone where the audience is mocked for having had even the slightest interest in second-rate, go-nowhere IP like the surplus superhero Gambit (Tatum). Reynolds and company flourish at the expense of the dummies they ridicule. A joke in the film sums it up. Told he has shit himself while unconscious, Deadpool offers a correction: "I wasn't unconscious."

Twisters

Right away, Lee Isaac Chung's *Twisters* won me over with a twist I did not expect: it killed off almost its entire cast of young STEM jerks in the first big scene. I'm so sick of these chipper teams of Spielbergian science kids in everything. Read a real book for a change. "Five years later," they've been replaced by an alternative group of gnarly storm-chasing tornado wranglers—older STEM kids in disguise, but a slight improvement.

The film borrows heavily from the classic *Only Angels Have Wings* playbook, in which an experience-hardened daredevil (Glen Powell/Cary Grant) tutors a skittish female newcomer (Daisy Edgar-Jones/Jean Arthur) in the ways of danger and adventure (filming tornadoes in Oklahoma/delivering airmail in the Andes). Powell as Hawksian man works fine, but Edgar-Jones, a Brit playing a New Yorkified Southerner who sounds like Anne Hathaway, never quite rises to the challenge of having a personality.

The book somebody read here is *How to Blow Up a Pipeline*, by which I mean they saw Daniel Goldhaber's 2022 movie of it, which also features Sasha Lane in the cast, in the exact same role as one of the rebel wranglers. A pipeline and a refinery do get blown up in *Twisters*, but these storm chasers have substituted politics for meteorology, ironic since the real Weathermen were bomb-making radicals.

The wranglers here are trying to stop things from blowing up, and they sell T-shirts for charity like good philanthropist-capitalists. Their project is really just making a belated sequel more rad by blowing out the back wall of the movie theater, in a re-creation of a photo that went viral in 2021, the one a US Marine took of the interior of a Kentucky movie theater after a tornado hit, with the screen gone and the post-storm wreckage visible where the movie should be.

Just add someone yelling "This theater wasn't built to withstand what's coming!" and you've got a movie—and a prophetic cry about the cinema, which wasn't built to withstand the AI demolition now slicing through it. The use of diaper gel to stop tornadoes is like a joke out of *Deadpool*, but in the end the view of climate change here is real, because one aspect of it is certain: at the end of the world, wranglers with video cameras will be there, wranglin' (trying to upload video to YouTube without a signal).

The Linguini Incident

In *Twisters*, Maura Tierney plays Edgar-Jones's mother, a plainspoken Oklahoma woman who can't quite bring herself to say *climate change* but who knows things are getting worse. Thirty-three years ago, dressed in a silver lamé New Wave outfit, Tierney had a small part as a waitress at a restaurant named Dali in a forgotten movie called *The Linguini Incident*. The film's cowriter and director, Richard Shepard, who went on to direct other features, documentaries, and episodes of *Girls*, restored the film last year, as best he could. This summer it played in very select theaters.

The Linguini Incident is something of an East Coast version of another 1991 movie, Steve Martin's *L.A. Story*, similarly a romp on the cusp of a disappearing zeitgeist, a last expression of the previous decade just after it ended.

Rosanna Arquette stars as Lucy, Dali waitress and fledgling escape artist on the downtown performance scene, frequently tied up and wriggling to free herself; David Bowie plays Monte, Dali bartender and gambler on the run; and Eszter Balint is Vivian, Lucy's best friend, a designer of fetishy women's lingerie. The duo who own Dali are a pair of sub-Wildean wits in colorful suits played by André Gregory and Buck Henry, encouraged by Shepard to deliver lines like this week's guest stars on *Mr. Belvedere*. Their obnoxiousness makes them easier to take as marks when Monte involves Lucy and Vivian in a scheme to rob the restaurant on a night when it's at its busiest.

Arquette in *Desperately Seeking Susan* (1985) and Balint in *Stranger Than Paradise* (1984) were defining women of the cinematic New York 1980s, one starry-eyed, goofy, and yearning, the other deadpan and blasé. In casting them alongside Bowie, Shepard had the makings of a classic, but he didn't know it. This could have been the *Design for Living* (1933) of its day, a hipster screwball comedy about three thieves in love.

Instead, it's more like an enjoyable second-tier pre-Code Hollywood programmer, although one filmed in color by Robert Yeoman, who went on to shoot Wes Anderson's movies. Arquette, Bowie, and Balint hang out and walk around downtown, go to restaurants and bars, travel by half-broken bicycle, live in a crummy apartments. A Busby Berkeley feeling takes over near the end, in the water tank straitjacket escape routine that Lucy is fooled into performing despite her inability to extricate herself when bound.

Bowie, with his two differently colored eyes, was never quite a leading man. As a movie star he was always a character actor (a "Cracked Actor"). Trying to be semi-normal, a basic dashing cad, he becomes a touch bland and Ronald Colman-ish. A missed opportunity, the film did have a happy ending offscreen. The model Iman has a bit in *The Linguini Incident* as a guest at Dali. That's where Bowie met her. The rest is history, but not quite film history.

Close Your Eyes

Víctor Erice's fourth and probably last feature film begins as a film-within-a-film, one with the same basic set-up of *The Big Sleep* or *Mr. Arkadin*: An older man summons a younger private detective and gives him a mission to dig into his past. The scene refers explicitly to another film of that era, *The Shanghai Gesture*, but the gesture isn't complete. That's because *Close Your Eyes*, though clearly a late work and a cinema valedictory, never rises to the level of the classic. It comes across as work done in frustration, not recollected in tranquility.

There is something choked off and inaccessible about *Close Your Eyes*. It holds back even as it perseverates about its one situation: Years ago a famous actor (José Coronado) abandoned the film-within-a-film in the middle of shooting, and ever since then, the film's director (Manolo Solo) has been living with the ruins of his abandoned movie and his aborted career, searching for his lead actor, who has disappeared.

The film never hums or vibrates. The best scenes are the ones set at the director's beach shack, with the multigenerational residents of his threatened seaside community sitting around a table, drinking after dinner, and singing "My Rifle, My Pony, and Me" from Hawks's *Rio Bravo*, a gesture toward a lost world that for the time being they still inhabit. Too much of the rest of the film is old men whining about cinema's decline. Although I feel this sense of loss as acutely as anyone, I'm tired of this attitude in the older generation. Just go to the movies.

La Chimera

It's not like good movies are not being made and not playing in theaters. It's that men like the ones in Erice's film refuse to acknowledge they exist. Alice Rohrwacher's *La Chimera*, for instance, a film that's pretty casual about its brilliance and originality, also presents a lost soul. Josh O'Connor's Arthur, just out of prison and sick with a cough, returns to a small town in Italy. He's a disgraced British archaeologist with a sixth sense for buried antiquities, which he'd been incarcerated for looting. Young and handsome in a dirty linen suit, he is also reeling from the disappearance of his girlfriend, Beniamina (Yile Vianello), whom he sees in his dreams, pulling on the end of the film's literalized fil rouge.

All the vibrations absent from *Close Your Eyes* travel on this thread in Rohrwacher's movie, humming past gorgeous, decaying buildings in the Etrurian countryside. If there is one director who doesn't flinch before admonishments against so-called poverty porn, it's Alice Rohrwacher. She has a totally new way of filming, encompassing cities and nature, and she is especially good with wind on bodies of water at night. The way she tells a story is elliptical, satisfying, and makes the viewer feel in on things. Her characters never seem acted, no matter how weird or flamboyant. We want to know who these tombaroli are, how they exist.

O'Connor and the film are as fragile as the paintings on the tomb walls that fade the minute they are exposed to new air (as in Fellini's *Roma*). The revelation by flashlight, then candlelight, of a statue in shadow is the film's emotional peak. The statue—a young goddess holding a fish, with a panther at her feet, unseen for millennia—replaces the missing Beniamina of Arthur's dreams and is immediately beheaded so it can be removed from its tomb and sold on the black market, buried for transport in a crate of cheap toy soccer balls the colors of the Italian flag.

Substitutes for Beniamina proliferate and taunt Arthur. "Finally you can see my face," says Spartaco (Alba Rohrwacher), a glamorous art auctioneer heretofore only known to Arthur and his fellow thieves as a male voice. The headless body of "The Sibyl of Etruria" (as the statue is christened) is projected on Spartaco's dress as she explains to her wealthy audience that this ancient prophetess can be "the goddess of anyone." She can be "any one of us" because "she hasn't a face," not knowing Arthur has the Sibyl's marble head in a bag, that he and the other scroungy tomb raiders plan to extort her with it.

Arthur's tragedy is that this head, this face, will become as lost and buried as the missing Beniamina. In *Close Your Eyes*, a statue of the twin-faced Roman god Janus sits locked in a garden, and Erice cuts back to it several times to make a point about his lost actor. Rohrwacher brings her statue out into the open, into the light of day. She turns it into a better metaphor: the search for a close-up. *La Chimera* is the simpler, wiser, and newer film, with a more intimate connection to a larger, deeper past.

Do Not Expect Too Much from the End of the World

One day in the life of a production assistant in the Romanian film biz, shot in black and white, it starts at 5:50 AM when "Angela Răducanu from Forbidden Planet" (Ilinca Manolache)—blonde, thirties, not making it, working herself to death twenty hours a day—gets up so she can drive a Fiat Doblò van to the homes of injured workers, auditioning them for a part in a PSA in which they will have to tell lies for the company that maimed them. Angela wears the same sparkly 1990s-style club dress throughout the movie, not changing it after it's stained during a tryst with her boyfriend in the van. *Do Not Expect Too Much from the End of the World* is the anti-*Frances Ha*, a vulgar blast of contemporary political outrage and anger shot into the miasma of contemporary image production.

Angela's only breaks come when she adopts the persona of a sleaze named Bobiță, her TikTok alter ego, seen in color, a bald, perverted dirtbag with a dark brown beard and mustache. An avowed Andrew Tate worshipper, Bobiță broadcasts misogynist jokes during Angela's brief bursts of free time, spewing obscenities as a maker of short-form content for post-communist Romanian domestic consumption. Radu Jude, the film's director, contrasts her day with scenes from a 1982 Romanian movie about a woman cabbie, a communist film produced before the Ceaușescu Palace was built, a surviving document of better labor practices in a demolished neighborhood.

There is so much in this film, which is open to anything. In its 163 minutes, *Do Not Expect Too Much from the End of the World* encompasses both a silent color sequence comprised of 115 shots of roadside crosses and an unbroken, thirty-five-minute take, from a fixed camera position, of the workplace safety video being filmed (also in color). A fearless, intelligent, and generous filmmaker, Jude stops the film at its exact midpoint so Angela can interview the German filmmaker Uwe Boll—notorious director of the world's most interesting terrible movies—and make a Bobiță clip with him. I'd rather see ten movies by Uwe Boll telling everybody to fuck off than even one film by Edward Berger.

Angela and Boll briefly discuss face changes in the work of Robert Louis Stevenson, and later a producer, debasing the words of Samuel Fuller in *Pierrot le fou*, tells the PSA crew that there's only one word for what he wants in his corrupt production: *emotion*. A woman from the marketing department with the Godardian name Doris Goethe (Nina Hoss) explains that all he really means is he wants a close-up. It reminds me of something the film scholar Tag Gallagher once said. There is no such thing as a generic close-up—there are only close-ups made by individual filmmakers, and they mean entirely different things depending on who makes them.

Janet Planet

There are kits you can buy to add faces to your trees, and in playwright Annie Baker's first film, *Janet Planet*, we see a tree that's been faced. I think it's the first time I've ever seen one in a movie, though my neighbor down the road has one on a tree in his yard that I walk by all the time. Baker is supremely attentive to details like that, and in this film she and her cinematographer, Maria von Hausswolff, have captured the faded greenness of long-ago summers with a rare, delicate precision.

Janet Planet is also a movie for people who aren't crazy about summer, and it gets at the sometimes annoying quality New Englanders have of trying to figure everything out. The prime annoyance here is 11-year-old Lacy (Zoe Ziegler) a strange, matter-of-fact, friendless girl who says things to her mother, Janet (Julianne Nicholson), like "You know what's funny? Every moment of my life is hell." Janet ("I'm pretty unhappy too") seems tired of her daughter, but she's kind because she's distracted by her own life.

Lacy is a Baker stand-in, I have to assume, organizing the world by arranging her salt-and-pepper shaker collection in her dollhouse, moving through a summer of Bread-and-Puppet performances in fields. The film quotes Rilke's "Elegy IV": "Now at last there is a play," but the play is about her mother. We see Nicholson's Shirley MacLaine profile and watch as she goes through a couple of dicey relationships with men, played by Will Patton and Elias Koteas. Janet has bad taste in boyfriends, but Baker has excellent taste in character actors. Janet goes through friends, too, and I thought it was great that Baker allows the main one, Regina, to be played by Sophie Okonedo in her own British accent instead of trying to make her sound American. In fact, Baker forces no one to sound regional. That's a significant development for a New England movie, a throwback to a time when filmmakers weren't such maniacs for literalism and just cast people correctly in the first place, an easier and saner kind of perfection to achieve.

In addition to making the best use of a New England setting since Michael Roemer's *Vengeance Is Mine* in 1984, *Janet Planet* is also the best evocation of the early 1990s since Kalman and Horn's 2014 movie *L for Leisure*, another lost classic. Of course it ends as fall begins, with every sane person's "favorite smell in the whole world," the first sensory evidence that we've survived another hot one.

Longlegs

In *Longlegs*, Nicolas Cage plays a Satanist trans woman as a piggy bank–faced high school cafeteria lunch lady who is so clearly and dangerously off her rocker from the moment we first glimpse her that no child would spend more than a second in her presence, much less stand around listening to her lunatic phrase-making, as happens in this movie. Cage of course commits to the whole bit as only he can. He wears the shabby middle-aged homemaker outfit, red lipstick, and prosthetic makeup like it's something he does every day, playing this outrageous character with some subtlety and restraint, which means that when he repeatedly slams his head into a table, nothing explodes. "Dale Kobble" (a character name only Christopher Nolan could love), we learn, is an instrument of the Devil who causes fathers to murder their families just by speaking.

Osgood Perkins's horror film is artier than any other new movie I saw this summer. It's much more of an art film than, for instance, Bertrand Bonello's *The Beast*. Divided into chapters like *Janet Planet*, *Longlegs* takes place in the 1970s and the 1990s in rural and semi-suburban Oregon in winter, so everything is faded and stark. Perkins toggles the film's aspect ratio and presents images as color-drained slides while playing Marc Bolan songs on the soundtrack. He's a Wes Anderson who has reached the end of his spiritual journey and decided to get into Anton LaVey. A lot of "evidence" and historical records are tacked up as creep gallery exhibits. Ordinary things like birthday cards can start to feel off when they're handled by Satan's prop department.

Trap

Josh Hartnett is far less mannered as a serial killer in M. Night Shyamalan's *Trap*, and Shyamalan cuts out the middleman by making the good-looking nice-guy dad a villain who doesn't require a nudge from Satan. *Trap* is ingenious as a genre film, but it doesn't go much farther than that. It comes off as more of an exercise than one of the director's metaphysical outings. I preferred last year's *Knock at the Cabin*, which was more audacious if less fun. Like *Twisters*, which took the opening of Brian De Palma's *Mission: Impossible* (1996), *Trap* is also indebted to '90s De Palma, setting the action in an entertainment arena as in *Snake Eyes* (1998).

Trap was defended as a film of rare smarts that could only be truly understood by embracing its lapses and flaws. The message to Shyamalan was clear: don't try too hard, provide entertainment that works, twists will do. Here, Shyamalan sets up various spatial tricks in a huge arena where a pop star (Saleka Shyamalan) is playing to a packed house as the FBI hunts the killer, who has brought his daughter (Ariel Donoghue) to the show. The film moves through all of the arena's levels one by one, then relocates to a suburban house, finally limiting itself to a half-bath where Hartnett and Lady Raven, the pop star, struggle over her smartphone. Caught in this tiny space, Lady Raven's audience is even bigger than in the arena because she's livestreaming their fight.

Shyamalan has cast his singer daughter in the film, directing her to imagine what Tori Spelling would have done in the 1990s if she'd been told to guess what a pop diva might be like in 2024. He has also cast Hayley Mills as the FBI profiler trying to catch Hartnett. When she was 14, this British actress starred in the original 1961 version of *The Parent Trap.* Is her presence here the first example of casting by pun? In the end, plopped by the Feds in the backseat of an SUV, picking the lock on his handcuffs with a bicycle spoke, even Hartnett has to laugh it off.

The Becomers

Zach Clark has alarming ideas he turns into well-written screenplays and then directs on a tight budget, and he's great with actors. His 2016 film *Little Sister* was one of the best of the past decade, yet he is at a disadvantage, despite his talent, because there are no producers like Roger Corman anymore. If there were, one of them would bring Clark to Hollywood instead of Joe Swanberg bringing him to Chicago to make *The Becomers* for $100,000. There's no reason Clark isn't the next Jonathan Demme, besides a general, society-wide incompetence that can always find the money for anything as long as it isn't good.

Clark is one of the few American filmmakers at this level who shows no influence from Kelly Reichardt or Sean Baker. He's his own man. His new movie is a low-budget version of already low-budget movies, a version of *Invasion of the Body Snatchers* or *Not of This*

Earth. It's also the first original, insightful film about Covid and the Covid years—and the best film of this type since Amy Seimetz's *She Dies Tomorrow,* a neglected, misunderstood movie that came out to indifference during the first summer of the pandemic, which it had predicted by some kind of psychic osmosis. The premise of *The Becomers* is that the alien overlords who will take over our bodies deserve our sympathy. The film presents a circle of life in which identity and gender are totally fungible and homelessness is just around the corner.

The story starts out rather grisly, moving from actor to actor as bodies become inhabited and discarded, its purple-pink, green-blue palette giving way to the interior of a Motel 6 and the parking lot of a Home Depot. The movie's unexpected, poignantly low-key ending is inevitable here, and its ensemble is excellent, especially Isabel Alamin and Molly Plunk as the first two alien-ated women. The narration, read by Russell Mael of Sparks, is both banal and evocative, a witty report from the aliens' home planet. The narrator mentions that at one time he had been "accepted into graduate school for Vacuum Studies," a line that floated over my entire disembodied summer.

Green Border

The first shot of Agnieszka Holland's *Green Border* turns the green forest that separates Poland and Belarus black-and-white to let us know we are in the Europe of neorealism. The film's harrowing first half presents the refugee crisis there as both an intimate and large-scale tragedy, in which Syrian, Afghan, and African families are torn apart and people die in the woods, their bodies sometimes thrown over the high border fence like volleyballs or dead animals. Neither country wants these refugees, so soldiers at the border sic dogs on them and entice them to drink out of thermoses filled with broken glass. The soldiers steal their money and beat them as they huddle in tents in the snow.

This section of the film, the Rossellinian half, is harsh and unrelenting, presenting the families in full, detailed portraits. The plight of an unmarried, middle-aged Afghan teacher (Behi Djanati Atai) reflects the impossibility of understanding what's right in an extreme situation like this, in which people are treated without respect or dignity by armed bullies. She commits a series of tragic mistakes, each of which seemed like the best thing to do at the time.

Holland has made dozens of films in Poland and the US, starting in 1970, and she's directed episodes of *The Wire* and *Treme*. Her most well-known film remains 1990's *Europa, Europa,* but she also made the adaptations of *The Secret Garden* (1993) and the underrated *Washington Square* (1997), with Jennifer Jason Leigh. This side of Holland's work takes over in the second half of *Green Border*, in which a border guard (Tomasz Wlosok) with a pregnant wife at home (Malwina Buss) ditches his job, a psychologist (Agata Kulesza) living in a house in the woods joins a group of young activists, and an average Polish family takes in a group of teenage African refugees and integrates them with their own kids.

None of this is exactly phony, but it does put a positive spin on things, which Holland insists is more real than concentrating only on the anguish and atrocities that happen on the border. She may be right about that, but unfortunately it doesn't work, and instead of *Green Border* remaining a hard-edged film in which the depredations of an unfair, destructive system are exposed, it becomes something that makes viewers feel a little bit better about the agony she brought to life in the first half.

Reagan

Let me be the first and only critic to point out that *Reagan*, a three-year-old biopic on the life of the fortieth president of the United

States that's just getting released now—a film directed by a man whose other movies include *Casper Meets Wendy*, *Bratz*, and *Field of Lost Shoes*—is a better movie than *Deadpool & Wolverine*. It's based on a book called *The Crusader* and tells Reagan's entire life story, I mean all of it, solely through the lens of his anticommunism. It should have kept the title *The Crusader*, because Sean McNamara's *Reagan* is the last great epic of heroic Soviet socialist realism that the movies will see. In it, Dennis Quaid, whose performance as the Great Communicator is brilliant in its loopy detail and in its uncanny re-creation, totally eclipses anyone who played Stalin or Lenin in Soviet movies from the 1940s, when the USSR was a going concern.

The brazen worship of Reagan on display here, with all his little flaws intact and made lovable, befits an international order that is not supposed to think about him any other way. McNamara goes so far as to bring up Reagan's dismissal of the AIDS crisis, turning it into an unfortunate factoid that's part of Reagan's greater glory. Somehow, we are led to believe, if Reagan had done something about AIDS, maybe the Berlin Wall wouldn't have fallen. Penelope Ann Miller's Nancy is similarly perfect, recognizably Nancy, her hard-assed, conniving qualities only there to benefit Ron.

These two actors are not fooling around. Theirs is a grim job and they nail it with joy. So do the many other familiar actors here, a right-wing lineup done Oliver Stone–style, in which every important person Reagan met from boyhood to Hollywood, from Washington to Moscow, gets a bit. That includes the singer Pat Boone, who appears in the film as the Reverend George Otis while an actor (Chris Massoglia) plays him, a meta-fictional move as daring as anything Stone ever tried.

You do not have to be Jello Biafra to recognize that Ronnie always seemed like a sexless Howdy Doody, and the film makes room for that, too, by playing the Genesis song "Land of Confusion" and clips from its accompanying music video, which featured the hideous-looking Reagan marionette from the British comedy show *Spitting Image*. No criticism, we learn, can affect this man who survived an assassin's bullet and brought Gorbachev (a frowsy-looking Olek Krupa) to heel through the greatest charm offensive the world has ever known. Reagan, in effect, becomes in this movie the Soviet Union's last premier, the man who history tasked with bringing the whole thing down and who, as a child, identified its undoing as an historically inevitable process.

Reagan harps on the phrase "clarity is power," and it is clarity as a visual storytelling value more than patriotism or reason that makes this film into the most effective kind of propaganda. Its version of history is, in fact, the official one, and it hammers that point home Reagan-style, through folksy wisdom, fake niceness, and incredulity that any of it could have happened any other way. The cherry on top comes after Reagan's Alzheimer's diagnosis and his death. Twin poles of radicality and reaction meet in their shared showbiz realm. As the credits roll, Bob Dylan sings "Don't Fence Me In," recorded especially for the movie, cementing an era.

AGNÈS ALL ALONG

AGNÈS VARDA

THE BRITISH FILM CRITIC AND DOCUMENTARY FILMMAKER JOHN GRIERSON famously noted that when a director dies he becomes a photographer. Grierson meant that when a filmmaker runs out of ideas, he takes the easy way out, he falls back on visual beauty. The French filmmaker Agnès Varda, who spent a lifetime turning men's ideas upside down, reversed that. She started as a photographer, then became a film director, and in her later years ended up an installation artist. Varda refused to yield to linear notions of what a filmmaker's career should look like and where or when it should end.

Her contribution to film history is not just her status as "the godmother of the French New Wave," nor her centrality to the history of women auteurs, a history she in a real sense instantiated. It is her persistence, and the high level of the ideas behind her work, that made her one of the cinema's principal creators and prime artists. Varda started with visual beauty and never let it go.

She began young. She was already an established photographer when she made her first film, *La Pointe Courte*, a fully independent production, in 1954. Her last film, *Varda by Agnès*, came out in 2019, the year she died at ninety. In between, she was that rare modernist originator whose spiritual daughters were also her peers. In France, the filmmaking careers of Chantal Akerman, Catherine Breillat, and Claire Denis, all born about twenty years after Varda, would have been impossible without her as model and standard. Marguerite Duras, fourteen years Varda's senior, didn't make a transition from writing to film directing until the late 1960s, around the time Akerman began making films. (Does it mean anything that all three women were only five feet tall?)

Varda survived both Duras and Akerman, notably unembittered and aware she was still relevant. "She died while part of the cultural conversation," as the *Irish Times* put it in an obituary. Her career had lasted sixty-five years and bridged two centuries, encompassing many developments in the medium and seismic cultural shifts in both France and the US, the two countries in which she worked. Her innate sense of herself as unstoppable allowed her to gently mock tragic female creators who couldn't navigate these changes with her own sense of ease and her willingness to fight.

For *Lions Love (. . . and Lies)* (1969), set in Los Angeles, Varda hired the American filmmaker Shirley Clarke to play a composite Agnès-Shirley. In a scene in the movie, Varda had Clarke enact her suicide, supposedly in response to her Hollywood movie failing to get off the ground. On camera, Clarke refused to perform a scene in which she takes her life, so Varda took the part herself, for just that one scene, breaking the fourth wall, swallowing fake Seconals, and lying on the bed in a play-acted death pose. In reality, a film Varda was going to make in Hollywood had fallen through after a Columbia Pictures executive had denied her final cut, then pinched her cheek at the end of a meeting. Varda swatted his hand away and, far from getting depressed about it to the point of suicidal ideation, made *Lions Love* instead, outside the studio system.

It is significant that Mona's death in Varda's *Vagabond* (1985) is *not* a suicide but an accident, the outcome of her independence—and her neglect. Varda had, early on, resolved not to be neglected as an artist, no matter what else happened in her life. *Cléo de 5 à 7* (1962), Varda's first feature-length masterpiece and the film for which she is perhaps still best known, ends with Cléo reassured she will be able to survive the threat of cancer that has haunted her for the previous two hours (which the film fits into ninety minutes).

BY THE END, VARDA HAD MORE fans than ever, and "had assumed the position of subversive grandma," as Carrie Rickey points out in her compact, complete, and highly enjoyable book *A Complicated Passion: The Life and Work of Agnès Varda*, the first—and much needed—full-length biography of Varda in English. Rickey quotes the actor Jessica Chastain speaking at a Hollywood Oscars ceremony for Varda: as with tragedy and comedy, "the difference between an iconoclast and an icon is time."

Like her peer in the art world Yayoi Kusama, who also became an installation artist and has, like Varda had, a fixation on polka dots, Varda achieved an iconic status that was meme-able and could be cartoon-like. She gave in to this caricatured version of herself on posters for her late films and in their credits sequences, sometimes dressing as a potato. Potatoes were a frequent subject of her photography, and prominent in *The Gleaners and I*, her 2000 documentary. Rickey explains how Varda identified with potatoes, seeing herself the "unconventionally shaped and spotted produce abandoned in the field."

Varda's late-in-life look was essential to this process and to her ongoing status as an artist in the digital age. In Rickey's description of the look, Varda's dress was "aubergine, her leggings purple, and her slippers red, like the Pope's. Except for the skullcap of silver gray at its crown, Varda's hair and dress almost exactly matched." By the early 2000s, Varda had become a wise elder, always ready with a witty remark, like John Waters or Paul Schrader in the US today.

How did Varda get there? She was lucky in an important way. She had a successful father, a Greek engineer whose parents had emigrated to Belgium, where Varda was born, and who had become wealthy in the shipping industry before dying while gambling at a roulette table in a Knokke-le-Zoute casino. After his death, already established as a photographer of "skill and style," Varda convinced her mother to purchase two adjacent buildings for her in the 14th arrondissement of Paris, considered slum-like at the time. Both buildings were run down, one an empty framer's studio, the other a cheese shop that had gone bust—and for a cheese shop to go bust in Paris tells you something about the neighborhood.

For the equivalent of $55,000 in today's money, Varda bought the buildings in the rue Daguerre and made them her headquarters for the rest of her life—they still house her company, Ciné-Tamaris. At first she lived there with a sculptor named Valentine Schlegel, who became her lover; eventually Jacques Demy, the director of *The Umbrellas of Cherbourg* (1964), moved in and became her husband. The first thing Varda did when she took possession was plant a beech tree and a maple tree in the courtyard; later she began painting the building pink and accenting it with large purple polka dots and striping the door in mauve. "When you're a photographer in need of a studio and you find one in the rue Daguerre, that's a sign, isn't it?" Varda explained, referring to the inventor of photography for whom the street was named. It's no wonder *Cléo de 5 à 7* begins with a tarot card reading.

It's important, I think, to start with *Cléo*. People are often surprised to find out Varda had made films before it, and Varda's later films can be read as variations on its theme. *Lions Love* extends to feature-length and reimagines the scenes in *Cléo* with Michel Legrand and Serge Korber as Cléo's songwriters—Cléo is a pop singer with hits on the radio and on jukeboxes in cafés. In the later film, Varda puts the hippie creators of the musical *Hair* (James Rado and Gerome Ragni) in a ménage à trois with the Warhol superstar Viva, playing a version of herself, a New York actress-scenestress new to Hollywood. Fifteen years after that, *Vagabond* becomes a deglamorized, rural destruction of the city-bound Cléo, character and movie.

The way Varda made all three exemplifies what she called her four principles of filmmaking, which Rickey outlines in her book. One, "you don't make films to watch them alone"; two, "film quickly with the means at hand"; three, "nothing is banal if you film it with empathy"; and four, "you need a viewpoint to make a film." *Vagabond*, for instance, started as a documentary on tree plague before Varda met a cop on location who told her how a homeless young man in the area had recently frozen to death. She couldn't raise money for the film but shot anyway, with Sandrine Bonnaire in the title role, and it became her biggest post-*Cléo* hit.

To those four principles we might add two more, which Rickey's book makes clear: Varda never shot on a soundstage, and she never made adaptations from other sources. She shot on location, and her films, whether they were features or documentary shorts, were originals. It was Varda, along with Jean-Pierre Melville, who showed the New Wave that you did not need credentials to make films. She insisted anyone could do it, with whatever they had on hand.

In addition, she had what Rickey calls "the gift of unselfconsciousness," the ability to act and speak naturally onscreen, coupled with a related talent, the aptitude to speak well of her films without seeming to brag. When she describes an early short of hers, *Ô saisons, ô chateaux* (1958), she says she "stumbled into a sublime late fall, all golden, bathed in sunlight. I was taken with the gentleness of the Loire Valley, and the film was instilled with the melancholy of bygone epochs." She could be describing her late career.

RICKEY'S BOOK INCLUDES an eight-page section of black-and-white photos, showing Varda with Demy, at work and with her children Rosalie and Mathieu, accepting various awards, in her potato costume from the 2003 Venice Biennale, and at the 2018 Women's March at Cannes, which the festival's director announced to the press by explaining that "a large group of women were going to do something that affirmed their presence."

Agnès Varda: Director's Inspiration is the catalogue for an exhibition of the same name at the Academy Museum of Motion Pictures in Los Angeles, which is on display through January 2025. The show and the book cover Varda's work as a photographer, filmmaker, and visual artist. The book is generously illustrated with color photos, and includes short essays from critics, filmmakers, and Rosalie, as well as an excellent 2017 interview with Varda by the Gabonese filmmaker Manouchka Kelly Labouba that concentrates on Varda's time in Los Angeles, from 1966 to 1969 and again in the early 1980s. In those two periods Varda made five films: *Lions Love*, the short feature *Documenteur* (1981, one of her most affecting and personal films, though a fiction in which she does not appear), the documentary feature *Mur Murs* (also 1981, about public art in the city), and the short documentaries *Uncle Yanco* (1967, on her colorful long-lost uncle, a noted beatnik painter living on a houseboat in Sausalito) and *Black Panthers* (1968, an important early document of the Black Panther Party in Oakland). The book makes one long for another large art book dedicated solely to Varda's photography, which would include her pre-LA work in Cuba and China. Along with potatoes, Varda appears to have been the best photographer of hippies.

Varda and Demy lived in Los Angeles because Demy had been invited there to make films. His stay resulted in *Model Shop* (1969), a rare example of a French take on Hollywood that isn't mean-spirited (though it's a little downbeat). The couple lived in Beverly Hills and rented twin white convertibles, a trope from Demy's French movies, his dream of America. They made great use of their time, meeting everyone from the Doors' Jim Morrison to Andy Warhol—Varda appeared on the cover of the first issue of Warhol's *Interview* magazine. As she had discovered Gérard Depardieu in Paris, Varda also discovered Harrison Ford in Los Angeles. Rickey's book features dinner parties and get-togethers with Antonioni and Roger Corman, Henry Miller and Mae West. At one point a drunken Morrison face-plants into a plate of birthday cake at a party for Rosalie, a premonition of his death in a bathtub in Paris, where Varda would be the first person called to his apartment to witness his corpse, and a reminder of that scene in Oliver Stone's *The Doors* (1991), in which Meg Ryan yells, "Jim Morrison, you have ruined another Thanksgiving!"

Demy had made forays into Hollywood before. During one of them he took a trip with an agent to visit Bodega Bay, where

Hitchcock had shot *The Birds*, and the two men began an affair, the first of two covered in Rickey's book. Demy revealed this to Varda while she was pregnant with their son, Mathieu, and in 1972 Demy left her to go back to California and live in "a small cottage in Venice" with a 26-year-old Warner Bros. story editor named David Bombyk, who later, like Demy, contracted HIV and died of AIDS.

In America, Varda had immersed herself in the feminist politics of Shulamith Firestone and Kate Millet. "The feminists there were much more radical than those in France," she noted. Back in Paris, Varda devoted herself to women's rights and began to pursue her own projects away from Demy. They reconciled but lived separately after Demy got sick—she in her busy studio on the ground floor at rue Daguerre, he in an eighth-floor apartment across the street that Mathieu described as clean, white, marble, and futuristic. After Demy's death in 1990, Varda became his ardent memorializer. She made several films about him, including *Jacquot de Nantes* (1991), the best and the only true biopic about a film director, a work of great love and delicacy. In that film, Varda re-creates scenes, in black-and-white, from Demy's childhood in the occupied France in which they both grew up, edited with color footage from his last days.

THE COMMONPLACE VIEW OF Varda as the most understanding wife of all time, the most patient and the most accepting, is perhaps belied by moments in films she made both before and after Demy's infidelity. The title of her groundbreaking feminist musical *One Sings, the Other Doesn't* (1976) refers to the film's two female protagonists, but it could refer to her and Demy, too. He, a maker of triste musicals, sings; she, a documentary photographer, deals in reality. Note that unlike Demy's musicals, she purposefully gave *One Sings, the Other Doesn't* a happy ending.

In *Uncle Yanco*, her artist uncle speaks of how "between the desire and the painting there is a little bitterness, a passing shadow." If this shadow existed in her relationship with Demy, it is certainly also apparent in *Le Bonheur*, her 1965 movie that presents itself as a sunny picnic in the grass but is really "a ripe summer peach with a worm inside," as Varda described it. By the end, the film is more like a horror movie, though an exceptionally subtle one, than the Renoiresque outing scored to Mozart it at first appears to be. Martin Scorsese has said *Le Bonheur* exposes the alleged happiness of marital fidelity as a lie from a shampoo commercial, but Varda's dare to herself in making it is that the film could also *be* a shampoo commercial.

Le Bonheur's pastoral tone is clear, but the film is impossible to pin down, which is what makes it so chilling. An evocation of bliss, as the critic Amy Taubin described it, it is also a "vengeful act." It nakedly presents what Chantal Akerman called an extraordinary idea: that "one love is worth the same as another, a person can be replaced by another." "For me," Akerman said, "*Le Bonheur* is the most anti-romantic film there is." The film's penultimate scene of betrayal exactly and amazingly duplicates Demy's revelation of his infidelity seven years later. The wife in *Le Bonheur* does not survive that; Varda did.

The lingering effects of *Le Bonheur*'s remorselessness got her in trouble with feminist film theoreticians. The backlash continued for a decade. Varda said of *One Sings, the Other Doesn't* that "for once you have a film where women are without guilt, without shame, without dependency, without stupidity, fighting against laws and institutions, getting value and putting value into women's ventures." This was not enough for the British "cinefeminist" Claire Johnston, who hated *Le Bonheur*, calling it "unforgivably cruel," "reactionary," and a "retrograde step in women's cinema" that placed women outside history. Needless to say, this view of Varda and her work has waned.

AGNÈS VARDA HAD NOT SEEN more than twenty-five films when she made *La Pointe Courte*. She was not a cinephile like the critics from *Cahiers du cinéma* who made up the bulk of the New Wave. One can only imagine what these young men thought of her, a single mother, when they first met her. She became the godmother of the New

Wave even though she was the same age as them, because her first feature came out four years before theirs. In the heady rush of the New Wave's success in 1959 and 1960, she gained a reputation as a forgotten director, and so early on had to be defended as a precursor. By 1959, Rickey points out, the French critic Jean Douchet noted, in a review of her first retrospective, the injustice of Varda being ignored as a founder of New Wave. It was a strange situation. Varda was getting a retrospective just as the movement she had kick-started into being was getting underway.

Cléo came out in 1962. When it reached the United States that year, Stanley Kauffmann, writing in the *New Republic*, accused her of being a New Wave imitator. As angry as Claire Johnston, he called the film "a sedulous exercise in what could be called Cleo-realism" (you don't encounter the word "sedulous" much anymore) and a parody of films by Truffaut, Godard, and Chabrol. "The pat shape of the story," he wrote, "its very cleverness, the shallowness of its emotional exploration, the heroine's self-conscious dramatization, make it merely a flashily dressed up conventional tearjerker, a sob sister of the works of Fannie Hurst. The avant-garde trappings disguise nothing; it is Irving Berlin orchestrated by Stravinsky." Guess he didn't like it—nor did he know what he was talking about.

Varda herself was harsh on films. The first film she ever saw was *Snow White and the Seven Dwarfs*, in 1938. "What is certain is that I hated *Snow White*," she said as an adult, explaining that "its valorization of the heroine for cleaning the house of the dwarfs without pay" disgusted her. ("A sophisticated critique for a 10-year-old," writes Rickey.) Demy loved *The Sound of Music*; Varda did not. "How could you love a stupid, bullshit film like this, with that stupid babysitter who wishes to marry the father? I mean, is it interesting to see someone wash the pants of eleven children to get a man?" she asked. She thought Ingmar Bergman's marital dramas were also suspect. As late as 2013 she told an interviewer, "It's fine that they made *Gravity*, but I really couldn't care less." In *A Hundred and One Nights* (1995), one of her cinema-valorizing movies, Michel Piccoli, playing a man who is supposed to be the living embodiment of cinema, makes an anti-Bergman statement apropos of nothing, "Down with cries, long live whispers," demonstrating where Varda's heart lies.

I MUST CONFESS THAT WHEN I was young, my heart lied with Carrie Rickey, whose brief time as the film critic at the *Boston Herald*, before she went on to her long and distinguished career as the film critic at the *Philadelphia Inquirer*, coincided with my college years and my initial discovery of Varda's work during a French-cinema class. The professor began the semester with two films: Louis Malle's *Lacombe, Lucien* (1974) and *Cléo de 5 à 7*.

I had never seen a Varda film and was immediately hooked by the way *Cléo* purports to be in real time, and of course by the Paris of the Nouvelle vague and by the silent-film-within-a-film, starring Anna Karina and Jean-Luc Godard, that Cléo (Corinne Marchand) watches from a projection booth. A whole book could be written about the connections between Godard's work and Varda's, and the back-and-forth between them over six decades, that sadly ended in Varda's *Faces Places* (2017) in the scene in which Godard refused to see her when she went to visit him at his house in Switzerland. In *Cléo*, Varda made Godard remove his sunglasses and showed him with a tear rolling down his cheek. In *Faces Places* he returned the favor, causing her to cry by so coldly ignoring her.

He left a note on the door reminding her of the old times in the first half of the 1960s, when she and Demy had been witnesses at his marriage to Karina. So much in Godard, it now seems to me, comes directly from Varda or is a reaction to something in her work. The garbagemen and their sandwiches in Godard's *Weekend* (1967), for instance, now strike me as Vardian, but with Godardian spite and critique added. "She does not scold, she does not virtue signal," Rickey writes—unlike Godard, who made a career of the former and sometimes slipped into the latter. In Godard's penultimate movie (so far), *Trailer of a Film That Will Never Exist: Phony Wars* (2023), there's a title card that reads, in part, *le bonheur est/était une idée neuve en Europe* ("happiness is/was a new idea in Europe"). It's a quote from the French revolutionary Saint-Just, but seeing it on the screen not long after both Varda's and Godard's deaths made me think of *Le Bonheur* and ideas from Europe that had once been new.

Back to Rickey and Varda. *Vagabond* came not too long after I first saw *Cléo*. I believe Rickey was still at the *Herald* then, though I can no longer recall if she reviewed that movie, or if she did, whether I read her piece. I do know that at the time I considered her the only good newspaper critic in Boston, and I clipped an interview with her from a local weekly and put it on my fridge for inspiration. Wish I still had that—probably no library even has it. After Rickey moved to the paper in Philadelphia in 1986, I read her no more, until now. There was no internet then. I wouldn't go so far as to call her a "legacy critic," as Carrie Courogen does in her recent book on Elaine May, *Miss May Does Not Exist*, a book about another filmmaker we are constantly told people have forgotten about, never got her due, etc. I suppose "legacy critic" was meant as a compliment, but it didn't read like one.

Rickey's book on Varda reminded me of when I first saw Varda's films and when I read all the critics in all the papers in Boston. The return of Rickey, who first encountered Varda as I did, in a college class (though hers was taught by Manny Farber), is most welcome. Her book is moving because Varda's life was moving, and because its existence made me realize I'd been waiting for it. It brings to mind something Varda said about seeing movies and making films: "When I see a bad film, I think, 'Films are disgusting!' When I see a beautiful film, I think, 'That's what I must do. I must create a beautiful film!'"

OIL PAINTINGS AT THE DENTIST'S OFFICE

OSCAR MOVIES 2025

The Apprentice

This year's Oscar-nominated movies are a snapshot of a short, peculiar moment in American history: the Kamala Harris era. The Harris era exhibited contradictory properties usually associated more with quantum physics than with Hollywood movies: it was both brief and nonexistent. It was an era designed for awards-bait cinema, movies with good intentions, serious, un-self-aware, lacking in Harris's own campaign promise of "joy." Made to counter superhero movies and other franchised content, the films of the Harris era often relied on third-act jump scares as dramatic devices. Defined by wishful thinking, these movies presented the triumph of the sacrosanct in difficult, intractable situations that in reality did not offer clear resolutions or even cause for hope.

Or, like *The Apprentice*, these movies succeeded only in making the monsters they scrutinized stronger. *The Apprentice* gave us an accurate young Trump (Sebastian Stan), a grotesque, self-aggrandizing rapist ready to throw over anybody for fame, wealth, and power. In Ali Abbasi's film, from a screenplay by the journalist Gabriel Sherman, Trump's rise is inexorable. He is a man of destiny, like Reagan in last year's *Reagan* movie, but with no self-control, whose liposuctions and hair transplants we see performed onscreen.

To succeed, Trump must absorb the lessons offered to him by Roy Cohn (Jeremy Strong), the shady, anticommunist lawyer held over from the McCarthy years. When we meet Cohn in *The Apprentice*, he is prowling the celebrity-studded world of crumbling 1970s New York with his entourage of attractive young gay men. By the end of the film he is a husk used up by Trump. Dying of AIDS at his Mar-a-Lago birthday party as the future President mocks him, Cohn, barely able to stand, has to make a speech praising Trump and the USA. Lit from below by sparklers decorating an American flag cake, he's a figure in a horror movie extolling his master, Satan or Dracula.

"*The Apprentice* is first and foremost humanist, which makes it radically different from all the political noise," said its executive producer Amy Baer, a Hollywood veteran, describing it as though it were *Pather Panchali*. It was not, though nor was it something made by "pretend filmmakers" that belonged "in a dumpster fire," as an official Trump spokesman called it, unclear on how to use the phrase "dumpster fire" in a sentence. The film is, instead, a failed exposé. It will stand as a unique monument—a rebuke to the corruption of a past and future President that had no effect on anybody, but did get nominated for Oscars.

Conclave

As I write this, Pope Francis is in the hospital in Rome, likely dying of pneumonia. Right now the Holy Father is a type of pope we know well: the pope on his deathbed, not the Francis of *The Two Popes*, or the pope of *The Young Pope*, or *The Pope with an Exorcist on His Staff*. *Conclave*, which is about the election of a new pope, is therefore newly timely, like *The Apprentice* was, because of an upcoming election.

The wish of Cardinal Lawrence (Ralph Fiennes) in this movie is that God grant us "a pope who sins and asks for forgiveness and who carries on," and after two acts of fairly riveting election intrigue from

The film's light-pink and dark-green palette makes it look like Lilly Pulitzer was hired to design *Hook.* Jon M. Chu has directed it so dutifully that no musical number can become a showstopper, which doesn't really matter because the film's audience already knows the songs by heart. Heart, however, is what the film lacks. It contains nothing within a Kansas mile of Judy Garland singing "Over the Rainbow." There is no longing here, nothing *sad*. Emotions in *The Wizard of Oz* were anchored to Dorothy's dream of a world in which her relatives and the people in her town could be other than what they were. *Wicked*'s longing is to be a *Harry Potter* movie.

Jeff Goldblum's Wizard is underwritten considering that this was a novel before it was a Broadway show. He's a Roy Cohn figure, seeking to mentor and exploit Elphaba in order to control Oz. Back in December, Adam McKay, the director of *The Big Short*, tweeted that *Wicked* is so "nakedly about radicalization in the face of careerism, fascism, propaganda" that "if America keeps going on the track it is I wouldn't be surprised to see the movie banned in 3–5 years." The actual track we are on with *Wicked* is that Universal is about to make a billion dollars from it. The track we got off is the one on which Kamala Harris said during a televised Democratic debate in September 2019, "Donald Trump . . . you know he reminds me of that guy in *The Wizard of Oz*, you know, when you pull back the curtain, it's a really small dude?" Did we really think someone who couldn't convincingly describe *The Wizard of Oz* could be elected President?

Emilia Pérez

Idiotic cultural appropriation is paid back to Netflix, the distributor of *Emilia Pérez.* Netflix sent the French *Emily in Paris*, the French sent back this film—the titles are practically the same. A Mexico-set musical about a transgender narco (Karla Sofía Gascón) who starts an NGO to help the families of people murdered by the cartels, the film actually stars Zoe Saldaña as Emilia's lawyer and the facilitator of her gender-affirming surgeries. It is a thankless role, predicated on Saldaña taking seriously the idea that Gascón is, as a review in the *Los Angeles Times* had it, giving a "sensually charged portrayal [that] wouldn't be out of place anchoring a classic Hollywood woman's noir." Sure, Tommy Wiseau could play Philip Marlowe in *The Big Sleep*, too, if you gave him the chance.

The idea that this galoot would be unrecognizable to even her children requires a special suspension of disbelief. Therefore the director, Jacques Audiard, had to include a song about it called "Papa," in which the kid has an inkling that is soothingly dispelled by Emilia herself. If the film had anything of a fairy-tale element to it, which it does not, a scene like that might have worked. But everything in *Emilia Pérez* is too easy, a neoliberal cakewalk. It's the kind of movie in which Emilia makes sure to assure us her NGO is "not a replacement for public services." The film is a preposterous nightmare of first-world self-regard.

Beyond being an insult to Mexico and to the aborted film careers of trans performers like Candy Darling, *Emilia Pérez* is also an insult to French musicals, rendering the achievements of Jacques Demy and Michel Legrand into distant, unrecoverable memories. It is an astounding phenomenon that so many American critics praised this film, and Gascón's performance in it, before Gascón's long series of hateful tweets was revealed to the world.

At the end we are supposed to believe Emilia has become a martyr. An effigy of her with a bleeding hand and missing fingers, too obviously phallic for anyone to comment on, is carried through the streets to sainthood. This final transformation is more vainglory than ascension. The reality of *Emilia Pérez* is too stark: once a cheeseball, always a cheeseball.

The Substance

Coralie Fargeat's *The Substance* is another French fantasia of North American life, this one set in a place where the French are more comfortable than Mexico: Hollywood. As in Bertrand Bonello's *The Beast*, people in the contemporary Los Angeles of *The Substance* drive 1960s Ford Mustangs, sip cocktails, live in places with huge windows, try to get acting jobs, answer weird ads. A dark feminist satire that is also a big play for Hollywood acceptance, Fargeat's movie criticizes the exploitation of women's bodies and their disposability as performers as they age by using large, splashy servings of gore and Margaret Qualley's ass in high-def. The movie has its cake and eats it, too, and also smashes it and gets it all over its hands and smears it on its face.

The film is too long for its one concept, which is that Elisabeth Sparkle, a middle-aged actress played by Demi Moore, can buy and inject a serum that allows her to split into a younger version of herself, Sue (Qualley), who could be called Su Tissue like the singer in the Suburban Lawns because she is born from the sinew of Elisabeth's body, emerging through her spine and out her back, which then requires thick black stitches to sew up. This wonder drug comes with responsibilities, as fluids from the two bodies must be carefully extracted and managed, there are time limits on the use of the younger body, and side effects develop if the schedule is ignored.

Of course the lure of youth, which as we know is wasted on the young, proves too much. Elisabeth's toothsome counterpart is so telegenic she becomes a TV star on a morning exercise show. Predictably, dancercise is not a path to happiness. As things begin to melt into big gobs of chicken fat, Fargeat takes us on a trip through the history of fairy tales, 19th-century horror literature, and 1980s movies that used lots of crazy prosthetics before the term *body horror* came into overuse.

Fargeat is relentless and tiring in combining Hansel and Gretel and the David Cronenberg of *The Fly* and *Naked Lunch* with movies like *Street Trash* and *Society*, with Dorian Gray, Dr. Jekyll and Mr. Hyde, *The Nutty Professor* and *Freaky Friday* if Darren Aronofsky had directed them, *The Wasp Woman*, and on and on, often in arty, spare Kubrickian compositions. Soon Elisabeth starts to look like the Ice Cream Man from *The Pink Opaque*, and the whole movie becomes a reenactment of the *Triangle of Sadness* puking scene but with menstrual blood. The final image is graphically arresting but exhausting to contemplate. It's at least four things at once: a Medusa head, "they had faces then," "some of us are looking at the stars," and the poop emoji left on the street.

I'm Still Here

Walter Salles's *I'm Still Here*, from Brazil, has the virtue of dealing with political repression and state-sanctioned murder in a mature, adult way, but it does so by making it immediately relatable to people with families who live in big apartments in gentrified parts of town.

The first half hour of this cautionary tale sets up the perfect life of Rubens and Eunice Paiva (Selton Mello and Fernanda Torres), a husband and wife with five beautiful children who live in a spacious, multifloor, book-lined apartment in Rio. Rubens is a former liberal politician now working as a civil engineer, and he is part of a cell that helps radicals opposed to the repressive military government that ruled the country in the 1960s and '70s. It is 1970 as the film begins, and the kids are into Tropicália, the Beatles and Bob Dylan, Godard and Antonioni movies. They dream of cultured, Europeanized lives, but the dictatorship is cracking down in response to a series of kidnappings by the radicals. Rubens is swept up in this, taken from this happy home, and never seen again.

This is a true story, based on a book by Marcelo Rubens Paiva, Rubens and Eunice's son. The military police hold Eunice and the rest of the family hostage in their apartment and then take Eunice and one of her daughters (Luiza Kosovski) in for questioning. Fernanda

Torres's performance as Eunice is one of great tribute to this woman who spent decades searching for the truth about what happened to her husband. She and the children have to move because they can no longer afford their place, she gets a law degree, becomes a fighter for Indigenous rights, and leads a long, distinguished life as a human rights advocate.

Her happy ending comes, years later, in two parts. The first is that she finally receives Rubens's death certificate, proving he'd been killed by the dictatorship. The second is that in her eighties, suffering from Alzheimer's and confined to a wheelchair (and now played by Fernanda Montenegro, Torres's mother, also a distinguished actress and movie star), she sits alone in the living room at a family gathering and sees a documentary about Rubens on TV while everybody else is out on the patio reminiscing.

This section of the film is designed to elicit warm-but-bittersweet feelings of familial love, and to demonstrate that there is always hope that the truth will come out. But it makes TV the ultimate validator of history, which it is not. Even Brazilian baby boomers must know that. The ending is tragic—a silent old woman watching television alone when something about her murdered husband happens to come on and no one notices it but her.

The Seed of the Sacred Fig

Mohammad Rasoulof's *The Seed of the Sacred Fig* is a more immediate, less aestheticized, and not at all nostalgic version of *I'm Still Here*, set in the present, and banned in Iran, where it was made and from which Rasoulof had to escape to get the film shown. Written in response to the 2022 state murder of Mahsa Amini, who was killed by the Guidance Patrol for not wearing a headscarf, and the subsequent protests that erupted, Rasoulof's film indicts his country by describing the slow descent into paranoia and violence of a man (Missagh Zareh) who works as a judge for the Revolutionary Court.

Iman's actual job is to rubber-stamp state executions, and taking this new position has moved his family up in the world. He and his wife (Soheila Golestani) and their two daughters (Mahsa Rostami and Setareh Maleki) now live in a bigger place, so when his daughters begin to follow the news of the protests and timidly become involved in them, he and, at first, his wife put a stop to their activities. When he seemingly misplaces the handgun he's been issued, he turns his family's life into one of accusations and recriminations, mimicking what is going on outside their window as the protests grow. Soon he loses the trust of his new colleagues at court, who begin to monitor his activities, increasing his sense of isolation and paranoia.

Iman whisks his family off to his abandoned childhood home in the arid mountains, where he puts them on trial for stealing his gun. Sana (Maleki) emerges as the savior of her family, taking heroic action to protect them from her father's increasing madness. This section of the film calls for bravura performances and strives for the elemental quality of a 1950s Anthony Mann western, which it doesn't quite achieve. Rasoulof needed to call on an inner Sergio Leone here, but perhaps the nature of the way the film was made, hidden from the eyes of the government, didn't allow time for that. The shock ending and cut to news footage of the Amini protests is a Kiarostamian move that brings the film back into reality, but its indictment of Iranian patriarchy and repression was already clear.

September 5

A stand-in for *October 7* that is also a tribute to American sports coverage, Tim Fehlbaum's movie about the massacre of Israeli athletes by Palestinian terrorists at the 1972 Munich Olympics applies "the thrill of victory, and the agony of defeat" to geopolitics. The fact is that ABC Sports messed up their coverage of this hostage crisis, calling it for peace before nine Israelis were killed in a shoot-out at the airport between West German police and Black September, as the Palestinian group called itself. Five of the Palestinians and one cop died. In *September 5*, we do get a re-creation of the most infamous image of 1970s terrorism, the black-and-white photo of the kidnapper in a ski mask and sweater on the concrete balcony of a hotel, his head and body tilted down as he looks over the railing.

The small, transparent network logo that used to appear in the corner of TV screens was called a "bug," or "the bug," and it was invented by ABC Sports during this armed standoff, we learn here. That was the highlight of the movie for me. I'd always wondered about that. In the end, *September 5* is a tribute to Nielsen ratings. Nine hundred million people watched this tragedy unfold on live TV. Now that TV news has become unprofitable for the entertainment conglomerates that own it, and the Olympics are viewed piecemeal across many platforms, the film can be seen as nostalgic longing for a time when terrorism got everybody to watch the same thing at the same time. That is not what movies are for.

No Other Land

Part of the reason the Palestinian documentary *No Other Land* still doesn't have an American distributor may be that it shows up as useless the computer-generated nonsense of Hollywood and European films about inclusion. If big-budget film producers are happy with those, and writer-directors like Adam McKay call them radical, so what? What good are they? What have they changed?

No Other Land was made by a Palestinian-Israeli collective of four filmmakers headed by Basel Adra, a young Palestinian man from Masafer Yatta, in the West Bank, a place being forcibly evacuated by Israel under false pretenses. The Israelis claimed the army needs the land for military training, but that was later revealed as a lie. Palestinians were evicted, their houses bulldozed as they watched, to make room for settlers. The film, which was shot from 2019 to 2023, records this in great detail. As usual, the settlers come off as violent and dangerous, the most insane people on Earth, which in 2025 is saying something.

The more of this documentation, the better. Much of it was shot by Adra on his smartphone. The film stalls when Adra and Yuval Abraham, an Israeli journalist and a codirector of the film, pause for discussions about Abraham's presence in the village (though those scenes, and all the scenes of Adra's daily life, are beautifully shot by codirector Rachel Szor). A useless, showy visit to Masafer Yatta by Tony Blair and his entourage is a highlight of the film and a low point of this history recorded by Adra, a textbook pseudo-event that changes nothing.

Nickel Boys

I admit that I'm not convinced that the decision to shoot *Nickel Boys* primarily in point-of-view shots really works; and I confess that the film's beautiful, sunny cinematography and its extreme earnestness are not aspects of any movie that I ever appreciate the most. RaMell Ross's previous film, the documentary *Hale County This Morning, This Evening* (2018), struck me as more moving and more filled with mystery, and the last film I saw that was shot by Jomo Fray, Raven Jackson's *All Dirt Roads Taste of Salt* (2023), I found more unexpected and original. And while a film as sincere (and long) as *Nickel Boys* can't be called a commercial play, Ross still shocked me when he recently mentioned he'd work for Marvel Studios if he could help educate them. Has he talked to Chloé Zhao lately?

The clips included in *Nickel Boys* from *The Defiant Ones* (1958) made me want to rewatch and re-evaluate that most liberal of 1950s white vs. Black dramas, which I did, and I found that—as with so many movies—time has improved it because it was made with so much more serious-mindedness and professionalism than most Hollywood films today. The ending isn't great, and *Nickel Boys* does do something serious to correct that. In the same way, the use of

Martin Luther King Jr.'s "Funtown" speech was a signal that the movie was going to purposefully deny any kind of fun to its main character, Elwood (Ethan Herisse).

Shots of a cake knife scraping against the side of a bowl to get the frosting off it are as memorable in *Nickel Boys* as the story, and Aunjanue Ellis-Taylor, as Elwood's grandmother, has to do the same kind of acting that Audrey Totter had to do in *Lady in the Lake* in 1947, that previous POV adaptation of a novel that also dropped the *The* from the title. It is very hard to not overdo it when acting directly into the camera as if it is a person you are speaking to. And then to hug it? This was a risky proposition all around. That Ross and Fray have managed to make it work and have created a film unlike any other proves it was a risk worth taking. Yet I still want that two-shot of Elwood and Turner (Brandon Wilson) in the cafeteria of Nickel Academy, a place they never should have ended up. Some things in life you don't get.

The Brutalist

It seems to be generally understood by everyone who has seen it that *The Brutalist* is a deeply confused film that touches greatness by mixing disparate elements that have no business being mixed together, and that its success or failure in the mind of any individual viewer depends on how much they are personally offended by any one of those elements. Just in describing the character Adrien Brody plays—a Hungarian architect named László Tóth, who is a student of the Bauhaus, a Jew, a concentration camp survivor, a refugee, a heroin addict, a rape victim, a possible Zionist with a Black best friend, a great artist, and a stroke victim—it is possible to understand where all this could go very wrong, except in the minds of people who give out acting awards.

Brody's exceptional Greek tragedy mask of a face is perfect for a role like this, more tortured with age than it was in *The Pianist* in

2002, a movie in which somehow he had fewer issues than in this one. He can now fully inhabit the soul of a man carrying each and every one of the world's problems on his bony shoulders without appearing callow. His callowness made *The Pianist* more entertaining, but *The Brutalist* has pretty much dispensed with entertainment, even though Guy Pearce's gleeful turn as a pompous American industrialist livens things up, until it doesn't anymore.

Brady Corbet's films seem to be designed to impress viewers with high art allusions and to suck them in with Lol Crawley's exquisite cinematography at the same time as they announce they are for some other, more deserving future audience, just as Tóth's work is. What saves them is their clear element of madness. There is something really insane about these films, something beautiful (as in the marble quarry scene) but opaque, which Corbet and his co-screenwriter wife, Mona Fastvold, often subvert and ruin (as in the scene after the marble quarry scene).

During the speech at the end of the film made by Tóth's niece (Ariane Labed) as she picks up an award for him—one of many scenes that drove architects and writers about architecture around the bend, if I am using the proper architectural term when I say "bend"—she announces about Tóth's buildings that "the inherent laws of concrete things such as mountains and rock define them. They indicate nothing. They tell nothing. They simply are." That isn't true of Tóth's work, which is revealed in the film to be ideological and full of hidden meanings related to his imprisonment in Buchenwald. And I can't think of anything less true of Corbet's movies than that, either. But making such an outrageous claim will definitely get me to see his next one.

Flow

If animated cats, dogs, and lemurs are your thing, *Flow* is the movie for you. Thankfully these animals don't talk and it isn't a musical. Instead, this story of climate change reminds us that after nature has finished with mankind, no one will ever have to hear Josh Gad sing again.

A Real Pain

A journey from New York to Majdanek with the most annoying person in the world, the effusive but morose, joyful guilt tripper Benji (Kieran Culkin), here being indulged by his rigid, neurotic cousin, David (Jesse Eisenberg, who also wrote and directed). Early in the film, at the airport, David surreptitiously tosses in the trash a yogurt Benji has bought for him, which led me to dislike David for the rest of the film and to immediately understand that by the end he would get an important life lesson about privilege from his emotionally incontinent cuz.

A Real Pain is well directed, but the scenes in Poland had me wishing for a Kieślowski *Dekalog* film about pride with American tourists really fucking up in a life-ruining, terrible way, which is not at all what happens here. The two boy-men honor their late grandmother with a visit to her old place of residence, there's lots of contemplative Chopin on the soundtrack, and Eisenberg gave a good part to Jennifer Grey. These nice boys in their nice movie made me miss Steve Coogan and Rob Brydon, and Wallace Shawn and André Gregory, in their talky two-handers, in which dudes with opposite personalities and worldviews get together for meals and hash things out in a melancholy and uncertain way. It even made me miss *Old Joy*, which is a true downer of a movie even without a stop at a concentration camp.

A Complete Unknown

Bob Dylan is to Pete Seeger as Donald Trump is to Roy Cohn in this version of *The Apprentice*, the same story of discarded mentorship. *A Complete Unknown* is the positively charged interpretation that mirrors the negative one about Trump; both dramatize the same kind of relationship. Seeger and Cohn come from the same red-baiting era, one (Seeger) on the side of good, the other (Cohn) evil, and Seeger, we learn early in *A Complete Unknown*, was called before the House Un-American Activities Committee, the kind of semi-fascist panel run by Cohn for Senator Joseph McCarthy. (Seeger was found guilty of anti-American subversion, but won his case on appeal.)

Ed Norton plays Seeger as a musician and activist so kind and patient he could be Mister Rogers, the folk scene his West Village neighborhood. When he meets Timothée Chalamet's Bob Dylan, he knows he has a star on his hands, just as Cohn knew that about Trump in *The Apprentice*. Like Sebastian Stan in that movie, Chalamet makes his Dylan an evil genius chosen by history to succeed. A devilish self-made modernist unconcerned with the truth, he makes his story up as he goes along. Chalamet's performance is a success, a real feat of acting in which he thoroughly inhabits Dylan-ness without slipping into parody, speaking in a voice that's somehow as distinctive as Bill Skarsgård's in *Nosferatu* without losing himself in it.

James Mangold's film is as great as Hollywood musical biopics get. As with all of them, including his Johnny Cash and June Carter movie, *Walk the Line*, now twenty years old, the question is how much of it is really memorable beyond the superficial but not at all easy feat of getting it right, which Jay Cocks's screenplay does manage. Johnny Cash appears in *A Complete Unknown*, played here by Boyd Holbrook, not Joaquin Phoenix, linking the two films across two decades.

Cash is central. We hear him in voice-over before we meet him as Dylan reads his letters. He's more important to Dylan than the two women in his life, Elle Fanning's Sylvie and Monica Barbaro's Joan Baez, because being accepted by the most badass white musician alive means a kind of recognition that only the gods can confer. Baez is a competitor who Dylan knows can't write songs as good as his. To her face, he calls them "oil paintings at the dentist's office." It doesn't sting because *A Complete Unknown* has established that Joan only slept with him because of the Cuban Missile Crisis, an example of the film's attitude toward history.

Sylvie, as ignored and sad-faced as she becomes, sums up this movie and the whole adventure of Hollywood movies like this one, when they work. She compares Dylan to a French performer they saw on Ed Sullivan once, who could spin multiple plates on sticks and keep them all going at the same time. "I kinda like that guy!" says Dylan. "Yeah," Sylvie responds, "it's fun to be the guy. But I was a plate."

Anora

The first section of Sean Baker's *Anora* is fast-paced, sexed up, and makes you want to know what's going to happen next, as stripper and escort Anora (Mikey Madison, called Ani) marries her john, Vanya (Mark Eydelshteyn), wastrel son of wealthy Mill Basin Russians. In the second section Vanya scampers off, but we lose the Ani we'd come to know, as she sits passively in the back seat of a car, dragged around by Vanya's father's fixer (Karren Karagulian), who's hunting for Vanya but yells at strangers in restaurants for no reason, wasting screen time. In the third section, Vanya's horrible parents (Aleksei Serebryakov and Darya Ekamasova) show up and demand Ani accompany them to Vegas to have her marriage to Vanya annulled. They drag her onto a plane with transparently idle threats I could not believe she fell for. In the end, the oligarchs win, and Baker presents us with a hopeless world in which the only solace is fucking in grandma's car.

I don't know any Brooklyn girl who would've gotten on that plane. Ani doesn't even have a prenup. The parents offer her $10,000 to piss off, but she's already made $15,000 from a week with Vanya. Pretty sure she can do math. Mikey Madison calls to mind a roster of Brooklyn actresses, starting with Barbara Stanwyck, who wouldn't have put up with any of that. The 1930 Frank Capra movie *Ladies of Leisure* has a very similar plot to *Anora*, and even though it contains one of Stanwyck's more passive lead roles, she still maintains her dignity. Madison is "the kind of woman that makes whole civilizations topple," as somebody says about Stanwyck in *Ball of Fire* (1941), but here nothing topples. And when the Russian mother takes Ani's brand-new sable coat, a gift from Vanya, and throws it in the face of a Las Vegas courthouse worker and lets this random woman keep it, I didn't believe it for a second. Wilder and Brackett would have crumpled that up right after they typed it.

Dune: Part Two

This second *Dune* movie—who knows how many more there will be—begins with bodies being burned in a pile and exudes a general ambience of old-style fascism, which it combines with tropes from 1950s cardboard Roman epics and Youssef Chahine's 1963 *Saladin* film, which is incredibly dull and which I watched once out of boredom. It strives for a Langian *Nibelungen*-ian quality that it is too glacial and pompous to grasp, even in the black-and-white gladiator sections with eyebrowless Austin Butler refusing to take drugs or use AI to kill his opponent. How many gladiators do we need in movies? As the Lang films prefigured German fascism, the *Dune* films prefigure some kind of North American fascism, but they also seem like ads for a fictional French-Canadian oil conglomerate that is destroying the planet.

I can only take so much messiah talk in science fiction, especially when it's coming from Javier Bardem and Timothée Chalamet, both of whom I generally like, but here all I could think about was that they'd played Desi Arnaz and Bob Dylan. Did those two ever meet? This movie takes place in the year 10,191, and once I knew that I kept wondering if movies from the 10,180s and 10,170s were better.

Anya Taylor-Joy shows up, a refugee from *Furiosa*, a much better film set in a much more interesting desert wasteland in a time closer to our own. On the other hand, there is a scene in *Dune: Part Two* where we learn that the Fremen's food is too spicy for some people.

David Lynch

The death of David Lynch in January unleashed a great outpouring of love from cinephiles and other fans unlike anything that has ever happened when any other great film director died. It was immediate and massive, encompassing hundreds of written tributes, hundreds of thousands of posts online, piles of flowers at the Bob's Big Boy where Lynch ate lunch every afternoon for years, with similar tributes at the real-world locations from his work: the Deep River apartment building in Wilmington, North Carolina, where Dorothy Vallens (Isabella Rossellini) lived, the café in North Bend, Washington, that the world knows as the Double-R Diner from *Twin Peaks.*

This spontaneous, worldwide homage to Lynch and his work gave the lie to Hollywood's refusal to back his films and TV series, proving once again that they only make what they want to make. Does anyone actually think that unfilmed Lynch screenplays like *One Saliva Bubble* or *Ronnie Rocket* would have done less well than such unnecessary garbage as last year's *Madame Web*, *AFRAID*, or *Borderlands*? And every Lynch film has grown in stature with time.

It's important to remember that even as Hollywood was ignoring Lynch, much of the mainstream, middlebrow critical establishment in the US was also disparaging his work. It wasn't just that it was too weird. It elicited really hateful reactions from Siskel & Ebert, among others. At the *New Yorker*, one of the film critics instantly dismissed *Twin Peaks: The Return* as soon as the first episode ended, tweeting that Lynch had been superseded by Wes Anderson, and their TV critic simply refused to watch it, while at the same time insisting it was TV, not cinema. Even the highest-browed American,

Fredric Jameson, who died four months before Lynch, saw in Lynch's work some kind of threat, writing against him in *Postmodernism, or, the Cultural Logic of Late Capitalism* by calling his work "evil." Just last summer, Phillip Lopate's latest collection of his film criticism, *My Affair with Art House Cinema,* came out, and included a piece on the inadequacy of *Mulholland Drive* in which this dean of American film critics described Lynch as "prone to jejune self-indulgence, capricious phantasmagoria, and vulgarity."

Such big, dismissive words! As for me, my mind was blown open by *Blue Velvet* when I saw it college-aged in first run in 1986 at the Nickelodeon Cinema in Boston with my then-girlfriend. We could not speak when we left the theater, so rattled were we by this terrifying new thing that had come into the world (the same summer and fall as *Down by Law, She's Gotta Have It, Big Trouble in Little China,* and *Something Wild*). This filmic world of smashed TVs, diners, wood paneling, the ominous hum of electricity, and rose-pink wall-to-wall carpeting was not, as some viewers may now think, an alien place. It was the actual America of that time, put on screen by David Lynch in a way no one had ever seen before.

I was working at the Nickelodeon then and I wanted to learn to be a projectionist. The guy who ran the booth would let me come in and watch him make up the reels for the platters, and I heard *Blue Velvet* as much as I saw it. I know every line in it, the famous ones of course ("Do it!"), but also things like "If you want to spray for bugs, it causes us no pain" and "Oh, you're from the neighborhood?" and "I'll go one, two, three, four," which have really stuck with me.

"Hell arrives tomorrow when we bring in the cardinals." Seeing *Conclave,* which also features Rossellini, this same season in which the Los Angeles wildfires shortened David Lynch's life recalls something else Laura Dern says in *Blue Velvet*: "There is trouble until the robins come." As for the Oscar-nominated movies of 2025, a line that Bob, the director in *Mulholland Drive,* not the all-pervasive evil presence from *Twin Peaks,* says to Naomi Watts comes to mind: "I mean, it was forced, maybe, but still humanistic."

ENEMY OF THE GOOD

AI IN FILM

THE NOTION OF AUTHENTICITY IN THE MOVIES HAS MOVED A STEP BEYOND the merely realistic. More and more, expensive and time-consuming fixes to minor issues of screen realism have become the work of statistical data renderings—the visual or aural products of generative artificial intelligence. Deployed for effects that actors used to have to create themselves, with their own faces, bodies, and voices, filmmakers now deem these fixes necessary because they are more authentic than what actors can do with just their imaginations, wardrobe, makeup, and lighting. The paradox is that in this scenario, "authentic" means inhuman: The further from actual humanity these efforts have moved, the more we see them described by filmmakers as "perfect."

Is perfect the enemy of good? It doesn't seem to matter to many filmmakers working today. These fixes are designed to be imperceptible to humans, anyway. Director Brady Corbet's obsession with "perfect" Hungarian accents in his Oscar-nominated architecture epic, *The Brutalist,* is a case in point. Corbet hired the Ukraine-based software company Respeecher to enhance accents by using AI to smooth out vowel sounds when actors Adrien Brody and Felicity Jones (American and British, respectively) speak Hungarian in the film. Corbet said it was necessary to do that because, as he told the

Los Angeles Times, "this was the only way for us to achieve something completely authentic."

Authenticity here meant integrating the voice of the film's editor, Dávid Jancsó, who accurately articulated the correct vowel sounds. Jancsó's pronunciation was then combined with the audio track featuring Brody and Jones, merging them into a purportedly flawless rendition of Hungarian that would, in Corbet's words in an interview with *GQ*, "honor the nation of Hungary by making all of their offscreen Hungarian dialogue absolutely perfect."

The issue of accents in movies has come to the fore in recent years. Adam Driver and Shailene Woodley were, for instance, criticized for their uncertain Italian accents in 2023's *Ferrari*. Corbet evidently wanted to make sure that would not happen if any native Hungarian speakers were watching *The Brutalist* (few others would notice the difference). At times, Brody and Jones speak in Hungarian in the film, but mostly they speak in Hungarian-accented English. According to Corbet, Respeecher was not used for that dialogue.

Let's say that for Corbet this will to perfection, with the time and expense it entailed, was necessary to his process, and that having the voice-overs in translated Hungarian-accented English might have been insultingly inauthentic to the people of Hungary, making it essential that the movie sound, at all times, 100 percent correct when Hungarian was spoken. Still, whether the Hungarian we hear in *The Brutalist* is "absolutely perfect" is not the same as it being "completely authentic," since it was never uttered as we hear it by any human being. And, as it turns out, it was partially created in reaction to something that doesn't exist.

In his interview with the *Los Angeles Times*, Corbet said that he "would never have done it any other way," recounting when he and his daughter "were watching *North by Northwest* and there's a sequence at the UN, and my daughter is half-Norwegian, and two characters are speaking to each other in [air quotes] Norwegian. My daughter said: 'They're speaking gibberish.' And I think that's how we used to paint people brown, right? And, I think that for me, that's a lot more offensive than using innovative technology and really brilliant engineers to help us make something perfect."

But there is no scene in Alfred Hitchcock's 1959 film *North by Northwest* set at the United Nations or anywhere else in which two characters speak fake Norwegian or any other faked language. Furthermore, when Corbet brings in the racist practice of brownface makeup that marred movies like 1961's *West Side Story,* he is doing a further disservice to Hitchcock's film. The UN scene in *North by Northwest* features Cary Grant speaking with a South Asian receptionist played by Doris Singh, not an Anglo in brownface.

Corbet's use of AI, then, is based on something that AI itself is prone to, and criticized for: a "hallucination" in which previously stored data is incorrectly combined to fabricate details and generate false information that tends toward gibberish. While the beginning of Hitchcock's *Torn Curtain* (1966) is set on a ship in a Norwegian fjord and briefly shows two ship's officers conversing in a faked, partial Norwegian, Corbet's justification was based on a false memory. His argument against inauthenticity is inauthentic itself.

AI WAS USED LAST YEAR in other films besides *The Brutalist.* Respeecher also "corrected" the pitch of trans actress Karla Sofía Gascón's singing voice in *Emilia Pérez.* It was used for blue eye color in *Dune: Part Two.* It was used to blend the face of Anya Taylor-Joy with the actress playing a younger version of her, Alyla Browne, in *Furiosa: A Mad Max Saga.* Robert Zemeckis's *Here,* with Tom Hanks and Robin Wright playing a married couple over a many-decade span, deployed a complicated "youth mirror system" that used AI in the extensive de-agings of the two stars. *Alien: Romulus* brought the late actor Ian Holm back to onscreen life, reviving him from the original 1979 *Alien* in a move derided not only as ethically dubious but, in its execution, cheesy and inadequate.

It is when AI is used in documentaries to re-create the speech of people who have died that is especially susceptible to accusations of both cheesiness and moral irresponsibility. The 2021 documentary

Roadrunner: A Film About Anthony Bourdain used an AI version of the late chef and author's voice for certain lines spoken in the film, which "provoked a striking degree of anger and unease among Bourdain's fans," according to the *New Yorker*. These fans called resurrecting Bourdain that way "ghoulish" and "awful."

Audience reactions like these, though frequent, do little to dissuade filmmakers from using complicated AI technology where it isn't needed. In last year's documentary *Endurance*, about explorer Ernest Shackleton's ill-fated expedition to the South Pole from 1914 to 1916, filmmakers used Respeecher to exhume Shackleton from the only known recording of his voice, a noise-ridden four-minute Edison wax cylinder on which the explorer is yelling into a megaphone. Respeecher extracted from this something "authentic" which is said to have duplicated Shackleton's voice for use in the documentary. This ghostly, not to say creepy, version of Shackleton became a selling point for the film, and answered the question, "What might Ernest Shackleton have sounded like if he were not shouting into a cone and recorded on wax that has deteriorated over a period of 110 years?" Surely an actor could have done as well as Respeecher with that question.

Similarly, a new three-part Netflix documentary series, *American Murder: Gabby Petito*, has elicited discomfort from viewers for using an AI-generated voice-over of Petito as its narration. The 22-year-old was murdered by her fiancé in 2021, and X users have called exploiting a homicide victim this way "unsettling," "deeply uncomfortable," and perhaps just as accurately, "wholly unnecessary." The dead have no say in how their actual voices are used. It is hard to see resurrecting Petito that way as anything but a macabre selling point—carnival exploitation for the streaming era.

BESIDE THE REANIMATION of Petito and the creation of other spectral voices from beyond the grave, there is a core belief that the proponents of AI enact but never state, one particularly apropos in a boomer gerontocracy in which the aged refuse to relinquish power.

That belief is that older is actually younger. When an actor has to be de-aged for a role, such as Harrison Ford in 2023's *Indiana Jones and the Dial of Destiny*, AI is enlisted to scan all of Ford's *old* films to make him *young* in the present, dialing back time to overwrite reality with an image of the past. Making a present-day version of someone young involves resuscitating a record of a younger version of them, like in *The Substance* but without a syringe filled with yellow serum.

When it comes to voices, therefore, it is not just the dead who need to be revived. Ford's *Star Wars* compatriot Mark Hamill had a similar process done, but only to his voice. For an episode of *The Mandalorian*, Hamill's voice had to be resynthesized by Respeecher to sound like it did in 1977. Respeecher did the same with British singer Robbie Williams for his recent biopic, *Better Man*, using versions of Williams's songs from his heyday and combining his voice with that of another singer to make him sound like he did in the 1990s.

While Zemeckis was shooting *Here*, the "youth mirror system" he and his AI team devised consisted of two monitors that showed scenes as they were shot, one the real footage of the actors un-aged, as they appear in real life, and the other using AI to show the actors to themselves at the age they were supposed to be playing. Zemeckis told the *New York Times* that this was "crucial." Tom Hanks, the director explained, could see this and say to himself, "I've got to make sure I'm moving like I was when I was 17 years old."

"No one had to imagine it," Zemeckis said. "They got the chance to see it in real time." *No one had to imagine it* is not a phrase heretofore associated with actors or the direction of actors.

Nicolas Cage is a good counter example to this kind of work, which as we see goes far beyond perfecting Hungarian accents. Throughout 2024, Cage spoke against AI every chance he got. At an acceptance speech at the recent Saturn Awards, he mentioned that he is "a big believer in not letting robots dream for us. Robots cannot reflect the human condition for us. That is a dead end. If an actor lets one AI robot manipulate his or her performance even a little bit, an inch will eventually become a mile and all integrity, purity, and truth of art will be replaced by financial interests only."

In a speech to young actors last year, Cage said, "The studios want this so that they can change your face after you've already shot it. They can change your face, they can change your voice, they can change your line deliveries, they can change your body language, they can change your performance." And he said in a *New Yorker* interview last year, speaking about the way the studios are using AI, "What are you going to do with my body and my face when I'm dead? I don't want you to do anything with it!" All this from a man who swapped faces with John Travolta in 1997's *Face/Off* with no AI required—and "face replacement" is now one of the main things AI is used for.

In an interview with Yahoo Entertainment, Cage shared an anecdote about his recent cameo appearance as a version of Superman in the much-reviled 2023 superhero movie *The Flash*. "What I was supposed to do was literally just be standing in an alternate dimension, if you will, and witnessing the destruction of the universe. . . . And you can imagine with that short amount of time that I had, what that would mean in terms of what I could convey—I had no dialogue—what I could convey with my eyes, the emotion. . . . When I went to the picture, it was me fighting a giant spider. . . . They de-aged me and I'm fighting a spider."

Now that's authenticity.

MOVIE STARS IN BATHTUBS

48 MOVIES AND 2 INCIDENTS

Les Vampires (Louis Feuillade, 1916, France)

The fifth episode of the mysterious saga alternates scenes of people returning to consciousness and people losing it. The thief Moréno (Fernand Herrmann), archrival of the Vampires criminal gang, swallows what appears to be a suicide pill. Reporter Philippe Guérande (Édouard Mathé), conked by the Vampires, awakens in a basket tumbling down a long flight of stairs. Most memorably, the Grand Vampire (Jean Aymé) and Irma Vep (Musidora) disguise themselves as a baron and his niece to host a society ball where they gas dozens of rich people, taking their jewels and fat wallets when they succumb.

Feuillade's camera dollies past the hands of party guests clawing to escape the sealed room. The Vampires, silhouettes framed in doorways, led by Irma in her skintight black suit, descend on the sleeping guests like the gas or like dreams. This French serial introduced the supervillain and the sexy accomplice who wear disguises and turn the devices of modernity against the people they were invented to help. It made criminal anarchy and terror into entertainment, which Feuillade made into art.

Feuillade filmed his exteriors in Paris locations that the First World War had emptied of people. The idea that places and objects recorded by the movie camera shimmer with life and might be trying to tell us something dates from encounters with Feuillade's crime serials. "It is in *Les Vampires* that one must look for the great reality of our century—they are beyond fashion and beyond taste," wrote the surrealists Aragon and Breton.

Nanook of the North (Robert Flaherty, 1922, USA)

Flaherty got the idea to make a film of Inuit life while working as an explorer for a railway company in northern Quebec in the 1910s. A fur company set him up with movie equipment, but he rejected his initial efforts as amateurish, and he lost other attempts in a fire. Working slowly in the cold of the "illimitable spaces which top the world," aided by the Inuit who appeared in his film as versions of themselves, Flaherty finished his work, which he conceived as a story film as much as an ethnographic record, and released it to theaters. It succeeded and made Nanook the Eskimo a household name; the man who played him (Allakariallak) died of starvation "in the actual Arctic" six months after the film came out.

Nanook enters our consciousness from within the white of the frame. He pushes himself out from inside an igloo he has just built. The film ends in a nighttime so real it's like science fiction. We leave Nanook as he falls asleep.

Almost ninety years after its release, *Nanook of the North* is still controversial; Flaherty is taken to task for exploiting his cast and for not making a "real" documentary. But it is a harsh writer who would criticize the scene—a remarkable scene about sound in a silent movie—in which a white trader plays a gramophone and Nanook takes off the record and bites it. Who hasn't loved a record so much they wanted to bite it?

The Docks of New York (Josef von Sternberg, 1928, USA)

Not a lot is known about Jules Furthman. He was a Chicago newspaperman who got to Hollywood about ten years before Ben Hecht did and wrote screenplays for von Sternberg and Hawks. Leigh Brackett, who wrote scripts with him even though she was thirty years his junior, said he was the kind of writer who didn't like to write things down. He wrote over a hundred films, the first in 1915, the last in 1959 (*Rio Bravo*, with Brackett). In his Hawks biography, Todd McCarthy describes Furthman as cantankerous and quotes Hawks as saying only he, von Sternberg, and Victor Fleming would work with him. "He was such a mean guy we thought he was great," Hawks explained.

Furthman specialized in unclassy tales of redemption in tawdry settings, featuring charming semi-brutal men and glamorous women who were a little ruined, people in trouble who rise to the occasion against their instincts. His women could be Dietrich or Bacall, his men Bogart or John Wayne. In *The Docks of New York*, George Bancroft's stoker and Betty Compson's Mae are more primitive versions, violent, romantic, and drunk. The originals, concocted out of who knows who or what, lived in Furthman's head. Certain gestures of theirs cross between the films of the directors Furthman worked with, gestures that must be attributable to him. They can be seen in everything Furthman worked on: *China Seas* (1935), a Clark Gable movie directed by Tay Garnett, plays like knock-off von Sternberg or Hawks wafting over MGM.

1932: Shiro Kido tells Mikio Naruse he doesn't need another Ozu

Only one of the first sixteen films Mikio Naruse made survives. It's called *Flunky, Work Hard!* After ten years at Shochiku, after being passed over for Heinosuke Gosho and Yasujiro Ozu, who'd started in the film industry after him, in 1930 Naruse finally got to direct a film. He had to shoot it non-stop in thirty-six hours. When he finished he collapsed.

According to Audie Bock's book *Japanese Film Directors*, in the early 1930s Naruse was making the equivalent of $360 a month as a salaried director at Shochiku and living in a rented room over a sushi place. He got meal tickets from the studio, which he traded for cigarettes, choosing to eat alone in cheap bars. One film he made was shelved because studio boss Shiro Kido thought it was too much like an Ozu movie. Kido kept Naruse on, but in 1932 he took him aside and explained that Shochiku didn't need two Ozus. While he was at it Kido threw in that Naruse shouldn't imitate Hiroshi Shimizu, Gosho, or Yasujiro Shimazu, either.

Today it's hard to believe this happened. Imitations of hit films are exactly what producers want. Kido's insult forced Naruse to look for stories in the harsh world where he was eating lunch. The name of the film Naruse was working on when he had his conversation with Kido? *Be Great!* For the next thirty-five years Naruse made films "with the thought that the world we live in betrays us," poignant films that stand on their own next to the best ones made anywhere.

Scarface (Howard Hawks, 1932, USA)

Among other things, Ben Hecht was a Chicago newspaperman, a playwright, author of maybe the funniest American novel, recipient of the call-to-Hollywood telegram from Herman J. Mankiewicz that read "millions to be grabbed out here and your only competition is idiots," and screenwriter of the original *Scarface*.

Hecht arrived in Hollywood at the end of the silent era. He wrote Sternberg's *Underworld*, the first gangster picture, then worked on thirteen dozen other movies, often without credit.

He told *Scarface* producer Howard Hughes he could double the body count of any previous gangster film and write one twice as good, then worked out a payment arrangement designed to add to his image as a hired gun. Hughes had to pay him a thousand dollars in cash every night at six until he finished the first draft. He finished in eleven days. He wrote the final draft with Hawks on a train to New York on their way to test Paul Muni for the title part, Tony Camonte.

Hecht defines the writer-producer relationship in a speech Camonte makes to his boss. "There's only one thing that gets orders and gives orders, and this is it," Camonte says, indicating his machine gun. "That's how I got the South Side for you and that's how I'm gonna get the North Side for you. It's a little typewriter, right? I'm gonna write my name all over this town with it, in big letters. Get outta my way, I'm gonna spit!" he yells, and starts firing.

It's a Gift (Norman Z. McLeod, 1934, USA)

There isn't a better illustration of unsparing W. C. Fields comedy than this portrait of Mr. Muckle, a hostile, uncontrollable blind man. While scrambling to fill an obstreperous customer's order for "ten pounds of kumquats," Fields notices that outside a black-clad figure in sunglasses is making a beeline for his store carrying a cane. Fields immediately stops what he's doing, points, and yells "Open the door for Mr. Muckle!"

Already something has been set in motion that has happened before and is too late to stop. Suddenly Muckle is upon Fields and us and the world. Muckle crashes his cane through the store's glass door, points out that "you got that door closed again," and falls into a stack of boxes. To add to the scene's audacity, Fields tries to placate and console this intractable old man, who is also partially deaf and has to be shouted at through an ear trumpet, by calling him "honey" and "dear." When he hands Muckle the five-cent pack of gum he came in for, the blind man refuses to "lug that with me" and insists it be delivered.

Here Fields sets up his world, where slow-moving forces of mulish humanity become like the objects (light bulbs, coconuts, ice picks) they use to bedevil him. For Fields, Depression-era America was a combination of *The Grapes of Wrath* ("Shades of Bacchus!" he exclaims at one point) and *L'Age d'or*, with all the frustrating sadness and bitter absurdity that coupling implies.

The Awful Truth (Leo McCarey, 1937, USA)

Near the start of *The Awful Truth* McCarey cuts to an insert of a toy that Jerry Warriner (Cary Grant) shows his dog, Mr. Smith (Asta, of the *Thin Man* movies). It's a tennis-size ball in the form of a Chihuahua's head with poppy eyes. Breaking into a scene that way was unusual in a Hollywood film then, but the ball gets a closeup all its own. Jerry's wife, Lucy (Irene Dunne) throws it for Mr. Smith, who chases it.

Jerry and Lucy have decided to separate. In the next scene, divorce proceedings are ending, but the matter of who will get custody of Mr. Smith isn't settled. The judge (Paul Stanton) orders the fox terrier into court. "Custody of the dog will depend on his own desires," he tells the couple. "Will you each call the dog?"

Jerry and Lucy position Mr. Smith between them, imploring him with here-boys and clapping. Jerry seems to be winning, so Lucy surreptitiously nods the doghead toy at Mr. Smith. He jumps in her lap. Case closed. Now we see why McCarey highlighted the toy earlier.

Jerry and Lucy compete for Mr. Smith's attention the way Grant and Dunne compete for ours. They are so captivating that without realizing it we willingly put ourselves in the position of a dog choosing between masters. McCarey's doggie reaction shots aren't too cute; Mr. Smith doesn't cock his head or whine. He's a sober audience conned by a little trick Lucy uses to make him love her more.

Grand Illusion (Jean Renoir, 1937, France)

Englishmen in drag singing "It's a Long Way to Tipperary" is not exactly what you'd expect in a French prisoner-of-war film, but this famous scene from Renoir's *Grand Illusion* achieves a resolute toughness that explains its classic status. The film breathes where other prison-camp movies stifle.

The scene begins in full-on goofiness during a prisoners' variety show. A tuxedoed prisoner named Cartier (Julien Carette), a music-hall comic in civilian life, leads a troupe of English officers dressed as showgirls. Their performance erases the difference between the prisoners and their German guards by reminding them of the world they've left behind for the Great War's mud: the city life of women and music. As Cartier good-naturedly thumbs his nose at a guard, Renoir cuts to French prisoners Maréchal (Jean Gabin) and Rosenthal (Marcel Dalio) backstage reading a newspaper. Maréchal takes the stage: "Stop! Stop! We've retaken Douaumont!"

One of the Englishmen removes his wig and requests that the band play the "Marseillaise." He begins to sing in his lipstick and off-the-shoulder dress. The camera pans past the musicians, including a trumpet player who rolls his eyes upward like he's trying to remember the song. Maréchal and Rosenthal, in black sweaters, look down toward the German guards. The camera follows, crossing a pillar to find the audience of prisoners on their feet, singing the anthem sternly but almost placidly. Unstructured, amateurish nonsense coalesces into meaning and beauty. The variety show's foolishness doesn't just stand in for the civilization the war leaves behind—it becomes its living proof.

Ninotchka (Ernst Lubitsch, 1939, USA)

In 1939 Shirley Temple, age 11, was tops at the box office. Glamorous stars like Greta Garbo were considered unwholesome. The year before, the *Hollywood Reporter* had declared her "box office poison." But Garbo laughed in *Ninotchka*, and America went through a spell of adulthood that lasted until *Gone with the Wind* came out—about two months.

We meet Nina Ivanovna Yakushova (Garbo), special envoy from Moscow, on a Paris train platform. She wears a plain suit, a hat with the brim down, and men's shoes. When a porter (George Davis) explains it's his business to carry her bags, she tells him, "That's no business. That's *social injustice*." Three comrades (Felix Bressart, Sig Ruman, and Alexander Granach) take her to her hotel room, passing a fancy hat shop in the lobby. She looks in the window: "What is that?" "A woman's hat," answers one of the Russians. "How can such a civilization survive which permits their women to put things like that on their heads? It won't be long now, comrades," she says, raising an eyebrow at the doomed frivolity of the capitalist West.

Lubitsch predicts the history of the Soviet Union in the story of this hat. Ninotchka shakes her head at it a second time before we meet it again as she takes it out of a locked drawer to wear on a date with a handsome Frenchman (Melvyn Douglas). This is the cinema's lightest and sharpest appraisal of communism. Only Lubitsch would have the nonchalance to reject it, by the end of the film, for making an omelet fall.

The Magnificent Ambersons (Orson Welles, 1942, USA)

In the spring of 1942 when Orson Welles was in South America making *It's All True* at RKO's behest, the studio previewed *The Magnificent Ambersons* after a showing of *The Fleet's In*, a musical comedy. Kids in the audience who had come to see Betty Hutton sing and dance hooted Welles's bittersweet masterpiece and wrote they didn't like it on preview cards. An RKO producer sent Welles a mewling telegram right away: "Never in all my experience in the industry have I taken so much punishment or suffered as I did at the Pomona preview."

RKO removed over fifty minutes of Welles's cut and threw away the negative. In Welles's absence the producers demanded that editor Robert Wise and the Mercury unit shoot a couple of new scenes to patch up what was missing and tack them to the end of the film. The studio released *The Magnificent Ambersons* in July 1942 with a running time of eighty-eight minutes—there's something insulting about that number, like a full ninety minutes wouldn't have left enough room for *Mexican Spitfire Sees a Ghost*, the movie RKO tied to *The Magnificent Ambersons* in a double feature before they dumped it into theaters.

The butchering of *The Magnificent Ambersons* is indefensible, yet Welles critics have been making excuses for it for years. Significantly, it happened during wartime, when hysteria becomes internalized and can leach into anything. "There aren't any times but new times," says the automobile inventor Joseph Cotton plays in the film. Editing by preview card is still with us. This was its low point, the most final cut in film history.

***The Woman in the Window* (Fritz Lang, 1944, USA)**

It's based on a novel that ends with the protagonist's suicide, unacceptable to Hollywood in 1944, so Lang contrived to end *The Woman in the Window* in a dream instead.

Richard Wanley (Edward G. Robinson), a professor of criminal psychology with a wife and two children, has a problem. After Wanley kills a man (Arthur Loft) in the apartment of a woman (Joan Bennett) he barely knows, he's embroiled in a blackmail scheme from which he can't escape. Desperate, this middle-class everyman drinks poison, then takes a seat next to a table holding photographs of his family. As he loses consciousness the phone on the table rings—it's a call exonerating him. He doesn't answer it. The clock behind him chimes. The camera dollies in for a closeup—Wanley is dead. Then a hand enters the frame and shakes his shoulder: "It's 10:30, Professor Wanley."

Wanley wakes up. He's in his club, not at home. The camera pulls back. Without a cut Lang has changed the set and Wanley's outfit. The glass in his hand is no longer poison but brandy. Wanley stands, finishes his drink, and exits. The people he meets on his way out—the hatcheck guy, the doorman—are the villains from his dream.

Lang acknowledged "it was only a dream" endings were old hat. Yet this well-executed ending adds something that would not have been there had Wanley killed himself. The dream ending is a negation that moves the film out the door and back into real life.

White Heat (Raoul Walsh, 1949, USA)

Before *White Heat* no gangster film had featured anybody like Cody Jarrett (James Cagney). The film is set in the prewar Warner Bros. tradition but takes place in a postwar world still reeling from Hitler and Hiroshima.

Walsh sets the scene quietly for Cody's possibly epileptic prison breakdown. There is nothing wasteful here. The scene runs exactly three minutes. Three hundred convicts file silently into a mess hall under guard. A whistle blows. Cody sits and notices a new prisoner, a member of a gang that works the same territory he does, and under his breath he passes a question about his mother to him, down the line of cons sitting next to him until it reaches the new guy. The camera dollies across the men and back as they whisper the words "she's dead" one after another until the news reaches Cody. We know Cody is neurotically dependent on his mother, but we can't predict his reaction. He slams down his cup, stands on the table, slides himself across it and attacks the guards. They manage to subdue him and carry him out as he makes animal noises, the only sounds we hear as the other prisoners gape silently. Cagney didn't tell Walsh what he was going to do in this scene, so the extras didn't know either. Their stunned reaction mimics ours.

Cagney's performance is not gratuitous. It is structured, formidable. That Cagney decided *White Heat* was what he should do after twenty years in movies is a testament to his originality.

Los Olvidados (Luis Buñuel, 1950, Mexico)

In 1929, after the Paris theater where it was booked refused to screen it, Buñuel and Salvador Dalí's *Un Chien Andalou* became a succès de scandale. At showings of 1930's *L'Age d'or*, Buñuel's next film, angry Parisians threw ink at the screen and yelled "Death to the Jews!" at this film by a Catholic from Spain. A friend of Buñuel's won a lottery, so in 1933, Buñuel made *Las Hurdes*, a documentary about a backward region of Spain promptly banned by the Spanish government. Buñuel left for Hollywood and New York, where he looked on as his erstwhile partner Dalí became a celebrity who resembled, according to Max Ernst, "those horrid jellies Americans eat for dessert."

Frustrated, in 1945 Buñuel moved to Mexico. The reputations of his three films grew, but as far as anyone knew he was out of filmmaking. In Mexico he made a couple of low-budget genre films. One flopped, but one did OK and in 1950 Buñuel made *Los Olvidados*, a story of Mexico City street kids that synthesized Val Lewton horror and neorealism—it put the realism back in surrealism, mixing poverty and nightmares. One of the kids in it tosses a raw egg into the camera lens.

Buñuel had stayed true to his vision through bad jobs, short funds, and seventeen years of projects that never got off the ground. While *Los Olvidados* was met with protest in Mexico, it won two prizes at Cannes and allowed him to make twenty-six films over the next twenty-six years.

In a Lonely Place (Nicholas Ray, 1950, USA)

In a typical case of tone-deafness, studio publicity described the ending of *In a Lonely Place* when it came out as a "stunning surprise climax." Only in Hollywood could somebody's innocence be touted as shock. But if what they meant was that the climax was emotionally devastating, and that emotional devastation was unexpected in a studio film, they had a point. Inner conflict structures every scene in this film. By its end, everything, even the way Humphrey Bogart puts down a telephone receiver to make two black holes in the frame, adds to its heartache.

"Can't you relax for a second?" Gloria Grahame's Laurel asks Bogart's Dixon Steele. He can't. Steele, a Hollywood screenwriter, exists in the tension between creative work and real life. His fear of being misunderstood and punished for being right plagues him, makes him lash out, and poisons his relationships. We see it happen in wrenching closeups of Laurel's face as she looks at him. In the film's last scene, Ray keeps subtly emptying the frame until Dix and Laurel break up and disappear, he through an arch that leads to the street, she behind a door she closes.

It's not just the end, but the film's whole last half hour that wrecks you. Ray couples anger to tenderness. Dix beats up a guy, then delivers the film's (maybe any film's) most romantic lines. He describes a "good love scene" to the woman he loves even as she realizes she has to leave him.

1951: The first issue of Cahiers du cinéma

When book reviewers read in Colin McCabe's biography of Jean-Luc Godard that *Cahiers du cinéma* was "the most significant cultural journal of the 20th century" they couldn't wait to jump on him for laying it on so thick. What do they know? There is film criticism before *Cahiers du cinéma* and film criticism after it. Because of the tremendous impact of the Nouvelle vague, which sprang from its pages, there is visual culture (and the analysis of visual culture) before and after *Cahiers du cinéma*, too.

The magazine's presiding figure was André Bazin, a tireless worker in the postwar French ciné-club movement who contributed to the *Revue du cinéma* and other journals. When the *Revue*'s editor died, Jacques Doniol-Valcroze and Bazin found financing and in April 1951 began publishing *Cahiers* in Paris. The magazine hired young writers from ciné-club newsletters, the habitués of the Cinémathèque Française who later formed the nucleus of the French New Wave—Eric Rohmer, Jacques Rivette, François Truffaut, Claude Chabrol, and Jean-Luc Godard. They favored Rossellini and Hollywood genre movies over the "quality" films they saw stultifying French cinema.

Unlike film critics today, these writers did not complain that they were powerless. They defended the movies they loved and excoriated the ones they hated. For them film criticism was a confrontation, its goal to change how films were viewed and how they were made. The magazine's polarizing "auteur theory" was attacked with the vehemence that heralds artistic breakthrough. By the decade's end the group's first films came out.

The Big Knife (Robert Aldrich, 1955, USA)

Rod Steiger, as magnetic as fellow Method actor Marlon Brando, wasn't handsome like Brando. In the 1950s he didn't get leads in prestige pictures like Brando did. Bitter or not, in *The Big Knife* Steiger unleashed all the contempt he could muster for "profession: movie star." As studio head Stanley Hoff he slides like an anaconda into the Bel-Air pad of star actor Charlie Castle (Jack Palance) and squeezes him to death.

Steiger, who was 31 when Aldrich filmed this Clifford Odets adaptation, plays an older man. He's hardened with a Mabuse-like armor: sunglasses, hearing aid, black suit, white crew cut. The air fills with Hoff disparagement before he shows up. We're told he's crass, that he's not one of the producers who make movies with "guts and meaning" like Stanley Kramer. By the time he arrives to blackmail Charlie into renewing his contract, talk like that has paradoxically won him our sympathy. Steiger's great philistine totally dominates his two long scenes. Even cowering like a turtle before Charlie's manliness he turns himself into an X that blots out everything. Then he explodes like a neutron bomb, leaving the set standing but obliterating the people.

"Who *are* you?" he howls at Charlie. "Some kind of special aristocracy because the female public wants to make love with you? I built the studio! I ripped it out of the world with *my* brains and *my* hands and *who—are—you?*" He exits exulting in himself like he's holding a shell to his ear to catch echoes of his greatness.

Ride Lonesome **(Budd Boetticher, 1959, USA)**

The characters in *Ride Lonesome* cross the desert toward a dead tree that's ghostlike, the destination of a bounty hunter named Ben Brigade (Randolph Scott). Brigade insists he's taking the killer he has in custody to a town called Santa Cruz, then the tree appears. Boone (Pernell Roberts), an outlaw competing with Brigade for his captive, knows this tree, a "hang tree" with a "jury limb," and so does Brigade. Night falls (an indigo day-for-night) and the men make camp near the tree with Mrs. Lane (Karen Steele), a young widow they've saved from marauding Apaches.

If *Ride Lonesome* is the best of the seven westerns Boetticher made with Scott, it has a lot to do with this night scene, a dark idyll before the film's showdown. The tree looms in the background as the woman they've rescued crosses between the two men. While Boone stares at her, Brigade's gaze is fixed on the dead tree, which Boetticher contrasts with the blonde's shapely form. For Boone Mrs.

Lane represents the possibility of a new life. For Brigade she embodies a past he's come to avenge. And for both men the tree is a death they may not escape.

Nothing is wasted in the stripped-down clarity of *Ride Lonesome*'s eighty minutes. This is the apotheosis of the classical western, which ends with Boetticher. The hang tree burns in the film's last shot, taking the genre with it.

Eyes Without a Face (Georges Franju, 1960, France)

Images of trees define Franju's black-and-white horror film, which is saying a lot considering a young woman's face is surgically removed in it. Lit by the headlights of a car, trees emerge from the inky night like bioluminescent coral. During the day they are silhouettes against the cloudless late-autumn sky.

White trees are the first things we see in the film, and the last. A dead woman's white legs remind us of them; they stick out from behind the shiny black raincoat of the woman (Alida Valli) dumping the corpse in the Seine. Cinematographer Eugen Shüfftan is careful to get the reflections of trees on the hood of the surgeon's (Pierre Brasseur's) sedan whenever he pulls up—black on black. At a funeral bare trees point above the crosses stuck in the ground. The surgeon and his assistant lure a young woman (Juliette Mayniel) to his suburban clinic by mentioning trees: "You'll love it there, it's surrounded by trees." The film is matter-of-fact about everything, but the word starts to sound ominous: "I'll show you your room, it looks out over . . . *the trees*."

Franju and Shüfftan denature these trees. Without leaves they are skeletal, bodies without flesh. The sounds of nonmigratory birds and chained dogs barking dot the soundtrack like the trees line the picture. In *Eyes Without a Face*, the natural doesn't exist anymore, but it hasn't been replaced by anything.

Breakfast at Tiffany's (Blake Edwards, 1961, USA)

The party in Holly Golightly's (Audrey Hepburn's) one-bedroom Manhattan apartment starts out slowly with Holly's agent (Martin Balsam) telling stories about her to her new neighbor, Paul (George Peppard). Is she a fake phony or a real phony? It's better to be a real phony. She's a real phony, they decide. The place begins to get crowded. Somebody's hat catches fire. Mag Wildwood (Dorothy Whitney), a loud model, shows up with a couple of rich guys (José Luis de Villalonga and Stanley Adams). Mag gets trashed and collapses. Nobody cares. When the booze runs out a delivery boy brings more. Oh yeah, lots of smoking. The mambo music is loud and the upstairs neighbor (Mickey Rooney, in an infamous performance) calls to complain. The phone is hard to get to—it's in a closed suitcase. The place is wall-to-wall people, well dressed but not stiffs. You can't move. People are making out in the shower. This is what people move to New York for and what they want out of a party once they're there: proximity!

The party scene is slapstick relief after a lot of talking and setting up, which is what a party's supposed to be. Edwards doesn't cut it into pieces. It's all easy, loping group shots following people from place to place. Before this scene, Paul was a writer-schnook-gigolo. Now he starts to seem decent. Not so Holly, who exits on the arm of a fat, giggling millionaire and directs the cops upstairs to her own apartment to shut the party down.

Contempt (Jean-Luc Godard, 1963, France)

Earlier in *Contempt* Fritz Lang (playing himself) asks translator Francesca Vanini (Giorgia Moll) the Italian word for "strange." The word lingers over unhappy husband and wife Paul (Michel Piccoli) and Camille (Brigitte Bardot) as they arrive at a movie theater where

Paul, a writer, is meeting Lang and an American film producer (Jack Palance) to discuss their screen adaptation of *The Odyssey.*

They enter under a poster for *Rome Adventure* and leave under a marquee announcing *Voyage in Italy.* This is the transition scene between their stay at Cinecittà and their departure for Capri. Auditioning a girl singer to play a role in *The Odyssey* provides an excuse for the movie-theater setting. Italian pop blares as they take their seats across the aisle from each other, Camille next to Lang, Paul next to the producer. Francesca, translating their conversation, and a photographer taking flash pictures divide the space between them. The camera dollies back and forth as the singer dances across the stage mouthing the song's lyrics out of sync in front of the movie screen. As the foursome talk the camera dollies across the aisle, too, but Godard cuts out the music so we can hear them speaking. It's simple, but jarring in the way it's "wrong."

This veiled criticism of dubbed sound in Italian movies, along with Lang's explanation of unity in Homer, mirrors the couple's break. Everything is separation: between image and sound in dubbed movies, between mankind today and in *The Odyssey,* between wholeness and Godardian fragmentation, between integrity and corruption, between lovers drifting apart.

The Killers (Don Siegel, 1964, USA)

When Siegel made this adaptation-remake of Hemingway's short story, Lee Marvin was starring on TV, but in movies he specialized in playing violent, sarcastic men for directors who valued his ability to smash people in the mouth. His understated acting style and silver-gray hair conferred intelligence and authority on the rash, amoral hoods he played. These contradictory impulses came together in Charlie Strom, a middle-aged hit man looking to answer a question, then cash out.

We first see Strom reflected in his associate hit man's (Clu Gulager's) sunglasses as the two men, both in shades and tailored suits, march into a school for the blind. The poised, angular Strom listens with his head up but cocked, an arched eyebrow, slit-like eyes. He looks like he's staring with his lower teeth.

Small signals he makes control the film, directing the other characters so he doesn't have to raise his voice. Seating himself across from Sheila (Angie Dickinson), an untrustworthy mob wife, he crosses his legs, removes his hat, shoots his cuffs and crosses his arms. "What do you want?" she asks. "The money," he answers, giving the definitive interpretation of those two words but sounding like he's ordering lunch.

We leave Strom clutching a briefcase, bleeding on a suburban lawn. Lee Marvin is the un-McQueen. Not handsome, unconcerned with the audience and therefore compelling, he is distant and takes things personally. He's too smart to be monumental like other movie stars, but when he falls it's like a world got killed.

The Patsy (Jerry Lewis, 1964, USA)

In the last half of *The Patsy* a team of showbiz handlers teaches a bellboy named Stanley (Jerry Lewis) a simple joke to tell onstage. The joke concerns a dog chasing a car who catches and buries it. Stanley rushes it backwards, yelling "I got a car that chases dogs!" "Slower!" instruct the handlers. He tries it slower: "I . . . got . . . a dog . . . that . . . "

Later, at a try-out, Stanley offers, "Like, my dog chased a car a lot." The handlers record another appearance at the nightclub and listen to the tape later. "Remember about my dog who was always chasing cars?" Stanley asks. "He finally caught one, a Mustang. And he buried it in the backyard." No matter what, it doesn't work. Stanley can't grasp the rudiments of stand-up.

Why does the movie harp on this lame joke? The handlers train Stanley to replace a famous comedian who died as the film began. The dead comic, a version of Jerry Lewis, is like the car in the joke Stanley can't tell: The handlers can't bury the comedian any more than Stanley can get the dog to bury the car. Nor can Stanley lip-sync in the record act Lewis resurrects from earlier in his career. In the movies Lewis directed he struggled not to conform to playback, and his comedy is so exasperating it makes people watching it break things, the way his handlers drop cups and overturn bottles watching him in disbelief at his one-of-a-kind incompetence.

Masculine Feminine (Jean-Luc Godard, 1966, France)

What untold depths will Miss 19 reveal to us now? Winner of a teen-magazine beauty contest, Elsa Leroy stands before Godard's camera with her back to the light like her hands are nailed to the windowsill and answers offscreen questions about socialism and birth control in an unbroken take six-and-a-half minutes long. Often regarded as an indictment of plasticity or misogynist cruelty, Godard's "interview with a Consumer Product" is one of the things that stops *Masculine Feminine* from being the yé-yé movie some music buffs would prefer.

Miss 19 is nice to Paul (Jean-Pierre Léaud), "a pollster for the IFOP." She seems a little nervous but not defensive, and aware she's being punked. She admits she doesn't know much about politics. When she expresses admiration for American women, Paul cuts her off: "Does the word *reactionary* mean anything to you?" When he sees his questions about love are going nowhere he asks her if she can name a place where a war is going on. "No," she laughs. "But I don't care."

We sense Paul asks Miss 19 questions he wishes he could ask Madeleine (Chantal Goya), the girl he loves. Earlier in the film he shouted "I want to live with you!" into a recording he never gave

Madeleine. Over shots of Paris street life, Paul reflects on his work: "Polls quickly veer from their true goal, the observation of behavior, and instead insidiously go for value judgments." His exposé of Miss 19 was as much about him as her.

The Good, the Bad and the Ugly (Sergio Leone, 1966, Italy)

Tuco (Eli Wallach) and the man he calls Blondie (Clint Eastwood) pursue gold across the Texas desert in a stolen Confederate coach. Disguised in the gray uniforms of dead Rebels, they know the blue-clad Union Army is chasing a Confederate regiment across the same terrain. Tuco rouses the napping Blondie to tell him he's spotted a cavalry platoon moving in their direction. "Blue or gray?" Blondie asks.

Tuco lifts the eye patch he's wearing to get a better look. "They're gray like us!" he shouts. "Hurrah for the Confederacy! God is with us because he hates the Yanks too!"

Blondie pushes back his hat and squints. "God's not on our side because he hates idiots also," he informs Tuco as the soldiers approach covered in the desert's gray dust. They watch as the officer leading the troops beats the dust off his jacket with a pair of gloves, revealing his blue uniform underneath. By yelling about which side God was on, Tuco invalidated the special protection granted men who pursue their own goals during wartime. Cut to Blondie and Tuco chained in a prison camp.

The film insists there are two kinds of people in the world. Leone's penchant for contrasting two kinds of shots, close-ups and long shots, finds its corollary in the gray or blue of the two kinds of soldiers who move toward Blondie and Tuco from afar. Leone turns gray soldiers blue in the simplest way possible. Movies were invented for ideas like that.

Fahrenheit 451 (François Truffaut, 1966, UK)

A simple idea motivates Truffaut's credits sequence: Reading is banned in the world of *Fahrenheit 451*, so the titles are spoken, not printed. We listen to the credits the way characters in the film receive the programs they watch on TV, and we see a series of photos like the picture-comics they look at instead of reading newspapers.

Truffaut brought more cinematic acumen to this minute-long sequence than many filmmakers deploy in an entire feature. Washed-out pastels overlay seventeen black-and-white stills of TV antennas as the camera zooms in on each. Offscreen, Alex Scott (who also plays one of the "book people") announces the film's title and the principals' names in the clipped tones of British radio, accompanied by Bernard Herrmann's ethereal score.

Truffaut turns the spoken credits from Sacha Guitry's *Story of a Cheat* or *The Magnificent Ambersons* or *Contempt* into a kind of Hitchcockian intro reminiscent of Chris Marker's *La Jetée*, science-fiction dealing in memory. The sequence follows the film's path: The first thirteen shots show suburban roofs cut off from nature, the last four set the houses among the trees; the film's protagonist flees suburban emptiness by escaping to the wintry forest of the book people. Even before the credits, Herrmann's music imparts a mystery and romance denied the turning globe of the Universal Studios logo-snipe in other Universal films. This is music of the spheres broadcast through a swirling aurora into homes only dimly aware of the cosmos.

Zontar the Thing from Venus (Larry Buchanan, 1966, USA)

Zontar, which endures as a thing of ridicule, started life as a remake of Roger Corman's *It Conquered the World* (1956). AIP needed filler to complete a TV sales package and contracted Buchanan, a Texas filmmaker known for ambitious if substandard exploitation fare, to quickly remake several of its '50s sci-fi monster movies in color and 16mm for about $30,000 each. Shown on late-night TV for years, the films are remembered by insomniacs as cheesy and boring. They're also so much less than that.

If, as Godard said, "the definition of the human condition should be in the *mise en scène* itself," then *Zontar*, which plays like an industrial documentary on Dallas living rooms and shopping centers, puts it there in negative. A dead-watch-battery miasma pervades the film, a three in the afternoon of the soul.

Much of the film consists of an embittered scientist (Anthony Houston) speaking into a radio wall-unit he's installed behind a checkered sliding door in a closet in his den. That's how he communicates with Zontar, a Venusian invader hiding in a nearby cave. We don't hear Zontar respond, though, just static and a low hum. "Yes, it's true," the scientist says to Zontar with his back to the camera. "I *am* your only friend." *Whrr bzzz*, replies Zontar.

The inadequacy of the film's world seems normal and accurate, snapshots of the time as it was. In the end it's a valid document of a place that did survive some kind of attack, but kept on going the same dull way, learning nothing.

The Rise of Louis XIV (Roberto Rossellini, 1966, France)

Rossellini ends his examination of the Sun King's rise with a three-minute shot following Louis (Jean-Marie Patte) through his bedroom as he removes the trappings of his power. The camera pans with the king as he crosses to a table in highwater pantaloons, black stockings, and gold shoes. He removes his black gloves, hat, wig, medallion, sash, and frilly jacket. By convincing the aristocracy to dress in this finery he has diverted its attention from the matters of state he now controls. By inventing a fashion he's instituted a reign of what Rossellini biographer Tag Gallagher calls "totalitarianism via consumerism."

Alone in his room, he reads aloud from La Rochefoucauld's *Maxims*: "There is a loftiness that does not depend on fortune. It is a certain air of superiority that seems to destine one for great things. . . . This quality enables us to usurp other men's deference and places us further above them than birth, rank, and merit itself." He sits behind his desk and continues: "Neither the sun nor death can be faced steadily." He puts the book down and repeats the last line. Fade to black.

The scene has a melancholy, even morbid finality; the quotation is an epitaph; the book is like a mirror. Louis has made himself like the sun and like death. He can't be faced or challenged. Yet the scene isn't exactly heavy. Rossellini's moving camera keeps it lively even as he criticizes the kind of spectacle Louis uses to rule, the kind movies make of history.

Kill, Baby . . . Kill! **(Mario Bava, 1966, Italy)**

This gothic horror is genuinely forbidding. Bava's vivid camerawork, with its emphatic zooms and vivid '60s color, creates a shut-off atmosphere suited to the movie's Carpathian town, a blighted place dominated by a ruined villa. The story spirals around the ghost of a little girl whose appearance, announced by a bouncing white ball, predicts the deaths of those who see her. The little girl is a manipulable symbol the villa's baroness, her mother, uses to instill fear in the villagers who caused her daughter's death.

Bava analyzes the way fear breeds violence. When the villagers see the little girl they become so afraid they commit suicide. Science enters this world in the form of a coroner (Giacomo Rossi-Stuart) sent to perform an autopsy. His self-assured, enlightened attitude only increases the death toll. Lured into the villa, his psyche begins to crumble like everything around him.

Responding to a woman calling his name from offscreen, the coroner bursts into a room where a painting of the villa covers one wall. He runs through the room to another door and bursts through that one—back into the same room. He continues this circuit eight times, getting closer to himself with each pass, until he grabs the shoulder of a figure running ahead of him and spins him around to find he's staring himself in the face. Bava does this through editing and pace, with two actors dressed alike. It's utterly convincing, a reminder that cinema had all the tools it needed before computers.

Just for the Hell of It (Herschell Gordon Lewis, 1968, USA)

Just for the Hell of It is a juvenile-delinquent shocker the director of *Blood Feast* slapped together in Florida the same year he made four other films. It is unconcerned with quality, but within its context of indifference its destructiveness is triumphant. The film is a blur of flailing. Long, desultory group fights filmed indifferently through a dirty lens alternate with scenes of absurd rampage where the cast puts a baby in a trash can or tears up magazines in a waiting room.

The violence begins before the credits. A prank at a house party triggers a dozen post-teenagers to break mirrors, rip up sofas with knives, smash tables and lamps, and chop a piano to bits. They smear the walls with red paint in this pseudo-happening that would shame an Action artist, and which predates the Manson murders by a year. The scene plays without music; Lewis fades out on it coldly.

Herschell Gordon Lewis was a literature professor who switched to advertising before making nudie and gore movies. Currently he's a big shot in direct marketing who has said his fondest wish is to conduct a symphony orchestra. No filmmaker has insisted he is not an artist and that film is not an art like Lewis has. He says it in every interview; his films shout it in the streets, from Ozark mountaintops and from the top of Florida motel signs. *Just for the Hell of It* is cheap and ugly, but if it isn't art, nothing is. Which is exactly Lewis's point.

Les Biches (Claude Chabrol, 1968, France)

Scenes of people listening to records have a special quality. Maybe it's because the black disc spins like a film reel. (Bowling is like that, too.) In *Les Biches* Chabrol makes that quality unnerving. The characters may want to hear the record they're playing, but instead of enjoying it with them we watch and listen like the only person not drinking at their party.

By the time they ask the curiously named Why (Jacqueline Sassard) to put on a record, it's already clear Frédérique (Stéphane Audran) and Paul (Jean-Louis Trintignant) have made her their servant. They ask her for things all the time: *Get me a beer, Why, bring me the butter, pour me some cognac.* The music she puts on is what they already have on their turntable, easy listening music for rich perverts, a cross between Poulenc and Les Baxter featuring a high-pitched, wordless vocal. As the three of them drink and fondle each other, the record gets stuck in a groove, and they ask Why to get up and fix it. The music follows them as they stagger to Frédérique's bedroom, where Frédérique shuts the door on Why, who loved Paul first.

Les Biches, a clearing of the decks for Chabrol, ushered in six years of great filmmaking. Chabrol used it to push himself past the Nouvelle vague. Its ménage is *Jules and Jim* gone sour in 1968. In *Les Biches,* those who have are given more, while what little the homeless street artist Why has is taken away.

L'Amour fou (Jacques Rivette, 1969, France)

Rivette made three films in the 1960s, fewer than other major figures of the French New Wave. The third, *L'Amour fou,* came out in 1969 and can stand as an end-of-the-decade summation of the Nouvelle vague aesthetic in a time of confusion and change. It's also the film in which Rivette's previously murky aspirations as a filmmaker coalesced, revealing his true direction.

The film is recognizably New Wave, but in a broken way. Shot in black-and-white in 1967 and '68, it takes place in Parisian cafés and apartments that belong to the mid-'60s more than the post-'68 world of Rivette's later films. It seems to balance on the exact point between two eras, and serves as a record of the transition between them.

In *L'Amour fou* the relationship between a theater director, Sébastien (Jean-Pierre Kalfon), and his girlfriend, Claire (Bulle Ogier), disintegrates during rehearsals for his production of Racine's *Andromache*, which are being recorded by a documentary film crew. The boundaries between life and art and film and theater are not the only ones broken down. In one amazing scene Sébastien and Claire prove you can spend the whole day in bed and methodically destroy your apartment at the same time.

A stark shot of two folding chairs on the play's white stage goes out of focus and then back in, breaking this four-and-a-quarter hour film in half. Somehow the film is anchored by these two empty chairs, which represent Sébastien and Claire and seem lost and otherworldly in their absence.

Twitch of the Death Nerve (aka *Bay of Blood*) (Mario Bava, 1971, Italy)

American slasher movies like *Halloween* and *Friday the 13th* imitated this bloody thriller set around a bay, the first film of its kind. Bava's European original includes youthful characters killed in the woods, but its interest lies elsewhere, and its multiple victims come from several classes and age groups. Two of them, Renata (Claudine Auger) and Albert (Luigi Pistilli), tow their young children (Renato Cestiè and Nicoletta Elmi) to the bay in pursuit of an inheritance.

Today mechanical plot twists and pointless reversals pad the last reels of thrillers long after they've meaningfully ended. Bava's shock ending, however, is an exclamation point that throws the whole film into relief. As the murderous couple Renata and Albert smile and hug, congratulating each other for achieving their goal

("It's the least I could do for my family," says Albert), Bava's camera zooms out and a double-barreled shotgun enters the frame from the right. *Blam blam.*

Cut to their 8-year-old holding the shotgun, his younger sister beside him. "They're good at playing dead," she observes, then the children skip off like they're in a soap commercial as a happy chorus of *yeah-yeahs* fills the soundtrack.

"Children should stay with their parents," Albert told Renata before they left them alone in their camper. A shot of the kids breaking a ceramic head links them to the film's mayhem, then Bava deserts them, too, and we worry about them. Where are they? Are they in danger? This *Weekend*-like movie's harsh ending somehow recalls the sunny domestic horror that finishes Varda's *Le Bonheur.* It's just as radical and surprising.

Wanda (Barbara Loden, 1971, USA)

Always described as Elia Kazan's wife who played the wild sister in *Splendor in the Grass,* Barbara Loden should be remembered as the director of *Wanda.* This bleak film follows a lower-class woman named Wanda Goranski (Loden) through a series of numbing encounters in narrow bars serving quarter beers, downtown hotels where the sink is next to the bed, and all-night restaurants where people eat spaghetti while smoking. The film hurts. Its plodding grimness reduces life to getting money and eating.

Shot by a documentary cameraman in 16mm color in Pennsylvania coalfields and in Waterbury, Connecticut, *Wanda* has the brute intensity of *Harlan County USA.* Wanda is disconnected. She loses her family in divorce court and can't hold a job. After she's pickpocketed in a movie theater she wanders into a bar during a robbery and leaves with the thief, a Mr. Dennis (Michael Higgins), who calls her "Hey, stupid" and slaps her in the face.

Subsumed by the broken people they're playing, Loden and Higgins don't appear to be acting any more than the non-professionals in the film's other roles. Wanda tells Mr. Dennis she's never had anything and never will. "You don't have anything, you're nothing," he explains. "You're not even a citizen of the United States." Then he gets on the roof of his car with a bottle of bourbon and swipes at radio-controlled airplanes like King Kong. Loden deglamorizes his bank robbery scheme into a series of pathetic incidents, denying her heroine a movie ending.

The Heartbreak Kid (Elaine May, 1972, USA)

The restaurant scene opens with a shot of a waiter's finger tapping a live lobster on a plate, prodding it to show it's alive before it's boiled and served. Elaine May does the same thing to the couple about to eat it, Lennie (Charles Grodin) and Lila (Jeannie Berlin), newlyweds from New York honeymooning in Miami Beach. Lila is unaware Lennie wants to dump her for Kelly (Cybill Shepherd), a blonde co-ed from the Midwest he met on the beach while Lila recovered from a sunburn in their hotel room. Lennie is determined to tell Lila their marriage is over, to finish the meal with a piece of the restaurant's famous "Florida pecan pie" and no hard feelings, and get to Minnesota to claim Kelly.

This may be the only scene in an American comedy that really qualifies as brutally funny; it's like a punch in the stomach. Lila's humiliation, as unbearable as it is, is worsened by our perception of her as a slob whose abandonment is inevitable, and by Grodin's feigned deflective ire at a waiter (Erik Lee Preminger) who tells him the restaurant is out of pie. This is screwball comedy without redemption, an underdog comedy where the underdog is a jerk.

Neil Simon's screenplay, from a Bruce Jay Friedman story, must be given credit along with May's direction and the film's priceless performances, including Eddie Albert's as Kelly's father, a man who (in another dinner scene) doesn't buy Lennie's talk of beef that doesn't lie, sincere potatoes, and undeceitful cauliflower.

The Discreet Charm of the Bourgeoisie (Luis Buñuel, 1972, France)

Triggered by minor annoyances, the dreams and memories of civil servants invade the lives of Buñuel's upper-class characters whenever they sit down to eat. Bloody anecdotes, related by the people who maintain order in their world, animate their unease.

Simone (Delphine Seyrig), her sister Florence (Bulle Ogier), and their friend Alice (Stéphane Audran) go to a café for tea. Florence, annoyed by the presence of a cellist, makes Simone change seats with her so she won't have to look at him. As Alice notices a soldier (Gerald Robard) staring at them, a waiter (Bernard Musson) arrives with news the café is out of tea. They switch their order to coffee with milk. The soldier joins them. He relates a macabre story, which we see in a flashback: as a child his dead parents appeared to him and convinced him to murder his stepfather with poisoned milk. The waiter returns. The café is also out of coffee—and milk.

Florence, who is single and seems to prefer alcohol to sex, can't stand to look at a cello. Alice, whom we've seen cavorting in the bushes of her estate, is the first to notice the soldier. Simone, off to an assignation, allows him to hold the door for her as she leaves. Yet the soldier's confession makes less of an impression on them than the café's lack of tea and coffee. Protected by haute couture and polite smiles, these unflappable women have an uncanny ability to ignore the poetic. Eventually it opens fire.

F for Fake (Orson Welles, 1974, France)

"That's her real name, you know. *Oja.* Oja Kodar." Welles pronounces these syllables like they're hard facts. Why? We already know his costar's name. But it isn't her real name. He doesn't tell us it's a name he gave her long before they made *F for Fake.* Welles uses her name to introduce a confession: Everything he said in the film's last seventeen minutes was a lie. "My job," he says, "was to try to make it real."

"Not that reality had anything to do with it." He utters these words over a shot of a man we know as Oja's grandfather. More precisely, over a shot of her grandfather's legs floating in the air over a grassy field, the rest of his body out of frame. "Reality?" asks Welles. "It's the toothbrush waiting at home for you in its glass. A bus ticket, a paycheck, and the grave."

The grandfather winks and nods at Welles on the word "paycheck" as Welles passes his black cloak over the levitating old man like he's dead. The grandfather, Welles reveals, never existed. He was a fiction, too, an actor. The old man disappears in mid-air; before he's gone we just glimpse a chicken-wire figure under the sheet where the grandfather was supposed to be.

Did Welles write those marvelous lines about reality himself? He must have. Yet after seeing *F for Fake* who would be surprised to pick up a book someday and find them there? And would it make any difference?

The Killing of a Chinese Bookie (John Cassavetes, 1976, USA)

If you pay them off you'll lose some more; if you build it they will come to take it. This lesson, learned at the hands of gangsters, sinks in for strip-club owner Cosmo Vittelli (Ben Gazzara) as he returns, bleeding, to his cabaret. Why try at all? When Mr. Sophistication (Meade Roberts), the club's bedraggled emcee, begins his goodnight version of "I Can't Give You Anything but Love," Cassavetes provides an answer.

Instead of violence, *The Killing of a Chinese Bookie* ends with a musical number. Mr. Sophistication throws fake money into an audience that's shouting "take it off!" at the half-naked De-Lovelies on stage. He snappishly changes the song's lyrics to reflect petty demands: "Happiness, great success / All the things you always *whined* for." As his song grows triumphant, he exclaims "Love, love, love—*hot love*!"

Then one of the De-Lovelies (Haji) needles him by lighting a novelty explosive on his shoulder. He sighs and heads backstage, where a hand is extended in comfort or congratulation; his singing resumes over the end credits. Sometimes the message of love (*hot love!*) can come delivered by a pissed-off little fat man in sweaty whiteface. We leave Cosmo bleeding on the sidewalk, hurt but on his feet. His bullet hole rhymes with Mr. Sophistication's shoulder explosion. In Mr. Sophistication, Meade Roberts, a screenwriter Cassavetes tapped to act, created an unforgettable figure. He is the humiliated professor of *The Blue Angel* on stage with ex-ultravixens, consigned to awkward grandeur in LA.

On Top of the Whale (Raúl Ruiz, 1982, The Netherlands)

The polyglot cast of *On Top of the Whale* delivers its lines like they learned them phonetically. They speak six European languages and one made-up for the two surviving members of an Indigenous Patagonian tribe (Luis Mora and Ernie Navarro). Beginning in a near-future Netherlands Soviet Republic, the film follows an anthropologist (Jean Badin) and his family to a house in Tierra del Fuego (actually Holland), which cinematographer Henri Alekan photographs like a landscape in Murnau. By the end of this "film about survival" it's unclear whether Ruiz meant the survival of Indians facing extinction or Europeans who betray their own past.

The Indians believe "one is an even number" and speak a language of sixty words whose meanings vary with inflection and change daily. At first the anthropologist is excited to be studying these men, but his enthusiasm wanes as they repeat the same word to him whether they're shown binoculars or a tape recorder. Isolated in this lonely spot where the Indians bury mirrors, the family loses itself in "metaphoric images" of Lacanian psychoanalysis becoming a religion.

In this moody, hilarious film's last scene the anthropologist approaches the two Indians in long shot as they back across a gully. They sit opposite each other talking about the future, Ruiz cutting between them in a shot-reverse shot. When the anthropologist gets up to leave, Ruiz cuts back to the long shot and we remember how far apart they are. The strange effect of this simple, unexpected cut reverberates as the scene fades and the film ends.

The King of Comedy (Martin Scorsese, 1983, USA)

Pretending he's scheduled a working weekend, Rupert Pupkin (Robert De Niro), an amateur comic desperate for fame, takes Rita (Diahnne Abbott), a girl he knew in high school, to the home of Jerry Langford (Jerry Lewis). The nighttime talk-show host is Rupert's idol; Rupert is his stalker. Langford has definitely not invited him over.

Rupert's hostile disregard for other people pours out in this scene, aggravated by joking and wheedling. His refusal to acknowledge the gap between his own life and what he knows from TV humiliates Rita, infuriates Langford, and unnerves Langford's butler, Jonno (Kim Chan). Rupert makes it worse by using Rita as a shield. When she insists they leave, he begs Langford to correct her: "She's a girl who works in a bar. Tell her she's wrong, Jerry, please."

Langford's patience reaches its limit when Rupert admits he's made a mistake. "*So did Hitler!*" Langford yells back, golf club in hand. Rupert, flinchy and petulant, rears back, making even more of a spectacle of himself. "I'm going to be fifty times more famous than you!" he yells at Langford, confusing talent with fame.

There's something epic in the confrontation between Robert De Niro and Jerry Lewis. The modern sculptures it takes place around lend it a Greek quality. Langford, dressed in shorts and sneakers, is stoic and regal. Rupert, with his little mustache and two-toned shoes, is a jester heralding a new regime of shamelessness. Rita's peach chiffon dress and Jonno's white coat further isolate Rupert in this living room where there's no TV.

Stranger Than Paradise **(Jim Jarmusch, 1984, USA)**

Jarmusch's mournful examination of emptiness renews a longing for emptiness in a world stuffed with crap. *Stranger Than Paradise* captures what in retrospect turned out to be a last moment of unbranded American reality. It was the end of the non-branded American film, too, and arrived just before Sundance-ification engulfed non-studio filmmaking in the USA. Jarmusch looked at the world and noticed there was nothing instead of something. Today we wonder why there's everything instead of nothing.

The Lake Erie scene comes near the end of the film's second third. The shady hipsters Willie (John Lurie) and Eddie (Richard Edson) leave New York to visit Willie's teenage cousin Eva (Eszter Balint) in dead-of-winter Cleveland. When Eva, newly arrived from Hungary, told Eddie back in New York she'd come to America to move there, he assured her she'd love Cleveland, a beautiful city with a big beautiful lake. "Have you been there?" she asked. "No," he answered.

The film's black-and-white Cleveland is a dead-end America of train tracks and old-man bars, the hot dog stand where Eva works, the interior of a movie theater showing a kung fu flick to practically no one, not much different from the trio's New York. Eva takes Willie and Eddie to see the big lake. The three of them stand there with their backs to the camera. It holds on these black figures shivering in hats and coats, whipped by the snow and wind. The lake is a white void, a blank, the horizon erased. "It's not always frozen," says Eva.

They Live (John Carpenter, 1988, USA)

John Carpenter emerged from the same California milieu in the 1970s as George Lucas and Steven Spielberg. He has worked in the same Hollywood as they have, in the same genres, but in many ways he is the anti-Spielberg and the anti-Lucas. *They Live* is the most extreme example of this. It criticizes not only spectacular entertainment but commercial image-making in general. That it does this in a cheap, blunt sci-fi flick starring a professional wrestler is nothing to sneeze at. Here Carpenter reveals himself as an enemy of what one of this film's villains calls "our ongoing quest for multi-dimensional expansion."

They Live addresses what another character in it calls "the annihilation of consciousness." Carpenter means class consciousness, too. Roddy Piper plays an out-of-work construction worker who finds sunglasses that expose what billboards, magazines, and product labels really say—OBEY; MARRY AND REPRODUCE; CONSUME; WATCH TV—and what the overlords who put them there really look like (they look like metal skulls wearing toupees).

When Piper wears the sunglasses, he sees the OBEY world in black-and-white. Carpenter cuts between two ordinary views, one in color and filled with signs, the other in black-and-white and also filled with signs. He keeps them separate and makes no attempt to optically integrate them. This radical simplicity is meat-and-potatoes semiotics as arresting as anything in Cronenberg. After seeing *They Live* it will be hard to forget what it says on the black-and-white dollar bill: THIS IS YOUR GOD.

Anjaam (Rahul Rawail, 1994, India)

This Hindi stalker musical proceeds through the usual melodrama and songs, but what it builds toward in its first two hours is the violent, almost unimaginable revenge tragedy of its third. Madhuri Dixit, as *Anjaam*'s heroine, Shivani, loses the child she's carrying after she's beaten by the warden of the prison where she's incarcerated on false charges. From then on she becomes Charles Bronson trapped in a movie by Mario Bava. Against a backdrop of rain and fire and a relentless song that's sung onscreen by her cellmate, Shivani sets out to avenge every wrong ever done to her.

Dressed in either all white or all black, she hangs the warden, bites the veins from her brother-in-law's wrist, kills a rapist cop in a graveyard, and goes after her now-wheelchair-bound stalker (Shah Rukh Khan) with a scythe. When she realizes she can't bring herself to kill a quadriplegic, she decides to rehabilitate him by bouncing a ball off his head, doing a love dance as he stares on helplessly, and pushing him into a swimming pool, chair and all. I don't know if any of Rawail's other movies reach the frenzied pitch of *Anjaam*. Maybe Dixit's possessed pulchritude sent him to a frightening, dizzying height he's never known before and hasn't since.

La Cérémonie (Claude Chabrol, 1995, France)

Something telling, something vital to the film, happens in *La Cérémonie*'s first few seconds. But it's the kind of fleeting moment that doesn't register, and can't register, until the film is over. By then it will probably have been forgotten.

A woman (Sandrine Bonnaire), a tiny figure seen in long shot, stops in front of a bar, looks at the door, and turn to ask a passerby for directions. He points across the street. The woman proceeds in that direction and enters a café, where another woman (Jacqueline Bisset) is waiting for her. We've been watching this scene from inside the café, from the second woman's point of view. Our point of view is hers. It's a viewpoint *La Cérémonie* will come to indict. But that's not the telling detail.

The woman in the café is Catherine Lelièvre, a bourgeois housewife and art-gallery owner waiting to interview Sophie Bonhomme for the position of housekeeper. Catherine is friendly, Sophie all business, but the two women, dressed professionally, seem on equal footing. The plot of this thriller hinges on the consequences of Sophie's illiteracy. She had to ask directions because she couldn't read the signs: she couldn't tell the bar from the café.

Chabrol undermines the concept of "the reveal" by getting it out of the way before he does anything else. It's the first sneaky move in a subtly radical film.

I Shot Andy Warhol (Mary Harron, 1996, USA)

In this compelling portrait of Warhol's would-be assassin, Lili Taylor plays Valerie Solanas, author of the *SCUM Manifesto*, like she's a newsboy from a '30s movie looking for someone to talk to. With her choppy haircut and black cap, looking sideways and smoking, she hangs around a New York newsstand and hustles "finks." That's how she meets her publisher, Maurice Girodias of the Olympia Press (Lothaire Bluteau). "Give me fifteen cents and I'll give you a dirty word," she tells him. "What's the word?" he asks. "Men," she says. Girodias promptly offers to buy her a drink.

Taylor's voice prevails over the tragedy of Solanas's life. Harron wisely allows her to recite passages from the *Manifesto* in black-and-white monologues meant to evoke Warhol screen tests. No matter how nutty Valerie's ideas, Taylor's delivery lends them credence.

Her voice cuts through the complacency of Warhol's entourage. Her asides are memorable. "An exquisite mosaic!" she remarks to a john showing her the scabs on his chest made by high heels.

After Valerie dolls herself up in a red dress to sign a book contract with Girodias over dinner (the film's most affecting scene), she begins to unravel. She doubts herself and reverts to the angry student who answered a letter about corsages for her college newspaper by scrawling FUCK YOU on it.

"All I know is I want a piece of the groovy world myself." She never gets one. "Where do you live?" a cop asks her after her arrest. "Nowhere," she answers.

Taste of Cherry (Abbas Kiarostami, 1997, Iran)

A man (Homayoun Ershadi) drives around the slag-heap outskirts of Tehran in a Range Rover propositioning laborers and soldiers. He wants to pay someone to check on him after a suicide attempt to make sure he's dead, then fill his grave with dirt. The man, Mr. Badii, never divulges his reason but finds someone to accept his offer, a taxidermist (Abdol Hossein Bagheri) who understands melancholy and knows that "what you get is a matter of luck. Birds don't fall into the net to make you happy."

As *Taste of Cherry* ends, Badii swallows sleeping pills and lies down in the hole he's dug to await his death. It is night. Thunder rumbles in the distance. A couple of lightning flashes illuminate Badii in medium close-up, but the screen is otherwise black. We hear rain falling. It appears the film is done.

It isn't. Kiarostami fades in to video footage of soldiers marching up a hill in long shot, accompanied by a Louis Armstrong recording of "St. James Infirmary" (no vocals). He cuts to scenes of the crew at work, including Ershadi, who smokes and offers Kiarostami a cigarette. This unexpected break in the narrative deepens the film's ambiguous ending and makes it more powerful. There is no definitive explanation for why it's there. It is several things at once: a scene of mournful tranquility, contemplation of the happiness of being alive, relief from the film's tension, rejection of sentimentality, a scene of rebirth, and an invitation to leave the theater.

American Job (Chris Smith, 1997, USA)

Chris Smith made his debut film in the Midwest for $14,000 with writer Randy Russell playing a version of himself, a guy drifting in a perpetual fog of lousy minimum-wage jobs. The gangly, bespectacled Russell looks like Kevin, the nerdy stock clerk from *Repo Man*, but his performance is self-effacing, not unctuous. *American Job* was barely released and got little support from critics. Shot in 16mm in the fading colors of a Wisconsin autumn, it's a real achievement in independent filmmaking, socially conscious, formally daring, and unpretentious.

The film moves steadily among low-paying jobs where conversations with coworkers mostly turn to what you'd do if you won the lottery. Russell starts the film as a lever puller in a factory, ends up as a telemarketer, and in-between tries washing dishes in a chicken joint, housekeeping in a motel, and third-shift warehouse inventory. Private time is almost nil. At one job, Russell's lunch is a slice of meat wolfed down in a men's room he's supposed to be cleaning.

Non-professional actors make up the rest of the cast, picked because they had experience as hourlies or managers in the film's workplace settings. Uniformly excellent, they help Smith blur the line between shambling indie and vérité documentary, crafting a low-key tragicomedy that's like a working-class *Office Space* with less hope and no plot. At the chicken place they hose down the day-old rolls before they throw them out. It's a fitting image for the forgotten level of American life the film explores.

The Last Big Thing (Dan Zukovic, 1998, USA)

Shot in 1995 but unreleased until 1998, *The Last Big Thing* follows alienated anti-hipster Simon Geist (Dan Zukovic) as he drives his purposefully damaged car to fake interviews for a nonexistent magazine called *The Next Big Thing*.

Geist has an agenda. His dedication to exposing the "LA fame need" infecting his city attracts the attention of an unhappy trust-funder named Darla (Susan Heimbinder). The two move into a "personality-less, non-individualistic" house near the desert, where they drink beer in their backyard over the *Los Angeles Times* and plot Geist's forays into town. In their spare time they bark monosyllables at a nightclub comic or sit in a movie theater glowering at blockbusters. As Geist's aphoristic confrontations begin to backfire, he becomes increasingly megalomaniacal. Soon a crisis is upon him—he's asked to direct a music video.

Few satires really blister; this one does. Geist's clipped, controlled rants, often delivered into a tape recorder as he drives, are incisive monologues filled with unrivaled hatred for the vacuous. Punctuated by fender benders and the whine of car alarms, Geist's indictment of a "culture finally going down on itself" where "all meaning has been neutered" and "all mediums are pointless" is an analog yawp of despair poised on a digital abyss. Heimbinder's red-haired Darla, in her olive-drab jumpsuit, drags the pop-culture detritus of a loveless world heroically behind her. The two of them are strangely resilient, and so is the film, a gem from an era of manufactured cult items.

Eyes Wide Shut **(Stanley Kubrick, 1999, UK)**

When it was released its mere existence was an affront to the audience and, therefore, in those days when Americans weren't supposed to stop cheering the Dow, to the pocketbook of Warner Bros., the studio that paid for it. Bad for business, it was bad, period. *Eyes Wide Shut* has survived the opprobrium of the bubble era that was a sign of its distinction. It's a reminder of that dumbed-down audience, eager to congratulate itself for being bored.

It was a knockout in the first round. Kubrick's fluid camerawork lulled them. The modulated performances of Tom Cruise and Nicole

Kidman seemed to waste the stars of *Days of Thunder*. The film's evocation of Christmastime New York as a lonely city of sexual conspirators seemed fake in a world of yet-to-be-indicted CEOs. When *Eyes Wide Shut* was released on over 2,400 screens in the summer of 1999 it was guaranteed to tank, almost as if a major studio had wanted to prove it could kill the auteur film for good and make it look like a marketing accident. Was it meant as a sacrifice, like the one the drug-addicted girl makes for Bill Harford at the orgy?

LUCKY TO BE ALIVE reads a newspaper headline in *Eyes Wide Shut*. Kubrick died four months before it came out.

Vanilla Sky (Cameron Crowe, 2001, USA)

If *The Matrix*'s "welcome to the desert of the real" ended the 1990s, Tom Cruise's plunge from a New York skyscraper began the 21st century with a hyperreal splat. Released three months after the Twin Towers fell, *Vanilla Sky* is both the last pre–September 11 and the first post–September 11 Hollywood movie. It posits a world where the disfigurement of Cruise's face is a global catastrophe and his coming to consciousness is an act of lifesaving suicide. "Things are very different now," as tech-support avatar Edmund Ventura (Noah Taylor) tells Cruise's narcissist publisher David Aames. "Forgive me, I'm blowing your mind."

Crowe's baby-boomer fantasy tinkles with notions like a jostled perfume counter. By the film's end, when Aames ascends in an elevator with Ventura like he's Lon Chaney starring in *The Fountainhead*, the viewer is prepared to have his mind blown in the worst way. After a bittersweet parting with Penelope Cruz as love-object Sofia ("wisdom") Serrano ("mountain"), a woman who lives every moment to the fullest even though she's dead, Aames jumps from the roof and plummets through the Monet-inspired CGI clouds into the canyon of Manhattan.

While comparison to Wile E. Coyote is as apt as to the victims of September 11, Ventura describes this (everything in *Vanilla Sky* is described by its characters at least four times) as "a brilliant journey of self-awakening." A montage of rock-era imagery accompanies Aames as he descends like one of the parade balloons we'd seen pass his apartment window, only this time made of lead.

Femme Fatale (Brian De Palma, 2002, France)

There is a picture book called *Movie Stars in Bathtubs*, but there aren't enough movies with movie stars in bathtubs. De Palma's *Femme Fatale*, which stars Rebecca Romijn, does much to correct that.

Romijn plays Laure Ash, a jewel thief thrown from a hotel balcony by her accomplices. When the parents of a missing girl named Lily find Laure unconscious on the hotel floor they whisk her home and put her to bed in their daughter's room. In a typical De Palma touch, Laure is a blonde disguised as a brunette, making her Lily's double. (Romijn plays her, too.) Laure awakens, sees Lily's photograph, and realizes she can use her lookalike's passport to escape the men she's double-crossed. Before she leaves she decides to take a bath.

Laure's bath frames at least half the film's action. Drinking tequila and smoking, Laure drifts off as the tub begins to overflow. Thunder strikes outside, waking her up (again) as Lily returns, loads a gun, and puts it to her head to commit suicide. A fish tank overflows as Lily pulls the trigger. Now Laure can take Lily's place for good.

De Palma brings a lifetime's contemplation of cinematic trickery to this, his most abstract and satisfying thriller. When Laure is thrown from a bridge into the Seine she finds herself suddenly without her clothes and awakens in the overflowing bathtub again. Again Lily returns and puts a gun to her head, and for once De Palma denies himself a victim.

ACKNOWLEDGMENTS

Mark Krotov worked without tire to assemble and edit this book, and Rachel Ossip designed a striking, electric cover. I was fortunate to work with them again. Lisa Borst was as ever a constant source of good editing and good advice. Also at *n+1*, Alan Dean, Nicole Lipman, Dani Oliver, Dayna Tortorici, and Colin Vanderburg provided aid and insight. I am indebted to Wick Hallos for his excellent indexing.

Great thanks to the editors and staff at other publications in which the pieces in this book first appeared: Daniela Shreir and Missouri Williams at *Another Gaze*; Emily Carroll, JW McCormack, Jonathon Sturgeon, Zach Webb, and especially Ted Jouflas, for his wonderfully twisted full-color illustrations, at the *Baffler*; Michael Miller at *Bookforum*; Liz Helfgott and Ben Mercer at the Criterion Collection; Max Ufberg at *Fast Company*; Melissa Anderson and Ania Szremski at 4Columns; Caroline McCloskey at Galerie; David Marcus and Emmet Fraizer at the *Nation*; Max Nelson and Willa Glickman at the *New York Review of Books*; Craig Keller and Francesco Simeoni at Radiance Films; and Durga Chew-Bose and Olivia Whittick at SSENSE. For commissioning pieces for books, I thank Jon Dieringer and Chris Fujiwara, and at Semiotext(e), Hedi El Kholti, Christine Pichini, and Janique Vigier. For pieces first published by art galleries, thanks to Claire Barliant, and Daniel Merritt and Laura McLean-Ferris at the Swiss Institute.

For their encouragement and assignments, for their help in times of need, and for talking to me in public settings and inviting me places, even on Zoom, I am grateful to Stacey Allan, Jessica Almereyda, Michael Almereyda, Lili Anolik, Michael Baker, Miriam Bale, Kate Bolick, Roudi Boroumand, Annabel Brady-Brown, Nick Bruno, Christopher Byrd, Deb Turcotte Carragher, Pelle Cass, Holly Chambers, Rebecca Curtis, Ricky D'Ambrose, the Diagonale Festival of Austrian Film, Dan Doody, Chris Dumas, Andrew Durbin, Bilge Ebiri, Nina Eichacker, Lee Eichelberger, Sarah Fan, Devika Girish, Manuel Gnam, Leo Goldsmith, Micah Gottlieb,

Marlowe Granados, Michael Grodner, Elizabeth Gumport, Carol Hayes, Joan Hawkins, Gillian Horvat, Gary Indiana (RIP), Daniel Kasman, Irena Kovarova, Jennifer Krasinski, Clinton Krute, Justin LaLiberty, Abby Lee, Light Industry, Chloe Lizotte, the *Los Angeles Review of Books*, the Lotos Foundation, Christopher Lydon, Kate MacKay, Whitney Mallett, Jen Marshall, Ed McCarry, Mary McGrath, the Mar del Plata International Film Festival, Hind Mezaina, Sarah Miller, Jennifer K. Mitchell and Jim Terhune, Yuka Murakami, Morley Musick, Minh Nguyen, Sophia Niehaus, Amy Ash Nixon, Now Instant Image Hall, Maxwell Paparella, Jay Patrikios, Nicolas Pedrero-Setzer, Kate Perkins, Jake Perlin, Jenny Perlin, Richard Porton, Andy Rector, Chris Richards, *Rīgas Laiks*, Max Rippon, Vadim Rizov, Eric Roberts, Toni Russo, James Schamus, Ingrid Schorr, Randall Sellers, Ethan Shantie, Erin Sheehy, *Sight & Sound*, Nora Smith and Glenn Jones, Soda Jerk, Will Stephenson, Will Tavlin, Chip Thomas, Stephanie Verme and Heriberto Yunda, Richard von Busack, Jeremy Wang-Iverson, Al Warren, Anna Zagala, and Kit Zauhar.

Suzanne Smith and Geoffrey Clark deserve special thanks for guiding me and making me feel welcome in St. Lawrence County, NY, which is where I wrote about a third of this book, in an A-frame house the same color as the one in *Midsommar*.

The essays in this book originally appeared in *n+1* and in the following:

Another Gaze: "Postcard from Home" (No. 05, October 2021).

The Baffler: "Money Is an Iron" (February 7, 2020), "The Other Guy Being Socialism" (Issue 51, April 2020), "Zero Hour Contracts" (Issue 52, July 2020), "In Three Years We Can Quit Chicken Sexing" (April 22, 2021), "Time Is a Rabid Dog" (January 13, 2022), "The World Was Just an Address" (March 24, 2022), "Riding the Elephant" (as "Riding the Goddamn Elephant") (March 9, 2023).

Bookforum: "Double Squibs with Hamburger Meat" (as "There Will Be Fake Blood") (February/March 2019), "Dutch Angles" (as "He Found It at the Movies") (September 3, 2019, September/October/November 2019), "Thread Count" (as "Inherent Nice") (November 30, 2020, December/January/February 2021), "Slime Regained" (March 1, 2021, March/April/May 2021), "The Bitter with the Sour" (as "Some Like It Fraught") (March 1, 2022, March/April/May 2022), "Time to Face Reality" (July 2, 2024, Summer 2024), "Agnès All Along" (October 29, 2024, Fall 2024).

The Cinema House and the World: The Cahiers du Cinéma *Years, 1962–1981*, by Serge Daney, translated by Christine Pichini (Semiotext(e), 2022): "Cinema Is Never on Time," a foreword to the book.

The Criterion Collection: "All We Got in Common" (*Matewan* Blu-Ray, October 29, 2019), "Stay Near the Tree" (*Taste of Cherry* Blu-Ray, July 21, 2020), "The Captain's Dinner Is Coming Up" (*Triangle of Sadness* Blu-Ray, April 25, 2023), "A Young, Honest Guy Like Himself" (*Real Life* Blu-Ray, August 27, 2024).

Fast Company: "The Business of Nostalgia" (as "'Unfrosted' is the latest in corporate nostalgia, Hollywood's favorite new genre" (May 7, 2024), "Enemy of the Good" (as "Hollywood's obsession with AI-enabled 'perfection' is making movies less human") (February 28, 2025).

4Columns: "Every Moment Between Human Beings" (as "*The Conversation*") (March 20, 2020).

Galerie: "Sound Sleeper" (July 5, 2023).

Horror Caviar: A Cookbook, edited by Jon Dieringer (A24 Films, 2021): "All-Consuming Horror" (as "Cleanup on Aisle 9: Consumerism as Horror").

"Movie Stars in Bathtubs" originally appeared in different form in *The Little Black Book: Movies*, edited by Chris Fujiwara (Cassell Illustrated, 2007). It appears here as published online by *n+1* on November 7, 2018, including the addition of a short entry on the movie *Anjaam*, which first appeared on the website Tripod.com in 1998.

Museum Memories, edited by Claire Barliant (Quick and dirty, fast and cheap, 2019): "The MoMA Gramercy," published untitled in this pamphlet as part of Katarina Burin and Farhad Mirza's exhibition *a low storey between two others* at the Anthony Greaney Gallery, Somerville, Mass.

The Nation: "Beyond the Visible" (February 6, 2024/March 2024 issue).

The New York Review of Books: "Persistence of Mission" (August 2, 2023), "Objects in Space at a Moment in Time" (February 3, 2024).

Radiance Films: "Inside the Special People Club" (*Welcome to the Dollhouse* Blu-Ray, May 15, 2023).

SSENSE: "The Old Bamboo" (Issue 3, October 20, 2020).

"The Work of Fate" was written as a lecture for the Swiss Institute Contemporary Art New York, and was delivered before a screening of Jean Cocteau's *Orpheus* at the Quad Cinema in Manhattan on December 18, 2019, as part of the exhibition *Jill Mulleady: Fight-or-Flight*. It was published online by *n+1* on January 14, 2020.

INDEX OF TITLES

C

D

G

Q

R

S

T

U

Y

Z

INDEX OF NAMES

A

B

C

E

F

G

H

L

M

N

Q

R

S

T

X

Y

Z